PRAISE FOR *Stranger in a Strange Land*

"What a wonderful book this is: gripping, illuminating, beautifully constructed, and full of the communicative energy that comes from things long in gestation but written with fire and speed. It does so many things so well—the portrait of Scholem himself, the account of his work, the study of friendship that comes about through the sustained presence of Walter Benjamin, the evocations of Jerusalem and New York, above all the paralleling of Prochnik's own story with Scholem's. The extraordinary affinities between author and subject give the book an emotional intensity that complements its erudition and lends power to its final, audacious, inspiring claim on the reader's capacity for hope."

—JAMES LASDUN, author of *The Fall Guy*

"In his previous book, George Prochnik gave us a moving portrait of Stefan Zweig, the Viennese Jew who wrote tenderly of the 'world of yesterday'—the liberal Europe that collapsed with apocalyptic consequences in the 1930s—and killed himself in his Brazilian exile rather than die in its flames. In his powerful new book, Prochnik offers us a portrait of a Berlin Jew, fifteen years Zweig's junior, who made a very different choice: to renounce the dream of a liberal Europe and remake himself, and his people, in Palestine. Gerhard Scholem, who would become the famous scholar of the Kabbalah Gershom Scholem, upheld a cultural version of Zionism, and spoke of the need for Arab–Jewish coexistence; yet over time he accommodated himself to the often brutal practices of the Jewish state, which turned Palestinians into strangers in their own land. In the late 1980s, as Palestinians in the Occupied Territories launched their first Intifada, Prochnik, an American Jew from the suburbs, settled in Jerusalem with his family, inspired

by Scholem's vision of a renewed Jewish cultural vitality, only to discover that this vision lay in ruins, no match for the muscular, expansionist Zionism with which it had made a marriage of convenience. In *Stranger in a Strange Land*, Prochnik writes of Scholem's dream — and of his own — with a rare and affecting combination of authority and vulnerability. This is a deeply felt work of critique and elegy, a probing examination of the subject of our time: the temptations, and the dangers, of belonging."
—ADAM SHATZ, contributing editor at the *London Review of Books*

"George Prochnik's book presents an uneasy political-mystical tour through Scholem's writing and his own Jerusalem, now lost forever. What makes it a unique and brilliant contribution to current debates about Palestine is that in his reading of Scholem, Prochnik finds simultaneously both the echoes of the forces — messianic, national, and colonial — that keep tearing the region apart, and also the kernel of something precious to be salvaged. From the abyss of our despair, Prochnik manages to do what so few others can: imagine a future of living together."
—EYAL WEIZMAN, author of *Hollow Land: Israel's Architecture of Occupation* and director of the Centre for Research Architecture at Goldsmiths, University of London

"Prochnik is a great practitioner of the art of auto-nonfiction, the writing of intellectual history in which a past life is quickened again by the keen presence of the author. Yet Prochnik never obtrudes; rather, his beautiful sentences guide us, gently but surely, through both the often-complex thinking of his subjects and the often-traumatic events of their lives. As in his biography of the mercurial Stefan Zweig, alienation is foregrounded in this account of the scholarly Gershom Scholem (who inscribed it in his adopted name, Gershom, meaning "stranger in a strange land"). But loss is lightened here by the Scholemian conviction that the Kabbalah, the mystical tradition of biblical interpretation of which he was the world expert, offers not only a key to the broken past but also a call to its healing. If the Kabbalah appeared to Scholem as an allegory of Jewish exile, Zionism was his way to bring this wandering to an end. As a young man Prochnik was fired by similar hopes, and in what he describes elsewhere as a 'shadow-arc' of his subject, he too emigrated to Jerusalem—only, like Scholem, to be disillusioned by the state politics he encountered there. Yet even that loss is lightened somewhat, for Prochnik came to discover what Scholem had also learned: how we are then mandated to 'live responsibly, inside history.' That ethical invitation is heard in every sentence of this inspiring book."

—HAL FOSTER, author of *Bad New Days: Art, Criticism, Emergency*

"Reading this utterly absorbing book, I felt like the stranger in the title, led by the hand through the complementary landscapes of two lives: Gershom Scholem's and the author's. Moving between them with deftness and artistry, Prochnik holds the reader's attention at every turn. In the process, he casts new light on Kabbalah and develops a critique of Zionism that is as thought-provoking as any I have read."

—BRIAN KLUG, author of *Being Jewish and Doing Justice: Bringing Argument to Life*

Stranger
in a
Strange
Land

Searching for
Gershom Scholem
and Jerusalem

GEORGE PROCHNIK

 Other Press New York

Production editor: Yvonne E. Cárdenas
Text designer: Julie Fry
This book was set in Legacy.

10 9 8 7 6 5 4 3 2 1

Library of Congress Cataloging-in-Publication Data

Names: Prochnik, George, author.
Title: Stranger in a strange land : searching for Gershom
    Scholem and Jerusalem / by George Prochnik.
Description: New York : Other Press, 2016. | Includes
    bibliographical references and index.
Identifiers: LCCN 2016034545 | ISBN 9781590517765 (hardcover)
    | ISBN 9781590517772 (e-book)
Subjects: LCSH: Scholem, Gershom, 1897–1982. | Jewish
    scholars — Germany — Biography | Jewish scholars —
    Israel — Biography
Classification: LCC BM755.S295 P76 2016 | DDC 296.092 [B] — dc23
LC record available at https://lccn.loc.gov/2016034545

For Yona, Tzvi, Zach, and Rafael

always and afterward

*In his commentary on the Psalms, Origen quotes a "Hebrew" scholar...
as saying that the Holy Scriptures are like a large house with many,
many rooms, and that outside each door lies a key—but it is not the
right one. To find the right key that will open the doors—that is the great
and arduous task.* —GERSHOM SCHOLEM

*And she bare him a son, and he called his name Gershom: for he said,
I have been a stranger in a strange land.* —EXODUS 2:22

INTRODUCTION

LET ME BEGIN at the end.

I fought my way back down a staircase outside the building, pushing through dense branches, trampling on garbage and broken glass, clutching at crumbly stucco, scratched and slapped by a riot of foliage. At a window, I peered through metal bars into a dark room in which the ceiling had partially collapsed. A few pieces of splintered wooden furniture lay in shadows, amidst a chaos of torn paper and plastic. I began descending again, pausing once more before a tattered, moldy book that had been discarded near the bottom of the steps, open to a line drawing of two boys at a bookshelf. One, dressed in an old-fashioned sailor suit, stood bent over, hands on his knees. The other, who looked older, knelt on one leg, withdrawing a volume. The caption beneath the image read, in Hebrew, "And three rows of books came into sight…"

I continued down until I reached the ground level, which was buried in refuse, and forced my way through the hard limbs and prickly brush that had taken over the narrow path to the sidewalk. When at last I'd made my way back out the rusted gate, I was panting. Twisting back, I gazed once more toward the building: Abarbanel Road 28 — though the number set into the façade was so worn it could only be seen up close, and the entire structure was screened by a tangled wall of wild shrubbery.

I still couldn't really believe it. On this pristine, elegant little street, at the heart of expensive Jerusalem's costly Rehavia neighborhood, one building had reverted to the anarchy of primeval nature — and this building was the former home of Gershom Scholem, the greatest scholar and one of the most formidable intellects to inhabit the city in the twentieth century.

A bearded man in a bright white shirt and dark pants with a big bunch of keys dangling from his belt and a black velvet yarmulke on his head was moving into the large gleaming building under renovation next door, transporting boxes from the back of his car with the help of a couple of young men dressed in the same Orthodox apparel. He halted a moment not far from me on the sidewalk.

"Excuse me —" I had to call over to him. I had to tell somebody. "Did you know this used to be Gershom Scholem's house?"

The man turned to me, scanning my features with a mix of apathy and mild suspicion.

"Gershom Scholem — the great writer — the rediscoverer of the Kabbalah." I said.

He continued to eye me coolly. I couldn't tell whether he had never heard the name, or was simply indifferent.

"Gershom Scholem?" I made the name a question.

I forbore from adding that some readers of his work think that Scholem's achievement surpassed even that of Sigmund Freud. Cynthia Ozick, the essayist and novelist, once argued that whereas Freud "dared only a little way past the margins of psychology, Scholem, whose medium was history, touched on the very ground of human imagination." Scholem, Ozick declared, "went in pursuit of the cosmos." Harold Bloom, the literary critic, had gone farther still, declaring that for many contemporary Jewish intellectuals, "the Kabbalah of Gershom Scholem is now more normative than normative Judaism itself. For them, Scholem is far more than a historian, far more even than a theologian. He is not less than a prophet."

Admittedly, these remarks were made some time ago. Both the essays from which they're drawn were anthologized in 1987, the year

I first visited Israel. Still, while Gershom Scholem's legacy might have been pecked at since then, it had never been dismantled. By conducting a herculean analysis of countless texts long viewed by Jewish historians as nonsense — the mad, titanic systems concocted by religious figures dancing on the brink of heresy, intent on grappling with the most profound, irrational mysteries of the universe — Scholem had single-handedly created an academic discipline out of an obscure theological tradition, and challenged academia itself with a lush, alien spirituality. Nor, despite the prodigious scale of this scholarly achievement, had he remained cloistered in the sanctuary of his book-lined study. Having moved to Palestine after the First World War as an idealistic, if idiosyncratic, Zionist, he'd thrown himself into the fray of Mandate-era political struggles, becoming among the most active members of the Brit Shalom movement, which sought to create a binational Jewish-Arab state in Palestine. After that movement collapsed, he continued to weigh in as a major public figure on subjects ranging from the dangers of messianism in state politics, to the meaning of evil, and the nature of the public intellectual's responsibility to his or her people in the shadow of historical catastrophe.

Arriving in Palestine in 1923, in the early years of rising Jewish immigration, continuing to write, teach, and lecture through all the subsequent riots and wars almost to the day of his death in 1982, Scholem's life had unfolded in tandem with the creation and ideological evolution of the State of Israel. It was one thing for his name to have largely disappeared in the United States, but here — in Jerusalem? To find Scholem's house not only unmarked, but utterly derelict?

When I explored the story of Stefan Zweig for an earlier book, I was following one line out from the ruins of twentieth-century European history — a hopelessly snarled thread, as it proved, which never truly escaped that labyrinth of destruction. Zweig's wild, zigzagging exile across Europe and the New World after the advent of Hitler, culminating in his suicide in Petrópolis, Brazil, embodied the predicament of the cosmopolitan humanist who could not abandon his idealized vision of European culture, even after he'd been forced to acknowledge its illusory character. More finally than in Vienna, Salzburg, or even Paris, Zweig had made his home in the palace of the European imagination. For all that this domain was always, of necessity, an intellectual construct, it proved no less consuming an attachment than that a "blood and soil" nationalist might feel for the physical ground of the homeland. Zweig's experience dramatized, on an operatic scale, the distinction between worldly nomadism and legally defined statelessness. His story offers an object lesson in the different forms of homelessness conferred by the conflict between the nation and the individual — some of these conditions psychologically chronic, even when the native land is at last supplanted by a materially fruitful new life on fresh shores.

Gershom Scholem's life trajectory seemed to present not just an alternative but an antithetical narrative: the founding of a home where there'd been no home before. Rather than engaging in a rearguard action to conjure "the world of yesterday" (the title Zweig gave to the memoir he wrote in exile), Scholem left Germany for good, entirely of his own volition, ten years prior to Hitler's appointment as chancellor. Declaring that he'd never felt any greater sense of home in the conceptual than in the concrete Europe, Scholem made his bid to escape through Zionism, which he described as "a calculated risk" aimed at bringing about "the destruction of the reality of Exile." By his own account, Scholem's path had led in a straight line: *From Berlin to Jerusalem* was the title he gave his autobiography. Resettling himself some eighteen hundred miles from Berlin, the city of his birth, Scholem established a home that, for all its remoteness, appeared to physically and psychologically complete him. On reaching Palestine, he changed his name from Gerhard — the German name his parents gave him — to Gershom, the Hebrew name Moses bestowed on his son after first fleeing Egypt. If Zweig's story revealed a dream of paradise lost, Scholem's tale at first suggested a dream of paradise found. "The building of the land of the Bible and the foundation of the State of Israel represent, if you will allow me to use a daring formulation, a utopian retreat of the Jews into their own history," Scholem wrote. He considered an exclamation by the philosopher Hermann Cohen against the Zionists — "Those fellows want to be happy!" — the most profound statement ever made by an opponent of the movement.

Not only was Palestine spiritually rejuvenating, it rewarded Scholem with invigorating practical opportunities as well. Shortly after his arrival in Jerusalem, he was named director of the Hebrew Division of the Jewish National and University Library, "which itself serves to prepare the way for a great academic undertaking that will be closely connected with the rebuilding of this land by Jewish hands," as he wrote to a professor under whose tutelage he'd taken his degree in Semitics at the University of Munich. Noting the difficulties for Jewish scholars in Munich in the wake of Hitler's 1923 Beer Hall Putsch, Scholem said that it was best for him to establish his life "on a foundation and in a context that promise, despite shortages and obstacles, to develop securely and steadily in all areas of life." In Jerusalem, he concluded, young people like himself would be liberated from the panoply of torments and anxieties poisoning their existence in the fatherland.

A photograph of Scholem taken a year after his emigration shows him standing in a slim-cut black suit before a wall of rough-hewn Jerusalem limestone. Hands jammed in his jacket pockets, head crowned by a shock of tousled black hair, he's making a sour

face. He looks much younger than his twenty-seven years — lanky, brash, and defiant. There's a rock-and-roll insolence to his pose. He's carving a place for himself and knows it.

Indeed, the fate of those he left behind in Germany seemed to confirm the inspired prescience of Scholem's choice. "Oh how lucky you are — and how wretched *we* are," his friend Erich Brauer wrote after receiving one of Scholem's first reports from Palestine. In Jerusalem, Brauer remarked, "One needs only the right amount of decisiveness (and naturally the proper talents)." Of life back in Berlin, he said, "There's nothing new to report here; we all make our way, twisting and turning, through Germany's ruins." Sentiments like these were echoed with far greater pathos by some of Scholem's former compatriots after National Socialism's ascendancy, as these ruins became a defining motif of the age.

But if, on one reading, Scholem's post-European story offers a textbook-perfect, life-affirming counterpart to Zweig's disastrous plunge, the question of Israel—slipping so neatly into the slot opened up by "the Jewish question" in Scholem and Zweig's youth—complicates matters. On closer study, the dense problem of the Jewish homeland proves to be only the most conspicuous of many factors, historical and psychological, complicating Scholem's clean one-way version of the narrative arc "from Berlin to Jerusalem."

For one thing, there's no question that Scholem's overwhelmingly intense—and only intermittently requited—friendship with Walter Benjamin persistently displaced his consciousness from Jerusalem. After Scholem's death, his widow, Fanya Freud, remarked that Benjamin was the only person Scholem had ever truly loved. The debate the two men conducted, which pitted Benjamin's Marx-inflected universalism against Scholem's Judeocentric particularism, ultimately concerned nothing less than the question of how to create the most profound life work possible—how to avoid misspending one's time on earth. Do we mine down as deep as we can go into the shaft of our own personal origins? Or do we strive to disseminate our energies and insights as broadly as possible across the panorama of human production?

Though on the most literal level, Scholem's choice to remain in Israel indicates that he did not concede to Benjamin, their arguments continued to whirl through his thoughts long after Benjamin's death, finding explicit and cryptic expression in letters and books—never truly resolving. Scholem stayed on in Jerusalem, but he was too clear-eyed and repelled by sanctimony to deny the dangers of politically actualized Zionism. Only two years after arriving in Palestine, Scholem wrote a friend back in Berlin, "No one should foster the illusion that what happens here and will occur in the future…has the slightest thing in common *in substantia et essentia*, with Zionism, in whose name your faithful servant is here. In the battle between the building up of Palestine *coûte qu'il coûte* and Zionism, the latter is hopelessly outgunned." During the years leading up to establishment of the State of Israel, his writings struck an increasingly somber, prophetic note on the topic. "There would be no use in denying that the countenance of the Zionist cause has darkened in catastrophic fashion," he declared to Martin Buber, his onetime spiritual mentor, in 1930. Acknowledging that the cause to which he'd devoted his life might prove irredeemably flawed, he wrote that the anguish of this disappointment was almost unendurable. "After all, we have to realize that our interpretation of Zionism does no good if someday (and there is no mistaking the fact that the decisive hour has come) the face of Zionism, even that which is only turned inward, should prove to be that of a Medusa."

Scholem's own ambivalences were surely part of the reason his failure to persuade Benjamin to join him in Jerusalem, despite years of ardent effort to make this move philosophically and logistically palatable, remained an open wound. Not only did Benjamin's resistance frustrate and hurt Scholem—fueling a lasting antipathy toward Benjamin's historical-materialist friends on the left whom Scholem viewed as having tricked Benjamin out of his true calling in Jewish studies—it also brought Scholem up against his own limitations.

The critic George Steiner—himself hardly a poster child for intellectual humility—described what it was like to visit Scholem in his final years and confront the master's "Voltairean mien, the needling eyes, the bat's ears ever alert, the lips given to twists of sardonic dismay." Scholem's countenance, wrote Steiner, "composed a mask of reason"—one that discomposed virtually every person who came into his presence. Steiner himself, by his own admission, "could not engage Scholem's sustained interest" and was relegated to being a listener. Yet when the subject of Benjamin came up, Scholem himself yielded to a kind of awe. In Benjamin, Steiner wrote, Scholem "experienced an intuitive clairvoyance into the fabric of language and symbolism, a reasoned though metaphoric revelation as to the meanings of history, which he judged superior even to his own."

Lecturing on Benjamin in New York in 1964, Scholem contrasted him with all those Jewish authors writing in German, like Stefan Zweig and Arthur Schnitzler, who had looked upon themselves "unquestioningly...as forming part of German culture and tradition, as belonging to the German people." Having subscribed to "a lurid and tragic illusion," Scholem said, they all might have echoed the cry of the author Berthold Auerbach, who famously lamented on his deathbed, "In vain have I lived, in vain have I suffered." Benjamin, however, "never succumbed to the illusion of being at home." Attesting to Benjamin's terminal alienation in Europe might have tempted Scholem to parade the righteousness of his own choice, but in fact he admitted that he didn't know whether Benjamin or Kafka (his other signal exception) would have been at home in the Land of Israel either. "I doubt it very much," he concluded. "They truly came from foreign parts and knew it."

These "foreign parts" must be understood as the transcendent realm. And thus, while the choice to live in Israel might have been preferable in Scholem's eyes to entertaining the fantasy of being at home in Germany, Benjamin's refusal to join him in Palestine reminded Scholem of a yet higher path than that pointing to Jerusalem: a consecrated philosophical vocation, which lay beyond his own sphere of action. In this sense, Benjamin's life choices constituted a permanent rebuke to Scholem—felt by him, on days when the wind blew the wrong historical direction, like an aching in the metaphysical joints.

A friend described a scene from Scholem's final years, when all but one of the dazzling German-born scholars and philosophers who'd known both Benjamin and Scholem well, and who could grasp the nuances of Scholem's eclectic strain of Zionism, were dead. Every week, Scholem would convene with this last revenant, Werner Kraft, and there, in the shadows and lamplight, the men would resume their endless conversation about Walter Benjamin. "Both of them cursed him, week after week, year after year," the friend reported. "I think it was only because they never felt loved by him. Walter was like a deity who let them down. Or maybe they thought they had failed him."

The feelings of adoration, betrayal, overidentification, and mourning that Benjamin inspired make Scholem's development at key junctures comprehensible only as a love story. "He's just like me, only five years older," Scholem wrote of Benjamin, adding that this made him "the paragon of the way one should struggle and wrestle."

I find myself haunted by the image of those Jerusalem gatherings. Kraft and Scholem drawn back into each other's company time and again at the home of the educator and religious philosopher Ernst Simon, another old friend from Germany, not just to nostalgically rekindle memories of the absent comrade and mentor of their German youth, but also to curse the dead—struggling with some profound, unanswerable need. These three elderly figures, seated, pacing, gesturing in the quiet shade of Rehavia, amid their vast, grave libraries of old German books and their little brassy souvenirs of the new country they now called home. Kraft with his melancholy, deep-set eyes and egg-shaped bald dome; their host, Simon, dapper, genial, with a penetrating dark gaze; Scholem—tall

and gangly to the end, wizened and spritelike, a kind of hypereru-
dite Jewish Puck on stilts — reaching out to snatch another of the
little chocolates of which he was inordinately fond, fluttering his
long, eloquent fingers together beneath pursed lips as he prepared
to expound on their vanished past.

Almost all the apartments in that neighborhood share a family
resemblance: modest in size, boasting thick stone walls and tiled
floors, ringed by balconies fragrant with pots of herbs and flowers.
I picture the trio of remarkable castaways in a window open to the
tingling mountain breeze of nighttime in Jerusalem, trading allusions while the wind carried scents of jasmine and, sometimes, the
summons to prayer from muezzins in the Old City.

The enchantment of the setting is palpable to me, since I lived
in Rehavia from the late 1980s through much of the '90s, initially
on Rehov Alfasi, where Kraft was still living at the time of my
arrival. I only just missed the possibility of looking up one night
on my way home from the university to glimpse these men in some
glowing room, too lost in conversation to notice the student who'd
stopped on the sidewalk below, straining to hear their voices. The
neighborhood as a whole retained at that time the proud, slightly
fussy, scholarly character of its many German-Jewish immigrants.
Piano scales drifted from the windows. Old courtesies wove
through casual sidewalk conversations in which avid curiosity vied
with elegy. Poppy-seed pastries at the tiny bakeries were exquisitely
layered.

And yet my intimacy with Scholem's chosen city doesn't fill me
with any sense of ease in telling this story, for all that visions of the
place remain piercingly vivid to me. Instead, my own experience of
Jerusalem exerts a violent pressure on this history — jams forward,
demanding its own voice in the drama. Rather than making me
feel sanguine about writing about Gershom Scholem in Jerusalem,
my familiarity with the city infuses me with sorrow and alarm.

After I turned away that fall afternoon when I found Scholem's home in a state of abandon, I wandered back toward the small compound of two-story apartment buildings around a courtyard at the intersection of Gaza and Arlozoroff streets, where I'd spent most of my years in Jerusalem — writing, teaching, and helping to raise a family. Light filtered down through tall trees, beams and curtains that shifted slowly over walls of pale gold stone, magenta bougainvillea, and blazing trumpet vine. The neighborhood could not have been more dreamily peaceful — just as it had appeared when I first walked its passageways. Here and there, traces of antiquity nestle in shady recesses. On Rehov Alfasi, almost directly across from the garden flat where my eldest son slept as a newborn in a bed made from a dresser drawer, a Maccabean tomb, chiseled from bedrock in the Second Temple era, juts up, boxy, pointy, fiercely archaic.

It always seemed just amazing to me that I could walk out of my door whenever the mood struck and in moments be staring into those dark chambers constructed more than two thousand years ago, back at a time when this area was the heart of Jerusalem's "City of the Dead," a vast necropolis in the limestone basin surrounding the Old City. The walls of the tomb are covered with writings and images. Most are illegible now, but it's still possible to make out a few charcoal pictures of warships manned with archers. An Aramaic lamentation bidding farewell to the tomb's namesake is inscribed on one wall, along with lines in Greek: "Those who are alive — rejoice."

Those who are alive — rejoice . . . The phrase reverberates in Jerusalem, striking a note somewhere between admonition and mockery. So often it's the dead who are groomed here for rapturous celebration, while the living mourn. It's thrilling to be able to visit such ancient memorials on a whim, but when one considers how these constant interruptions of the present by the importunate dead fray the attention of contemporaries in Jerusalem, it appears a more ambiguous blessing.

Although the physical setting of my former neighborhood is much the same as it was when I arrived, if more expensively manicured, the human cast here has transformed. I don't refer to the inevitable action of time on any population. In my passage through Rehavia that day, almost every man I saw wore a black fedora and dark suit. The women hid their hair beneath wigs, scarves, or hats. They wore long dresses and clutched small, worn prayer books.

If, when I lived in Rehavia the neighborhood was largely populated by older, mostly secular *yekkes* — Jews of German descent — today it is almost entirely religious, and becomes more Orthodox all the time. Playgrounds are flocked with religious families. The certificates of rabbinical approval on its shops grow more prominent, numerous, and arcane. Whereas previously one or two cafés opened on the Sabbath, all businesses now observe the laws dictated by the rabbis. In virtually every aspect of its public comportment, the neighborhood proclaims that God's manifest command rules here.

There's nothing unique to Rehavia in this transition. Virtually the whole of West Jerusalem grows more consumingly religious every year. On visit after visit, friends whose families were staunchly faithless for generations tell me that a brother, a sister, or a child has just become observant. They reveal this with bewildered, apprehensive gazes, as if they'd been struck on the head with a blunt object while sleeping. In the eyes of some nonbelievers, Orthodoxy's spread through the city bears a resemblance to the proliferation of plague through the North African town Oran in Camus's novel. Inscrutable and ruthless. Shrouding women in layer upon layer of concealment. The Haredi, "those who tremble in fear of God," produce children at a rate so far above the reproductive pace of their secular counterparts that before long a majority of the city's schoolchildren will be ultra-Orthodox. Their trembling declares the community's righteousness before the world and heralds the ultimate triumph of their vision of the holy city, along with the promised defeat of those resisting this conception of the universe.

But the forms of faith pumping through the channels of the nationalist movements are more disturbing. For these latter believers seek to sanctify the here and now through the action of territorial expansion. And if their numbers are not growing at quite the same rate as the Haredi in demographic terms, they soar beyond them with respect to power in the political arena.

While I walked through Rehavia, I wondered what Scholem would have made of all these changes in the city. The complexity of his thinking makes it hazardous to draw conclusions. He was repelled by what he called "traditional national Jewish theology," but his life's work centered on the effort to revivify a vast corpus of religious ideas, partly to make Jews aware of their power to reimagine and seize control of their destiny. Whereas post-Enlightenment Jewish authorities had effectively buried mysticism, Scholem relished the notion that by bringing Kabbalah out of the murky, disreputable underground to which it had been consigned by mainstream guardians of the faith he would be reintroducing an explosive element into a neutered spiritual and historical consciousness. Even if he danced the fence on the question of whether it was still possible to actually *be* a Kabbalist, Scholem felt that the jolt normative Judaism would receive by confronting its mystical substrate could only be salutary—potentially even salvational for the contemporary disassociated religious self. The parallels with Freud's project are obvious, but Scholem was seeking to recover from the depths of institutionalized repression the demon-and-sex-rife netherworld of an entire culture. And he was doing so not to buttress reason by elevating awareness of what lay below the veneer of civilization but to puncture that surface with a vitalizing shot of the irrational.

It's not surprising, then, that although Scholem himself could never bear to live under the yoke of the commandments, he nevertheless saw secularism as a transitional stage of Zionism. He believed it contributed to the idea of a Jewish renaissance that moved the young builders of the state but nonetheless marked a phase that would ultimately be superseded by some new, as yet undetermined expression of religiosity. Myth as a political predator did not beat its path into modernity through religious tradition, Scholem contended, but on the wings of the belief that humanity would one day progress *beyond* faith to some glimmering, benignly rationalist universalism. In the mid-1970s, Scholem gave an interview in which he described as foolish the notion that

Jews should form a nation like other nations. "Even if we wish to be a nation like all the nations, we will not succeed," he said. "And if we succeed — that will be the end of us." Rather than a nation like others, he subscribed to the sentiment expressed in Exodus, "And you shall be unto Me a kingdom of priests, and a holy nation." This, he said, had always been *his* definition of Zionism.

But what in practice does such a definition mean? At the moment I began to write this book, decisions being made in Jerusalem were translating into bloody mayhem in Gaza, and acts of terror and deadly riots were erupting around the country. I found that I could not cordon off that destruction from the historical narrative before me. There was no way to write about Scholem in Jerusalem, or about his intellectual journey to that city, without reflecting on the convulsions still unsettling the Land.

It's not only that these events were too full of anguish and ecstatic fury to be repressed. Whether at his most scholarly or most political, Scholem never stopped insisting that Jewish history could not be approached as a sealed book. It must be treated as an element in molten flux — taking shape now before our eyes, through our hands, in ways that fire meaning backward and forward in time. Throughout his career, Scholem argued for the imperative of what he called "living responsibly, inside history," which as a contemporary Jew meant wrestling with the Zionist project as that continued to unfold on the ground. What are we to make of this injunction today?

In a lecture he gave about messianism in 1959, Scholem asserted that "the utopian return to Zion" signified "a readiness which no longer allows itself to be fed with hopes. Born out of the horror and destruction that was Jewish history in our generation, it is bound to history itself and not to meta-history." He went on, "Whether or not Jewish history will be able to endure this entry into the concrete realm without perishing in the crisis of the Messianic claim which has virtually been conjured up — that is the question." The question remains, and we owe Scholem the respect of believing he meant us to take it seriously. His outspoken, lifelong engagement with the Zionist project matters not only for understanding his own psychophilosophical development but also for the effort to fathom the State's own trajectory.

Stefan Zweig renounced the concrete realm and withdrew from living history into an ersatz version of the world of yesterday in the Brazilian wilderness before departing from this world altogether. Gershom Scholem dared to stake everything on the wager that Jewish history could transcend what he saw as its own death wish, born of generations of suffering, by reincarnating at the point where it began. Standing at the crossroads between these positions, knowing all we know today, which way should we turn? Surely we must choose the path of life? *Those who are alive — rejoice . . .*

My thoughts keep winding back to the dreamlike vision of Scholem's Rehavia home swallowed in wild vegetation. Does Scholem's intellectual legacy now lie similarly abandoned and subsumed? If so, what might this say about my own life choices made in response to that legacy?

Setting out to follow in Zweig's footsteps was a conscious, authorial decision. But in the case of Gershom Scholem, I had already followed in his footsteps many years before contemplating a book about him, not in order to conduct research but in the attempt to create a life of my own.

When I moved to Jerusalem, at the age of twenty-seven, in the summer of 1988, I brought with me an old, battered paperback edition of Scholem's *On the Kabbalah and Its Symbolism*, with the pink, yellow, orange, and white Tree of Life on its cover suggesting a hallucination of cotton candy from the heyday of Haight-Ashbury.

I might not quite have been waving my little psychedelic volume in the manner of a protorevolutionary with Mao's little red book, but the comparison is not altogether off base. With respect to my decision to relocate to Israel, Scholem's work effectively substituted for the Bible—which I did not carry along. Though I hadn't yet read Bloom on Scholem, and though I would never have consciously framed the matter to myself in these terms, I was one of those for whom Scholem loomed as a kind of prophet. I found in his work if not faith, yet something closer to revelation than anything I could discover in normative Judaism.

His books, which I read insatiably over the course of the year preceding that move, seemed to make an end run around many of the obstacles I encountered when trying to imagine life within the framework of my father's religion. Not that my father himself was observant. To the contrary—he labeled practicing Jews perfect examples of people who, however smart they might be, "don't have enough sense to step inside when it's raining." But the bemused indifference, alternating with sarcastic hostility, that he displayed toward all formal aspects of Judaism was part of its appeal. My interest in the Jewish faith contrived to be at once a classic first-born son's revolt against the father and an identification with the long tradition that his own father had continued at least in part to abide by. (By embodying both conservative and revolutionary forces, this posture thus unconsciously aligned me with one of the key dialectical features Scholem identified in Zionism itself.)

I saw my father having let the flame of his Jewish identity burn down as low as it could go without altogether extinguishing. My own mother was not Jewish, after all! There was something magically intoxicating in the notion that I might choose to blow on that flame through the actions of my own life and so magnify its blaze no end. Too many Jews died in the Holocaust to countenance the idea that our family would just step forever outside the nimbus or noose of Jewish history as casually as they might step out of the car in a supermarket parking lot. Almost all the history of my father's family had been lost in the upheaval of their flight from Europe, for God's sake. Too much of the past had been surrendered to the conflagration of evil to let what remained get lost like crumbs between entertainment-room couch pillows. I owed a debt to the dead, and I meant to pay.

But my sense that this debt should be addressed through a greater identification with Judaism than could be acquired strictly through cultural reference points—bageloxy—made my actual encounters with observance all the more dispiriting. I hated praying. Orthodox synagogues were endlessly problematic in their intolerances. Reform services were intolerably denuded of authenticity. Either way, the services bored me silly. And though, when I set out to study the canonical texts of Jewish belief, I discovered potent flashes of ideas and imagery, there seemed at last just too much dross to plow through before getting to the sparkly bits. The books of the Bible were one thing, at least minus Deuteronomy, Leviticus, and Numbers. But the ritualized law seemed for the most part an object lesson in how to nurture obsessive-compulsive disorder.

And this is where Gershom Scholem's writing came in. His portrayal of the Kabbalists evoked a realm of mystics who succeeded in being absolutely subversive of the tradition while somehow remaining within its historical folds. The Kabbalah in Scholem's rendering appeared to embody, indeed, nothing less than a rich Jewish tradition of the subversion of Jewish tradition. Perhaps best of all, there was a hint carried through his writing that the intense study of this covert history might somehow replace the obligation to worship.

The potency of Scholem's work wasn't limited to the content of what he wrote. It was also a factor of his tone, which could sometimes be exacting but always projected a seductive authority. Scholem's first degree was in mathematics, and the lucidity of hard logic girds his writing. Against the muzzy realm where the mystic urges I'd hitherto encountered swirled and twinkled,

Scholem wielded a textual mastery that gave his subject the weight of stone and force of iron. Here was mysticism for the age of heavy metal.

Through all the provocative ideas that glittered through his writing, there was one concept that cropped up repeatedly, as a kind of choral refrain, which I found galvanizing: Kabbalah preserved the frame of monotheism while shattering the idol of monolithic truth. Scholem's notion of truth's absolute multiplicity was epitomized in a commentary he treasured from the sixteenth-century mystic Isaac Luria: "Every word of the Torah has six hundred thousand 'faces,' that is, layers of meaning or entrances, one for each of the children of Israel who stood at the foot of Mount Sinai. Each face is turned toward only one of them; he alone can see it and decipher it. Each man has his own unique access to Revelation." Elsewhere Scholem wrote, "The binding character of the Revelation for the collective has disappeared."

This is a formula for religious anarchy. And Scholem was perfectly aware of that implication. As a young man he'd been attracted to political anarchism, especially as embodied in the work of Gustav Landauer, a leading German-Jewish theorist of the movement. Though Scholem ultimately could not overcome his skepticism about the social-governance program of anarchist doctrine, based on what he saw as its unduly optimistic assumptions about human nature, these reservations did not apply in a theological context. Indeed, *religious* anarchy might be said to be grounded in deep spiritual pessimism. (However cruel one all-controlling, singular-Revelation-bestowing God might be, life became infinitely more lonely in His absence.) While Scholem left behind his youthful political idealism, he continued to draw on aspects of anarchist thought in his meditations on the Kabbalah. Elevating the notion of the individual's ability to take responsibility for the historical tradition into a transcendent faith, Scholem came, over time, to define himself explicitly as "a religious anarchist."

The concept might be unstable and elusive, but still it captured my imagination. Looking back, I think I went to Jerusalem in search of a guide to religious anarchy. Gershom Scholem helped plant the seed for this contrarian yearning — the wish for a God-less god, and an outlaw's Law, and a revelation that could be stolen from the gilt vaults of orthodoxy, broken up, and redistributed among the poor in faith.

Part I

ONE

1915 RADICALIZED EVERYTHING. In one year, Gerhard Scholem sealed his passion for Zionism, discovered the Kabbalah, got thrown out of high school, met Walter Benjamin, and tried to kiss his first crush. For a time, he also thought he was the Messiah.

That winter, he spent whole days in his room in his parents' apartment at Neue Grünstrasse 26, opposite the garden of St. Peter's Parish, watching the snow fall in mad swirls. "Earth is a snowflake's destiny," he wrote in his journal. "For snow, fate is an unknown, inexplicable, and 'terrestrial' power." He could apply this principle to humans as well, he realized: "We also put up resistance when we plunge into an unexpected abyss, and we also melt. We are snowflakes with a bit more distinction."

Ideas were exploding inside him. He read like a maniac. For months on end he strove to acquire what he described as a total perspective on every variety of poetic longing. He wrote unremarkable verse and brought out an underground newspaper titled *Blue-White Spectacles*, whose purpose was to examine the world through the lenses of Zionism. And he felt bitter disappointment at almost everyone around him. Everything about his stuffy, small-minded family circle—exemplars of the Jewish middle class—nauseated him. The old men who glared disapprovingly at him as a nebbish were the stereotypical provincials who'd come to Berlin as pants salesmen and ended up wealthy manufacturers of bathtubs and sausage skins. Later, he wrote his friend Werner Kraft that the

definition of the word "bourgeois" was simply "all things abomi-
nable." His father Arthur's canny management of their print shop
didn't translate into a shred of wisdom about anything vital to the
human spirit. What could you say about someone who spent his
free time grandstanding in professional associations and immersing himself in minutiae of health insurance plans for the graphic
arts trade? Yes, after war was declared, he'd had the shrewd realization that Germany's bureaucratic apparatus would swell beyond
measure. He promptly established a Forms Division in the shop,
which flourished. The family would probably sail through this
revolting bloodbath—a "petty-bourgeois war...draped with the
mask of a holy war," Gerhard said—and come out on top.

But the man's only higher value was eager conformity to everything German. He was an extremely advanced assimilationist, no
question. Arthur worked on Yom Kippur, and fasting was out of
the question. The sole reason he might have gone to the Grosse
Synagogue on the Jews' holiest day would have been to savor the
moment when, upon stepping out midmorning with the other
worshippers, he'd hear the cheeky headwaiter at the restaurant
next door announce, "The gentlemen who are fasting will be
served in the back room."

Christmas was observed as a national holiday, with roast goose,
a decorated tree, lots of presents, and a recital of "Silent Night" by
a piano-playing aunt who merely pretended to be catering to the
gentile cook and servant girl. Arthur strictly forbade the use of any
Jewish idiomatic expressions at home—a proscription Gerhard's
irrepressible mother, Betty, flouted at every opportunity. *"Hat sich die
Kose bemeikelt!"* she would say. So the goat shits on itself! (In other
words, "What else is new?") His mother brought that phrase to Berlin straight from her ancestral roots in the Grand Duchy of Warsaw.

Betty was the flash of light in their home—sharp-witted and
willowy, literary and beautiful. (Whereas his father was stocky and
myopic, with a droopy mustache and a cannonball head.) Gerhard

had inherited Betty's long countenance, sad eyes, and arched brows. Her letters were masterful. She could compose poems and plays for family events in a trice. And she read everything from Schiller to Stefan Zweig's quite impressive translations of Belgian poetry. Gerhard's tenderest memories were of the intimate hours he spent with her. After the noonday meal, she would stretch out on the elegant chaise longue in her bedroom and Gerhard would swaddle her in a voluminous camel blanket. He continued the ritual until his twentieth year, in 1917, when he left home for good. But he kept that blanket all his life. Once he'd wrapped his mother in, he would be permitted to pinch a bar or two of fine Swiss chocolate from a special drawer and then unburden himself of deep grievances beside her.

His father was a reactionary drudge and a hypocrite. When he lit his cigar on the Sabbath candle while intoning the mock blessing *"Br'ei pri tobacco"* — blessed is the fruit of tobacco — Gerhard wanted to howl. Arthur would rise from the dinner table once or twice a year and deliver a thundering speech about the holy wonder of the Jews' mission on earth: "We brought monotheism to the world! We introduced to humanity a purely rational morality!" ("Reason is a stupid man's longing," Gerhard wrote in his journal. "These people think that in the messianic age everything will be rational. God forbid!") And then — the pièce de résistance of his father's sermon — "Baptism is an unprincipled and servile act!" A line likely as not to be followed by some after-dinner tirade against Jewish backwardness.

Even as a child, he'd been aware that the bad faith of it all stank to high heaven. It was no wonder that he had grabbed every opportunity to escape the house. Once roller skates hit Berlin, Gerhard took off. Only about half the city was paved, but he skated every bit of it — streaking fearlessly between carriages, streetcars, and automobiles, not to mention the bicycles, which Joseph Roth described

flying all directions through the streets of Berlin "like arrows shot from a bow." Every intersection was a pedestrian nightmare, Roth observed. "One man stopped, another sprinted, arms across his chest, cradling his life." Then came "the wailing hoot from a policeman's cornet" commanding a rapid march amid "a whole assembly of trams, cars crushing one another's rib cages, a flickering of colors, a noisy, parping, surging color, red and yellow and violet yells" beneath a sky wildly crosshatched with electric wires.

When he wasn't on roller skates, he'd played pickup games of marbles with other freewheeling boys in Märkischer Park, then wandered down to the banks of the Spree and watched the long-distance trains roll by, intoxicated by the names on the individual cars that spelled out exotic-sounding destinations—Hoek van Holland, Eydtkuhnen, and Oświęcim, the latter a border station that would become well known as Auschwitz. Or he'd dash off to explore the latest chalk graffiti on the fences of nearby storage lots: *"Gustav ist doof!"* (Gustav is a dufus!) He liked the rude vigor of the pure Berlin dialect he found there, just as he reveled in his mother's ungroomed Jewish idioms. The raw and primordial always enchanted him.

By his early teens, Gerhard was taking flight from his surroundings inside Berlin's new movie theaters. These *Flimmerkisten* (flicker boxes) were often built to suggest palace temples, sometimes in the Moorish style. The Orient peeked through the hurly-burly of Berlin in the form of painted backgrounds at the carousel and in the Orientalist Art Nouveau that was inspiring the work of some avant-garde Jewish writers and artists. Entire sections of Berlin's Jewish Quarter—especially the more economically lackadaisical and lyrically pious streets—evoked the Orient. The Eastern European Jews who populated these places, with their shabby robes, curlicue sidelocks, and velvet caps, their melancholy, elevated gazes and aura of antique wisdom, were all the more beguiling to Gerhard and his peers because their parents found them repellant. Martin Buber's hugely popular anthologies of Hasidic tales stoked the cult appeal of Eastern Jews for the bourgeois offspring of assimilated families, serving as a gateway fantasy to the Levant.

Buber lectured frequently, with a charismatic radiance that mesmerized his listeners. In 1912, he gave a speech titled "The Spirit of the Orient and Judaism," which identified the contemporary Jew as an Oriental, along with the Indian and Chinese. Where the Occidental saw only the world's fixed, objective multiplicity, the Oriental was able to perceive limitless motion. To the Oriental, in Buber's vision, everything was processes and relationships, mutuality and community, action and decision, against the atomized, petrified Western man of the senses. And everything Buber attributed to the Oriental at large, he said, was especially true of the Jew. "We need only look at the decadent yet still wondrous Hasid of our days; to watch him as he prays to his God, shaken by his fervor, expressing with his whole body what his lips are saying—a sight both grotesque and sublime; to observe him at the close of the Sabbath as he partakes, with kingly gestures in concentrated dedication, of the sacred meal to which cling the mysteries of the world's redemption, and we will feel: here, stunted and distorted yet unmistakable, is Asiatic strength and Asiatic inwardness."

Buber's talk reads now as perplexing, bombastic, and racially outrageous, even when laudatory. But with this paean, along with other addresses on Judaism he delivered at the time, he stirred the passions of a generation. Buber held that Judaism, as a religious system in the Oriental spirit, activated inner experiences that transcended the fractional character of sensory data, thereby unifying the self, uniting the self with world, and—at the most elevated level—merging the self with the Absolute. This idea resonated, especially at a time when human experience in general and urban Jewish experience in particular appeared ever more disjunctive. Summing up the magnetism of Buber's ideas in his youth,

Scholem wrote that he "diagnosed and combated the 'illness, distortion, and tyranny' of a disfigured Judaism in exile." Early on, Buber coined the phrase, "Not the forms but the forces." He never tired of repeating it, and this romantic, revolutionary disdain for Jewish Law, coupled with the vision of visceral faith he embodied, held electric charm for the young — partly through the challenge it posed to the authority of age.

Buber's project was not intended simply as a thought experiment. Rather, he averred that having gone through heaven and hell in the Occident, the Jew with his ineradicable drive to total unity — the now dormant but unbroken Jewish spiritual prowess — could be reawakened only in Palestine. Once that strength "comes into contact with the maternal soil it will once more become creative," Buber promised. It was as if, in the hippie era, all those Westerners who sought Indian gurus had been told by some formidable spiritual guide that not only were they going to encounter fonts of unimpeachable wisdom in the East, they were of the same blood tribe as those sages: They were returning home

when they entered the ashram. Buber made his devotees feel the Other throbbing inside their own skin.

For Scholem, the allure of the Orient as the axis of what might be called magical authenticity—the antipode to his father's bourgeois Berlin—took hold early on. "You are Orientals and not Europeans," he wrote in his diary toward the end of 1914. "You are Jews and humans, not Germans and degenerates, and your God is named *Ha-Shem* [the Name] and not the belly." This faith soon crystallized into a battle cry. The future belonged to the Orient, and revolution would be his guiding principle. "Revolution everywhere!" Gerhard demanded some weeks later. Above all, "we want to revolutionize Judaism," he added. "We want to revolutionize Zionism and to preach anarchism and freedom from all authority." Whereas the old adage warned that if you bashed your head against a wall, your head would split, he and his spiritual compatriots believed it was imperative to smash against the wall—and the wall, not their skulls, would crack open. This was the credo of their Zionism. Through the spiritual dynamism of Martin Buber's personality Gerhard had come to understand "the deep streams of inner connection that bring us together with other creative peoples of the Orient. And where others have seen only death and decay, he has seen life and rebirth; where others saw graves, he has seen resurrection."

Reading Scholem's words about the opposing visions of death and resurrection, I find my thoughts shadowed by two memories connected with my own would-be immigration to Jerusalem. One involves the closest thing to a mystical experience I've ever had. Just before moving to Israel, I traveled to Boston to see friends, and while there I became seized by conviction that I needed to visit the graves of my paternal, Viennese grandparents, which I had not done since childhood. I knew, in some way that went beyond what

I could then articulate, that it was for my grandparents and their own aborted line of European history that I was now preparing to transplant myself to Jerusalem. I drove there in a hard downpour, late in the day, despite my father's warnings that I would never be able to find their burial place. Upon arriving, I stepped out of the car into the vast, poorly signposted cemetery, and right before me, on the grass between the stones stood a large fox, the color of fire. The fox began to move across the dark path and underbrush. I followed it. Faster and faster. We moved between the graves, through what seemed an endless sea of granite and marble; then suddenly the animal switched course and disappeared into bushes beyond the trail, and I was alone. I found myself standing directly before three black stones — the graves of my grandfather, Jonas; my grandmother, Edith; and my father's brother, George, for whom I am named.

This happened, just so. And it seemed inconceivable to me then not to understand the experience as a kind of biblical sign, affirming the rightness of the enormous move I was about to make in my life.

The other memory is of an occasion almost exactly nine months before this visit to my grandparents' graves, on the first trip I ever made to Israel. After having obsessively read Scholem's works, I flew to Jerusalem with my wife, Anne — partly on a whim, partly to see the place at the center of so many mystical yearnings. Our first attempt to enter the walled Old City was repulsed. In our rental car, we kept trying to find a gate, but the roads all seemed to veer away at the last moment. Suddenly, we were shooting down into a valley, then up a narrow, steep, dusty street lined by low, blunt cement houses into what I now realize was part of Silwan, in East Jerusalem. The next thing we knew, we were bouncing across a field on a faint track, pocked with stones and holes. Ahead of us was a crowd of people. Even from a distance, the motionless assembly suggested a solemn occasion. As we drew nearer, we realized that we were barreling into a funeral ceremony. But there was nowhere to turn around. Dogs were chasing our wheels by now. I pressed the brake to reduce the dust. Barking ricocheted from all directions. People were twisting our way. We waved stupidly. Children were coming around the car, followed by a couple of young men. The entire group of mourners now seemed to be staring at us. I stopped. We sat a moment, smiling out at the onlookers. Then I threw the car into reverse, carefully backing away. It seemed an eternity before we came to the end of that field.

I still hear the dogs. I still see those eyes. And looking now at these two recollections, it seems to me that—rather than tying the experience of being led by the fox to my grandparents' graves with the specter of their European exile—I might instead have linked it with the scene in which I could not find the entrance to the Old City of Jerusalem and ended up at a Palestinian funeral. If I was so given to discerning mystical signs, perhaps it was these more proximate moments that should have been placed in conjunction. What would the message have been then?

Of course, the world may be layered at every turning with esoteric signals, but we're the ones who draw the connecting lines, and these can go any direction, forward and backward in time, west to east, or the reverse. Where do we break off the lines and where do we elect to extend them? An enchanted animal leads us to some profound communion with the dead. Missing our way, we are led by ignorance into the funeral of a person from a people as unknown to us as the dead must remain. How can we weigh the respective measures of truth and responsibility trembling at the margins of these encounters?

Some nights now, when I cannot sleep, I see that funeral in Silwan. The burial was taking place almost in tandem with the start of the First Intifada. Who, I now wonder, was the person being lowered into the ground? And why there, on that lonely patch of earth, were the death rites being performed? I wish that I could zoom in slowly on each image and moment — come to understand the multiplicity of worlds brought together that day, each individual's life: how they came to be there, where they would return to at the end of the funeral, and what would happen to each of them in the ensuing years of Jerusalem's transformation and stagnation. But when I try to move closer, to rewind and change angles, the dust starts rising, as though it were being torn from the earth by an onrushing vehicle, until the whole picture is clouded by that haze of history we discover we've passed through only after the fact.

"The first impetus for my Jewish consciousness was provided by my interest in history," Scholem recalled in his memoir. And his deepening identification with Judaism also became the engine of his escape from home as he began to mature. In 1911 his religious-studies teacher had introduced him to a three-volume edition of Heinrich Graetz's *History of the Jews*, a popular abridgement of the eleven-volume original. Gerhard burned through the chronicle, which made Jewish history out to be one long train of fearless heroes and ravaged martyrs, like a young person today devouring some apocalyptic fantasy series. At the end, he wanted more. From there, one thing led to another. The study of his people's ill-starred wanderings ignited a passion to track the energy that kept the Jewish spirit alive.

He asked his teacher to teach him Hebrew. He didn't want just to read *about* things. He sought a way back to primary truths. Gerhard and a friend began staying after school twice a week to study the language. And he fell completely in love with it. He started trotting around to different Berlin synagogues for Friday night services just to hear Hebrew chanted by the city's gifted cantors. This language was something undeniable, steeped in the long history of the people — and not just absorbing but actively shaping Jewish destiny. The future tense in Hebrew is a *command*, just as commands in the present are an injunction "to *be*," he observed in his diary later on. For example, "*Kedoshim thuju*" — You should be holy — means both that you will be holy in the future and that you are holy now. "You *are* holy because I am holy," God said. With the Hebrew language, "*Time is transformed through fusion*: the past is in the future and the future is in the past," Gerhard noted. This was nothing less than messianic Time revealed.

One day he barged in on his father and burst out, "Papa, I think I want to be a Jew."

"Jews are only good for going to synagogue with," his father snapped, citing that infuriating maxim so popular among German Jewry.

"That's a lie!" Gerhard exploded.

"You want to return to the ghetto?" His father asked.

"You're the ones who are living in the ghetto," Gerhard countered. "Only you won't admit it."

That got him. When Papa flared up, with those giant Scholem ears sticking out like jug handles, Gerhard felt himself staring into a mirror of genetic humiliation. At least his father could wiggle his own pair. Gerhard might not have experienced anti-Semitism personally in Berlin, but his ears got plenty of ridicule. And even without firsthand exposure to anti-Semitism, he developed a fascination with the literature, reading everything from tracts by notorious racists like Houston Stuart Chamberlain, who praised the German soul against Jewish money-grubbing legalism, to vitriolic anti-Jewish speeches by distinguished parliamentarians, and reports by farmers' associations full of accusations against the degenerative Semitic influence on the pure Teuton. It was all highly instructive. Gerhard took the slander not as a threat but as a goad to lash back, *To hell with you*. The only response to such claptrap was Zionism, he resolved. He'd never felt himself at home in Germany anyway. These writings just confirmed his sense of estrangement—while also increasing his disgust with the self-deception of his fellow Jews. When everyone in the family kept chanting at him, "You want to go back to the ghetto?" he finally shot back, "Where are the Gentiles! I've never seen a single one of them come to your homes for a social call!"

He announced that Hebrew studies were only the beginning. He would study the Bible also. And from there he'd plunge deeper still. His father just shook his head.

"Forget my family," he scribbled later in his diary. "Is it my fault I was born into these surroundings? If I had been born as a worker or the son of a poor but ambitious Jew (and who cares if his name is Yitzhak the Rag Dealer) I would have the world at my fingertips. But as it is! Ugh!"

He started loading up on Jewish literature of every sort, reading as far and wide as his pocket money would take him. In used copies of Zionist pamphlets and books by Theodor Herzl, Leon Pinsker, Max Nordau, Nathan Birnbaum, and other activists, he discovered Zionism as a movement beyond Buber's shimmering Oriental vision.

And when he informed his family that he, too, was a Zionist, the arguments really got fiery: This was no longer just about back-sliding into the ghetto; Zionism meant being a traitor to the German nation! So be it—Gerhard was charging ahead on his own. His mother finally acknowledged his passion by giving him a portrait of Theodor Herzl, the founder of the Zionist Organization. Unfortunately, she had the gall to nestle Herzl's picture amid the gifts piled under their family Christmas tree. Gerhard nailed the portrait in its thick black frame to the wall of his bedroom. And when he paced back and forth, pondering that proud, bearded countenance, all sorts of thoughts roared through his brain. One day he wrote a poem to Herzl, proclaiming: "He spoke for those who had repressed their longing/And for those devoured by silent grief,/And they all bowed their heads, now belonging/To him who had come to slake their disbelief."

Did *he* belong to Herzl? What was the soul, anyway? He thought it was dynamic. The soul might be the force that existed between things. Staring at the Herzl portrait, Gerhard wrote in his diary, "I have the impression of 'Theodor Herzl,' along with certain memories and associations." But "along with the material transmission there is something 'between-the-things'—an immaterial essence of some sort that could reach the mythological 'Self.'" Nietzsche had written that in the absence of myth, "every culture loses the healthy natural power of its creativity." His romanticism had "rattled heaven," Gerhard declared, and that sacrifice for truth had been rewarded with "blessed lunacy." Why hadn't the Jews gone crazy too fifteen hundred years ago? he mused one day. "If we had we would have spared the world and ourselves a great deal of evil!"

At times, his journal reads as though he's pacing beneath the Herzl portrait in his bedroom with the Bible in one hand and Nietzsche's *Zarathustra* in the other, reciting from both simultaneously, as one single text. In fact, he described them in identical terms as holy books that no matter how often you dipped into them would always reveal something fresh and profound. *Zarathustra*, after all, *was* a new bible, he decided. Yet in one critical respect Gerhard diverged from Nietzsche: Nietzsche apparently "wanted everything for our world and detected in the idea of a World to Come traces of world-flight and world-dissatisfaction, which he immediately fought against," Gerhard reflected. "I'm of the opinion that the World to Come is the object of our longing; it is perfection and fulfillment." He didn't *believe* in it—not as anything floating out there all crystallized and prepared to receive us. Humanity was created for this earth, which people had been denying for too long. Yet the dream of ideal purity might still prove an inspiration, even if one couldn't hope to attain it. This was not about becoming one of those "preachers of death" whom Nietzsche bemoaned—the sickly advocates of renunciation—but about being absolutely of the world while *also* having the visionary will to find seeds of the Beyond in the here and now. These seeds were meant to be cultivated. For his part, Gerhard declared his ambition to write a *Zarathustra* for the Jews. What would Herzl think of *that*? Well, a new Herzl was needed as well!

Zionism was fertile enough to embrace multiple lines of radical thought, Gerhard maintained. Along with his affinity for figures like Nietzsche, Strindberg, and Ibsen, he cherished Kierkegaard and Tolstoy as giants who'd unconsciously "destroyed heaven through their deep religiosity." Expansive speculation about what the movement might one day encompass remained possible then. Yet the young Scholem still sometimes sounds as if he wants to have things all ways at once.

Truthfully, Gerhard's Christmas portrait of Herzl wasn't the only picture of Herzl in the family. And Gerhard wasn't completely alone among the Scholems in his Zionism. One of Papa's brothers, Uncle Theobald, kept a Jewish National Fund collection box for the purchase of land in Palestine hung conspicuously in his flat. Whenever his siblings lost a bet to him, he made the loser flip a one-mark coin into it. Of course, everyone in the family always ribbed him for such eccentricities. Uncle Theobald was a scholar manqué. His big oak bookcase in the apartment in Friedenau was stuffed with books about the Far East and India, along with studies of Buddhism and Islam. For Theobald's wedding, Betty penned a play called *Ex Oriente Lux*, which satirized his fascination with all things Oriental. Six-year-old Gerhard played the Hindu, with a plumed turban.

The problem for Gerhard was that Uncle Theobald didn't actually *know* anything, despite his colorful books and enthusiasms: He'd had to quit school early to take up a business apprenticeship. Theobald's idea of Zionism was wrapped up in vague notions of spiritual emancipation expressed through extreme physical fitness. A founding member of Bar Kochba, the Jewish gymnastic association, Theobald was a subscriber to what the early Zionist theorist Max Nordau had dubbed "muscular Judaism." Bar Kochba, in Nordau's estimation, was nothing less than "the last world-historical embodiment of a war-hardened, weapon-happy

Judaism." Uncle Theobald's portrait of Herzl was taken at the Basel Zionist Congress of 1903; it showed Herzl among a bunch of Bar Kochba gymnasts.

This notion of Judaism was about as far from Gerhard's burgeoning ideals as you could get. At his uncle's house, what Gerhard waited for was the moment when the last of the noonday meal had been sopped up and his uncle would trudge off for a snooze, leaving Gerhard free for a tête-à-tête with his sympathetic Aunt Hedwig. She was thrilled when he began telling her of his plans to immigrate to Palestine and wanted to come along herself. But despite Uncle Theobald's sporty, bold Judaism, shrewd business calculations intervened when it came to the question of actually moving to Zion. They never took the gamble.

Some of the ambivalences diluting the strength of muscular Judaism also showed up in the Jung Juda (Young Judaea) organization, which Gerhard first became involved with early in his Hebrew education. The Zionist youth movement had its roots in the larger Central European youth movements of the era, most particularly the Wanderwogel, which sought to forge new communities of young people through shared mystical communion with nature. When the Wanderwogel grew increasingly anti-Semitic before the outbreak of the First World War, parallel Jewish groups began to be formed. These preserved much of the ideology underpinning their German models, including the idea that nature hikes would catalyze a symbiotic process whereby spiritual enlightenment would be nurtured through fellowship, and fellowship would be fostered by spiritual enlightenment.

The Jung Juda members met in the back room of a hotel called At the Sign of the Golden Goose, where they discussed political events between recitations of poetry. Unlike his brother Werner, who had introduced him to the group before declaring it too limited, Gerhard criticized it for not being particularist *enough*. Judaism demanded something more substantial than emotive spiritual consciousness. Where were the Hebrew studies, for starters? When he attended the group's drinking parties, he felt he might just as well have been pounding his tankard in synchrony with some random gang of plastered German patriots. Not to mention all the pipes and cigarettes at Jung Juda meetings! He was getting a reputation as an asocial anarchist, but this was partly just because he couldn't stand smoke-filled rooms.

However, Gerhard didn't dismiss the group. Pathetic though he considered most of its participants, Jung Juda provided the only real framework for nurturing Zionist consciousness among students at a time when the whole enterprise was basically a youth movement. Instead of decreasing his commitment, he spent *more* time at their gatherings, often adopting a pugnacious attitude in an effort to save the movement from itself. And when its deficit of authentic Jewish content became too upsetting, he visited the new youth wing of Agudat Israel, the Orthodox association, which he soon joined as well.

In the spring of 1913 he began studying Talmud, with a wonderful teacher, Dr. Bleichrode, who taught Gerhard without accepting a pfennig in payment. Among the religious studies crowd, Gerhard was considered a prodigy and almost immediately got elected to Agudat Israel's executive committee. Less than half a year later, everyone was up in arms, accusing Gerhard of being false to the Law. A huge fight erupted, ending with him being basically excommunicated. (He took a certain pride in triggering boycotts of himself.) But six months among the pious had been long enough for him to fall in love for the first time.

Yetka was the exquisite, devout daughter of a tailor from Russia. Her blend of flirtatiousness and pure faith transfixed Gerhard. He started going to services at the Alte Synagogue just to watch her silently rocking in the first row of the empty women's section, with "curls resplendent." All day Gerhard ran around with fantasies of their future together. Sometimes the thought of how lucky people like Yetka were to grow up in an observant household over-whelmed him. He tried to make his friends grasp how beautiful Jewish rituals at home were, but they couldn't get it. Who wants to be bound by commandments to do this or that? they scoffed. You're missing the point! he objected. It was all about beauty. You couldn't revitalize Judaism without beauty. And what could be more poetic than the Friday evening meal? The father raising the brimming kiddush cup on high; the mother fluttering her hands to bless the candlelight. Such peace. What would it be like to one day introduce his own children to these graceful ceremonies that were mocked by the secular and twisted by the Orthodox? Before the hearth would be his wife, making all the Sabbath preparations so that their home would appear lovely and holy. And he would come home and put his hands on the inky-haired heads of the little ones and say the blessings. Then they would all sit down together at the table in pure-minded simplicity...(*"Gerhardchen ist nebbich so anständig"* [Jerry is such a decent boy, poor thing], sighed his Aunt Grete, a reproof he never forgot.)

Notwithstanding his reveries, he couldn't stay observant. If he was going to write a Jewish *Zarathustra*, he had to renounce Agu-dat's program in favor of Buber's line. He also became a Socialist. Yetke didn't drop him after he confessed this. Neither did Bleich-rode. But his inner turmoil kept mounting.

Then came Sarajevo.

The Great War might have been happening inside his brain, yet his appearance of self-possession concealed everything. "There is no one in my immediate vicinity with a stronger mask than mine," he wrote. "I allow myself to be driven about my choices, and I end up putting one person after another on a throne, only to knock him off again." His best Zionist friend, the dark and silent Edgar Blum, received his military orders to report immediately for duty. It was so monstrous, he couldn't think about it. His brother Werner's friend Jansen got shot dead on the battlefield. It was the old men who should have been shipped off to the front. They would do better to blast one another. "They just shouldn't rob youth of its blood, which is a vicious act against the future," Gerhard raged. Why did young people put up with it? That was the worst part: Youth thought it had to submit to martyrdom or be disgraced for cowardice.

Then came news that Martin Buber himself was endorsing the war. In a speech delivered at a Hanukkah gathering in December 1914, Buber compared the conflict's liberating energy to the struggles of the Maccabees: The concept of the *Volk* had never manifested itself so powerfully as now, and this sweeping feeling belonged to the Jews also. What was this? Some cockamamie version of Uncle Theobald's gymnastic Judaism, vaulting headfirst into the firing line?

At the same time, Gerhard crashed against Herzl's theoretical limitations. Herzl was really to blame for the state of Zionism, "a movement that instead of going forward looks backward, an organization of shopkeepers that grovels in the dust before the powerful!" Gerhard scribbled in his diary. Herzl's Zionists tackled "the Jewish problem merely as a form instead of in its inner essence. Its only thought has been the Jewish *state*. We preachers of anarchism reject this." He did not seek to go to Palestine to found a state, Gerhard wrote, "thereby forging new chains out of the old. O you miserable little philistines! We want to go to Palestine out of a thirst for freedom and longing for the future."

Increasingly, he realized that he had to be *against* someone in order to think. He required an adversary to spur his own inspiration.

Everything was crumpling and unfolding simultaneously. At a bookstall by the synagogue, Gerhard found a copy of the Zohar, the foundational text of Jewish mysticism. He could make no sense of it but kept reading anyway: "In the beginning — when the will of the King began to take effect, he engraved signs into the heavenly sphere [that surrounded him]. Within the most hidden recess a dark flame issued from the mystery of *Ein Sof*, the Infinite, like a fog forming in the unformed —"

Whatever it meant, he felt captivated by its strangeness — also revolted by its primitive nature. But he persisted with the book, which he later decided was a great "proto-novel." Then one day, in the midst of everything, he met Yetka in Treptow Park, with its allées and fountains alongside the Spree. They walked down the broad paths with their old, majestic overarching trees. Gerhard's thoughts wouldn't stop racing. The Kabbalah was not Truth — God forbid. But it might be philosophy. Yetka was so beautiful! He could stand it no longer. He moved to kiss her. At once she turned coy. That was it. Unbearable! They split up. He was alone.

In February 1915, some wretch from another youth group took up Buber's war chant and published an article declaring that Zionists made superior German citizens. In the surge of mass emotion, "We sensed our melody and suddenly community engulfed us," this fraud wrote. "So it came about that we were drawn to the war not despite our being Jews but because we were Zionists."

Gerhard felt poisoned. That was *it*. He immediately penned a protest laying out all the reasons why Jewish interests were totally distinct from those of Germany. Everyone he showed it to begged him not to print the screed. Fine, but he'd already brought it into class to collect signatures, and one day while he was out in the schoolyard at recess, a nasty little fink snatched it from his briefcase and reported him to the authorities. Gerhard was booted out of the gymnasium for antiwar attitudes.

His father went berserk, shouting that he would pack Gerhard off to be a herring tamer (Berlinese for becoming a grocer). Not long thereafter, "Mr. Big Shot," as Gerhard now called him, announced that he would no longer even bother doing a seder that year. When this war was done, he would sever his connection to the Jewish community once and for all, he swore.

Excellent. But why wait for the end of the slaughter? Gerhard asked. The man would never follow through on his threat. He was too frightened by the prospect of his shop being blacklisted.

All the convergences were tangling in knots. Whom was Gerhard meant to follow? Perhaps he was meant to follow himself!

In May he finally allowed himself to articulate the idea that had been gestating inside him for months. Over the course of a long journal entry in which he referred to himself in the third person throughout, he rehearsed each phase of his *Bildung* to date: the moment when he discovered that there was no soul in Herzl's writing, only the desire for one; the period when he'd joined Jung Juda and gained esteem as "a walking conversation lexicon." The growing realization that this miserable lot of would-be Zionists didn't know how to search for, let alone find, anything. The period when they started mocking him as "Scholem the Buberian." The hour when he finally stormed forth on his own road to Zion.

"This was an unusual time when the dreamer awoke and got to know his own longing," Gerhard wrote. "Longing is the mother of renewal." Buber had felt this longing, but he was not the redeemer. "The quiet youth living within the walls of a Berlin home felt how the embryo was growing within him," Gerhard continued. He trusted in the "unchanging mystical facility of his people that he found in himself" and sought the truth that would prepare him for a great act of emancipation. "The young man went alone through the world and looked around to find where the soul of his nation awaited him," yearning for "the One who would have enough audacity to free it from banishment" and lead the people on the path to redemption. "And who is this dreamer, whose name already marks him as the Awaited One? It is Scholem, the Perfect One."

That summer, thank God, Scholem met Walter Benjamin.

TWO

IN 1915, Walter Benjamin was twenty-three years old, rich and rebellious, with a reputation among Berlin's radical youth for precocity, intense seriousness, and a tendency to reason himself into abstractions that left others mystified. Musing about relationships and human nature, he declared that "there is no such thing as an unrequited love" — an aphorism that at first seemed profound but then left his young friends scratching their heads. Another time, considering shame, he suggested that since people excrete in solitude they ought logically to eat alone as well — a deduction that provoked one friend to jeer at Benjamin's chronic obliviousness. During this period he was publishing difficult essays at an industrious pace, mingling with all sorts of intellectual circles, and striking out in search of new friends.

Among the groups Benjamin spent time with was the enticingly named Neopathetic Cabaret, a neoexpressionist group that staged events around the call to subvert rational modernity with spiritualized aestheticism. A big woodcut of Walt Whitman graced the cover of the movement's new journal, and Stefan Zweig — who may have coined the term "Neopathetic poetry" — was vaguely involved with it. Benjamin enjoyed the company of Kurt Hiller, an essayist and arch-Nietzschean, who was one of the cabaret's founders. He found Hiller winning and decent, though Scholem later claimed that, for his part, Hiller always despised Benjamin. In photographs, Hiller appears glum, balding, and churlish; but he was known for

being sharp and gregarious with a special table at the Café Grössenwahn, where he indulged his taste for adolescent male camarade-
rie while waxing on wittily about the irrelevance of history.

Gerhard read Hiller's book *The Wisdom of Boredom* with interest, and one night that summer he decided to attend a lecture
Hiller was giving. Most of the time in those days, when he wasn't
haunting Berlin's synagogues, full of longing and ambivalence,
Gerhard just pored over his books. But every so often he skulked
out of what he called his "cloud-cuckoo-land" to hear lectures by
intellectual bigwigs. They gave him nothing and only squandered
time from his studies, but he couldn't relinquish the search for
live revelation.

In this instance, Hiller's fatuous reduction of everything to
trivialities affronted Gerhard. Hiller proposed that *all* obstruc-
tions to human progress were surmountable by sheer willpower.
Wish away your headaches and wish forth a new universe. He'd
managed to reoccupy Nietzsche's most problematic positions
concerning the past's paralyzing effect on man's vital spirit. "Why
bother with millennia of rubbish when we live with the generation
we're born in?" Hiller demanded.

"We carry the burden of history in our blood and our consciousness," Gerhard fumed. History makes all of us ancient, and
at the same time we're young and all of a now-ness. With every
step, we must contend with this irreconcilable paradox.

When Hiller's lecture was subsequently advertised as the subject of discussion at the Free Students' Meeting House, on the
edge of affluent west Berlin, Gerhard raced to the meeting and shot
up on his feet at the first opportunity to protest. Why did words
always spill out of him so clumsily? At one point when he stumbled, he was simply cut dead by the chairman, a friend of Hiller's.
The humiliation made his ears burn all the hotter when he became
aware that Walter Benjamin was in the room.

He'd seen this mysterious, intimidating man speak once before in 1913. Now, as then, Benjamin became still as a statue on reaching the lectern, lifting his eyes above the audience and addressing a stream of lofty, letter-perfect sentences to the ceiling. Though decidedly not good-looking, with his hieratic pose and extreme concentration, there was yet something arresting about him. Benjamin "assumed a virtually magical appearance," Scholem wrote later. He was very slender then, with feathery dark hair and a noticeably high brow. His face was rose tinged, but otherwise "his skin was absolutely white," Scholem recalled. He wore powerful eyeglasses, which he often took off in conversation to reveal "a pair of striking, dark blue eyes. His nose was well-proportioned," while the lower half of his face was very gentle, with a full, sensuous mouth. "His hands were beautiful, slender, and expressive." When he spoke, his face took on "a strangely reserved, somewhat inward expression." Taken as a whole, Benjamin's "physiognomy was definitely Jewish, but in a quiet, unobtrusive way as it were," Scholem noted, in language tinged with its own racial bias.

His manner was, anyway, so intense that Gerhard could no more absorb the substance of his remarks than he had on the previous occasion when he'd heard Benjamin make some torturous reflections on Zionism. While not exactly dismissing the movement, Benjamin had relegated it to a profoundly secondary position. Judaism should not be considered an end in itself but rather a vehicle of broader spiritual rescue, Benjamin believed. The Jewish people might seek to reengage their ancestral identity so that it could be enlisted as a larger repository for culture—a kind of ark that by virtue of its great age and visionary premises was linked to the origins of civilization as such. The capacious intricacy of Jewish historical consciousness might accommodate other vulnerable cultural forms, affording them refuge beyond the reach of present-day catastrophe.

Benjamin would later write of the shock incurred when a word somehow points us "to that invisible stranger—the future."

Whatever precisely Benjamin said in his speeches, his language gave Scholem that kind of jolt.

A week after the fiasco at the Meeting House, Gerhard was browsing in the card catalog room of the university library when suddenly right smack in front of him appeared the charmed speaker, "my Herr Benjamin," as Gerhard called him in his journal.

Benjamin raised his eyes to Gerhard's and held them there. How was one supposed to respond to that stare, which Scholem realized only much later had more to do with myopia than attitude? Gerhard did his best to appear studious, flicking through index cards, until at some point he looked up and discovered that Benjamin had disappeared. Excellent! Just as it should be, he thought to himself. We go our separate ways and I don't have to deal with him.

A moment later, the door swung open again and Herr Benjamin strode right up to him, swooping down in an exquisite bow.

"Are you the gentleman who spoke at the Hiller discussion?"

"Yes!" Gerhard answered.

"Well, I would like to speak to you about what you said. Would you give me your address? I will write you next week."

Scholem wrote down his house number and passed it over, whereupon Herr Benjamin at once spun about and trotted off again.

Soon thereafter, Gerhard paid Benjamin a visit at his family home in a suburb built at the end of the nineteenth century beside the Grunewald forest, enclosing small lakes and parkland. The bankers and industrialists who'd made this neighborhood their own constructed pastiche palaces that referenced neoclassicism, rococo, and the bulky heft of the Central European Renaissance. Grunewald's historical free-associating evoked Vienna's prize avenue, the Ringstrasse. And like the Ringstrasse, Grunewald became home to intellectual and artistic luminaries, a sizable proportion of whom were Jewish — so many, indeed, that its commuter train was nicknamed the "Roaring Moses."

Rancor simmered among those Berliners who came to Grunewald on Sunday outings and registered the success with which Jews had taken over the greater German idyll of a "return to the forest," where tired city dwellers could manage just a few hours of leisure — inhaling the perfume of the pines without actually owning the property. Describing his excursions to Grunewald as a child of privilege, Vladimir Nabokov recalled that one was always coming upon strange junk in those woods: a dressmaker's dummy, an iron bedstead, a disfigured mirror. How did they all get there? "Perhaps such intrusions on these burgherish pleasure grounds were a fragmentary vision of the mess to come, a prophetic bad dream of destructive explosions, something like the heap of dead heads the seer Cagliostro glimpsed in the ha-ha of a royal garden."

Walter Benjamin, for his part, noted that his neighbors lived "in a posture compounded of self-satisfaction and resentment that turned it into something like a ghetto held on lease." He abhorred his confinement within this oasis of opulence.

For Gerhard, the whole outing must have been an adventure. Masters of real fortunes, like Benjamin's auctioneer-entrepreneur father, kept aloof from prosperous scrabblers like Arthur Scholem At precisely five thirty in the afternoon, he stood before the two bronze lions' mouths set with rings that jutted out from Benjamin's front door. On being admitted, he was ushered over Oriental carpets, past paintings and porcelains, into the large room with a balcony that served as Benjamin's bedroom and study. Its main piece of furniture was a massive desk overhung by a long mirror, which meant, Benjamin noted, that one could never raise one's eyes while writing. The walls of the room were richly arrayed with books. Where Gerhard hung a portrait of Herzl in his bedroom, the dominant picture in Benjamin's chamber was a print of Matthias Grünewald's Isenheim Altarpiece, an early sixteenth-century religious masterpiece renowned for the harrowing realism of its depiction of Christ's death—livid, bony arms and fingers twisting off the wood of the cross, away from the nails in his palms; blood streaming from his emaciated rib cage. Benjamin told Scholem that when he'd seen the original, he'd been stunned by the expressionless character of the panels. Mistrusting psychology, he found that this neutralizing of affect heightened the picture's chromatic potency. He was in the process that year of developing a mystical theory of color that located the spiritual basis of the image on the surface of paintings. "Color is first of all the concentration of the surface, the imagination of infinity within it," he wrote.

The chamber struck Gerhard as a "very respectable room," a proper "philosophical hermitage." Whereas at his own home he always felt porous to the family clamor—exposed as the brick wall of a public house to every indignity—here everything was swaddled in fine fabrics, hidden behind the luster of myriad beautiful objects.

To Benjamin, the luxury his family lived in had other connotations. "The arrangement of the furniture is at the same time the site plan of deadly traps, and the suite of rooms prescribes the fleeing victim's path," he wrote of his milieu, describing "gigantic sideboards distended with carvings, the sunless corners where palms stand, the balcony embattled behind its balustrade, and the long corridors with their singing gas flames...On this sofa the aunt cannot but be murdered."

Where for Scholem the Orient conjured Buber's Palestine phantasmagoria, Benjamin eulogized the "rank Orient" inhabiting the typical bourgeois interior, with its "Persian carpet and the ottoman, the hanging lamp and the genuine Caucasian dagger. Behind the heavy, gathered Khilim tapestries the master of the house has orgies with his share certificates, feels himself the Eastern merchant, the indolent pasha in the caravanserai of otiose enchantment, until that dagger in the silver sling above the divan puts an end, one fine afternoon, to his siesta and himself."

Benjamin's "deep, inner relationship to things he owned" impressed itself forcefully on Scholem's consciousness. He describes Benjamin placing books, works of art, and curios into the hands of visitors, "as he mused over them aloud like a pianist improvising at the keyboard." On one occasion, Scholem noted a blue-glazed tile emblazoned with a three-headed Christ on Benjamin's desk. Elsewhere lay an old farmer's pipe with an amber mouthpiece and silver-studded bowl. Enigmatic objects filled Benjamin's rooms and his consciousness, becoming amulets and genie lamps under his touch. He multiplied his collections in the course of his travels. In Moscow he bought a silver poniard. At his apartment in Paris he hung a tattoo artist's pattern sheet from Copenhagen. The word "Jerusalem" appears exactly once in Benjamin's childhood memoir. Recalling a butterfly hunt near his summer home at Potsdam, he writes of "mourning cloaks and admirals, peacocks and auroras...scattered over one of those glistening

Limoges enamels, on which the ramparts and battlements of Jerusalem stand out against a dark blue ground." Jerusalem, too, under Benjamin's spell, became something that fit in the hands as a gleaming, intriguing material object.

Indeed, Benjamin's collection not only set his mind going in countless directions but also allowed him to pay his ontological farewells to dead cultures, forsaken states of consciousness, and the fallen nature of Creation as such, in the manner of the stones Jewish mourners place on graves. When he put his treasured bibelots into the hands of his visitors, or the palm of the reader's eye, the act of physical possession and of transubstantiation — of metaphysical *dispossession* — became one. Like the potent images of home he would later conjure from exile, his voluptuous descriptions of objects are ultimately intended to provide an inoculation against longing. "I sought to limit its effect through insight into the irretrievability — not the contingent biographical but the necessary social irretrievability — of the past," he wrote in his memoir. One feels this quality when reading him, as his guests must have felt it when they were in his presence: the administration of a vaccinal nostalgia that simultaneously tingles the senses and disintegrates the context of consumption. Walter Benjamin's relationship to things allows us to have our cake and not eat it too.

Scholem tied Benjamin's fascination with things that could be cradled in the hand to an urge to find perfection "on the small and very smallest scale," which Benjamin expressed also in his obsessive devotion to micrography. The idea that "the greatest is revealed in the smallest" was an axiomatic truth to him, Scholem asserted. He later recalled Benjamin dragging him to the Musée de Cluny in Paris in August 1927 where, in the collection of Jewish ritual artifacts, Benjamin showed him "with true rapture two grains of wheat on which a kindred soul had inscribed the complete *Shema Israel*" — the core prayer of Jewish liturgy.

A photograph of Benjamin taken that summer has earned a spot on the intellectual-icon spectrum somewhere between Che in his red-starred beret and Albert Einstein with his hair looking like he's just stuck his finger in a socket. Benjamin's eyes are cast down and averted behind wire spectacles that rest on an aquiline nose beneath a luminous brow and mussed locks of dark hair. A cigarette projects from the first and second fingers of his right hand, which folds gently against his chin, below his sealed lips and full mustache. He appears literally lost in thought—transported from the present by discontent and wonder, with nothing left behind but the afterglow of refined concentration.

Chic, barely incarnate, beguilingly alone—if the young Walter Benjamin's image had a sound track, it would be a loop of Cage and cool jazz.

I don't know where I first picked up *Illuminations*, Walter Benjamin's best-known collection of essays. I was too young and ignorant to understand much of it, but I found something captivating in the book's voice. Its language had the sound of authority and mystery, even when it was theoretically critiquing both categories.

Above all, I lingered on the notion of the sacral aura adhering to the unreproducible work of art, which Benjamin called inseparable from its "contextual integration" in a tradition, and upon the image of the pile of debris mounting higher and higher before the Angel of History. "Where we perceive a chain of events, he sees one single catastrophe which keeps piling wreckage upon wreckage and hurls it in front of his feet," Benjamin wrote. Between these two visions—of the aura and the ruin—hides a key to my conversion to Judaism, I now believe. Not that I was anywhere near this move at the time I first read Benjamin. Then I had no idea even that his letters would prove the gateway to my discovery of Gerhard Scholem.

Conversion. The word sticks inside me, and I feel myself blush when I confess that I've done so. What are the last words of Kafka's *The Trial*? "It was as if the shame would outlive him." None of my friends in New York have done such an odd, regressively flamboyant thing. God is a crutch that doubles as a truncheon in the eyes of most of them. What am I saying? Often in my own eyes as well.

And Judaism? Isn't converting to Judaism in these times a bit like announcing one doesn't believe in Palestine? Or at least of cluttering the sight lines to a contemporary political imperative? The assertion of Jewish identity has become so conflated with the actions of the State of Israel in the view of many people who consider themselves politically progressive, as well as people from the extreme right, that there's hardly a slit of light visible between the two. Simply to deny the equivalency no longer suffices. But what's the alternative?

Perhaps another kind of faith is called for, not simply an insistence that we are falling farther and farther from the golden tree of some ethically pristine Jewish cosmopolitan past — the never-never land of nostalgic humanism. As to the nature of this new faith, if we had the vocabulary, we'd have the belief. However it's worth pondering in this context a comment Scholem made about the Kabbalists in a late interview, when he was trying to sum up their abiding importance.

"If you ask me, I say that the Kabbalists had a fundamental feeling that there is mystery — a secret — in the world," Scholem remarked. What attracted him was the way they'd managed to convert this intimation into powerful symbols. They charted the cosmic repercussions of Jewish suffering. "A rather small group of people were able to create symbols that expressed their personal situation as a world situation," he wrote. In contrast to the modern individual who, according to Scholem, lives "in a private world of his own," coining subjective symbols that do not "obligate," the Kabbalists had managed to create symbols that served "as an objective projection of the inner side of a miserable, grotesque, and weird Jewish externality."

These lines hide metaphysical possibilities that still resonate. Perhaps there are other symbolic reserves we've not yet tapped out, corresponding to the inner truth of the strange externality we find ourselves living today—symbols that obligate us in new ways to contemporary ethical dilemmas. Scholem spoke of the rising generation in Israel falling prey to a "technological assimilation," which he saw as the latest iteration of a false universalism. A new synthesis might yet emerge, he argued, but it was also possible that the higher dream could "just smash itself up on technology." What he insisted on was that Judaism had to be engaged as a living phenomenon, without uniform content, defying formal definitions, and containing "utopian aspects that have not been revealed." As to the question of whether Kabbalah could play a role in nurturing spiritual vitality in the future, he said he could not answer this, but invoked certain kinds of poetry, "steeped in elements of naturalistic, atheistic and pantheistic mysticism," as a model for creating new symbols responding to dimensions of the world that doctrine had neglected. He would not foreclose the possibility that for young people in the coming years, what he called "naturalistic" forms of consciousness, which seemed to lack any relation to traditional religious concepts, would become the true home of mysticism, the place where "mystical experience still exists, and is preserved and echoing."

Scholem's acknowledgment that he took up his studies of the Kabbalah "not merely as a chapter of history but from a dialectical distance—from identification and distance together" is linked to the spectrum of lingering symbolic potential that he saw extending through contemporary society into the larger universe. Lifting back the mask he generally kept tight to his features when the subject of his own religion crept into conversation, he abruptly told an interviewer, "My secularism is not secular."

My secularism is not secular. The formulation makes me smile with the tingle of self-recognition. For I feel and always have felt the same. But why, then, bother to convert? And why, having done so, the feeling of shame? Since I wasn't seeking to pretend that I'd attained any kind of enlightenment, and since my act of willed identification was not predicated on notions of a "Chosen People," or any sacred right to the Land, I must accept that there is something shameful in my embarrassment. I must try to examine what did lead to my conversion, the embrace of Judaism that eventually also brought me to Jerusalem.

My discovery of Benjamin preceded both my historical and theological educations. And when I wonder how Walter Benjamin's ruins could have resonated so powerfully for a child of the American suburbs in the late 1970s, what comes to mind is an image of myself and my best friend in high school perched atop a mound of rubble in the bulldozed remains of one of the last undeveloped tracts of land in the heart of Fairfax City, our home. We stare out angrily over the toppled trees, Medusa locks of uptorn roots flaring from red earth that once held dense woodland and crumbling stone walls, reputed to date back before the Civil War. Cursing the mustard-yellow caterpillars and heedless developers, we plotted to sabotage their missions of destruction. But none of our schemes ever stopped anything. Long before my conversion to Judaism, I felt that I'd been forcibly inducted into a patriotic consumerism that I wanted nothing to do with — from which I wanted to *de*-convert, into some form of being that spoke to my nature — to Nature and History. It was the ruin of ruins that I grew up with, the transformation of nature's open-ended, wild anarchy into closed, sterile commercial space. Only later, as my knowledge deepened, did I graft onto the ruination of nature that I'd witnessed the ruins of European history that my father's family had fled.

As a child, what I knew of the latter world manifested most evocatively in the guise of a few objects in my grandmother's apartment that had been smuggled out from Vienna. These gleam for me now in a perpetual moon glow: a lamp of twilight-blue-and-white crystal that my grandmother made out of an old handblown vase; a Biedermeier dresser with undulating drawers; books with gilt gothic script on their bindings; a large painting of children arrayed in beach grasses, a boy playing an accordion, a girl with a wreath of indigo flowers in her hair.

What I knew, without knowing the words, was that these objects had preserved the aura of enchantment, what Benjamin calls authenticity, through all their perilous migrations. I sought, in Judaism, to recover the aura I'd touched in these fragments of their vanished world. And this search was in part motivated by and a response to the ruins of the natural world I lived through growing up. In place of the forest, the history of the Tree of Life.

I converted to Judaism in my midtwenties, and it was a slow, halting process that unfolded without any singular moment of revelation. Rather than a lightning bolt of recognition, the image that comes to me is geological: the accretion of layers of historical perspective that left me both uplifted and subsumed by questions I could not escape from.

How could the experience of exile happen over and over to the same people in ways that were always different, yet correlative, and always generative of new insights into the texts around which Jewish identity first came to be constituted? Might it really be possible, as one rabbi suggested to me, that the antihierarchical structure of Jewish worship promoted an egalitarianism among congregants that nurtured a broader Jewish commitment to equal rights? What did it mean to pronounce certain blessings at certain times in exactly the words that had been spoken on the same occasions for thousands of years? Though in the abstract I might dismiss this practice as a historical stuck record, the actual experience proved affecting in ways I found myself unprepared for. When you speak words that echo so far back in time, self-consciousness flickers down before the collective past.

Along with questions having to do with ritual and time were others concerning historical catastrophe. If I could not believe in any kind of God I had language for, there yet seemed to be historical tragedies of such magnitude that they bore a transcendent character. The dark dimensions of the Shoah seemed *untranscendable* — suggesting the possibility of a negative theology. (If the contours of absolute evil were visible in attempted genocide, might there be a counterpart in some unimaginable good — a symmetrical opening in the rational universe for another kind of absolute?) W. G. Sebald's comment on the Holocaust, "No serious person ever thinks about anything else," still catches me up short and would have seemed to me then sufficient explanation for the path I was on. Hadn't this unassimilable tide of destruction swept up my own family?

Still, I wonder why it is that past tragedies float with such incandescent authority over the second and third generations. Sometimes the vision proves an evil deity, a Moloch devouring the children, triggering crippling obsessions and lust for vengeance; other times it may serve as a muse inspiring acts of profound restoration. Either way, there always seems to be something verging on the mystical in the call those born belatedly feel to engage with some wrong that's already happened; the pain once suffered; the blow fallen, the blast gone silent, the gas released, the lives long ago expelled from this world by violence. When Benjamin writes that the only historian who can fan the spark of hope from the past is the one "who is firmly convinced that *even the dead* will not be safe from the enemy if he wins," he brushes the border of theology. The particular tangle of history and faith that Judaism presents can make the move from recognition of catastrophe to religious affiliation — along with the reverse move from theology to catastrophe-inflected politics — seem almost reflexive.

Despite its materialist concerns, Benjamin closes "The Work of Art in the Age of Mechanical Reproduction" with a reflection that juxtaposes death with his themes — and forces us to reconsider the meaning of the work of art in terms of human life. "The destructiveness of war furnishes proof that society has not been mature enough to incorporate technology as its organ, that technology has not been sufficiently developed to cope with the elemental forces of society," he writes. "Instead of dropping seeds from airplanes, it drops incendiary bombs over cities; and through gas warfare the aura is abolished in a new way."

So the notions of aura and ruin find new forms for new times — though these, too, encompass the destruction of nature and aftershocks of the European collapse. And when I think now of conversion, I think of converting to Judaism again, through a wider river of history that leads to another vision of Jerusalem, in which the city's neighborhoods and faiths crisscross and reconstellate.

I think of how Zion itself can be converted into a state of exile, of how everything changes, in one endless process of conversion, converting and converting to new forms of conviction, despair, and responsibility, until flesh converts to the earth. *What can I make of my conversion now?* Not what have I done, but what can I do?

From the moment Scholem first encountered Benjamin, he felt some overwhelming attraction. And as soon as the two men began to speak in Grunewald, Benjamin plunged deep. "I am occupying myself a great deal with the nature of the historical process, and have also been reflecting on the philosophy of history," he said, staring intently at Gerhard. Right away, they were discussing subjects with which Gerhard had been intensely preoccupied for years, even if he was only seventeen. And Gerhard found himself able to talk unrestrainedly. Thank God, with Benjamin as his sole audience, he didn't garble his points.

Gerhard expounded his theory about the different lines of influence forming individuals: the blood inheritance that conveyed spiritual essence and certain core traits, along with the heritage that came through intellectual ancestors to whom one bore no biological relation. Spotting a book by Friedrich Theodor Vischer—the writer-philosopher who had the splendid nerve to declare that there was no God and earth was created by the devil—Gerhard announced that he considered Vischer a spiritual forefather.

A lengthy debate about blood and metaphysics followed. Benjamin circled and paced while he spoke. After acknowledging that certain oppositions appeared intrinsic to the dynamic of history, Gerhard found himself daring to propose a resolution that Benjamin didn't seem to have considered: simultaneously advancing along the two paths of anarchist socialism and Zionism. This was the task he'd set himself, Gerhard confessed.

He was thinking aloud with a freedom hitherto confined to

his journal. And Benjamin, who communicated, Scholem said, an "immediate impression of genius," was listening intently to everything he said. They discussed the war: Benjamin revealed that he was completely on the side of the pacifists, backing the radical Socialist Karl Liebknecht, who'd fought against war loans and been shipped off to the Eastern Front for helping to found the revolutionary Marxist Spartacus League. This prompted Scholem to reveal that he himself had gotten expelled from school for making antiwar statements. He also talked about the work he'd been doing with Werner's faction of the Social Democratic party.

The enthusiasm gushing out of him for Socialist activism might have startled Scholem himself. Something in Benjamin's manner invited such disclosures. Gerhard defended anarchism as the true form of socialism, because it didn't try to make historical change conform to scientifically verifiable laws.

Then the subject of Lao-Tzu came up. Thank God, Gerhard had read him! It was incredible the way Benjamin spoke — presenting several contradictory positions in turn, as though he were conducting a laboratory experiment. Over and over, he would begin with the phrase, "It's a metaphysical truth that..." followed by remarks that were "deeply enmeshed in the theological and frequently surprisingly odd," Scholem later wrote. At some point, Gerhard told Benjamin of the plans for his Zionist periodical, *Blue-White Spectacles*. It was time for Zionists to proclaim that their ways were not those of their fathers. The warmongers needed to understand that "we do not have great numbers of people for you to throw freely into the furnace like Moloch." He was planning to print his subversive journal right in the belly of the bourgeois beast, at Papa's own printing house. Benjamin, in turn, pressed on Scholem the first nine issues of *Der Anfang* (The Beginning), an influential periodical founded by Gustav Wynecken, whose disciple Benjamin had been in his student years, writing under the pseudonym Ardor. Perhaps these would furnish material for Gerhard to reflect on as he prepared to launch his own magazine? Wynecken had been instrumental in developing the rallying cry for a youth congress two years earlier, at which delegates avowed, "Free German Youth seeks to shape its life according to its own principles, on its own responsibility, and in inner truthfulness." This motto was not so different from positions Scholem was advocating in connection with anarchism—and Zionism.

Both of these, Gerhard argued, necessitated an absolute commitment to antiwar activity. That was the main thing. Benjamin agreed. When Gerhard began talking about secret meetings he'd attended with Werner at the Neukölln restaurant, where they dissected the German domestic situation for revolutionary purposes, Benjamin became fascinated. He announced that he wanted to become involved with the radicals immediately.

Gerhard told him to drop by his home and he would show him some incendiary magazines that he and Werner distributed illegally.

Benjamin promised to come. And at last, gathering up his nine copies of *Der Anfang*, Gerhard took his leave—withdrawing past the glimmering art; absorbing once more the shelves upon shelves of precious books; stepping out into the pine-scented night as the doors closed behind him and the twin lions glowered.

THREE

BACK HOME, Arthur Scholem constantly sniped at Gerhard and Werner for being chickens who wouldn't rush down to the recruiting office and do their part for the country. Werner screamed at Arthur for being a doltish subscriber to the Nibelungen code of honor. Gerhard yelled at both of them for betraying their Jewish identity. Reinhold, the oldest brother, scorned the lot of them, enlisting with a right-wing battalion and looking coldly even on Arthur for not being assimilationist enough. While Erich, the second born, tiptoed in the shadows, trying to keep the peace by not committing to anything. And Betty swept out of the house in her big plumed hat and boa on endless rounds of social calls that exasperated Gerhard for their bourgeois hypocrisy. She'd make nice with anyone just because she was by nature cheerful and flexible. What was she doing babbling a bunch of random opinions to conciliate her hosts? he chided. *"Mein Sohn, moniere mich nicht"* (My son, don't you admonish me), she replied. Those words still rang in his ears when he was an old man. By then he understood how much she'd done for him, even at the cost of bitter marital strife. The richer the family got, the more Betty indulged her taste for travel — and she almost always took off alone or with a lady friend. Maybe she hadn't been so happy after all, Scholem finally thought to himself.

At night, Gerhard sat brooding in his room, listening to shrieks and rotten piano playing from somewhere up the street. Was there really a God behind the dark blue night sky, planted on some unfathomable throne? Venus made the only sparkle of light. "It is lonely in heaven," he wrote in his diary. God could not possibly be up there directing anything. The shade above the rooftops was too pure and remote to have been created by any feeling sensibility. It was liberating not to have to think about some unknown immensity backstage of the stars disrupting the eternal harmonies. "God is insufferable," he abruptly declared.

Sometimes, mathematical meditations were all that could soothe him. The mechanical view of nature was spectacular. He loved necessity and the vision of everything in its proper proportions — the grander the better. "A law becomes more accurate the larger the dimensions that are observed and employed in its operations," he concluded after gazing for hours at the sky.

A thick mantle of dust powdered the trees that summer. Newsreels showed blind soldiers being conducted onto buses for outings. Men cast their heads around like frightened birds while female chaperones clasped their arms. Military bands sporting bright-spiked helmets marched through the Brandenburg Gate. Matrons and maidens wearing hats ringed with blossoms visited the hospitals, distributing cigarettes and flowers to men wrapped in bandages with their limbs all in traction. Women operated the trams and the omnibuses. The Socialist press noted the numbers of broken men in uniform hobbling along the streets. Copper roofs were being ripped off buildings to feed the factories making artillery shells and cable. Business, too, had become "toned with the colors of war; from the cinemas to the chocolate shops, it is all War, War, War." Public houses and restaurants were shuttered. Bars were cobwebbed. Dead flies cluttered the glasses. Though a food shortage was denied, rationing grew more severe. Ten thousand live reindeer were being sent from Norway to Berlin for slaughter.

"The state is violence," Scholem wrote in his journal, "from which follows that we have to extricate ourselves from it."

Some intellectuals perceived in the devastation wrought by this war the summons to a commensurately great utopian transformation of society. So much death might be a harbinger of some glorious rebirth. Even before war broke out, Gerhard had been drawn to anarchist tracts, especially the works of Gustav Landauer, who'd described the true mission as a form of social creation that didn't restrict the spiritual independence of individuals. "In these times when routine has become a malignant scourge," Landauer thundered, "it is spirit that must lead the revolution, spirit that overnight performs miracles." Many young Zionists took inspiration from Landauer who, with his long face and stalactite-cluster beard, resembled a holy man dreamed up by Tolstoy, his hero. Socialism couldn't simply be plastered over an established system of "national wealth and sumptuous economy," Landauer argued. "It must be created out of nothing amid chaos." His listeners embraced the notion that the new age might be launched immediately just by beginning to relate to one another differently, while the old structures of the state moldered away overhead. "We no longer believe in a gap between the present and the future," he proclaimed. "We know: America is here or nowhere!"

The lunatic slaughter of the Great War intensified Gerhard's determination to break free of German society. The philosopher Ernst Bloch, who became a provocative associate of both Scholem and Benjamin, declared that once the country had undergone "the destruction and defeat of its military autocracy...its deeply buried currents of beclouded, dreamy piety" would rise to consciousness, catalyzing the country's political and spiritual resurrection. In a later reflection on messianism, Scholem noted, "The apocalyptists have always cherished a pessimistic view of the world. Their optimism, their hope, is not directed to what history will bring forth, but to that which will arise in its ruin, free at last and undisguised." The powerful Jewish mystical concept of "the birth pangs of the Messiah" made historical disaster an essential prelude to the Redeemer's emergence.

Indeed, scholars have argued that although a romantic anticapitalist rebellion against reason and authority was pervasive among the generation that came of age as war broke out, the messianic expression of this revolt was peculiar to its Jewish proponents. This new form of messianism was simultaneously secular and religious. It involved the repudiation of orthodoxy, of the nontheological Judaism of the middle classes, *and* of the religion of personal revival championed by Martin Buber. In place of these, Jewish artists, intellectuals, and activists found their own paths to the conviction that *everything* had to change.

But the coming transfiguration was to be restitutive as well as salvational. The messianic revolution would entail a recovery of lost truths. Karl Kraus's aphorism "the origin is the goal" became a favorite line of Benjamin's. Scholem, for his part, liked to recall that the root of *teshuva*, the Hebrew term for "repentance," meant "to return" — a Jewish penitent was required to go back to the place where his evil ways began. Just so, Scholem insisted that his people needed to return to the spot on the road where they started and undertake the total refounding of society on grounds that excluded the use of force in favor of a harmonious existence centered on higher freedom, always recalling that in the universe, "violence-free cooperation obtains among revolutionizing powers." He was enamored of the writings of the cultural Zionist Ahad Ha'am, who sought to rekindle the Jews' prophetic moral spirit. Ha'am's book *At the Crossroads* tackled head-on the question of whether the answer lay in continuity or a radical new beginning. The abiding moral profundity of Judaism made of the Jews a "Supernation," predating and transcending Nietzsche's "Superman" individual in Ha'am's eyes. But while the Jews' national creative power had not completely vanished in exile, "every atom of that power which is severed from its original source and floats away into a strange world is an irreparable loss to the nation," he wrote. Only as a concentrated people could the Jews fulfill the mission of the Hebrew prophets, who'd "preached the gospel of justice and charity for the whole human race."

Above all, Gerhard inveighed against the callow disregard in which the Bible was held by fellow German intellectuals. They missed the whole point when they sneered that "God" would surely have created better stories than these shepherd folktales. People had forgotten how to read the book, for all that it could be found in every home library. He wished he could teach them how to study the work for its own sake, for its stupendous myths rather than for the laws. Genesis, Gerhard believed, revealed the most profound truth a person could discover: the divinity of everyday life. Peasants and commoners were enveloped by a sacred glow through its verses. The brilliance of Judaism was precisely to have brought "heaven down to earth and to recapture it in daily life," Gerhard wrote in his journal. He deplored his generation's deficit of *reverence*, by which he meant the mystical intimation that "behind everything yawns the 'great abyss' and one must surrender to the power that animates it."

In the days after his visit to Grunewald, Gerhard pored over Benjamin's magazines — with dismay. Even Benjamin's own essays for the periodical weren't much good. Their reverence was lavished exclusively on youth. One of Benjamin's tracts contended that the mask adults wore called "experience" was "expressionless, impenetrable, and ever the same." The meaning of this mask was that grown-ups had already experienced everything (ideals, hopes, women) and found everything to be illusory. Lifting the mask, Benjamin wrote, one discovered that the essence of this experience that adults lorded over young people was just that they too had once been young, disbelieving their parents — but their parents had been *right*. Life was meaningless and brutal. Youth knew a different experience, Benjamin averred, the experience of "spirit," and they could never be without spirit while they remained young. Remaining loyal to this principle, they would yet attain greatness.

The critique part was fine, but Gerhard balked at Benjamin's conclusion. It was right to denounce the concept of "experience" when it was invoked by philistines to dismiss the dreams of youth, but Benjamin apparently supported the idea that youth *as such* guaranteed the ability to catalyze social renewal. Wasn't this claim akin to Hiller's bankrupt position that we live only in the present? While Gerhard recognized that much of Zionism's strength lay in its young membership, all the time he'd spent with Dr. Bleichrode reading ancient texts — his growing relationship to Jewish *knowledge* — counterbalanced the idealization of juvenile energies.

Complicating matters was the moral breakdown their generation had suffered in consequence of the war. Youth now existed in a state of confusion—even if this discomposure was not of their own making. How could today's young people be granted oracular authority?

There would be no basis for true friendship if he concealed his reaction, Gerhard thought. So when Benjamin turned up at Neue Grünstrasse several days later, Gerhard burst out that the radical antihistoricism of "The Beginning" was anathema to Zionist thinking. Did Herr Benjamin really hold to the ideal of an autonomous youth culture? Wasn't the Zionist insistence on historical consciousness superior to *that*?

All my association with Wynecken and the youth movement ended with the outbreak of war, Benjamin said. He no longer saw his former comrades, and the movement itself had collapsed. In November, Wynecken—like Buber—had delivered a speech calling on youth to serve the fatherland. Thereafter, Benjamin published an open letter in which he called Wynecken's speech a disgrace and charged him with the unforgivable crime of having sacrificed young people to the state. This from the man who'd introduced him to the life of the spirit.

It was true, Benjamin acknowledged, he himself had once sought out younger companions from a sense that his peers had too much life behind them to have direct access to ideas any longer. He still treasured two lines from Goethe's "Marienbader Elegie": "Only where you are let everything be—always childlike/Thus you are everything—you are invincible." But he'd never been a "card-carrying member" of the student union, or a believer in the fixed innocence of youth. Innocence had "to be earned anew every day, *and as a different kind* of innocence," Benjamin told a friend at that time. This, in truth, had always been *Der Anfang*'s challenge: how to help youth overcome its reputation for instinctual goodness. Some accused the journal of corrupting youth's innocence, but there'd been no signs of this innocence, even before the war. The condition of being beyond good and evil that youth enjoyed was permissible for animals, but it led human beings invariably to sin.

Benjamin had been close to the poet Fritz Heinle, who was also part of the movement, he revealed. They'd spent many hours together in Freiburg, when Benjamin had been a student there: reading, climbing the slopes of Mount Schönberg after sunset, walking in the Black Forest long after midnight and discussing the notion of dread. He and Heinle understood each other better than anyone else ever could; perhaps because they were also forever at odds. Once he'd told Heinle, "Each of us has faith but everything depends on how we believe in our faith." He'd been thinking not as a Socialist but "of the multitude who are excluded and of the *spirit* that is in league with those who sleep and not with those who are brothers." And Heinle responded, "fraternity almost against one's better judgment." Benjamin didn't know any word that could describe his relationship with Heinle, but he contented himself with the idea of taking "pure delight in the pure struggle."

In a picture taken around this time, Heinle is seated in profile in a room piled with books, gazing thoughtfully down at a photograph of a woman who appears to be holding a brush and palette. Crisp and angular, his handsome, alert face seizes the light. "He confronted me in the name of love and I countered with the symbol," Benjamin remarked to a friend who knew both of them. When they returned to Berlin, the two men continued to meet, and Benjamin continued to find ever greater beauty in Heinle's poetry. Sometimes they rendezvoused at cafés. And often they met in the Free Students' Meeting House in Tiergarten. "Assemblies of bourgeois intellectuals were then far commoner than nowadays, since they had not yet recognized their limits," Benjamin remarked of this period. But they had *felt* those limits even then. They felt them when they were compelled to hold their literary gatherings in beer halls, spied on by waitstaff. And they felt them when they were forced to entertain their paramours in furnished rooms with doors that did not lock. And they felt them in their relationships with the landlords of public rooms, with family, and with guardians.

A week after war was declared, Benjamin awoke to a telegram from Heinle. "You will find us lying in the Meeting House."

Nineteen-year-old Fritz and his lover, Rika Seligson, sister of one of Walter Benjamin's best friends, had turned on the gas in the Discussion Hall. The press wanted to make the suicides a romantic sensation, a doomed lovers' pact born of thwarted passion. But their deaths, Benjamin knew, had been a radical protest against the war. They had chosen those rooms to exemplify the abject failure of the dream of the Free Students' Union. And the remnants of the youth movement who had clung to the *idea* until that day felt their limits once more in the aftermath of the double suicide, when those who'd been closest to Fritz and Rika could find refuge "only in a seedy railway hotel on Stuttgart Square," sharing their grief over dirty glasses. This was the curtain fall, so far as Benjamin was concerned. Wynecken's idea of transcendence through community had always been predicated on youth's patriotic allegiance to a national entity. The man could not think of Spirit beyond the borders of State.

When Benjamin thought back on the neighborhood of the meeting house, slashed by the bulky iron-and-stone girding of Berlin's municipal railway, at the verge of a steep slope leading down to the Landwehr Canal, where a vein of stagnant water divided Tiergarten's properties from the workers' realm of Moabit, he saw those buildings as "the last of their line just as the occupants of those apartments were the last who could appease the clamorous shades of the dispossessed with philanthropic ceremonies." The location graphed in space the historical end point of the true bourgeois elite. He realized now that it had lain as near to the apocalypse of the Great War as to the dark waters of the torpid canal.

Benjamin's youth in Berlin was defined by a chafing against confinement no less fierce than Scholem's sense of being caged. But whereas Scholem's rejection of the bourgeois world was shot through with conviction that the roots of the German-Jewish misalliance ran deeper even than those of economic inequality, Benjamin's isolation in the cocoon of the haute bourgeoisie allowed him to feed his hunger for escape closer to home. While still young, he began frequenting prostitutes, finding in this pursuit opportunity to trespass into secret parts of the city.

Where Scholem wanted to bust out of Berlin, Benjamin wanted to make himself more pervious to the place, mingling unrestrainedly with its diverse socioeconomic paradigms, partly in order to better understand and expose their systemic injustices, but also to locate the hidden entrances to illicit thrills that never much caught Scholem's fancy. At moments, Walter Benjamin sounds like a brilliant rich kid staring out the window at street urchins swinging sticks and cursing on the pavement below, resolving, come what may, to run riot through the refuse-strewn alleyways in a spirit of sublime solidarity. Scholem, on the other hand, sounds just that much closer to the lower classes to be exempt from even a nuanced idealization of their play.

On Revolution by Landauer jumped out at Benjamin as he was scanning the bookshelves. Gerhard was happy that Benjamin seemed to agree with Landauer's repudiation of Marx in favor of a vision of history as a perpetual, unpredictable becoming. "The past itself is future. It is never finished," Landauer wrote. "Each utopia contains the passionate memories of all former utopias," and every investigation "into the human past or present creates the future" by reactivating dormant revolutionary memories.

Benjamin's curiosity about revolution stoked Gerhard's enthusiasm. He gave Benjamin the first issue of *Die Internationale*, along with copies of *Light Beams*, the organ of the pacifist Socialists. They traded radical magazines the way people now exchange playlists.

When Benjamin left for an appointment with a woman, Scholem accompanied him all the way down Berlin's showiest boulevard, Unter den Linden, talking incessantly, and at some point the conversation turned to Gerhard's Jewish interests.

"Judaism occupies me greatly," Benjamin said. He'd recently likened the Jewish people to builders of an upside-down Tower of Babel. The Jews "handle ideas like quarry stones," he wrote the poet Ludwig Strauss. But they "build from above, without ever reaching the ground." Benjamin proposed that there was something unbalanced in the way that, to the extent they were both Jews and Germans, all their energies went to the German side, while the Jewish part became alien—or worse, sentimental: a sprinkling of "Jewish aroma in our production and our lives." It intrigued him that a young man from Scholem's background would embrace the study of Talmud without becoming Orthodox. This was virtually unheard of.

Gerhard was eager to pass on his thoughts about how the honesty of Holy Writ contrasted with the sloganeering of contemporaries. Here they were, approaching the second anniversary of what he called Europe's funeral, and most German Jews were still cheering on the godless death orgy. Jews had a relationship to Europe "only to the degree that Europe has acted upon us as a destructive stimulation," Gerhard told a friend.

How could he convey the relief he felt opening an old, grave book in a cool, silent room alone, and finding between its covers words that expressed who the Jews were: strangers to Europe, with no need to appease anyone but the Absolute. Perhaps not even Him. Maybe when a new heaven and a new Jerusalem were instated, there would be a "new God, a renewed God," he reasoned.

Benjamin never challenged Gerhard's devotion to Jewish learning. "God was real for Benjamin," Scholem later insisted. Nor did Benjamin debate Scholem's belief that Jewish theology provided a medium through which to engage with the people's historical development. That's why being a Jew and being a Zionist are one and the same, Gerhard said: Zionism is the latest form of Jewish development.

But here Benjamin demurred. Zionism interested him exclusively as a cultural endeavor. Yes, Western Jewry needed to be brought to self-consciousness, but the requisite self-consciousness would reinforce their commitment to internationalism. Anywhere Jewish cultural values manifested, he could express his Judaism, Benjamin maintained, including the much-scorned literati cafés. Even witty aestheticism should not be underestimated for its "penetrating, captivating power," which was both "forerunner and foe of religious feeling." Being a Jew, "if I live as a conscious human being, I live as a conscious Jew," he'd said. Zionism, meanwhile, seemed invariably to end up in the business of political organization. The Zionists "propagandize Palestine and [speak] German," Benjamin observed to Strauss, which made them effectively "half-human."

Gerhard felt the same way about the current state of the movement — hence his commitment to learning and teaching Hebrew.

"Have they ever thought through school, literature, inner life, or the state in a Jewish manner?" Benjamin wondered about Germany's Zionists.

This was the very problem Gerhard had diagnosed, which was why he was dedicated to revolutionizing the movement.

Benjamin told Gerhard he'd like to attend a meeting of Jung Juda in order to watch Scholem rouse some opposition. He'd seen too often that when a noble idea became politicized, "out of God develops a fetish."

But Zionism had the potential to become something much greater, Gerhard countered, blaming Benjamin's limited Jewish education for his "middle-of-the-road Zionist line." If he knew more, he'd grasp the imperative of taking a position on Jewish matters as radical as the one he instinctively adopted with respect to Socialist issues.

He would have brought Benjamin to Jung Juda the next week, but Benjamin couldn't make that meeting, and after this deferral, Gerhard grew ambivalent about the introduction. Later he claimed that despite Benjamin's professed interest, he sensed that Benjamin "would not be very comfortable in that circle, so I did not pursue his suggestion further." But in his diary at the time, his concern focuses on the visit's implications for himself: "Next week I'll have to see if I can squeeze something fruitful out of this. One must only maintain one's balance." Perhaps Scholem recognized an element of fantasy in his fledgling Zionist outlook that needed to be shielded from the analytic jolt of an outsider like Benjamin.

Instead of pressing Benjamin further, Gerhard immersed himself in *Don Quixote*. His inner strings played the melodies of Cervantes and the Romantics, he noted in private.

When Anne and I turned to Judaism, we were attracted not just by the religion's historical-philosophical intrigue but also by the aesthetic retreat of the home ritual. There was a modesty and observant stillness before Creation that moved our spirits. And the Friday night Sabbath at home *was* beautiful, as the young Scholem asserted — with the silver kiddush cup lifting on high in my hands and Anne's fingers beckoning inside the flickering candlelight, and the sound of the blessings in Hebrew so ancient the syllables might have passed through the looking glass to the verge of some original utterance. Like Scholem's Kabbalists, I had "a fundamental feeling that there is mystery — a secret — in the world" that these experiences seemed to bring closer.

But once I began actually attending synagogues, frustration with the different real-world communities of Jewish worship kicked in to counter the attraction of practicing the religion. The only congregation Anne and I felt the least bit at home with consisted of a handful of elderly parishioners, Holocaust survivors as well as lifelong New Yorkers, who prayed in a tiny, drab upstairs room of a cavernously grand, drafty Brooklyn temple. Picturing those faces now, hollowed, deeply wrinkled, with wide eyes and wild trails of gray and white hair, they seem like the personification of the icy winds that blew through the poorly taped panes of cracked stained glass in the deserted hall of worship below. But the people were kind and warm: a congregation of the grandparents we never had, charmed by our youth and sincerity. One man who must have been close to eighty took on the task of beginning to teach us Hebrew, refusing payment and working with meticulous diligence to give us a grounding in the language that had already gotten under our skin. The big cards with letters of the alphabet printed on them seemed to have floated off some eye exam chart in a dream, turning to black flame in the hands of that patient, large-boned man as he held them before us one by one: *Aleph* is the first letter, and it looks like an *X* struck by lightning. *Bet* is next, and it's a contrarian *C* that's traded its curve for three burnt matchsticks, then turned around the wrong way.

There was beauty in the generosity of his teaching, and the embrace of that poor tiny congregation stranded with their new hips and stooped backs in the empty synagogue where yellow marble, dim bronze, and dusty names of deceased members engraved in plaques by little burned-out lightbulbs seemed to cast a monumental sepulchral glow over the whole of Judaism. We felt a sense of purpose just in the practice of showing this lonely remnant that they had not been utterly deserted.

But the weekly visit to the temple and the hours we spent with the elders was not enough to compose a life with. We didn't know how to join their community in ways that translated beyond those twilight rooms of prayer and learning; if the worshippers were like grandparents, that meant we were the grandchildren. This temporal gap kept us in a state of youthful promise and innocence. (So we were fixed in their eyes, and so, seeing ourselves through their gazes, we preserved our own image.) Every so often, part of me suspected that our inability to find community with a congregation of our peers represented some deeper kind of evasion, or even denial. Perhaps the huge castaway synagogue was a sanctuary also in the sense that it shielded us from having to confront what it would mean to live the religion more openly.

Regardless, we felt increasingly estranged from our life outside that chamber. It's easy to romanticize late '80s Manhattan from the money-drugged perspective of today, but at the time it seemed to us marked less by edginess than by icy narcissism that left as much room for the spirit as a pinhole at a peepshow. Wall Street and the real estate titans were less proficient at sanitizing the city's street life than they've since become, and it seemed a little more plausible that the cash in this town would circulate toward its artistically unruly flip side. But the capital was hardly distributed with any great sense of overall justice, and was perhaps even less likely than it is today to find its way to the unaesthetic realms of deep socioeconomic disadvantage. We didn't feel we belonged to any New York world we knew, and hadn't yet learned to find in this not-belonging the basis for other kinds of sociopolitical attachment. The Judaism that Anne and I sought seemed a way out of a way of life that kept bad faith with the universe.

In our discontent, when the opportunity arose to borrow the cottage of Anne's stepmother in a wild swath of County Clare, we seized it. There I moved from reading Benjamin to Scholem, having gotten hold of his summary work *Major Trends in Jewish Mysticism* along with *On the Kabbalah and Its Symbolism* in the weeks before we fled New York.

I dipped in and out of them at first, trying to orient myself in this strange new realm of ideas. Scholem himself seems to have flitted back and forth in the field when he began studying Jewish mysticism, moving between a wide range of sources: various nineteenth-century German-Christian exegeses and reimaginings of the Kabbalah, the censorious pages on mysticism in Graetz's history of the Jews, and fragments of primary texts, especially the Zohar.

Near the opening of *Major Trends*, Scholem outlined a simple three-stage process that applies to the development of all forms of mysticism. At first the world was full of gods; humanity experienced the Divine at every step without the need for ecstatic petition and meditation. In this phase, marked by faith in the essential unity of all aspects of the universe, "Nature is the scene of man's relation to God."

Then religion, in its classical, monotheistic form, burst onto the picture. "Religion's supreme function is to destroy the dream-harmony of Man, Universe and God," Scholem declared. It signified "the creation of a vast abyss, conceived as absolute, between God, the infinite and transcendental Being, and Man, the finite creature." Why, exactly, religion committed this act of violence against the dream-harmony humanity once enjoyed wasn't quite clear to me. Scholem said the earlier, holistic state pertained only to "the childhood of mankind"—yet what exactly did that phrase mean? Were we really grown up now? Anyway, the abyss *was* there, and God knew I'd not crossed it when I went to synagogue in New York.

After the intervention of formal religion, Scholem wrote, the scene switched from Nature to the moral and theological activity of individuals and groups. Their engagement with the great moral questions produced history as "the stage on which the drama of man's relation to God unfolds." Given that humanity's perfect intimacy with God had been destroyed, the drama being enacted was essentially tragic.

Enter mysticism. Mysticism, according to Scholem, acknowledged the existence of the abyss, then embarked on a quest for the hidden bridge that might span this gap. Confronting the rupture between man and God engendered by the religious cataclysm, mysticism strove to piece together the shards, "to bring back the old unity which religion has destroyed, but on a new plane, where the world of mythology and that of revelation meet in the soul of man." Now the soul became the scene of the great drama, and the journey of the soul back "through the abysmal multiplicity of things to the experience of the Divine Reality...became its main preoccupation." The ascent of mysticism, Scholem wrote, coincided with "the romantic period of religion." It marked humanity's attempt to change the genre it was condemned to act in from tragedy to something more like the magic-infused reversal-of-fortune dramas typified by Shakespeare's late romances. Rather than a Yahweh out of Macbeth or Lear, give us God as Prospero.

Mysticism did not, then, restore the original wholeness; it sought instead to forge a new unity that overcame the duality that had arisen between man and God, at a higher stage of consciousness. Critically for Scholem, the moment when mysticism emerged did not indicate that classical religious forms had become altogether moribund. Otherwise, mystics would simply crack the shell of the official religion to found a new faith. Sometimes, to be sure, this *did* happen. But Scholem's interest lay in how mystical yearnings found expression in a fresh interpretation of old values, often characterized by a deeper, more personal relation to the religion's foundational tenets. As an example, Scholem cited the Revelation at Sinai. The mystic viewed this as a real event, but not a singular one, since its full meaning had not been disclosed at the hour of transmission. The event repeated as a private scene for mystic after mystic through the ages, and the secret revelation thus received was both novel and decisively anchored in the original sacred texts.

Because of the specificity of the different canons to which each mystic sought to connect his or her individual revelation, Scholem insisted there could not be "mysticism as such," only the mysticism of particular religious movements. It was only in recent times, he argued, that the trend toward abandoning specific dogma in favor of an abstract, universal faith had caused the historical aspects of religious mysticism to be "treated as corrupted forms of an, as it were, chemically pure mysticism."

In the case of Judaism, individual mystical experience was always filtered through the central motifs of the Orthodox religion, such as God's unity, the Creation of the universe out of nothing, the Revelation at Sinai, and the promised final redemption, with all its messianic and apocalyptic features. Many mystics from different faiths, he said, were moved by the sentiment of the psalmist who sang, "Oh taste and see that the Lord is good." They wanted that kind of personal, experiential contact with the Divine, but the flavor of the radiant fruit was a factor of its institutionally localized spiritual terroir.

This was all interesting enough intellectually, and I could relate on a visceral level to the idea of existing in a forlorn, broken world far from God: Our desultory life in the Burren was stark and withdrawn. Home felt ever farther away. But where did that leave us if we lacked knowledge of how to construct the grand mystical bridge to something beyond?

I rose from my hard chair to poke the guttering fire and stare out once more at the dripping magenta fuchsia blossoms hanging by the doorway. It rained and rained. The landscape beyond was all shattered rock. A water-drenched moon, in which countless miniature orchids quivered, lost fingers of pink and lavender. A farmer wearing peat-moss tweed said he'd never seen such floods. Black outside by three. Never light. Hard wind, and flickering oil lamps above a spitting wet log flame. Struggling to keep writing as we shivered side by side, Anne and I felt trapped in some cramped, thatched-cottage version of *The Shining*, without even any shining for light.

It was when Scholem turned to the question of how Jewish mysticism manifested its particularity that something began to really grip me. The Kabbalists, Scholem declared, were distinguished by their overwhelming, "metaphysically positive attitude toward language as God's own instrument." For them, God was literally — and literarily — the *author* of Creation. He had constructed the world through particular configurations of letters, still legible in the Torah, which itself was nothing less than "a living organism animated by a secret life which streams and pulsates below the crust of its literal meaning." While different mystical systems might envision a divine realm underlying the world of sensory data, if a Kabbalist turned the skin of creation into glass, he would see streaming letters and words beneath every surface—alphabets ribboning inside every limb of the body; Hebrew characters scrolling under the exteriors of stones, stalks, and leaves. All creation, according to the Kabbalists, was "from the point of view of God, nothing but an expression of His hidden self that begins and ends by giving itself a name, the holy name of God, the perpetual act of creation." Speech reached God because speech came from God—words bridged the cardinal divide. Humanity's own language "reflects the creative language of God. All that lives is an expression of God's language."

From the beginning, Scholem made clear that Kabbalah is a writer's mysticism.

Living in the middle of nowhere, amid biblical deluges, we made little effort to engage with our immediate environment. I was striving rather to *escape* where I was through writing—through language. When Scholem recounted how kabbalistic meditations enabled one mystic to perceive the world of letters as "the true world of bliss," while every language, not only Hebrew, became transfigured "into a transcendental medium of the one and only language of God," I daydreamed of our own writing as a vehicle through which we might ascend somewhere high above the rising waters and our own sinking spirits.

Still, when not reading Scholem, I spent a lot of time reading little travel advertisements at the back of the local newspaper. One day there was a good deal on flights to Jerusalem, and we just thought, *Why not?*

I didn't travel to Israel in search of a Jewish revelation, nor did I have one. But the jagged enjambment of different peoples, histories, and beliefs caught our imaginations by surprise. The trip was only ten days long, but so sharp and bright, with time-tripping descents into ancient sites and dramatic flourishes of natural beauty up above, that visions of the country lodged inside us, Jerusalem most of all.

When we returned from Ireland, we came back to Northern Virginia, not far from where my parents lived. Whatever else, writing had not opened a path, mystical or otherwise, to material survival. I'd thought I might eventually earn a living by following the example of my mother's grandfather, James Jackson Putnam, a neurologist and psychologist who'd befriended Freud. As a first step, I began working at a network of group homes for the chronically mentally ill. And it was in the context of administering this care that Judaism again began to draw me as a practice. For the job drove home the emptiness of what could be offered patients even as a final goal. Working as a night clerk in a cheap hotel and living "independently" in a ghastly apartment compound belted by highways, devoid of human interaction outside of symptom checklist meetings with exhausted social workers? These were the ones who made it? An image fixed in my mind of one poor resident named James, a little man with a toothbrush mustache and brilliant flash in his light green eyes, whose bed in the group house was surrounded by half a dozen alarm clocks, all ticking frantically away, to ensure that one clock at least would manage to go off and wake him for his shift under a bitter stock clerk at a supermarket of pharaonic dimensions. Shouldn't James's heroic struggle to wake on time be devoted to rising for something more meaningful than that? No wonder so many of the men and women who lived in these homes preferred not even trying to get out — claiming *any* outside work was too stressful.

I kept thinking of my great-grandfather, who'd sought to convince Freud that helping the analysand find some higher sense of purpose was essential lest the patient, once stripped of delusions, simply felt cast into the void. In the epigraph to one essay, my great-grandfather had cited the Bible, "The people who do not see visions shall perish from the face of the earth."

Perhaps it would be more effective to work as a psychotherapist within the context of a religious tradition, I concluded. And

I discovered a program in Jerusalem offered by the Jewish Theological Seminary that would supply the preliminary course work should I decide to seek training as a rabbinic chaplain. It would also give me an excuse to follow Gershom Scholem's path and see whether in Israel there might be some more galvanizing external form of Judaism than what we knew from New York or Washington. Anne was ready to radically upend the life we'd been leading in the name of anything even nominally higher and purer — even if what exactly that anything was remained phenomenally vague. She thought about teaching but wanted our germinal faith to somehow be part of the instruction she gave. Our life back home seemed make-believe, like we were playing some pasteboard version of the bourgeois lifestyle we'd formerly anathematized. It seemed easier to believe that we might make a real life somewhere utterly strange to us.

The hope I brought to Jerusalem of finding some more substantial way of helping people overcome psychological suffering was a dream of compassion. But sometimes now I think back on the congregation in the little room in the giant synagogue that first took us in as we began exploring the meaning of a Jewish life. And I wonder whether we were too quick to spot the element of "hiding from the real world" in our presence there, and too slow to fathom the depths of real empathy that might yet be tendered.

Though the people we'd come to know at the temple said they understood our leaving, telling us we had to lead our lives, and though I know our tears were real at the gathering when we saw them for the last time, we did, also, desert them. Sometimes I wonder whether we didn't take away more than we gave — the young couple who blew in from nowhere one frozen day, becoming part of their lives and hopes and then, on a summer evening lit by heat lightning, disappearing. What would have happened if we'd resolved to kindle our Judaism there, instead of five thousand miles away, instead of allowing that breath of humanity right before us to fade? *The people who do not see visions shall perish from the face of the earth.* And sometimes the people who do see visions shall cause others to perish from the face of the earth. By their hand, or by neglect. By not seeing what lies before them here and now.

FOUR

A PLAGUE OF LOCUSTS descended over the Holy Land in March of 1915. By late November, newspapers reported fields covered with the insects as far as the eye could see. Men, women, and children lined the roads dividing fields from gardens, attempting to drive the locusts into tin-lined traps sunk into the the earth. The green and black mass advancing through Jerusalem made its streets resemble flowing rivers. Orchards and vineyards were decimated. The markets were bare.

Hearing of the ruinous onslaught, Gerhard felt tempted to move to Palestine immediately. It would be a praiseworthy act, he decided, to build a hermit's shack on the Jordan River and subsist on a diet of locusts while absorbed day and night in his holy books. Part of him was always drawn to the ideal of the solitary mystic, perfecting his spiritual being in preparation for some higher destiny. But the bliss of the locust eater was something he had to deny himself, he resolved, since life in an isolated hut could not lay the foundation for a national community. The rewards of an ascetic retreat could be reaped only *after* the struggle for greater renewal had been won. "The way for the Jew of action is fight not flight," he reminded himself. And the purpose of being in Palestine was communal resurrection of the Jewish people.

Not that this goal constituted an ideology, exactly. In truth, Gerhard decided, no one actually knew what Zionist ideology consisted in, since it didn't yet exist. The first order of business was just to recognize that it was essential to compose this doctrine. The task would involve integrating four elements: a stringent historical consciousness, a sense of social responsibility regarding all humanity, misery over the condition of Europe, and general spiritual anguish.

It's an interesting Zionist wish list, almost fantastically alien to contemporary definitions of the movement.

Walter Benjamin said there was a simple, dependable criterion by which to gauge the spiritual value of a community: Does it allow *all* of an individual's efforts to be expressed? Is the *whole* human being committed to it and indispensable to it? Gerhard craved such guidance. Hovering over him, he always felt "the sneering face of the angel of insecurity." It goaded him on, his destiny and doom, master and muse. Insecurity was the mother of action—"action as flight from the flaming sword and as an attempt to reach salvation in the meadows of paradise."

Whenever Benjamin was in town, he and Gerhard spent long stretches of time together. They talked about everything from

German philosophy and myth to the Jewish spirit and dreams. They played chess, and Benjamin moved so slowly and played so blindly that Gerhard couldn't sit still, and the moment Benjamin's piece had found its new square, Gerhard's itchy hand sprang into action. Basically it was always Benjamin's turn.

He gave the impression of being infinitely patient, but there was no virtue involved, Benjamin confessed in his memoir. As a child, he'd often been sick, and this had accustomed him to seeing everything he cared for approach as from a distance, the way the hours drew near the sickbed to which he was confined. Even Benjamin's helplessness was cultivated. As a child walking with his mother, he'd drive her crazy with his slow pace, always loitering a half step behind. With no sense of direction, no ability to read a street map, Benjamin claimed not even to know his right hand from his left with any reliability until he was thirty. But the more his mother castigated him for maladroitness, the more Benjamin saw the advantages of not being able to keep up or find one's way — the freedom conferred by the pose of total ineptitude.

Whenever Benjamin traveled, he lost the most pleasurable part of the journey if he couldn't wait for great stretches of time in the station. He traveled frequently, and the places that touched him he'd return to repeatedly. To Basel to see the originals of the most renowned Dürer prints: *Knight, Death and the Devil* and *Melancholia*. To Venice for the Accademia. He knew Paris well and once had a vision in the Café des Deux Magots of his entire past diagrammed in a series of labyrinthine family trees, which he proceeded to transcribe, and then lose.

At home in Berlin, almost a quarter million men were now missing from the city, burrowed into frozen trenches along endless jagged battle lines. Rumors were flickering through Germany that an entire "city of the blind" was being designed to accommodate legions of gassed veterans. Masses of women had begun rioting against the food shortages.

The assumption that things couldn't go on as they were would one day confront the fact that "for the suffering of individuals as of communities there is only one limit beyond which things cannot go: annihilation," Benjamin said later.

Benjamin loved to talk, and to talk at great length. But he was also a marvelous listener. Early in their friendship, he wanted to hear everything Scholem could tell him about the reasons why Germany bore responsibility for the war. In this respect, Gerhard had been heavily influenced by the opinions of his brother Werner, who'd been drafted but not yet called up. In the years preceding, Werner had become increasingly active with the youth wing of the Social Democratic Workers party. For Werner, socialism supplanted Zionism: Having discovered "Humanity," he said he'd embarked on "a broader, more comprehensive sphere of activity" than that offered "by the narrow little thing called Jewish nationalism."

Werner had developed a maddening habit of climbing onto chairs and delivering Socialist diatribes as if he were standing on a platform at a party convention. Gerhard swore that Werner's notion of "universal humanity" was a fantasy. Hadn't Werner himself written letters about how anti-Semitism pervaded the party even when the members weren't aware of it? Jews get kicked out of everything, even movements they themselves start and are most involved with, Gerhard reflected. This proved the correctness of Zionist thinking.

One day when Werner was declaiming from his chair, Gerhard broke out, "You're deluding yourself the same way Papa is deluding himself!"

Werner ordered his younger brother to be quiet and learn something.

"You are deluding yourself by imagining you represent Germany's exploited industrial workers," Gerhard persisted. "It's a lie. You don't represent a thing."

"The Revolution will solve everything," Werner retorted.

"You're the son of a middle-class bourgeois Jew," Gerhard went on. "That makes you furious, so you go wandering off into other fields. You don't want to be what you are."

"The Revolution will solve all problems," Werner repeated. "Especially national problems!"

"The Revolution! The Revolution! It's all sloganeering!" Gerhard wouldn't listen to another word.

Werner sprang off his chair, arms and fists thrashing. They'd come to blows at last. Truthfully, given their contrary dispositions, it's a wonder all four Scholem boys weren't cracking heads constantly. Tumbling down the halls and knocking into the heavy furniture. Mostly they just had nothing to do with one another. Storming off to their separate corners. While Arthur blew up and poor Betty muttered, "So the goat shits on itself."

The radical divergence in the brothers' life paths led Scholem to comment that such disparity in families was typical for their Jewish bourgeois milieu — and also proof of how little influence a common environment has on individual development. It's the

kind of paradox he savored: at once giving everything and nothing to nurture against nature.

Still, now and then Gerhard lent Werner a hand in his activism, out of solidarity with the Socialist movement's pacifist minority. The brothers shared a hunger for the wholesale overthrow of the status quo. Benjamin's intrigue with socialism's metaphysical possibilities further stirred Gerhard's sympathies. The Social Democrats' goal of liberating men was profound. But they set about pursuing this lofty aim by jamming people into a rigid, soulless "Organization" and pretending that the future could be scientifically determined. "'Organization' is a synonym for death," he'd informed Werner. "The only organization Zionism has—which is identical with the truth—is the unification of all those who possess the truth," he later contended. The mystical Hasidism of Galicia preached socialism "*sans phrase.*" They stood for wholeness and myth, and myth was life. The Eastern Jews still inspired Gerhard.

In conversation with Benjamin, he continued to defend Buber's contention that Jerusalem was a passageway between the Orient and Occident, where Jews could serve as the mediating people, fusing East and West. But it was not so easy to debate this point with Benjamin. He maintained that the proposition of Palestine was one thing for the afflicted Ostjuden who had as little opportunity to consider "where they will end up as a man fleeing a burning house," but saw the project to unify the cultures of Eastern and Western Jews as a "*Salto-mortale*"—a deadly leap—"in chaos."

As for Buber himself, in Benjamin's estimation there were simply too many holes in the radiant vision he offered his disciples. And how he did prize his followers! (Gerhard acknowledged that Buber "*sought* this influence," diffusing it beyond his own people. Gustav Landauer, who liked Buber, called him "the apostle of Judaism to humanity.") Benjamin remarked that the schematized psychological philosophy of history Buber espoused was meretricious, while Buber's "cult of experience" frankly disgusted him. If that fellow had his way, Benjamin remarked to Scholem, "You'd have to ask every Jew you met, *'Have you experienced Jewishness yet?'*"

This was a bit much for Scholem, who'd finally met Buber in December to discuss the journal *Blue-White Spectacles*, which Buber appeared to endorse. Surrounded by mystical cult objects in the inner sanctum of his tastefully decorated chambers, featuring a large oil portrait of Buber himself, Buber held court for an hour and a half. Gerhard had to perch on a stool the whole time, fidgeting madly. Close up, Buber looked very good, Gerhard commented, which was surprising, given his "horrifying, utterly bloodless white tint, shockingly tender hands and almost entirely bald head." He'd beamed lovingly at Gerhard and his coeditor, while offering hazy, if well-meaning advice. Gerhard began talking about the principle of collaboration, whereupon Buber made the solemn pronouncement, "Anonymous artists have the disadvantage that no one knows who they are." Then he got a phone call and that was it, time to go.

Almost his whole adult life, Scholem had a strained, condescending relationship to Buber. After having been hugely inspired by Buber when he first discovered Judaism, Scholem never really forgave him for having endorsed the war. Buber's lapse in judgment on this critical issue might have made Scholem more attuned to the questionable authenticity of Buber's voluminous studies of Hasidism, which he censured unsparingly in later years. One has the feeling reading Scholem on Buber that while he couldn't dismiss the enormous effect Buber had on world opinion about Jewish spirituality, he didn't think what Buber had explicated really *was* Jewish spirituality. There wasn't enough textual meat to the interpretations. Moreover, though Scholem never failed to credit Buber for his forceful denunciation of exile, he felt that what Buber wanted to replace exile with was nebulous and indulgently personal. Sometimes it seems that what Scholem really couldn't forgive Buber for was not being smart enough

to deserve credit for having set Scholem himself on the path to Jerusalem.

On the level of sheer intellect, Benjamin, by contrast, never disappointed. Often he would read poetry aloud in his mellifluous voice: Baudelaire, Pindar, and Hölderlin. "Myths, which take leave of the earth, /... They return to mankind," wrote Hölderlin in one of Benjamin's cherished verses. In time, Benjamin also started reading from a cycle of sonnets he'd begun writing about Fritz Heinle. There were to be fifty sonnets in all.

In the Talmud it is said that there are fifty gates of insight, Scholem interjected. All but the last of these were opened to Moses. Benjamin was immensely taken by this. Scholem's budding researches into Jewish mysticism earned nothing but praise from him.

At that time, Benjamin composed a mystical essay on Hölderlin, which he gave Gerhard to read. Gods and mortals passed in contrasting rhythms through Hölderlin's poem about the Poet's courage, Benjamin wrote. According to Benjamin, thinking about the nature of the "poeticized" in Hölderlin's verse led not to myth itself but to mythic connections that the work of art molded into singular, unmythic forms whose meaning could not be further penetrated. The duality of death and the poet was transmuted into "the unity of a dead poetic world, 'saturated with danger.'"

"Profoundly metaphysical" was Gerhard's enthusiastic assessment of Benjamin's reflections. The denser Benjamin's thinking became, the closer it seemed to verge on theology. It was religion without God, Law, or prayer. Everything stripped away but sublime opacity. As Nietzsche declared, "One does want to be understood when one writes but just as surely *not* to be understood."

At home alone, Gerhard read the prophets aloud to himself in their original Hebrew and often broke into song. Whenever he began Ezekiel, he was carried away in semi-ecstasy before he'd gotten through five chapters. It was no wonder that the Kabbalists defined God as the Ein Sof. Existing beyond every boundary, "Ein-sof is that which *cannot* be named," he wrote in his diary.

The beginning phase of Jewish mysticism resonates with Scholem's desperate youthful struggle to find words that convey infinite, ineffable epiphanies: Its early texts record a kind of exalted tongue-tiedness before the Divine. That period lasted nearly a thousand years, starting in the Second Temple era and ending in the tenth century. Palestine, Scholem asserted, was the cradle of the movement, which initially promoted speculation about the first chapters of Ezekiel that contain the prophet's vision of God's chariot-throne, the Merkabah. Ezekiel describes a great cloud coming from the north, flashing fire and glowing with colors, inside which appear four living creatures, sparkling like polished brass and shooting out lightning. Each has four faces — human, lion, ox, and eagle — and four wings, intricately configured around strange

emerald wheels. The vision is wild and bizarre, and a reminder that
the Bible itself contains purely mystical strata.

Judaism's seminal mystics identified the "living creatures" in
Ezekiel's chariot as angels and imagined a complex hierarchy of
angelic potencies occupying the Celestial Court. Such conceits,
mingled with passages from ancient apocalyptic literature, and
new cosmogenic revelations, were eventually grouped together
under the rubric "Merkabah mysticism." Scholem makes the
point that from the outset, the kind of knowledge conferred by
Jewish mystical thought was viewed as dangerous by some religious authorities, who sought to restrict its circulation. (A letter
of St. Jerome, for example, cites a Jewish tradition that prohibited
study of the beginning and end of Ezekiel before one's thirtieth
birthday. Subsequent rabbinic pronouncements opposed the
study of mysticism before the aspirant was forty, married, and had
mastered Jewish Law.)

The seminal mystical writings are concerned with marveling
at and detailing the appearance of God's chariot-throne, which
somehow embodies the whole of Creation. Although this literature is fragmentary and frequently survives only through corrupt
references in later texts, Scholem maintains that evidence for the
existence of a movement with its own teachers and concepts, distinct from Christianity and Islam's mystical schools, is conclusive.
He was forever striving to define a uniquely Jewish mystical tradition, even when the evidence suggested that many ideas were
syncretic.

The earliest texts chart the features of different "chambers" of
the Merkabah. Later tracts involve descriptions of entire heavenly
halls and palaces. Most of these works are classified as "Hekhaloth
Books," from the Hebrew word for "palaces," and recount the
wondrous passage of the soul into God's precincts. Various ascetic
practices, such as fasting and chanting special hymns, enable the
mystic to glimpse the interior of heavenly chambers and enter a

succession of divine dwellings. The soul journeys through seven heavens to the heaven containing seven palaces guarded by archons who represent the seven planetary spheres and resist the soul's ascent at every stage. Safe travel through the celestial halls is secured through the possession of magical seals composed of secret names, which function both as armor and weapon, frightening away demons. The higher the soul rises, the more elaborate the magical formulas required until, Scholem writes, by the end of the mystic's journey "whole pages are filled with an apparently meaningless recital of magical key-words with which he tries to unlock the closed door." Reading scraps of these ancient texts with their necromantic signs, arcane names, interlocking passageways, gatekeepers, fiery adversaries, and secret weapons evokes a conceptually crude, but graphically exciting, multiplayer quest game. Instead of Dungeons and Dragons, Palaces and Demons.

Scholem contends that in the realm of Merkabah mysticism there is almost no notion of God's immanence in the world, or of the mystic's ability to achieve ecstatic union with Him on high. There *is* ecstasy, but it's all the euphoria of a visitor to some magnificent royal court — of a traveler witnessing the glories of a divine emperor. These mystics, Scholem writes, retained "an almost exaggerated consciousness of God's *otherness*." Though they got closer to the Divine than people might ordinarily, Merkabah celebrants still contemplated the sublime at an absolute remove, in a state of verbalized awe.

Hymns praising God in these tracts were said by the mystic to be the same ones chorused by the angels — perhaps even by the heavenly throne itself. The Merkabah prayers were solemnly grandiloquent and represented, Scholem argues, a core paradox: "the climax of sublimity and solemnity to which the mystic can attain in his attempt to express the magnificence of his vision is also the *non plus ultra* of vacuousness." These liturgical expressions heap praise upon praise, attribute upon attribute, in repetitive jumbles to reach crescendos of fulsomeness, which express above all the *inexpressible* nature of God's alien majesty. "The pure word, the as yet unbroken summons stands for itself; it signifies nothing but what it expresses."

For the first thousand years of Jewish mysticism, Scholem indicates, the movement was struggling to find its voice and filling the void between people and the Divine with a kind of vatic babble. God was given a host of mysterious, obscure names — Zoharariel, Adiriron, and Totrossiyah, for instance. Overwhelmed by consciousness of His transcendence, the mystics' creativity was largely confined to the composition of outlandish phrases and word combinations, "sometimes entirely novel creations, all bearing a decidedly numinous character," which Scholem thought might represent the original iteration of the verbal renaissance that flowered in the first classics of synagogal poetry in Palestine. The original Jewish mystics left behind something like the experimental juvenilia of a great religious poet.

Whatever Scholem might have read of the earliest Jewish mystics in his youth, and however much his longing to find the "pure word" for sublime experience might have recapitulated aspects of their straining after infinity, his later writings indicate that he saw that first millennium as a prologue to the texts that would determine his life course. Indeed, the line between Jewish "mysticism" and the "Kabbalah" wavers in his presentation. Sometimes he writes as if the two are synonymous. At others he draws sharp distinctions, suggesting that Kabbalah came into existence only with the crystallization of certain mystical concepts in medieval France after the tenth century. Because the Merkabah literature was focused so exclusively on God and His aura, "it made no contribution to the development of a new moral ideal," he states. The historical tradition did not find expression in the writings of these ecstatic magi of longing, as it would for those he unreservedly called Kabbalists. Vision and knowledge of God's splendor represented "the essence of the Torah and of all possible human and cosmic wisdom," while the moral aspect remained "pale and bloodless." For the Merkabah mystics, history was pure darkness, a negative spur to get free of this world. The essence of the individual's position was expressed by the questions posed in one tract: "When will he see the heavenly majesty? When will he hear of the final time of redemption? When will he perceive what no eye has yet perceived?" In a depressed era when persecution by the church was escalating, the mystic turned from history "to the prehistoric period of creation, from whose vision he seeks consolation, or toward the post-history of redemption," Scholem writes. An "apocalyptic nostalgia" came to motivate these mystics.

The young Gerhard was similarly driven to find a path out of the present by revealing the next manifestation of the Jews' primal identity. He wrote in his diary that he dreamed of creating a giant flag emblazoned with "the stammering sounds of an unborn future and the echo of unsaid words." Salvation would burst from "the lamentations of echoing words spoken out of the past." The ideology of filth contaminating present times would drive a person mad unless he wheeled around backward and plunged into underground channels from which the reigning generation could be sabotaged, he maintained. But historical consciousness was always part of Gerhard's subversive vision. "No one has a right to speak who, in the midst of thinking, hasn't been overcome with the experience of *glimpsing the essence of history*," he declared. And it was unclear at first that Kabbalah would provide his escape route from either the debased German present or the moribund realm of conventional Judaism. Whatever Jewish mystical works Scholem might have been dabbling in during the first period of knowing Benjamin, they weren't a fixation. The range of the men's reading was panoramic and ecumenically inspiring.

Hegel. Socrates. Plato. Schelling. Herder. Nietzsche. Cervantes. Marx. Tolstoy. Kierkegaard. The list could be doubled and not cover half of what the pair devoured then. Never had Gerhard had a friend like Benjamin! There was nothing quite so wonderful as hearing Benjamin respond to an argument he'd made with the word, "*Ausserordentlich!*" Extraordinary! It was his highest compliment at the time, always pronounced with a studied intonation that Gerhard found infectious, as he frankly did many of Benjamin's turns of phrase and mannerisms. At times Scholem identified so intensely with Benjamin it sounds as if he were trying to merge with, or become him. And Benjamin had so many idiosyncrasies to embrace. The stares. The silences. The stillness. The stylishness. He alternated intense secretiveness with sudden confidential revelations. He balanced "personal radicalism" with a "Chinese courtesy" so pronounced that he alone in Berlin moved Gerhard to suspend his notorious "provocative deportment" and assume a reciprocal politeness.

In conversation with Benjamin, Gerhard felt his own ideas finding their place, even if they did not coalesce. He was a creature of Romanticism through and through, he realized—not such a bad thing, since Romanticism, he mused, could be considered a form of revolution born of yearning. In Benjamin's presence, the oppositions dancing in Gerhard's brain ceased to torment him.

But Benjamin was often traveling, and out of Benjamin's charmed company, Gerhard was thrown back almost entirely on Bleichrode and that vestige of Jung Juda not yet in uniform. In time, Werner was sent to the front line. It was horrible to think of his brother gone off to war—little Werner, who sported the same giant jug-handle ears and funny wizened look as Gerhard, but who was elfin in stature, feet dangling off benches and chairs, wearing baggy suits that his tiny hands barely emerged from. Sometimes Gerhard felt like a spent, exhausted old Jew. The feeling broke his heart, and he made himself claw his way back toward hope. But if he wasn't actually in danger of going crazy, that didn't mean he wouldn't one day kill himself, he asserted in his diary, adding that his suicidal thoughts were no game.

The effect of Walter Benjamin's friendship on Scholem's world-view made itself felt with remarkable speed, at first threatening to overturn everything. For the breadth of Benjamin's intellectual horizons was so expansive that uncertainties Scholem already harbored about what exactly Judaism meant to him — where Jewishness fit in the scheme of his cosmically mandated life trajectory — now began undermining his entire sense of identity. At one point he got in such a foul mood about God that he made the mistake of announcing at home that he'd cut his ties with heaven, a confession that sent Arthur Scholem into gales of laughter. The portly man with his dripping mustache and big bald brow began guffawing uncontrollably, shaking his head with vindicated glee.

"I am an atheist! One must keep pace with the progress of science," the enlightened Herr Arthur reminded his son.

Unbearable!

Gerhard rushed from the room to his journal: "These vermin should be killed, their necks snapped. As dead as dead can be. I can't put up with this any more." Not long afterward he dreamed that his father strangled him to death for resisting the call to the army.

With Werner gone, there was no one to back him up against Papa. Whenever the man wasn't at the print shop, he just marched around the house, extolling the holy virtues of war, puffing out his chest, aflame with patriotism. His mother's eyebrows might have arched sardonically, workers in his shop might have considered him a reactionary boor, but the man couldn't rein himself in. Proud as a peacock that even that archpacifist Werner was finally doing his part for the kaiser. Couldn't wait his own turn to parade down to the enlistment office. *Let me serve! Let me serve!* The gratitude of the Jews to the state — *that* was the true psychosis. And the gods meanwhile sat in their heavenly banquet hall bursting their sides at the folly of humanity below — massacring one another and hurling prayers at the clouds.

It's difficult not to feel twinges of sympathy for Scholem's father, who receives blistering abuse in his son's journal. Arthur's explosion of laughter was obviously unkind, yet it may have been less triumphant than a spontaneous outburst at the element of theatricality in Gerhard's passionate about-faces—and also relief at the thought that his son might be toning down his zealotry. If Arthur's fervor about the war was fatally misplaced, his yearning to belong to the German state—the overwhelming intensity of his belief that the state represented a higher cause—reveals a neediness fraught with transcendent hope.

Jewish businessmen and intellectuals both were disproportionately susceptible to martial euphoria in the first phase of the conflict. When Stefan Zweig wrote of feeling "purified of all selfishness" by the declaration of war, he expressed a sentiment that can also be understood as a longing to be purified of all vestiges of alienation from the homeland. His friend, the popular writer Emil Ludwig, stated at the time, "During the past few days every individual formed part of the whole, every subject wore the German crown." One Jewish theater critic who lived in a villa close to Benjamin rhapsodized in poetry, "Do you love Germany? What a question?/Can I love my own hair, my blood, my very self?"

Was Arthur's spiritually consuming wish to belong to Germany totally unlike Gerhard's spiritually consuming wish to belong to the Zion of his dreams? Arthur's wish depended on the fantasy of his having finally "arrived" in Germany, of there existing a genuine dialogue between Jews and the German people. Gerhard's depended on the fantasy of there being a natural place reserved for him among the indigenous peoples of "the Orient" in Palestine—of a dialogue in waiting with the Arab. Arthur was not as brilliant—and not remotely as learned—as his son. But it plainly felt wonderful to him to have escaped from the world of *his* fathers, still mired in old, rigid forms of the faith, still largely ghettoized, at least psychologically. Arthur reveled in having achieved material success in a materially advanced society where many socially liberal and most commercially progressive values cohabited exuberantly.

The way this conflict kept resurfacing throughout Scholem's career is so striking as to suggest a repetition compulsion—not coincidence, but internal forces propelling him into situations where he would have to brandish once more the torch of ethnic-historical particularity against the ambient moral glow of universal ideals. In his seventies, Scholem still found himself berating interviewers for rehashing the reproaches of Jews he'd heard in his youth. "What are you going to create?" the assimilationists mocked. "One small nation—while we are going to integrate with world development." To which Scholem always countered, "What is the great, worldwide cause you believe in and speak of?" And no one could give meaningful content to that mirage. These glorious utopian abstractions of the progress zealots represented their own non plus ultra of vacuousness.

Yet one reason this debate kept recurring for Scholem was that ultimately he wanted to have it both ways—not *denying* individual responsibility to the Universal Good, but believing it could be fulfilled only by descending back through the genetic and historical etymology of selfhood. His way to transnational humanism was through the looking glass, as it were. He might have found inspiration for this double move—toward maximal particularity in the name of all the world—in the core definition of the word "Kabbalah": Tradition. For the Kabbalist, Scholem asserted, mystical knowledge was neither a private matter nor a "new" truth, but an all-embracing restoration. The purer the individual's personal intuition of God was, the closer it came to the original stock of wisdom bestowed on all humanity. A Talmudic legend has it that in the womb every infant is taught the whole of Torah and all the mysteries of creation, but at the moment of birth an angel gives the infant a tap between the nose and mouth, whereupon it instantly forgets everything—and is left with the tiny dent we all

carry just above the upper lip. Scholem was attached to the reading of this story given by a Hasidic sage who said that "if the child
did not forget, the course of the world would drive it to madness in
the light of what it knew." But Scholem also understood the philosophical implications of the allegory that made the act of acquir-
ing knowledge always a matter of recollection, hearkening back to
some primal state of completeness. (A powerful prefiguration of
Freud's idea that the finding of an object is always a refinding.)

The total knowledge of matters human and divine that Adam,
the father of humanity, possessed could be regathered through
Kabbalah, the mystics said.

So it was also that Gerhard insisted his Judaism had to be *total*.
And once he'd rejected Orthodoxy and orthodox Kabbalah's mystical exercises, the sole path to this totality was Zionism — of which
he likewise said that the imperative was wholeness: "wholeness of
the dedicated person, wholeness of the way and the goal, wholeness of the demand and of the sacrifice."

Part of Scholem's problem was that, as a young man, he felt
himself literally in thrall to his name. The Hebrew word *Shalem*
means "complete," and Gerhard chose to read "Scholem" as the
word's German transliteration. In his journal he wrote that he
would be absolutely fulfilled if the inscription on his grave could
be "*He Was His Name* — which is to say, he was total, he was *Scholem*.
By living out his name…he was complete and undivided."

However, decades later in his memoir he admitted that in fact
family legend had it that their patronym emerged when Scholem's
great-great grandfather, who'd migrated to Berlin from Silesia,
reported to the town hall in obedience to the Prussian edict of
1812 obliging Jews to adopt permanent family names. Asked for his
name by the city official, Gerhard's ancestor couldn't understand
the question and said, "Scholem," the Ashkenazic pronunciation
of the Hebrew *Shalom* — meaning "peace" — a common saluta-
tion. Requested to give his first name, he impatiently, confusedly

repeated, "*Shalom.*" It was thus that "Scholem" entered the record books. Rather than indicating wholeness, Gerhard's family name thus in truth signified fragmentation between cultures — the condition of having no firm identity at all.

Gerhard's wish for the total realization *of* himself perfectly mirrored Werner's aspiration to serve the totality of humanity *beyond* himself. Both were numinous propositions, with a void at their core that threatened to suck in all manner of perilous dogma. But the early encounters with Benjamin undermined Gerhard's faith in the completeness of Judaism as a spiritual paradigm. Though he might have tossed off the occasional critique of Benjamin for not knowing more about Judaism, what Scholem called Benjamin's "aesthetic-associative delight" was suggesting other paths to the sublime. He listened rapt as Benjamin expounded the metaphysical interest of everything from the writings of the mentally ill to German Romantic poetry — while questioning the entire principle of "totality." (Benjamin saw this notion, along with "coherence" and "progress," as obstructing the view onto historical truth, contrasting them with fragments of thought that enshrined the halting pattern of philosophical contemplation itself, which like a mosaic acquired force by way "of the distinct and the disparate.") Such ideas challenged Gerhard's desire to wall off his spirituality from more richly cosmopolitan perspectives. He desperately tried to regroup in such a way as to preserve his core Jewish commitment while opening to the new vistas of knowledge Benjamin illuminated.

Rage against his father's rejection of Judaism helped sustain Gerhard's own devotion to the cause. But at times during the war it all became too much. With the entire world in so black a state, the possibility that the Jews might not, after all, have the spiritual resources necessary to rejuvenate themselves began to prey on him.

Late in 1915, after confessing to his journal that he was considering suicide, Gerhard wrote that for the time being he'd lost his faith that he was the Messiah. This recognition filled him with sorrow, he added, because the belief in his own anointment and in Zionism were inextricably fused. If he couldn't hope to achieve his own messiahship, at that instant he stopped being a Zionist—at least the kind of self-renewing Zionist he thought it essential to be.

It's a provocative confession. What does it mean to hinge the commitment to Zionism on identifying oneself as the Redeemer? Though he later condemned the messianic element in political Zionism, there are clues scattered throughout Scholem's writing suggesting that with regard to his personal belief system, rather than outgrowing his youthful extremism, he ended up just making it more esoterically intricate—holding on to versions of his original convictions in a subterranean fashion that echoed his interpretation of the workings of the Kabbalah itself.

At the end of November, Gerhard had to surrender to the recruiting office, as Werner and Benjamin both had already done. (He'd helped Benjamin evade conscription by accompanying him on an all-night bender of coffee, chocolate, and Benedictine, to induce symptoms of a bad heart.) On his way to register, a solider who accompanied him murmured, "My God, how can you commit such a crime."

After a few strange days in the barracks—befriending a waggish postman, gaining a reputation as a philosopher among the motley recruits, and trying to block out all their loud snoring—he went off for his physical. On the way, he told himself that the child he would bring into the world would have to have a name—meaning, no doubt, a magical, fate-conferring name like his own. (It's touching how often Gerhard writes of his plans for his future offspring. He never had a child.) At the examination, he made a display of weird, nervous breathing that astonished the doctor. This man called over another physician, telling him to listen to this sound.

"Have you got a condition?" they asked him.

"Neurasthenia!" he promptly replied (a "beautiful, one-of-a-kind and vacuous word" that he wanted to bash the doctor over the head with).

"We can see that," they said. And they temporarily released him from service.

He was free and totally lost. Before the year's end he was marveling at the complete volte-face he'd made over the past three years. Had someone shown him a picture of Gerhard Scholem today three years ago, "I would have totally rejected him," Gerhard wrote in his diary. "Back then it was precisely *this* type of person I so resolutely despised." All that remained constant, he declared, was a craving for knowledge — and a radical opposition to what had been considered knowledge hitherto.

In the midst of such turmoil, he might have surrendered his youthful dreams once and for all, deciding that the vision of Zion he'd clung to had been hopelessly fanciful. Instead of folding, he went into overdrive. If the passage of emotions and ideas across his mind formerly resembled cloud movements from sunrise to sunset, his diary entries at the end of 1915 more closely resemble fast-motion footage of the cosmos.

At one point he was able to project the debate raging inside him onto other young Jews he'd been associating with, noting that many of his cohort seemed to have forgotten that the statement "We are Jews" must be loudly complemented by the assertion, "We are also human beings." So long as you actually know something about Judaism, nothing could possibly injure you by virtue of its non-Jewishness. For that matter, he mused, no pursuit could take you away from Zionism. Rather, Zionism was the prerequisite for every pursuit. Having discovered his true family, he waited for the moment when all the ideas he'd explored would meld into a novel synthesis, whereby he would become "a New Jew, or Gerhard Scholem. I march bravely through the primordial forest in the firm belief that there is light at the other end. I don't even realize how happy I am."

Along with such elated outbursts, he dreamed of composing a novel about a young man who traveled to Palestine and was totally destroyed because the land had not yet become pregnant enough to bear him. Thinking about the collapse of Europe led him to picture the Land of Israel as a kind of womb, streaming with the ages, awaiting insemination. He wrote of wishing that the land were his son, "for I am a man who lives his most beautiful reality through silent dreams."

His dreams were not always silent. Scholem took solitary walks down the city's wide avenues and alongside its waterways, during which he would scream out speeches that he ordinarily whispered. People stared at him, and he blushed. In his diary he scribbled ideas for stories and arguments with himself. He imagined a novella about his own suicide, the plot of which unfolded with "shocking ease" in his spirit, if not by his hand, he wrote. "I would shoot myself after concluding that there was no solving the gaping paradox in the life of a committed Zionist."

Paradoxes, rages, fears, and desires were flying off the fabric of his being like burst buttons and seams. Raving on the street in some paroxysm of humiliation and fury, he might have hurled himself in front of a train or off a bridge. He might also have leaped on his father with any weapon at hand. He seems to come within a razor's breadth of some irrevocable act of destruction. Scholem's whole story might have ended before he ever reached Jerusalem. He craved too desperately for an impossible purity. The Zionist deed itself, if undertaken without a sufficiently complete Jewishness, would constitute a form of suicide, he wrote.

Not a word of the thousands of pages on Kabbalah Scholem was to write yet existed. Had he acted on impulse in the midst of one his emotional crises, the entire academic discipline of Jewish mysticism would have come into being through some completely different personality. What would this have meant for what we understand Kabbalah to be? There's no question that Scholem imported from Weimar Germany to Mandate Palestine a way of reading Jerusalem itself as a construct of Central European thought. Though he made attainment of "complete Jewishness" a prerequisite for his own settlement there, Gerhard was also explicit about his goal of reinventing Zion as a center for humanist philosophy surpassing even Athens: "In the temple for all my demigods and Caesars I'll erect in Jaffa, Herr Plato and Herr [Karl Friedrich] Gauss [a highly regarded mathematician] will rotate places daily; Herr Pascal, Newton, Leibniz, and Kepler monthly; and Herr Husserl will be sacrificed to every ten years. All others will have to make do with special mention in the book I've yet to write, *Jerusalem for a Thinking Humanity or a Large Measuring Rod in the Vest Pocket.* The book goes all the way up to the father of the Messiah."

It's a strange, unapologetically hybrid vision of the city — one I myself set off to seek, half unconsciously. What would have been lost to the world had the wings of the demon that beat so close before the young Scholem's eyes shut all the way over him? And what did I find on Jerusalem's unclouded hills that kept Scholem alive for me?

Blotchy gray lizards, resembling slivers of the moon, swirled away from my steps. The sky was blinding. Insects droned from bleached clumps of rosemary. Though it was already October, the Jerusalem sun gripped the scene like a claw. There wasn't a breath of wind that afternoon, as I made my way up to school from the Valley of the Cross. Suddenly, I heard a sharp rustling in the olive tree beside me. An elderly woman in a voluminous black dress with panels of flame-and-rose embroidery was skittering through the branches overhead. A younger companion was wielding a stick

to knock the fruit from between teardrop-shaped leaves into a basket. The pair seemed to have appeared out of nowhere, billowing
magically in the tree limbs. At that moment, a forlorn caw rose
from the crumbling walls of a monastery below. A group of ravens
flapped their wings in synchrony without taking flight. The whole
picture was savage, dreamlike — and beautiful.

As I prepared to study a Talmudic tractate about the laws of
marriage (how many more *zuzim* you pay for virgins than for widows and so on) — while Anne, eight months pregnant, lay swel-
tering in our tiny apartment in Rehavia, struggling to master the
Hebrew of hospital bureaucracy and wondering how on earth we
would finance the next chapter of our nomadic existence — I found
myself thinking of Gershom Scholem's essay "Kabbalah and
Myth." "Jewish philosophy paid a heavy price for its disdain of the
primitive levels of human life. It ignored the terrors from which
myths are made, as though denying the very existence of the problem," he wrote. "The demonization of life was assuredly one of the
most effective and at the same time most dangerous factors in the
development of the Kabbalah."

We were in Jerusalem at last. Everything was intense. Nothing
felt certain. Some nights we were woken by feral cats howling from
nearby back lots. And sometimes, when the wind was right, we
heard muezzins from the mosques in East Jerusalem summoning
the faithful to predawn prayers.

During the summer, both Anne and I had done an intensive
Hebrew program at the university. Then we'd begun studying
together in the program run by the Jewish Theological Seminary.
In the final period of her pregnancy, she'd stopped attending
classes. We'd planned for this. We'd not planned for my own early-
bird doubts about the program, which swelled and multiplied
with each passing week. What did this mean for our future?

The problem wasn't the Talmudic material we were learning. But the teachers with whom we spent hours each day, so far

from being inspired, seemed almost willfully dispiriting. Rabbi X, with the perpetual furrow on his bulging forehead, his iron-clamp beard, and little dark rectangular glasses, who sometimes appeared to have become so disengaged from what he was saying that he'd entirely forgotten he was speaking and would catch himself awake, as if he were jerking out of hypnosis. Big Rabbi Y, with his rolling-scroll beard and jangling keys: jolly, intelligent, and bored beyond belief by our ignorance. The drab building in a grove of twisted trees not far from the Israel Museum, smelling as though its walls, instead of being made of stone blocks, had been constructed from the bones of overboiled chicken. Few of the students became comrades. Straining to carve their own paths through the commentaries into uncertain vocations, they looked straight past us.

I'd come to dread going into that place and slowed my steps on the winding walk from quiet, shady Alfasi Street through the vale to the institute. Stopping to pick up an odd-shaped stone or gaze around at the harsh plants and sharply gouged terrain. Not paying attention to anything in particular but pervaded by the landscape. Some said the ancient monastery of the valley had been constructed on the site where the original Adam's head was buried.

The only teacher who had any fire was the young, newly ordained Rabbi Z, all shaggy black beard and zipping voice, stinging questions and lumbering aggravation: half bear, half bumblebee. He was the sole instructor to bring a wider frame of references to his lectures, to demand that we actually think about why we were learning this material. He liked me, and pushed on me handfuls of crumpled Xeroxed pages from the manuscript he was struggling to write about the cosmic implications of certain prayers. One weekend he invited Anne and me to spend the Sabbath at his home in an outlying neighborhood of Jerusalem — over the Green Line, though I didn't know enough to recognize this at the time. We eagerly accepted. On the few occasions when Anne and I had chosen to observe the Sabbath by not driving or using electricity, there'd been a wonderful sense of growing more and more conscious of the natural world beyond the confines of our apartment—of changing minutiae in sky hue and birdsong. The world beyond us grew bigger and grander the stiller we became. We were full of curiosity to see how a passionate, observant teacher conducted his life in the Holy Land.

The journey north of the Old City, on a bus next to soldiers drowsily readjusting their gun straps to doze less uncomfortably was long and desolate. But we had no idea what awaited us when sunset fell and all transportation ceased. Those thirty hours in the rabbi's cookie-cutter house, in a residential clump on an isolated ridge, were among the most claustrophobic I'd ever experienced. The place felt so preternaturally sealed off and precariously suspended that it was like being inside an early space station. At the rabbi's home, the blinds were drawn—and there seemed to be a proscription against even peeking.

This was a novel experience of aggressively doing nothing. Look how much nothing I can do! And the somethings we did do seemed all the more fiercely intent on demonstrating that there was nothing outside us. We sat around exchanging flat remarks about ritual in a sallow room, bare except for a few ritual objects and kitschy paintings: prayer-shawl-shrouded ghetto rabbis stretching their heads back to heaven, old Torah scribes bent with their quills over parchment. I don't remember the rabbi's wife saying a word—but what chance did she have to speak when she could hardly emerge from the tumbling ball of their snuffly children before being called on to serve another heavy meal? The food sat inside us like the stones of Jerusalem "in her fall," each meal curtly terminating with the demand, "Have you benched?" (This slang term for the postprandial blessing, repeated over and over, began sounding like we were being queried as to whether we'd performed some gross bodily function.) I don't know if the rabbi and his spouse got along, but the way he sprang to his feet to drag me out for endless prayer service after prayer service — the furious pace at which we strode off down blank streets lined by pale apartment buildings, to squeeze in once again among a bunch of sullen men in a bunkerlike synagogue — suggested that the urge to escape oppression of some kind helped fuel his piety. Meanwhile, poor Anne sat marooned in their living room with a stray copy of *Newsweek*, which was somehow acceptable Sabbath behavior, while curling in a quiet corner to read Kafka, or write in her journal, or study Hebrew, as she longed to do, somehow was not.

For the last service of the day, I found I just could not bear to sit and stand through the full menu of prayers yet again, and whispered to the rabbi partway through that I would find my own way back. On my dilatory walk home, I cut over to a street that bordered one of the slopes on which the settlement was built. The earth off the edge plunged into darkness. Far below glittered a small village marked by long fingers of minarets. I stood a moment, while light left the sky. A high breeze tingled my skin, and suddenly all the muezzins began calling; their rising, rippling crackle seemed the aural counterpart to the topography of the land.

When the third star at last became visible, marking the end of the Sabbath and the start of the buses that would rumble us back to Rehavia, we vowed never to repeat this experience. The decision seemed to lock a door we'd hoped to keep open at least a crack.

Crenellations of the Old City walls rose before us in the darkness as we rode, golden as gold in a fairy tale. Jerusalem itself was still a powerful presence, I reminded myself. And I found myself turning back to Scholem for some kind of solace that I couldn't give name to. Perhaps "solidarity in a state of demonized alienation" might begin to describe it.

I'd read "Kabbalah and Myth" in Ireland before my conversion. Now in Jerusalem, this essay, which presented the heart of Scholem's theory of Kabbalah, took on other dimensions. "We confront the old questions in a new way," Scholem wrote there. "But if symbols spring from a reality that is pregnant with feeling…and if, as has been said, all *fulfilled* time is mythical, then surely we may say this: what greater opportunity has the Jewish people ever had than in the horror of defeat, in the struggle and victory of these last years, in the utopian withdrawal into its own history, to fulfill its encounter with its own genius, its true and 'perfect nature'?"

Despite my disaffection, I was continuing to do well in the program. The rabbis pushed me to take more advanced classes in Talmud and Mishna. Gradually they began inviting me to stay after regular lessons were done to discuss the institute: taking me into their confidence, lamenting the school's dropping enrollment. One day they revealed that their outpost might not survive without an increase in applications.

I walked back through the open land to Rehavia that evening with an idea hatching: Why not start including the writings of key European intellectuals as part of the course choices — Walter Benjamin, Gershom Scholem, Franz Kafka, and so on? Why not teach great Central European Jewish works — the secular prophets — together with the actual Talmud? Perhaps I would even be able to teach in this postreligion theological section. The rabbis seemed to value my presence. Perhaps this would be how we could survive economically and remain in Jerusalem!

I don't remember Anne's response to my plan. The scheme came to me a few weeks before she gave birth to our first child, a son, whom we named Yona after my grandfather and the prophet Jonah. I don't think my brainstorm for reconceiving the seminary curriculum to include saturnine modernists was foremost in her thoughts. But after a few days of pondering, I was convinced this could become a unique pedagogical experiment, with the potential to rejuvenate the moribund Jewish Studies program. I mapped out a reading list, a thematic structure for the series of classes that would resonate with the canonical texts. I requested a meeting with the rabbis and made my pitch.

Poor Rabbi X sat staring in befuddlement through his little dark glasses as I rambled on, suggesting modernist works that could be taught side by side with the laws of purity. "*Sanatorium Under the Sign of the Hourglass?*"

There was silence.

At last Rabbi X cleared his throat. "But it seems to me that these are just the books American students already read." He opened his hands plaintively. "The whole point of this program is to give nonreligious students the experience of reading Jewish texts in the Jewish homeland."

"Yes, of course," I said. "But to read figures like Schulz and Benjamin here"—I waved my hand vaguely above my head—"given what happened in European history. The connection with Israel's origins..."

His brow creased in a thousand lines of commentary.

"To read Gershom Scholem in Jerusalem..."

Rabbi Y turned vaguely away. Rabbi Z's look became grim. Rabbi X seemed embarrassed.

At last he thanked me, rising heavily, and the meeting was over. From that point on, though I continued to succeed in the courses, I felt my status as the chosen student slipping away—the boosting touch of the rabbis' guidance first weakened, then turned into a soft push out the door of the capsule.

Yet to this day when I go back to "Kabbalah and Myth," I find I still take more from that one essay than I did from my seminary classes. And I still yearn to understand why.

FIVE

FIRST, there's Scholem's voice:

"By way of introduction I should like to tell a short but true story. In 1924, clad in the modest cloak of modern philology and history, a young friend of mine went to Jerusalem, wishing to make contact with the group of Kabbalists who for the last two hundred years have there been carrying on the esoteric tradition of the Oriental Jews. Finally he found a Kabbalist, who said to him: I am willing to teach you Kabbalah. But there is one condition, and I doubt whether you can meet it. The condition, as some of my readers may not guess, was that he ask no questions. A body of thought that cannot be constructed from questions and answer—this is indeed a strange phenomenon among Jews, the most passionate questioners in the world, who are famous for answering questions with questions."

The opening sentences are intimate, playful, and intriguing. They present the amusing tale of an innocent's pursuit of secret wisdom. Scholem pokes a little fun at stereotypes ("as some of my readers may *not* guess") and leaves the reader with more questions than answers—and with questions about questions, too. One thing the tone decidedly is not is academic, although at the time he wrote this essay, at the end of the 1950s, Scholem was among the preeminent humanist scholars in the world. He draws us in by presenting a puzzle in the form of a parable, rather than by advertising his learning.

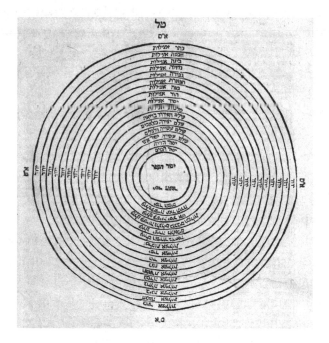

There are, in fact, even more games under way since Scholem himself is the young friend referred to, and the incident he describes would have occurred shortly after he came to Palestine. But why should he disguise his identity?

For one thing, acknowledging that he made this arduous search for a teacher among the remnant of Jerusalem's actual practitioners of Kabbalah might have laid Scholem open to suspicion that what he sought from within his "modest cloak" was something more than objective knowledge. The story hints that the young man himself may have been seeking kabbalistic illumination.

Two more sentences complete Scholem's introduction: "Here perhaps we have a first oblique reference to that special character, preserved even in its latest forms, of this thinking which expounds but has ceased to inquire, a thinking which might, as Schelling

put it, be termed a 'narrative philosophy.' To the great philosopher
of mythology, it may be remembered, such a narrative philosophy
was an ideal."

Suddenly, we may find ourselves fumbling for the light switch.
I didn't get far with those lines at first. But still, from this reference to the German idealist philosopher—a onetime roommate
of Hegel's who broke the chains of rigid dialectic to create what's
been called "visionary history"—I could glean the urbane sparkle
of Scholem's voice. The invocation of Schelling might require considerable erudition to parse, but it was not wedged into the text
like the allusive wadding in academic discourse I was familiar
with. Rather, Scholem drops the name with a casual fluency that
implies and inspires the reader's own textual command.

What *does* he mean? Well, Scholem could be invoking Schelling's late lectures on mythology, delivered in Berlin in the 1840s
before packed halls of perplexed students, at which the philosopher suggested that mythology's gods *literally* existed. Schelling
observed that however subjective the telling of the myths might
be, the origins and objects of these depictions "are actually and in
themselves theogenic powers." Thus, mythic narratives aren't susceptible to interrogative analysis since they constitute a form of
revelation, not argument.

Rather than criticizing the Kabbalist he'd located in Jerusalem
for having forbidden inquiry into his teachings, Scholem appears
to valorize types of knowledge that can't be plumbed through traditional question-and-answer exchange, even though the latter
might be definitively Jewish. These other categories find expression in images and symbols whose meaning can't be exhausted
through rational analysis.

By the end of Scholem's first paragraph, he's mapped entire
worlds of thought and done so in a voice that reflects his gifts as
a raconteur, historian, and high philosopher—all filtered mysteri-
ously through a chapter in his own spiritual autobiography. This

elaborate tonal glissando, with its conversational style mingling radical interpretation, cloaked personal allusions, subtle self-justifications, and lofty citations, calls to mind certain essays by Freud. There are many reasons for this resonance, not the least being that while Scholem followed Benjamin in professing little interest in Freudian theory, he inserts deep psychological conceits into his vision of Jewish theology. (Moshe Idel, the foremost revisionist of Scholem's Kabbalah, has argued that Scholem triangulated psychology with history and theosophy in constructing his interpretation of Jewish mysticism.) However, Scholem's own intellectual architecture reflects his attachment to the ruthless ethics informing the instructive myths of the Bible rather than the psychologically revealing but morally unedifying myths of the Greeks that Freud favored.

The start of the essay proper doesn't signal the onset of more traditional scholarly exposition, but instead introduces a deeper conundrum. Scholem announces that he will approach the problem of the relationship between Kabbalah and myth by recapitulating how Jews and non-Jews alike conventionally position Judaism in the history of religious thought. "Such an approach will help to elucidate the specific paradox which makes the thinking of the Jewish Kabbalists so attractive, but at the same so disturbing to the thoughtful observer," he adds. In the very process of declaring that he's about to examine a core paradox, Scholem ices the enigma with a further, emotional paradox: Kabbalistic thought is attractive and disconcerting at the same time.

Judaism, says Scholem, has always been understood as a reaction *against* myth. In contrast to "the pantheistic unity of God, cosmos, and man in myth, Judaism aimed at a radical separation of the three realms." Jewish theologians and philosophers alike concentrated on establishing God's absolute purity, which they achieved by stripping mythological and anthropomorphic features from His manifestation.

But this strategy proved a trap: In their effort to protect the transcendent Creator from adulteration by myth—to "reinterpret the recklessly anthropomorphic statements of the Biblical text…in terms of a purified theology," Rabbinic Judaism "tended to empty the concept of God." The less God has to do with the mucky scenes of life on this earth, the less there is to say about Him. "The price of God's purity is the loss of His living reality," Scholem writes.

More than is true with any other faith, Scholem contends, the history of Judaism is "the history of the tension between these two factors—purity and living reality." And the harder the religion's arbiters worked to articulate God's logically perfect, image-free unity, the greater the risk that they would provoke a rebellion bent on restoring the complex, dynamic life of a full-blooded divinity. Enter Kabbalah.

Scholem has not yet said a word about what the Kabbalah actually consists in. But the central agon of its development, as he's defined it, resonates also with his own desperate, youthful oscillation between the longing for ideal purity and a welter of ravenous, inconsistent desires. If the essay's opening anecdote hides a personal quest Scholem embarked on after reaching Jerusalem, the next passage surreptitiously traces the genesis of his migration to Palestine.

The first point Scholem makes about the Kabbalah itself is that there is no such thing. Not in the sense of a unified doctrine. Rather, the Kabbalah is made up of "widely diversified and often contradictory motivations, crystallized in very different systems or quasi-systems." There were untold numbers of rabbis developing kabbalistic ideas, some isolated, some in conversation with other mystics in circles at multiple Levantine and European centers, all riffing off a shifting, evolving network of texts, written over many centuries. Defining the Kabbalah is like trying to sum up the Internet.

Notwithstanding this radically decentralized, even anarchic view of the Kabbalah's character, Scholem identifies four chronologically sequential milestones in its development — even going so far as to hint at a teleological unfolding of mystical insights that culminates in nothing less than the rise of modern Judaism.

Before Kabbalah proper emerged, *Sefer Yetzirah* (The Book of Creation) appeared as a kind of cartographical sketch of its future zone of concern. This patchwork document of only sixteen hundred words, composed sometime between the third and sixth centuries, represents what Scholem calls "the earliest extant speculative text" written in Hebrew. Although connected formally to Merkabah literature, *Sefer Yetzirah* opened a new theological spectrum in Judaism with the doctrine of the *sefiroth*, which addresses the problem of the origins and development of the universe. Each of the ten *sefiroth* (literally "numbers," but kabbalistically closer to "spheres") encompasses dense constellations of God's potencies. Together, they delineate the process whereby "God emerges from hiddenness and ineffable being, to stand before us as the Creator," Scholem wrote.

In *Sefer Yetzirah*, the twenty-two letters of the Hebrew alphabet join with these ten primordial numbers to form "thirty-two secret paths of wisdom, through which God has created all that exists." Often the *sefiroth* are visually represented as circles on the branches of a cosmic tree: the mystical Tree of Life, which has its ultimate source in Ein Sof, "endlessness" — the hidden, unknowable Absolute. For true Kabbalists, the way to God involves reversing the sequence by which we have emanated from God. "To know the stages of the creative process is also to know the stages of one's own return to the root of all existence," Scholem explained.

But the *sefiroth* are not successive stages in God's emanation. Rather, says the *Sefer Yetzirah*, "their end is in their beginning and their beginning in their end, as the flame is bound to the coal — close your mouth lest it speak and your heart lest it think." He is neither "absolute being" nor "absolute becoming" but the union of both principles. Instead of a linear intervention, God's relationship to Creation is dynamically circulatory, ebbing and flowing from the invisible heart of pure monotheism, manifesting in diverse configurations of infinite potencies.

The first text Scholem designates as a work of true Kabbalah, the *Book Bahir*, which came to light near the end of the twelfth century in southern France, undertook a much fuller elaboration of the *sefiroth*'s symbolic character. It began, we might say, to map the interior of that capacious territory outlined by *Sefer Yetzirah*. *Book Bahir* is "one of the most astonishing, not to say incredible" texts of Hebrew literature in the Middle Ages, Scholem writes — although it's also a "wretchedly written and poorly organized collection of theosophical sayings." Only thirty-five pages in length, the work represents an altogether new force in Judaism, Scholem argues, and then he proceeds to illustrate that originality by quoting the vitriolic condemnation of it from an old-school rabbi who pronounced the *Bahir* devoid of truth. Again, Scholem tantalizes the reader with paradox: The book is one of the most astonishing Jewish texts from the entire Middle Ages — the book is horribly written and chaotic. It is an unprecedented force, and we can best get a sense of its novelty from the commentary of a rabbi who makes the case for its being worthless.

Then Scholem drops his bombshell. The reason the *Bahir* excited such outrage is that it marked the resurgence of brazenly mythological notions within Jewish theology. Mythical structures were adopted to monotheism, "no longer in the persons of the old gods" but in "the tree of the *sefiroth*." Thus, an account of the creation of angels, mostly cribbed from canonical commentaries on Genesis, abruptly devolves into a soliloquy by God: "It is I who have planted this 'tree,' that all the world may delight in it, and with it I have spanned the All and called it 'All'; for on it depends the All, and from it emanates the All, all things need it, and look upon it, and yearn for it, and from it all souls go forth." In some fragments of the *Bahir*, this tree of earth and souls switches from being an entity cultivated by God to becoming the embodiment of God's own generative attributes.

What has happened to the great separation between Creator and Creation on which the Jewish religion was theoretically premised?

No less startling are the *Bahir*'s commentaries on evil. A passage about Satan proclaims, "There is in God a principle that is called 'Evil,' and it lies in the north of God, for it is written [Jer. 1:14] out of the north the evil shall break forth upon all the inhabitants of the land." Wait—*in* God there is Evil? More confounding pronouncements follow: "God said: I love the gates of Zion when they are open. Why? Because they are on the side of evil, but if Israel does good in the sight of God as worthy that [the gates] be opened, He loves it more than all the 'dwellings of Jacob,' where there is always peace." As Scholem observes, this seems to contradict the foundation of Jewish self-understanding. The idea that the gates of Zion, that utopian structure through which Israel's creative force is traditionally expressed, are located "on the side of evil"—and more beloved of God than Jacob's peaceful dwellings—boggles the devout mind.

Though much of what's written in the *Bahir* defies interpretation, and its paradoxes are often explained by "similes and parables that are even more baffling than what they are supposed to clarify," Scholem argues that by abandoning the realm of allegory for a language of living symbols, the text effectively unlocks Judaism, restoring its protean fecundity. Symbolic expression, as Scholem writes elsewhere, allows the Kabbalists to turn mythic imagery from the Bible—like the oft-cited "arm of God"—into ciphers for decoding God's hidden life, and into a language in its own right, suitable for communicating with the Divine: "The mystical symbol is an expressible representation of something which lies beyond the sphere of expression and communication, something which comes from a sphere whose face is, as it were, turned inward and away from us." Instead of taking God's limb to be merely a figure of speech, the Kabbalists view it as "a symbol of a higher reality, an actual arm of God, although not in any way commensurate with a human arm." In the words of a thirteenth-century mystic, "All names and attributes are metaphoric with us but not with Him." Yet the divine reality, as well, is part of the chain of being in which "everything is magically contained in everything else." God's esoteric life merits surveillance because it directly impinges on human fate and can be influenced positively or negatively by human action.

Without grasping every twist in the kabbalistic narratives, we can still perceive how their charge of mythic content reorients the religion: away from a singular revelation happening under cloud cover at Sinai toward an exploded view of the universe that amplifies humanity's significance in transcendent systems, and factors historical change into dogma. From the beginning, Scholem notes, the Kabbalists approached Judaism "as a symbolic transparency, through which the secrets of the cosmos could be discerned." They vitalized and animated the structure of God's unity so that those elements in the Divine that had been perceived as static, ideal attributes now became active potencies and organic phases in a life process unfolding within God. The Torah itself was "re-mythicized."

Now the performance of the commandments didn't entail just *remembering* great historical moments like the exodus, but magically reenacting and thereby redeeming those events, as their aftershocks continue to ripple out through Creation. In short, the Kabbalists steadfastly observed the Law's dictates while completely reconceiving their purpose: "The Torah is transformed into a *Corpus mysticum*," Scholem comments.

Yet while the *Bahir* might represent a kabbalistic initiative to bring myth back into Judaism, Scholem argues that this process is not simply a matter of ancient religious strata being churned back up to the surface; it consists in sowing more recent layers of Jewish thought with seeds of what we might call "knowing mythology." In Scholem's telling, the segue between older mythology and kabbalistic imagery is a specifically Jewish strain of Gnosticism. (Scholem's definition of Gnosticism is notoriously fluid but revolves around pluralities in God's nature that find imagistic form in the Kabbalists' writing and play off one another to alternately harmonic and dissonant effect.) Through the Gnostic connection, Scholem was able to propose that instead of just reverting to myth, the Kabbalists achieved a dialectical advance — one that synthesized myth, the rational-philosophical reaction against myth, the variegated counterreaction against philosophy, *and* the actual experience of human beings. The latter encompassed both the individual's terror of life and death and the people's history of suffering.

A new kind of myth developed out of reflection on God's own inner being, which made the singular God into an operatic mash-up of primordial potencies. If Freud took the mythology of the Greeks and projected its narratives into the psychological structures of every man, woman, and family, Scholem's Kabbalah takes the sublimity and squalor of the postbiblical Jew's historical/autobiographical narratives and projects that back onto the cosmos, as the psychological drama of a new kind of God.

This new Scholem-Kabbalah deity proves to be a God defined by self-division, failed ambitions, ruins, strange dreams, and a brokenhearted dependency on the Jewish people for the redemption of His own creation. He is a profoundly disturbed God, so overbearing a presence that he must withdraw deep into the recesses of Himself in order to make room for anything else in Creation to exist. Scholem describes the *tsimtsum* — this original act of shrinking backward, which the Kabbalists made the prerequisite for everything — as "a primordial exile, or self-banishment."

Residing moodily in the "depths of nothingness," God sounds at moments like an incredibly lonely, brilliant, and tortured young man pondering a dark world during wartime.

I'm not suggesting that Scholem fabricated a new Jewish mysticism to suit his mental state. But what he found in the Kabbalah's spacious theories and what he chose to single out, correlated with key features of his own psychological struggles. And Scholem's life struggles were, in turn, sufficiently urgent and multifaceted that they share features with many people's battles with the demon. If we're anything less than zealous believers, the Kabbalah is not going to *explain* our sufferings, but it may enlarge and multiply our perspectives on them. By allowing us to envision cosmic variations on our inner strife, it may at least expand our sense of how our responses to those struggles affect the greater reality we inhabit. As Scholem notes in another essay, "In none of their systems did the Kabbalists fail to stress the interrelation of all worlds and levels of being…Nothing is without its infinite depths, and from every point this infinite depth can be contemplated."

The evolution of kabbalistic principles Scholem outlines (even while disavowing the idea of linear development) occurs in progressively more historically allusive stages. These begin with the *Bahir*, which reintroduces mythology into Jewish theology by reactivating the religion's Gnostic tendencies. The appearance in the thirteenth century of the Zohar, which Scholem describes as a kind of bible for the Kabbalists, inaugurates the next epoch of Jewish self-understanding through symbols. This is followed by the sixteenth-century system of Isaac Luria, which brought together and reconfigured many elements of kabbalistic thought to create a myth that gave cosmic significance to the Jewish experience of exile in the wake of the expulsion from Spain. Finally, the seventeenth-century movement centered around the mystical messiah Sabbatai Sevi lent voice to apocalyptic impulses and emancipatory ideals that were ultimately reconstituted into the building blocks of modern Judaism. Each of these phases reflects, in one way or another, Scholem's understanding of Kabbalah as a theology dramatizing God's struggle with loneliness.

Most of the mythological content Scholem cites in the essay has a very different narrative texture from that which those of us raised on Greek myths — or, for that matter, the Bible — are conversant with. Trees of unfathomable dimensions flicker alongside colored flames in hidden recesses. The "Creation out of nothing" is understood *literally*, thereby reversing its original meaning, which had been to emphasize God's freedom. Now the nothingness is understood to be a part of God, that interior abyss coexisting in tension with His fullness. (Kabbalah frequently takes canonical texts at their word to create what Scholem calls a "productive misunderstanding.") Its alien feel is due partly to the fact that kabbalistic mythology often concerns the universe *before* humanity's arrival — playing out across infinitudes where God and His agent Adam Kadmon, the primordial man, are the only characters. Often the action is wholly intradivine. This is a mythology of deep outer space, dazzlingly vast, and cold and remote. The Kabbalistic Absolute that Scholem presents in this essay finds expression through complexly balanced interplays of supernal light. Instead of gazing at an old master nativity scene, we're locked inside an endless Dan Flavin retrospective.

Within the space in which creation was waiting to happen hung amorphous vessels, themselves made of lower mixtures of light, intended to contain the divine rays as these projected from God's place of withdrawal to form the universe. The primordial man — identified with God the Creator — received streams of divine lights from above, and beams of light shot from his eyes, ears, mouth, and nose. But a disruption in the original equilibrium resulted in the upper light overwhelming the vessels — cracking them, spilling and scattering God's light all over creation. In trying to picture this primal scene, one might envision a largely

abstract gargantuan being sprawled across space, shooting light
rays from its orifices and being penetrated by shafts of light orig-
inating from some infinitely introverted, formless Divine. These
radiations, striking nebulous containers of luminescence, shatter
them, casting showers of sparks through the blackness. It's closer
to staring through the Hubble Telescope than to reading Ovid's
Metamorphosis.

But there's one great exception to all this masculine abstraction, which was not only compensation for but also the cause of
cosmic male disembodiment: The reason for God's overweening
loneliness, according to the Kabbalists, is that he's lost the woman
inside Himself.

In another revolutionary departure from Talmudic tradition, the Kabbalah identifies feminine potencies as essential parts of God's own constitution. Almost all God's problems across various kabbalistic systems, in fact, reflect discord or outright divorce between the Divine's masculine and feminine aspects — a separation that is variously accounted for, but that began with some flaw in God's own overambitious blueprint for Creation. The imbalances consequent on the divine split-up have permitted the masculine quality of "stern judgment" (including evil) in God's nature to gain disproportionate strength over the attribute of mercy. From the standpoint of ritual Law, the womanless, dictatorial God has turned the universe into a kind of hyperregulated police state. And the Jewish people are now charged with revolutionizing this monolithic governance by recovering God's own femininity. The people are, in fact, identified with God's female nature. Through the commandments and diverse mystical rites, the ecclesia gathers the holy sparks scattered through creation, recoupling God's male and female aspects.

Without graphing the whole labyrinthine process by which the Kabbalah establishes God's feminine potencies and their placement within the configuration of His masculine powers, it's possible to single out the appropriation of the concept of the Shekinah from Talmudic literature as pivotal. Shekinah literally means "dwelling," and the word was originally used just to signify God's presence in the world at large, and within Israel specifically. There is no orthodox distinction between this worldly manifestation of the Divine and the Divine Himself. But in the Kabbalah, the Shekinah "becomes an aspect of God, a quasi-independent feminine element within Him," Scholem writes. Through this identification between the Shekinah and the feminine aspect of the Absolute, "everything that is said in the Talmudic interpretations of the Song of Songs about the Community of Israel as daughter and bride was transferred to the *Shekinah*."

This correlation between the people of Israel and the Shekinah also meant that the Shekinah became the spiritual personification of exile. Given that, as Scholem puts it, "the real existence of Israel is so completely an experience of exile," the association carries manifold implications for Jewish history and theology alike. (For one thing, the link with exile precludes a simple idealization of the feminine, favoring instead meditations on a spectrum of unsettled states that enrich the categories of ambivalence and transience. For another, the notions of "dwelling" and of "homelessness" become provocatively co-identified.) The domain of the nomadic Shekinah was identified in the *Bahir* and the Zohar as the abode of the soul. Scholem observes that "the notion that the soul had its origins in the feminine precinct within God Himself was of far-reaching importance for the psychology of the Kabbalah." We might also infer that this condition has psychological implications for those invested in the Kabbalah, even if these possibilities have yet to be fully realized.

In one of the Kabbalah's boldest conceits, Scholem claims that the Shekinah's predicament means *"a part of God Himself is exiled from God."* Humanity's higher task is to end this exile by saving God's marriage, a process requiring self-purification in preparation for their own second-wife-style nuptials with the would-be Absolute—a ménage à trois of sorts between the Jewish people and the old married couple of God and the Shekinah, or at the least with a hermaphroditic split personality. It's a sensational mandate—an epic, melodramatic setup with room for further betrayals, pleas of repentance, enraged outbursts, and tearful reconciliations. The chronic bad behavior of the children of Israel is partly to blame for wrecking the divine domestic peace. But marital problems predated their birth. Regardless of who's really to blame for the state of things, every religious action the Kabbalists performed was supposed to include the formula: This is being done "for the sake of the reunion of God and His Shekinah." All kabbalistic rituals were "colored by this profoundly mythical idea," of bringing the masculine and feminine back to their foundational unity. In another essay, Scholem details some of these rituals, which involve changes in meditative intent rather than in practice so that, for example, the Friday night sexual relations encouraged by the Talmud became a prefiguration and summoning of the Divine's own conjugal rites.

I found all this enthralling. Many ancient mythological systems of course incorporate female attributes into their deity character, but it was almost as if Judaism had made the assumption of monotheism contingent on cleansing the Absolute of all feminine elements. And this purge had both conceptual and practical ramifications. One of my abiding dissatisfactions with the religion was its failure to be inclusive of women in a manner that didn't simply gut the doctrine of content. Orthodoxy effectively cut women out completely from nondomestic religious activity. Reform instead cut out the Law, partly to enfranchise women. But in just tossing out the awful harsh God with His bloody history of ill treating everybody, the Reform movement didn't seem to have held on to any power at all. Conservatism tried to finesse the problem by saying that women could do whatever men did in exactly the way men did it, and thereby gain equal religious status. But I felt there had to be a more meaningful role for women than just replicating male functions in ritual territory long ago demarcated and dust covered by men. What seemed essential was transformation from within, not just a franchised extension.

The Kabbalah seemed to present the gender-war equivalent of a binational solution — proposing that God's own character was of necessity simultaneously male and female. And until this dual nature was reembraced, God's *actions* would inevitably be violent and perverse. Humanity's part in fixing this relationship, the grand work of repair known as *tikkun*, was, Scholem wrote, "not so much a restoration of Creation — which though planned was never fully carried out — as its first complete fulfillment."

Here I was in Jerusalem, with Anne about to have our first child in which the male and female principles would be literally fused, delivering into this world a being who genetically embodied the future, with our own wedded union still finding its form. How could such ideas fail to move me?

We were walking through ancient landscapes, olive groves, crumbling stones, towers, cisterns, gardens, bells, sirens, and wails. These kabbalistic ideas about purposeful exile and the restoration of prelapsarian harmony, both erotic and communal, felt overwhelmingly powerful. Of course there is still mystery to the creation of life. Why not open a door in the darkness onto this encompassing mystical vision? One doesn't have to believe that the rites and prayers will literally achieve the magical redemption described in kabbalistic literature to find contemplation of these ideas stirring primal emotions. One way to think about this deep strand of Kabbalah is as a cosmic romanticization of marriage.

Only later did I confront the virulently misogynist positions and practices that accompanied kabbalistic speculations about the Shekinah (unsurprising historically, disappointing nonetheless). But I would still argue that these mystics wrote into core theological structures formulas for their own subversion. The kabbalists had foraged in the fields of archaic Jewish imagery like builders on the grounds of a collapsed ancient temple, picking up gleaming fragments of text and inserting them into the design of an elaborately heterodox, new symbolic edifice. What would come from the confluences thereby created could no more be legislated or fully engineered in advance than the nature of an unborn child.

As I read through these passages about God, the Shekinah, and the dream of sublime reunification now, I find my thoughts going back to Scholem's 1915 diary entry in which he conceives of a novella about a young man being driven to kill himself by the "gaping paradox" in living as a committed Zionist. "Lately I've been preoccupied with question of Palestine and mostly of marriage,"

he wrote before recording this fantasy. Dreams of Palestine, suicide, and marriage. "Mostly of marriage." He hasn't broached this
nuptial dream before now. There's no specific person to whom
the urge is directed, and yet Scholem is overwhelmed by longing
to join his fate with that of another soul. To what degree were
all his mystical yearnings and terrors then distorted expressions
of this elemental wish not to be alone? The prospect of marriage
stands at the apex of a triangle with Death and Zion facing off in
opposite corners underneath.

SIX

THE FIRST TIME Gerhard got called up for military service, he'd
trudged in a daze to the station, clutching his suitcase. Defeated.
His father strutted along beside him the whole way. In ecstasies.
Trying to stuff his pockets with banknotes at the end. Gerhard
took almost nothing. And once inside his train compartment,
his eyes were riveted by a group of wounded soldiers bitterly cursing the war. People were starving. Horror was everywhere. The
eighteen-year-old boy who got examined immediately before him
was sent home because of syphilis. Life ruined in his first youth!

The "lost condition of Europe," as Gerhard called it, made him yearn desperately, if abstractly, for the Land of Israel.

That was in 1915. The following year, the second time Gerhard was put through a military physical, he felt philosophically stronger because of his association with Benjamin. He entered the army offices with a thoroughly worked-out plan for dodging service. But the authorities were so dull-witted that he made fools of them at the first test, by again making strange noises when the doctor told him to breathe. The man asked what was wrong with him.

"Neurasthenia and a nose disease," he retorted.

A senior officer interjected that Scholem made a bizarre impression, "like a sleepwalker."

That was it. The doctor officially registered him as a neurasthenic and spun him back out the door.

Once more he'd triumphed over Moloch, Gerhard reflected after his release. He plunged into a new reading list, partly dictated by Benjamin, including works on immortality, sacrifice, Hebrew, and Arabic. "The Messiah will be the last — and *first* — philosopher of language," he announced — perhaps still sometimes imagining himself in that role.

But the third time he got called up, in June 1917, even though he was still considered a mental case, the great mouth of the German war machine finally sucked Gerhard in. He and his fellow recruits weren't even out of quarantine before conflicts began. His company was ordered to take Sunday walks in the forest for their health. The filthy talk of the soldiers as they ran around the woods like crazy animals disgusted him. So Gerhard reminded his superiors that he was a neurotic and got reassigned to postal duty. From that point on, the others despised him. The fact that he was a bit mad was something they'd been indifferent to before, but now that he'd earned special privileges, they mocked him and lorded it over him with their barbarian potency.

For Gerhard, the experience of having his military comrades

turn on him once they thought illness brought advantages provoked a fresh surge of repugnance for the Germans. And he
was genuinely shocked by what he described repeatedly as their
"smutty talk." It was inconceivable to live among such people,
he declared. He spent all his free time composing letters to old
friends from Jung Juda, trying to enroll them in the creation of an
elite secret society of Zionists who would cling fast to one another
religiously "and be active in Palestine as simple people in white
robes." Those who were left, that is. Edgar Blum, his dearest friend
among them — his only friend from childhood — had died in battle
of a pelvis wound. Gerhard had been unable to find a single word
of solace for Blum's mother because her son had been killed by the
most ghastly thing imaginable: "the absolute Satan," he wrote in
his diary. He longed for the day when he could erect a living monu-
ment to his friend who, despite his youth, had taught through his
inner calm the true purpose of Zionism, the lesson of reverence.
Blum had been fervently studying Hebrew, even on the firing line.
How could you find words for the wickedness that would snatch
so pure a soul from the world?

There were no German words, anyway. Increasingly, Gerhard
sought truth in the "heavenly alphabet" described in the Zohar.
He read "Hebrew, Hebrew, and more Hebrew," he told a friend
after Blum's death. Inspired by Benjamin's rarefied language speculations, he'd already become suspicious of utilitarian speech, which
both men saw as a tool of the state authorities who'd plunged
Europe into the abyss. At the time of his military induction, Gerhard sought to extend Benjamin's ideas about the true, elevated
purpose of language to the whole vision of Zion. "No one has the
right to have 'reasons' to become a Zionist," he wrote in his journal.
"The same goes for Hebrew: nothing is gained if someone has 'reasons' for learning it." His antipragmatic zeal was uncompromising. Even more than through fantasies about Palestine, Gerhard
now sought to distinguish himself from everything happening in

Germany by making himself out to be a creature of the Hebrew language on the deepest level at which Hebrew was Torah, and Torah was a fabric woven of divine names through which creation was mystically engendered. He sought proof everywhere that he was not *really* German. "Goethe has never spoken to me, which must mean something very important, perhaps that the Jewish genius in me demarcates itself somehow from the German world," he mused. Indeed, his need to define himself as constitutionally distinct from his fellow recruits found expression in a kind of racial linguistics so devoted to the unadulterated core of Jewish being that it proved no less essentialist than racial genetics, even if Gerhard's version was meant to extricate him from Germany, not to extirpate some alleged foreign parasite from his German home. The irony that one of the thinkers who most profoundly anticipated Scholem's whole approach to Jewish mysticism—someone whom he cited in his journal in the same breath as the Zohar for his remarks about Scriptures' holy letters as "the expression of spiritual powers with their roots above"—happened to be an eccentric early-nineteenth-century German Christian theologian named Franz Joseph Molitor was not lost on Scholem. Nor was this puzzle ever resolved.

On the army base he did everything possible to separate himself physically and psychologically from the other conscripts, begging his commander to be given work censoring Hebrew documents in seclusion. He'd had to witness the horrifying consequences of sexual impurity among the German conscripts with their *Volk*-building national fitness craze, he informed Aharon Heller, another Zionist comrade. "Obscenity blocks every passage to the holy in this place," he declared. Judged too unstable even for the mail service, he was soon reassigned to supervising hygiene at the toilets. He reported to a friend that he was forever hearing the "heavy footsteps of anti-Semitism…thumping behind my back." Once when someone muttered a slur, Gerhard became convulsed with rage and beat the man to a pulp. Since he'd made this "experiment," everyone preferred to keep quiet around him. He became known for having "fits," as he later confessed, without giving details. Two months after starting basic training, Gerhard was diagnosed as a total lunatic and kicked over to a military hospital.

Scholem later said that his breakdown was feigned, boasting that he'd hoodwinked the military doctors yet again, but it was more than a ruse. Whether he'd lost or suspended his reason, it was clear that he was out of control. Yet this psychopathology, by liberating him from war service, had also enabled him to pass the ultimate test of his Zionism, he avowed, proving that "Zion is stronger than violence." Perhaps in linking the attainment of a higher freedom to insanity, Gerhard had in mind what he called the "blessed lunacy," to which Nietzsche and Hölderlin succumbed when life proved too much for their pure strain of truthfulness. "Holiness is the rustling of madness in our blood," he'd written.

Removed from all duties, Gerhard spent the remainder of the summer recovering. In the fall, he began studying higher mathematics at the University of Jena. At the time, he was wavering "between the two poles of mathematical and mystical symbolism," he recalled later. But even after his army debacle—during which, one might say, Scholem theatricalized an episode of real craziness—he still wasn't given the official classification that would permanently discharge him.

Benjamin, meanwhile, had married, and he and his bride, Dora, had managed to get over the border to Switzerland. Using hypnosis, Dora had induced sciaticalike symptoms in Benjamin that bought him a few additional months' exemption from the draft. Eventually they reached a sanitarium in Dachau, where a doctor gave Benjamin the papers that would let him leave Germany. He and Dora invited Gerhard to join them in Switzerland as soon as he was at liberty, and this was his brightest hope. "Come as soon as possible, or you will incur the undying hatred of a cheated posterity," Dora wrote him in November 1917. They were doing splendidly, she said: commencing great works, or about to; living within their means thanks to a favorable exchange rate; attending unsavory theatrical performances and fine concerts. They lacked only company. For his twentieth birthday in December, they gave Gerhard the most wonderful gift: photographic portraits of themselves. He kept the two pictures on his desk in the spacious room he'd rented in Jena opposite the Botanical Garden. His eyes would move from the frozen landscape to the portraits. Dora was inexhaustibly lovely; Walter was so grave. Gerhard conducted imaginary conversations with the photographs. When Walter wrote in April to announce that Dora had given birth to a son, Stefan, Gerhard responded deliriously: "Your marriage is the most beautiful miracle taking place before my eyes." That evening, on his own, he dressed up in his best suit and celebrated the arrival of their baby in silence. Their marriage was before the gaze of his fancy the way perfect figures dancing in a snow globe revolve before a child.

The downward spiral in relations with his own family had been more or less continuous over the war years. Arthur might have taken a little pride in the fact that his son had succeeded in getting into the university after being expelled from the gymnasium. But once he heard that Gerhard planned to get a mathematics degree, his ironic scorn knew no bounds. Right in front of Gerhard he'd go off on a diatribe: "My son the gentleman engages in nothing but unprofitable pursuits. My son the gentleman is interested in mathematics, pure mathematics. I ask my son the gentleman: What do you want? As a Jew you have no chance for a university career. Take up engineering, go to technical college, then you can do all the math in your free time as you like. But no, my son the gentleman does not want to become an engineer, he wants only pure mathematics. My son the gentleman is interested in *Yiddishkeit*. So I say to my son the gentleman: All right, become a rabbi, then you can have all the *Yiddishkeit* you want. No, my son the gentleman won't hear of becoming a rabbi."

Werner almost made the ultimate sacrifice for Germany that Arthur commended. His foot got blasted during the 1916 Serbian campaign. He was laid up for months in the university town of Halle, and for a time it seemed to Gerhard that his brother was coming around to Judaism. He was so dissatisfied with him-self—unlike most Zionists—that there was actually room for his Jewishness to grow. "I intend to win him *fully* over to our side," Gerhard wrote his friend Erich Brauer. But as soon as Werner could hobble about, he got busy with the local Social Democrat crowd. The group staged a big radical-left antiwar demonstration on January 27 , the kaiser's birthday. Werner added a nice touch by wearing his military outfit. The police rushed in. Werner was immediately seized and hauled off to jail. Because he was in uni-form, the authorities charged him with treason. He managed to smuggle word of his fate out to Gerhard a couple of days later.

Gerhard realized all hell would break loose the moment Arthur learned he had a son locked up as a traitor. He grabbed his papers, journals, and letters and hightailed it over to a friend's house, where he deposited them for safekeeping.

Two days later, Arthur got news of Werner's impending court-martial. His rage at the dinner table was stupendous, and Gerhard got swept into the diatribe for objecting mildly to one accusation.

"Zionism and Social Democracy are one and the same!" Arthur yelled. "They are anti-German agitation and I will no longer coun-tenance them in my house. I never want to see you again!"

The next day Gerhard got a registered letter from his father announcing that he would have nothing further to do with him. In March, he'd send Gerhard a hundred marks and that was the end of it. "Turn yourself over to the authorities in charge of civilian affairs and you'll get some kind of paid work that fits your abilities," he advised. "What you call work is nothing more than a game," he added. The question of whether he would agree to pay for further studies after the war was contingent on his son behaving properly in the interim. Gerhard knew this meant stifling his Zionism, which was out of the question. Such self-abasement would only fuel his father's power lust. Arthur was already bragging around town about how he would agree to speak with Gerhard only after hauling him home "on a bridle." His mother was mortified but helpless, displacing her heartbreak onto pragmatic trivialities, like whether he was eating regular lunches and buying the right kind of soap.

Jung Juda got word of Scholem's exile. His friend Zalman Rubashov, an electric orator, scion of Russian Hasidic aristocracy, quipped, "A martyr for Zion! Something must be done." Rubashov found Gerhard a place at the boardinghouse where he was living for cheap, Pension Stuck, run by the female cousin of a famous German comedian who kept a rigorously kosher household for a ragged flock of Russian Jews who'd long ago given up any pretense to ritual observance.

It was a "purely Zionist" atmosphere, Scholem wrote, but one in which — because the movement was already so fractured — there were endless late-night debates in Hebrew, Yiddish, and Russian-accented German over the landlady's kuchen about what Zionism consisted in. As the only true Berliner in residence, he had a certain special stature — akin to "a multicolored dog," Scholem drily noted. In his memoir, Pension Stuck comes off as a rollicking Zionist hotbed. Black coffee, cake, and fevered talk of Palestine among bearlike Jews on the run from the czar. His journal for the period tells another story.

There he labeled his fellow residents profoundly debased petit bourgeoisie. So much did they repel him that it was only when he was shut up inside his own room that he could recover his equilibrium. Frau Stuck herself, with her ridiculous cultivated airs and vacuous prattle, filled him with loathing. It is no surprise that he was unpopular. When berated for making contemptuous remarks about the other pensioners, his response was, "Is it my fault that everyone around me actually *is* an idiot?" The truth was, he acknowledged, the pension triggered as much revulsion as did his parents' house. It was only because he was so hypocritical, self-satisfied, and bourgeois that he didn't spit in the faces of the other pensioners and storm out. If he really had integrity, he decided, he'd put a bullet in his brain and let God handle the rest.

Since Scholem preserved his journals, and cited them frequently, the discrepancy between these portraits of Pension Stuck cannot be a matter of simple misremembering. It seems more likely a reflection of his need to project a strict division between the corrupt, small-minded Western Jew and the spiritually vitalized Eastern variety.

Now and then Gerhard visited Werner in prison, where they shared their enthusiasm for the mounting drama of the Russian Revolution. The future of the Jews in a progressive, Socialist state looked promising—even Gerhard saw it. You didn't have to believe in the inevitability of a German Communist utopia to see that something was happening in Russia of world-historical significance. Werner told Gerhard that as soon as he got out of jail, at the end of 1917, he was going to marry his exemplary revolutionary girlfriend, Emmy Wiechel. Gerhard respected Emmy's authentically proletarian background and self-martyring radicalism. He found it charming that this plain woman refused to wear makeup.

The feminine quotient in Gerhard's own life had changed also. Girls now bobbed in and out of the picture, sometimes making things better, other times just aggravating his indignation at the state of reality. While still in Berlin, he'd begun frequenting the Jüdisches Volksheim, on Alexanderplatz, which provided support to refugees from the East and where a lot of Gerhard's young peers were volunteering. During working hours, the Jüdisches Volksheim was pretty much a day-care center for poor Jewish children from Eastern Europe. At night, the male and female volunteers gathered excitedly for talks.

The first time Gerhard showed up at the Volksheim, he was taken aback by the strange scene. A coterie of volunteers, many of them charming young women, were arrayed around their obvious leader, a graceful young lady with immense natural poise. Some perched on chairs. Some curled on the floor. The founder of the place, Siegfried Lehmann—a jaunty fellow who kept a spring in his step even after he later went fat in Palestine—was reciting a poem by Franz Werfel. The atmosphere could best be described as one of "aesthetic ecstasy," Gerhard concluded, the last thing he'd expected to find at a social work center for poor war victims.

On this next visit to the Volksheim, he was happy to see some familiar faces, including a party of melodious young women he'd encountered at another youth gathering. But Lehmann's speech about Jewish education was another matter. Lehmann began talking Hasidism—but it wasn't Hasidism. It was know-nothing Hasidism. No-history Hasidism. Hasidism purloined and diluted from Buber's superlyrical, ultraselective Hasidism. He spoke of *simcha* (joy) and *devekuth* (binding with God), and the audience quivered: "*Oh yes, oh religiosity, religiosity.*"

The next week, Gerhard attacked Lehmann head-on, demanding that people actually learn Hebrew and the Jewish sources rather than disbursing pious twaddle that bore no relation to Zionism. (Fifty years later, he would discover that one of the young women who'd seen him challenge Lehmann was Felice Bauer, Kafka's fiancée—and that Kafka himself endorsed his approach. "I am always inclined to favor proposals such as those made by Herr Scholem, which demand the utmost, and by so doing achieve nothing," Kafka wrote Bauer after receiving her description of the event.)

At the Jüdisches Volksheim, when he wasn't busy assailing its founder, Gerhard had admired its female constituency from afar. But now, in Jena, he found himself balancing the attentions of several serious women. Clumsily and unsuccessfully for the most part—but at least with some mutual intrigue.

He took long walks with Wally, at night through autumn woods. She'd been his first Hebrew pupil and was adorable. But she was also painfully vulnerable. He read psalms aloud in private with Meta, for hours, and sometimes began trembling uncontrollably before her. He talked ethics with Grete and pondered her doubts about his whole approach to resolving moral problems. Grete was his friend Erich Brauer's sister, and an ethical paragon. But Meta was more availably curious, with a warm physical touch: Just before his twentieth birthday, they kissed and caressed. Whom was he most indebted to?

In his descriptions, the women don't come across as ethereal, exactly, but they're oddly abstract. Juxtaposing sensual attributes with splinters of theory. Evocative of the Cubist art that came to obsess him after he visited an exhibition featuring Picasso's *Woman with Violin*, which he found transcendently formless. "All the girls I know have question marks smeared all over them," he remarked at one point. Meaning, bluntly, that he didn't know what in the world to make of them.

What *was* it about women and knowledge? When he thought about Grete, he realized that she knew far more than he did, but it was not a knowledge she could ever communicate—precisely because of her sex, which was also what gave her the knowledge. Only fools imagined this condition meant women in fact couldn't know things, and even bigger fools developed whole antifeminist philosophies on the basis of that sort of thinking. Perhaps, he speculated, women received as their birthright a symbolic language men could never acquire.

There's pathos to the young Scholem's efforts to both elevate and circumscribe the women he cares for—while simultaneously trying to overcome chauvinist stereotypes with some more substantial analysis of the difference between the sexes. But he gets so tangled in convoluted emotions (he feels more for Grete; he enjoys more intimacy with Meta), and seems so often tin-eared to the women themselves, that his relations become messier when he longs most for clarity. Falling back on the need for true Zionists to preserve "fanatical chastity," Gerhard ends up sounding just priggish and scared.

In his letters, he struggles to be absolutely candid with each woman in turn as his affections meander, but often he comes off as so maniacally driven to be naked about every single limitation or surplus of his feelings that honesty itself becomes emotionally toxic. Finally, shaking head to foot all the while, he tries to write Meta a brutally frank letter — and most of what gets onto the page ends up being a confession of overwhelming love for Walter Benjamin, whom he describes as the only man on earth who can truly be accounted a prophet of God. In the course of his paean to that sublime friendship, he also manages to sneak in a hint about another girl lodged in his heart who would have Benjamin's spirit if it were feminine. (That would be Grete.)

How did the gentle Meta feel as she tried to absorb this? Gerhard seems to suspect his letter won't rectify anything, for at the end he rather truculently asserts that if she doesn't understand him now, then a hundred more pages wouldn't help — after which he softens his tone by insisting that he is sure she *does* understand him, and that's why he loves her. "God has sent me your youth as the other face of my generation (to which in truth I don't belong) to show me whether there's a way to reconcile me with my generation (which I spurn)," he tosses off, like a spastic hand grenade, in closing.

The abstract, orphic key just doesn't work for Gerhard the way it sometimes will for Benjamin.

He began staking everything on Grete as a moral goddess. Even when she had nothing to say, her existence was a beacon to him. She was fluent in the profound language of silence. He sent a long letter confessing his anxious dependency on her, and avowing that the more she was encircled by "walls and locks," the more certain he became "in reaching into the center of your loneliness, directly

and immediately." She replied, tersely, that his letter failed to
entertain the possibility that she might simply be unable to fulfill
his hopes for her intervention. And by the way, things are tough
for me, too, she concluded.

Injured, outcast, keyed up, and productive, Gerhard returned
to his work: a study of the Book of Lamentations he'd been
immersed in for months. (He had told Grete those biblical verses
must be read "as a *confession* of my state.")

Lamentations had multiple theoretical resonances for Scholem,
but plainly also reflected the fact that he was in mourning for his
life, like a character from Chekhov.

The book was written after the Babylonian destruction of Jerusalem, when the Jews were in a state of total defeat, and Scholem
was interested in the ways that its expression of loss was so monumental as to take on a kind of negative transcendence. Lamentation "reveals nothing, for the being that reveals itself in it has
no content (and therefore one could simultaneously say that it
reveals everything) and keeps nothing silent, for its entire existence is based on a revolution of silence," he wrote at the outset
of a head-cracking sequence of negatives. This extreme instance
of what Gerhard called "the language of destruction" approached
the vanishing point at which word became silence. And for this
reason — since silence had not been polluted by use in the real
world — it was precisely what remained fertile in Jewish tradition.
"Language was indeed faced with the original sin but silence was
not," he wrote.

Gerhard and Benjamin had been exchanging thoughts on
what a redemptive language might consist in for years by this
point — and silence had always been integral to the project. "You
learn Hebrew in order to keep silent in Hebrew," he wrote just
before going into the army, and while there were many philosophical reasons for taking this position, part of what Gerhard
was trying to do was to stake out a linguistic sanctuary from the

present, as if Hebrew were a place you could retreat into, spiritually and historically.

In November 1916, Benjamin sent Scholem a letter that became the basis for "On Language as Such and on the Language of Man," a seminal essay that Scholem saw his own studies of Lamentations continuing. Humanity alone had been allowed to name its own kind, Benjamin wrote. All forms of language except the proper name were a means to an end and thus merely functional. Names represented "the communion of man with the *creative* word of God." But after the Fall, man "abandoned immediacy in the communication of the concrete, name, and fell into the abyss of the mediateness of all communication," reducing language to "a *mere* sign."

Benjamin's esoteric retelling of Genesis, in which the snake seduces man to a vain, nameless "language of knowledge," was intended partly as a warning against the manipulation of words for political purposes. The ongoing fall of culture in the war — manifest in the deluge of propaganda — brought urgency to this task. When Martin Buber solicited a contribution from Benjamin for his journal *Der Jude*, Benjamin refused, writing, "I can understand writing… as poetic, prophetic, objective in terms of its effect, but in any case only as *magical*, that is un-*mediated*."

Both Scholem and Benjamin saw the debasement of language as symptom and cause of society's morbidity. Violence and smut were gummed together. A purified language would serve as a weapon to liberate the creative conscience. Throughout the first years of their friendship, the pair traded insights in pursuit of a new metaphysical linguistics with a velocity evocative of the exchange between Picasso and Braque as they developed Cubism. But ultimately Scholem, playing Braque in this analogy, went deeper and deeper into his Cubist mysticism, seeing its multidimensional abstraction as fundamentally Jewish. "The *Jewish* image of a man *must* be cubist," he declared. "The Messiah will be a cubist," he added. Judaism's prohibition against semblance in art led to the split between nature and its representation through symbols, which he saw as a good thing. European art was "sham and vulgarity" because it desired "spirit through the flesh," whereas "Jewish art is cubism, which has abandoned the flesh." The Kabbalah's Tree of Life, too, had a "cubist feel," he wrote. Benjamin, on the other hand, turned again to the phenomenal — projecting their ideas back onto more and more features of the material world. He read the metropolis of modernity itself as a metaphysical book, while Scholem applied their new metaphysics of language onto more and more ancient mystical texts.

Not that the men's dialogue on these points was just a binary exchange in which Benjamin appropriated kabbalistic ideas to articulate his antipolitical yet revolutionary vision of language and Scholem imported Benjamin's personal glosses on Jewish commentary to deepen his own readings of kabbalistic texts. Scholem's thinking about the word of God as simultaneously devoid of specifiable content *and* the font of all meaning was indebted also to German Romantic and French Symbolist language theories, which had first influenced Benjamin. Schlegel, who loomed powerfully behind both Benjamin and Scholem's thought, had himself remarked that the "true aesthetic is the Kabbalah." In fact, the Christian Kabbalah, which developed out of Renaissance-era readings of Jewish and Greek Neoplatonic texts and sought to reconcile a heterodox reading of the Kabbalah with non-Jewish mystical

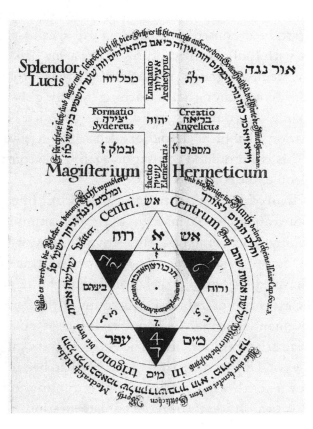

ideas, exerted a huge influence on subsequent kabbalistic speculation. (As well as on Christian thought: The fifteenth-century Flo-
rentine philosopher Giovanni Pico della Mirandola declared that
"no science can better convince us of the divinity of Jesus Christ
than magic and the Kabbalah.") Drawing on additional sources
culled from his vast reading, Scholem then regrafted distinctly Jewish elements onto this hybrid of esoteric Christian theology and
continental language philosophy as he built his own theory of mystical Judaism. Trying to sort out the ricocheting historical influences here is like charting the sound waves of screams in a cave.

But on a more personal level, Scholem's work on Lamentations
can be seen as a further step into Hebrew's mysteries as a route out
of Europe toward some higher state. "God is not interested in our
origins, only where we are heading," he declared in his journal. To
Werner Kraft, he promised, "My children will speak Hebrew." His
experience with foul-mouthed brutes in the army had confirmed
his most extreme diagnosis of the Jews' German problem. Jews
had lost their connection to the Teaching by selling themselves to
Europe. While the community of men was founded on "Silence
and Revelation," babblers, devoid of silence, could have no community. "This is a profound accusation against the contemporary
German people," he concluded.

As the chain of people disappointing or rejecting him grew, Gerhard lit more candles before his icons of the Benjamins until these
shone blindingly. Benjamin had sent Gerhard a copy of an essay he
wrote on Dostoevsky's *The Idiot*. The sublimity of this work completely unraveled Gerhard, for he at once thought he grasped its
secret: The essay comprised a veiled account of the demise of the
Youth Movement. Benjamin had doubled Prince Myshkin with his
beloved dead friend Fritz Heinle. The essay, with its "mighty sentences on eternal life" revealed how Benjamin had been able to sacrifice his own youth while miraculously continuing to live "with
the *idea* of youth." It was its own tract of lamentation.

Gerhard dashed off a letter to Benjamin explaining his revelation, and Benjamin responded with the most affecting lines Scholem said he'd ever received. "Since receiving your letter I often have found myself in a festive mood," Benjamin wrote. "I must celebrate with reverence the revelation in that which has made itself known to you. For it simply is the case that what has reached you and you alone must have been addressed to you and has entered our life again for a moment."

Gerhard was so overcome with joy by this disclosure that he declared his doubts about God's existence were over. For now he himself had not only met but had known God.

Benjamin's expectations for Scholem's appearance in Switzerland were not many notches below Scholem's own: He was grateful to Gerhard, he wrote, for "the replete sense of responsibility, the clarity, and the restraint, precisely because it is thoroughly responsive to me. I recently read the following words in Goethe: 'A real response is like a sweet kiss.'" He and Dora now expected that Gerhard would translate Benjamin's inner cosmos to the world—even, or perhaps especially, when Benjamin himself was not entirely sure what this plenitude consisted in.

Benjamin's heightened anticipation coincided with Gerhard's receipt of a formal diagnosis of dementia praecox—we'd say schizophrenia—which exempted him once and for all from the military. In tribute to the good news, Benjamin suggested, nearly three years into their friendship, that they begin calling each other by their first names. But Gerhard still lacked the documentation necessary to act on his release. He had to appeal to his mother to plead with his father to tell the authorities he needed to be treated by a doctor in Switzerland.

Reading furiously, writing madly, and dreaming endlessly about Walter and Dora, he became insomniac with anxiety about whether he would ever be allowed to travel. Finally, on April 17, his mother wrote that she was able to send the certificate that would enable him to see a physician who would have the authority to issue him a passport. Would the man come through? Would he himself remain alive? Was there any such thing as a Jewish death? he wondered. No, he decided, for in Judaism there was no difference between this world and the next. The very idea of such a distinction was shameful to Jews, he resolved. The world to come was nothing but the foundation of this world. And that was the reason why when someone transgressed, he was said to lose his place in the next world. From that time onward, his life had no foundation. In other words, his life had been destroyed from within.

I was sitting upstairs at the Café Atara at the end of the rainy season, huddled over my notebook and a poppy-seed strudel, when the realization came to me: *I've passed through the looking glass.* If I allowed my gaze to blur just slightly in that venerable coffeehouse, which had been founded by a German immigrant some fifty years before and had long been the haunt of authors and intellectuals, I might have been inside the world of yesterday. Brahms was playing softly. At the table behind me, two elderly gentlemen were bent over a chessboard. To my right, two elegant older women were conversing in German. *My grandparents would have found themselves at home here,* I thought.

I'd stopped at the Atara after a long afternoon ramble through a deep mist, in which I'd wandered down from the villas of the German Colony into Baka, then wound my way back into Rehavia — or Little Berlin, as it was called while Scholem lived there. Twice I'd come upon stacks of books neatly tied with twine and set before the entrance to stone apartment buildings. I'd learned by now to recognize these melancholy little offerings, frequently laid alongside a clumsy pair of scuffed black shoes, or the crumpled, dark bellows of old luggage. I'd take the books and leave the artifacts of wandering. In this way, I'd begun to amass a rather impressive library of classic German literature — Goethe, Heine, Nietzsche, Rilke — often with fragrant leather bindings and lovely thick paper. Once I found an edition of the works of Schiller in soft cream calf-skin, embossed with gold lettering.

Discarded books were common in Jerusalem during my first years in the city, because the generation that came there from German-speaking countries was dying; their bereaved loved ones, more often than not, had no use for these works. When I took the books home, I felt I was regathering sparks of the world my father had turned his back on. Sometimes, too, I found myself thinking of Scholem's descriptions of Jerusalem when he arrived in 1923: The city was "saturated with old Hebrew books the way a sponge is saturated with water." Jews had always come to the city "to pray, to study, and to die" he wrote. Now, since the years of the First World War — especially after the terrible famine of 1916 — a great many had died. No one had any use for the volumes of kabbalistic literature from the libraries of the dead, and he was able to build up an extraordinary collection for a song.

Scholem was living then just beyond the still intact wall seg-regating the religious neighborhood of Meah She'arim from the rest of the city. His home was "two rooms in an Arab house whose walls, believe it or not, were 4 feet thick." The sandy path on which it stood was already known as a Zionist center. "One could say that outside the walls of this Orthodox paradise, we lived almost allegorically," he observed. In those days, the walls of that district "were plastered with proclamations, and curses directed at the Zionists, all their schools, and other works of Satan." These "fanat-ics," as he called them, expressed violent opposition to every man-ifestation of the "national movement of renewal." Hence, "This Mea She'arim was a rather dialectical paradise, as is presumably in the nature of paradises. We represented the snake that crawled over the walls of this paradise."

Scholem believed that by plucking the knowledge of Kabbalah

from the moribund pious community that had abandoned it and feeding it to secular Zionists he could help fuel the movement's drive toward independence and historical responsibility. Without needing to actually promulgate the mystical practices outlined in these works, he could tap their latent insurrectionary powers, using them to develop a more explosive, polymorphous perspective on Jewish history. By cultivating broader engagement with these texts, and so expanding people's sense of the disparate potencies at work within Judaism, he would break down the walls behind which the Jews had sought to hide from history and so energize the Zionist project.

Today, when I think about those masses of books lying around Jerusalem after my own move to the city—the works of German Idealist and Romantic philosophers, of humanist novelists and Symbolist poets, which were abandoned by their owners just as the kabbalistic manuscripts had been cast off by the Orthodox in 1920s Jerusalem—I wonder whether these works might have their own productively seditious role to play in another kind of national renewal. For now it is the Zionist project itself that has become walled off and petrified, even as it walls in others. What if these forgotten books, which nurtured Scholem and Benjamin, were to become required reading once again? To live, as Scholem demanded, "responsibly within Jewish history" may now mean turning sharply outward, grappling with the vast multiplicity of the project, which was always fed by a world of textual sources and cultural influences, just as Scholem's own interpretation of Kabbalah was as indebted to Christian mystical thinkers and nineteenth-century German philosophy as to any specifically Jewish theological lineage—just as the medieval Kabbalists themselves were nurtured by everything from Aristotelian and Neoplatonic to Sufi, Christian, and Hermetic speculations. (For all that, in his fierce desire to mark off a Jewish space apart from European culture, he sometimes denied this polyphony.) And I sometimes wonder whether, with all his obsession with tracing the origins of Jewish mysticism—of his own Jewish identity—Scholem ever considered the genesis of his own home, that old Arab house with its inconceivably thick stone walls on the Abyssinian Road, which ended at the Street of the Prophets.

My whole walk through the mist had been magical. I'd paused before a building to listen to someone practicing cello. As I passed my favorite *yekke* bakery, a man was just carrying out a tray of fragrant rye loaves to a rickety old delivery van. It seemed everywhere I went I found sounds, smells, and shadows that evoked my Viennese grandmother's apartment. I could hear her voice rippling beneath the greetings of many elderly neighbors. And I realized now that part of what made me want to linger in the city, even though my program at the seminary was coming to an end and had led to nothing, was not a dream tied to biblical models of Jerusalem, but nostalgia for the musty, cultured air of Freud's Ninth District or Benjamin's constellation of West End cafés, which still collected in certain corners of the city, and in all those abandoned libraries—an aura that could be physically touched.

It was another day back at the Café Atara, now at an outside table on a beautiful spring morning, that something else I'd seen without seeing finally registered: How did it come to be, I wondered, that the tables were being cleaned by Palestinian boys who often didn't appear older than twelve or thirteen? Why weren't they in school? It might have been a tiny point in the scheme of things, but it troubled me. I asked my waitress how the boys busing tables had gotten the day free, and she mumbled something about it being a holiday. The next day, they were still there working, and the next day as well. One afternoon I met an Israeli acquaintance at the café and mentioned my concern. He sighed and said, "Yeah, it's terrible. Their families encourage them to miss school to make some money. They don't have enough in their economy. They're lucky to work here."

There were too many pieces missing from this explanation.

What was "their economy"? They didn't have their own country. Why wasn't the Israeli state "their economy" and committed to trying to make them go to school? What did it mean that
these children were forgoing an education so they could make a
few shekels cleaning tables for West Jerusalem café patrons like
myself? *Was* it such a small point if it concerned the prospects of
the next generation?

Rather than having passed through the looking glass into some
Old World coffeehouse idyll, I came to feel that I'd been holding
against my eyes a little snow globe of Habsburg Jerusalem, without even realizing that the globe was spiderwebbed with cracks
through which the snow had long ago drained away. It seemed
incredible to me that even as a fleeting fantasy I could have imagined myself in Berlin or Vienna of the 1920s.

But when I was in Jerusalem in the fall of 2014, when an anti-
democracy bill had just passed its first test in the parliament, and the
government was collapsing again; when the city's one Jewish-Arab
school was being attacked repeatedly by arsonists who painted on
the walls THERE IS NO COEXISTING WITH CANCER — when I
was told by a longtime Jerusalemite that one day walking near his
home he'd seen two old Palestinian men abruptly surrounded by a
group of Jewish girls joyously dancing in a ring, while singing, "Arabs
are dying! Death to Arabs!" and he'd started to keep walking but
stopped himself, thinking that if he kept going this *was* Germany —
then I wondered whether I'd been so wrong after all in my sense of
having passed through the looking glass. Maybe what I was seeing
did resonate with a lost Berlin or Vienna — but not from the Weimar era. The Café Atara, my old atmospheric haunt, was built in
1938, after all. The year of the Anschluss. The eve of the apocalypse.

When Gerhard at last received his passport, it was all he could do
to restrain himself from writing Walter immediately. He'd seen the

heavens open, but he didn't want to send word until everything was finalized. Instead, he fantasized about appearing on their doorstep as "a beautiful surprise." He would ring the bell. Dora would open the door. "Good day, madam, my dear lady!" he would say.

A few days after unloading his library in Berlin with his uncle, he stood on board the Lake Constance steamer, watching Germany recede in the boat's wake. The war was done for him. His prophet and his prophet's muse awaited him in freedom.

SEVEN

"I'M PLEASED WITH YOU."

Those were the words Walter met him with at the train station in Berne before escorting him to the apartment he shared
with Dora and their infant son, Stefan. From the moment they
met, he and Walter found their opinions converging, Gerhard
exulted. He scrupulously tallied in his diary the hours they spent
together. They talked about sin and responsibility, and fantasized
about creating a private academy dedicated entirely to their own
curriculum, in which Gerhard would be Beadle of the School of
Philosophy and Religion, and Walter would serve as Rector Mag-
nificus. They read Schlegel aloud and discussed Schiller. Walter
announced that the moment he passed his doctoral examination
he would begin studying Hebrew. Dora was simply "the most beautiful thing in the world," Gerhard declared. She and Walter presented him with a book of fairy tales by Ludwig Tieck, a muse of
the Romantic movement. Gerhard marveled at Dora's gentleness
with the baby. "Dora will be my mother," he wrote in his journal.

God permeated their conversations. According to Benjamin,
the Divine was the "unattainable center of a system of symbols
intended to remove Him from everything concrete and everything
symbolic as well." It was simple as that. Benjamin presented Gerhard with his essay "The Metaphysics of Youth," and Gerhard copied it out longhand like a scribe of the Torah. They talked about
Walter's program for a new philosophy, which would be based on a

theory of experience that embraced all man's intellectual and psychological links with the world.

In that case, you'll have to incorporate every variety of divination into your idea of experience, Gerhard observed.

"A philosophy that does not include the possibility of soothsaying from *coffee grounds* and cannot explicate it cannot be a true philosophy," Walter shot back. Even if Judaism condemned such pursuits, the profound interconnection between things demanded the inclusion of arcane forms of prophesying.

Sometimes Dora went to bed early, leaving Walter and Gerhard alone in Walter's large study to talk into the depths of night or take one of their nocturnal rambles. Other times, when husband and wife were particularly tender, fluttering and cooing, calling each other names in a made-up language, Gerhard found himself sidelined while they slipped into the next room. His own feelings stormed while they moaned and thumped.

In Switzerland, whole other dimensions of Benjamin's character began to emerge. One night Dora and Walter invited Scholem to join them at a recital by a distinguished pianist. When he arrived, Gerhard realized it was a society event, by the standards of Berne. He'd never seen the two of them so formally dressed. Here they were suddenly, his idols, bowing in all directions. Transformed into beings of the haute monde.

Was this the occasion that led to their first talk about money? Gerhard couldn't afford to mix with that kind of crowd, even had he desire to do so. Perhaps Dora or Walter had been chiding him to squeeze a little credit out of Arthur to help subsidize the rents in Muri, a small city nearby where they were planning to relocate while continuing to study full-time. *Something*, anyway, got them talking about how exactly they were going to underwrite their utopian retreat.

Benjamin made clear that he intended to cadge every mark he could get from his parents. Gerhard expressed surprise at Walter's willingness to be supported by parents whose values he despised. Benjamin made a point of indicting his family's materialism as symptomatic of an entire culture: the very particular circuit of shops he'd been forced to frequent with his mother — suits from Arnold Müller's, shoes at Stiller's, luggage from Mädler's, hot chocolate with whipped cream exclusively at Hillbrich's — that conspicuous tastefulness counterpointing the deep secrecy cloaking the financial underpinnings of their existence. Personally, Gerhard made clear, he felt repulsed by the idea of exploiting his own father economically.

Now it was Walter and Dora's turn to be startled. What on earth was he going on about? Benjamin felt no compunction whatever about taking advantage of his father's wealth for the sake of his work, and Gerhard should have no reservations either. "People like us have responsibility only to our own kind, not to the laws of a society we reject wholeheartedly," Walter said.

Gerhard was shocked. It was so unscrupulous! Didn't things become tainted if they were paid for by the enemy? How could Walter have such a transcendent, religious sensibility and speak in so nihilistic a fashion!

The only place where he recognized moral categories, Walter continued, was within the living sphere that he had created around himself and in the larger, purely intellectual cosmos.

It was outrageous, what he was saying.

Walter and Dora charged that *he* was the outrageous one, offending *them* with his "outrageous wholesomeness." How can you be so naïve? they reproached him. You allow yourself to be defined by gestures, they added.

It made Gerhard's brain reel, the way they were talking.

But then, when the night was over, for all the intensity of their row, he was no less disarmed by the placid cordiality Walter displayed on saying good night.

Perhaps it had all been a freak?

But the fights erupted over and over. Gerhard began noticing inconsistencies beyond those violating the moral code of self-reliance. How gleefully the couple lied about little things, for instance. Mendacity seemed to give them a conceited aesthetic delight, and one witnessed in their existence the terrible consequences of casual falseness. Walter's theories were surrounded by a luminous aura of theological gravity, but with respect to matters of everyday life, he was blithely amoral, even decadent. Everything that had so infuriated Gerhard about Jung Juda had to do with the movement's failure to live out its radical precepts. Was this another version of the same insincerity?

One evening, he read aloud to the couple his farewell letter to the Jewish Youth Movement, which he accused of having become so perverted by falsehoods and the drunkenness of "living experiences" that only silence could penetrate the shapeless community born of its pseudo-Zionism. "To restore language to youth: that is the task," he declared. "We are on a sinking ship, and no jubilation and no satisfaction about the 'general direction' can deceive us about the fact that we are not traveling to Zion but are going under in Berlin."

Gerhard probably expected applause when he put down the pages: He'd tried to apply Benjamin's ideas of silence and truth to the failure of Jung Juda. Surely this would elicit his friend's catchphrase: *Ausserordentlich!*"

Instead, Walter told him he shouldn't publish the screed, and a violent debate ensued. "In such matters, the key is to have the metaphysical laughs on one's side," he said. "You are loudly demanding silence."

But hadn't Walter made plain beforehand that he agreed with the thrust of this argument? Gerhard had no intention of withdrawing the letter.

"It's fine to write this kind of thing, but one doesn't print it," Walter persisted.

Gerhard knew there was something self-centered about his farewell. But metaphysics had made Walter insane. How were you supposed to ever act on your radicalism if you lived in such horror of having your ideas profaned?

And, by the same token, how could it be that, when it came to literature and philosophy, Benjamin resembled "a scribe cast out into another world, who has set off in search of his 'scripture,'" whereas in practical terms he came off as a feckless sensualist who'd sponge off his parents forever given half a chance?

If he was really so antibourgeois, why did he go into rhapsodies over the beautiful covers and typefaces of the volumes in his private library? "I deny that metaphysically legitimate insights can arise from this way of evaluating books on the basis of their bindings and paper," Gerhard cried.

Yet no matter what passed between them, compounding Scholem's confusion, at night's end Benjamin always reverted to his attitude of supreme courtesy. Once he held Gerhard's hand so long on parting, while looking deep into his eyes, that Gerhard suspected he knew he was going too far with his nihilism.

Undeterred, they all moved out to Muri. Gerhard rented a garret overlooking a wheat field framed by mountains just minutes from Dora and Walter. Walter teased Gerhard, saying that he crouched in his attic like a magician creating the weather with mysterious potions. The founding of their imaginary academy, the University of Muri, occupied them greatly. It would have a library stocked with made-up book titles, eventually including Pontius Pilate's *Hebrew for Prefects* and *Seven Titanic Cheeses*. They devised a rich study program, which Gerhard thought might allow for a department of demonology, though the Rector disputed this. They held endless discussions about a host of philosophers, and sometimes Walter recited at length from his epicurean dreams. In one of these, twenty people lined up in pairs and were given concepts like Rejection and Jealousy to act out. As they did so, appropriate costumes for each paradigm would magically materialize and outfit the performers. In Rejection, Walter was a round little Chinaman dressed in blue, with a troublesome partner who wanted something from him and wriggled up on his back. The dreams are opaque—and there were a lot of them. He had his own theory of dream interpretation, distinct from Freud's, which Gerhard couldn't get purchase on, but just listening to the weird visions was mesmerizing. They were of a piece with Walter's profound interest in clairvoyance, ghosts, and the whole "world of premythical spectral phenomena." All Walter's conversation in that gentle, harmoniously modulated voice, while he paced and gestured, stopping abruptly inches from interlocutors to stare up at them with his myopic cerulean gaze, cast a personal spell that whetted Gerhard's appetite for the mystical realm much as his theories did.

It was the different states between dreaming and waking that most fascinated Walter. He and Dora seemed to occupy that condition for Gerhard. Wrapped in mystery. Velvety. The knock of reality banging at the Benjamins' existence sounded faint to him. But the money at the couple's disposal was limited, and getting tighter. Dora as sublime maternal deity still had an infant to placate. Benjamin's graduate studies demanded arduous work, and there was no guarantee of a lectureship afterward. (In fact, Benjamin never received an academic appointment.)

Sometimes the couple exploded into terrifying fights. Screaming. Frantically racing around their apartment. Gerhard would try to quietly withdraw, but it wasn't always so easy. After the brawls there would be tearful, loving reconciliations—but still. When Walter wasn't a full-throated participant in the scenes, he would just recede and go cold. While taking their evening walks, Gerhard began to be conscious of Walter's basically depressive psychology. However shrill the pitch of the fracas, or however deep his subsequent withdrawal, Benjamin was still capable afterward of sententiously exclaiming, "There is no such thing as an unhappy love."

The whole thing shook Gerhard to his core. He wished he could cover his eyes and stop his ears. By midsummer he was ravaged. He'd staked everything on an idyll that was devolving into wild, shrieking quarrels about everything, about nothing. Nothing and everything. Everything is nothing. What had become of his teacher? They treated him like a flunkey. At times, Dora would fly into an hysterical fit for no discernible reason. Gerhard might be playing a quiet game of chess with Walter when Dora would leap up from her chair, run out of the room, and not show herself again the whole evening. Gerhard stared out his attic window in bewilderment, mediating on the 104th Psalm: "He looketh on the earth, and it trembleth: he toucheth the hills, and they smoke / I will sing unto the Lord as long as I Live: I will sing praise to my God while I have my being."

The landscape was tranquil, but he could never truly enter into it. That magnificent ocean of wheat rippling below him could be appreciated only at a distance. To attempt any more complete fusion with the scene would mean surrendering to the great hoax of pantheism. Which modernism had cast in the lazy key of aestheticism. Nature. God, Art, Madness, Death.

The infant Stefan began "writing" him letters. This was the pass they'd come to! The letters were in Dora's hand, but Scholem suspected Walter had much to do with their content. They might have appeared playful, but they were actually harrowing. The opening salvo complained that if "dear Uncle Gerhard" turned up at Papa and Mummy's place, "You will again tell me so many things that I won't be able to get a word in edgeways. Well then first I must tell you that you ought to know I no longer remember. For if I could remember, I certainly would not be here, where it so unpleasant and you are creating such a bad atmosphere; no, I long since would have returned where I came from." Stefan wanted to crawl back into the womb because of Uncle Gerhard! "I won't say anything about my mother, because she is, after all, my mother," the letter continued. "But I have all sorts of things to tell you about my father. You are wrong in what you write, dear Uncle Gerhard. I believe you really know very little about my Papa." A man like Benjamin, the letter went on, was born only once in an age. One just had to be kind to him, and he would take care of the rest on his own. "I don't want to be smart-alecky, for you know everything. That's the whole trouble," the letter concluded.

Gerhard was shattered. The idea that the man he'd designated as his prophet could accuse him of having failed utterly to comprehend his character flipped the world on its head. He tried to write back in a tone mimicking the note of lightly annihilating wit Benjamin and Dora had adopted. "Dear Stefan, the two of us know what's what," Gerhard began. "Let's continue to pretend that we still don't understand anything. After all, we are the youngest in the family and have to stand together against the older ones, who only want to suppress us. They're squeezing us dry, Stefan! But we won't stand for that..." Gerhard strains, but what he writes isn't really funny, and he knows it, and breaks off, ending by just composing a sonnet to the baby.

The strange exchange continued for weeks. Relations between him, Dora, and Walter got better, then worse. Worse, then better again. On the metaphysical plane, their dialogues were sublime; in the earthly dimension, they were deranged.

One evening shortly before the Armistice, he traipsed over to play chess. Dora was laid up in the next room, recuperating from Spanish flu. He and Benjamin chatted with her through the door while they played. Gerhard crushed Walter, and Walter was affable and recited sonnets to Heinle. They were planning to have supper together. Walter went into Dora's room around eight, and a fight broke out. Gerhard had no clue what precipitated it, but this one was a real smash-up. For a while Gerhard stayed glued to his chair, then he felt embarrassed being so close to the action and crept downstairs to the dining room. The maid had dinner ready. Usually, the couple got a grip fairly quickly and Walter, at least, would plod down eventually to retrieve Gerhard. But forty-five minutes went by and still he sat there alone. Should he eat without them? The maid was hiding in the kitchen. The soup was growing cold. You could hear Walter's feet creaking back and forth on the floorboards above. What was he supposed to do? He could hear all sorts of things now. He blushed. What were they up to? They didn't think about him at all! "I am not a eunuch to whom people expose themselves as they wouldn't to anyone else," he wrote in a frenzy. For two hours he sat there, listening and waiting, burning with shame, writhing in frustration. At last he forced the maid to go up and knock on their door. But no matter how hard she banged, they wouldn't answer. He left with no supper.

What anguish it was to be forced to witness a marriage like theirs turned monstrous! How could they treat him like an unfeeling nonentity?

Scholem watches the marital drama play out in the depths of a mirror mostly filled with his own horrified countenance. Unbelievably intense — happy to talk all night and all day — restless, judgmental, himself temperamental, prude and righteous, deaf to hints, blind to signals: Gerhard Scholem, for all his brilliance, was also the ultimate nightmare guest who won't go home until he's had the door slammed in his face.

Relations between him and the Benjamins swung back and forth manically for months, but gradually Gerhard began to find ways of placing a certain distance between himself and them — recalibrating the balance between his need for the physical expression of their friendship and the stimulation of their intellectual exchange, which required no proximity. It was Benjamin's *writings* that roused him to life, he noted in his diary. Gerhard observed that Hebel's aphorism, "If not everything is possible, the illusion of everything being possible is," was one of the most profound statements ever made. Their fantasy University of Muri glowed ever more radiantly as their real-life exchanges became cloudier.

When I think back on how I became involved with the Hebrew University, the logistics are shrouded in a fairy-tale mist of their own. It seems to me now that I more or less just wandered up Mount Scopus one day, scaling the rough, stony hill — passing the occasional Palestinian laborer smoking in the shade of a tree or rock overhang — into the walled garden of the university, found the admissions department, announced my intentions of studying there, and was immediately embraced.

I know that I'd reached my wit's end trying to think what to do next. Though I'd picked up a little freelance writing work, our economic situation was becoming dire. With the Jewish Theological Seminary apparently not my destiny, I had no idea what I would do on returning to the States. For we *would* have to return to America now, we assumed. And the realization made our hearts heavy. Where would we even go back to? Anne had grown up in New York, but mostly miserably, and our time together there hadn't further endeared the place to her. We weren't going to try the Washington DC area again, with its highways like the whorls on a hypnotist's coin. At some point the thought must have struck me that even if I couldn't impose my Central European literary curriculum on the religious program, I might yet pursue more traditional graduate literary studies at the university.

However it was that I first found my way there, it's no exaggeration to say that I'd never before found myself so warmly encouraged by any institution as I was by the School of Humanities at Hebrew University. I was offered a generous scholarship to study in the English and American literature departments. Before I knew it, I was enrolled in more advanced Hebrew classes and told that if all went well I would soon be eligible for an adjunct teaching position.

Indoors, the campus perched on French Hill was rather narrowly antiseptic — the jumble of newer buildings where most learning took place resembled those wings of an airport that are assigned to carriers from unprofitable countries — yet the university had an illustrious, feisty history. The school was initially funded largely by a cosmopolitan German banking family. Its first chancellor, Judah Magnes, a maverick American-born rabbi, infuriated many Zionists by refusing to advocate a Jewish homeland, instead repeatedly calling for a binational state in Palestine. "One of the greatest cultural duties of the Jewish people is the attempt

to enter the Promised Land, not by means of conquest as Joshua, but through peaceful and cultural means, through hard work, sacrifices, love and with a decision not to do anything which cannot be justified before the world conscience," Magnes proclaimed at the start of classes in 1929, just four years after Hebrew University's founding. The school's great mission, he said, would be to "reconcile Arab and Jew, East and West."

Magnes brought Scholem into the university as one of its inaugural scholars, legitimating Kabbalah as an academic discipline, and the institution became Scholem's lifelong home. Magnes also provided material support for Scholem's efforts to bring Walter Benjamin to Jerusalem, offering stipends and endorsing Benjamin's vague plans to become "a critic of Hebrew texts." There were interrupted traditions on campus that I felt drawn to revisit. I plunged enthusiastically into my studies. Before long, I was not only a student but also a junior faculty member. The idea of being paid to study and teach seemed magical.

Of course, this good fortune was not all the fruit of exchanges transpiring on the plane of higher thought. Though Anne and I came to Israel with no fixed return date, we'd never given much practical thought to the idea of becoming citizens. But by now people had made clear to us that there were all sorts of grants offered new immigrants, both at the university and beyond. Even without making a final commitment to the process of becoming Israeli, we could start getting some help — money toward rent, health care, and child support — on top of the payments I was already receiving from the university. It was great! No one, except our parents, had ever simply handed us money before. It wasn't so many thousands of shekels in the end, but it seemed like a lot to us then — and it made us feel good to be wanted in that materially substantiated way.

I didn't think about what this money meant regarding my relationship to the State as an entity. It barely crossed my mind to consider what State funds given to two New Yorkers from privileged middle-class backgrounds might *not* be financing as a result of having been allocated to encourage our settlement. I wasn't at the point of thinking in any but the most superficial fashion about what the State even consisted in. I needed money. I didn't scruple to take what I could get. Independence was not a virtue I'd ever much believed in, let alone prized. I wanted to write and to survive, and if the government of Israel was willing to help sponsor that undertaking, then my feeling was, to use the Hebrew vernacular, *bevakasha* — be my guest.

Zionism, it turned out, wasn't only a way of life; it could also be a way of making a living, or at least of starting to. How wonderful it seemed that when most countries were trying to seal off their borders, we found ourselves collecting checks to live somewhere foreign. (Similar financial considerations have played a role in

populating settlements in the Occupied Territories, where housing is often cheaper than in the major Israeli cities: I knew several young families who moved into settlements in the 1990s for
pragmatic economic reasons, despite their centrist politics, only
to edge farther and farther right over the years. When geography
is conceived as destiny, it becomes ideology, but simple financial realities can turn the same trick.) I felt good about being in
Israel. I didn't see myself subscribing to any compromised political
positions. Of course the Palestinians should have a state of their
own. Of course within Israel every ethnic group should be treated
as full, equal citizens. Of course the country should be a genuine
democracy. There. That was that.

Anne was soon pregnant again. We were making friends. We
liked the rhythm of life in Jerusalem: the slow slide into Sabbath
stillness, that charged pause each week. And I loved the fact that
the country wasn't only a Jewish homeland. Nothing was more
intoxicating about Jerusalem than being able to cross between
so many different temporal, ethnic, and theological worlds in the
course of a single walk. You could stroll from the Valley of Hin-
nom, where Moloch once devoured children in his fiery maw and
the Cinemateque now served up art-house films; to the eleventh-
century Armenian cathedral; on to the Wall, to the Rock, to the Gate,
to the Garden; up the Mount of Olives and down through East
Jerusalem, where there would still be time before nightfall for tea
in the Ottoman mansion that became the American Colony Hotel.

I was not oblivious of the reality of Palestinians being part of
the fabric of the world I'd entered. But their existence wasn't something I thought about much, beyond feeling glad that the presence
of another people stopped the place from being a monoculture. I
liked the Arab shopkeepers and the key holders to various semi-
hidden antiquities I'd come to be acquainted with in the course
of my Old City walks. Sometimes in those years it still happened
that older Palestinian women in traditional dress would appear in

the streets of Rehavia bearing great baskets filled with grapes, like bubbles of the sea nestled in vine leaves, crying in accented Hebrew as they walked, *Anavim, anavim.* Often it happened that when I was walking in the Valley of the Cross, or through one of the jagged ravines outside the Old City walls, a whistle or clinking bells would alert me to the passage of a flock of goats, shepherded by a couple of young Palestinians. The young men generally averted their gazes. But it was beautiful to see these remnants of an agricultural world wandering the margins of the city.

Yet slowly, even with the baby, work, and efforts to navigate this new society, some consciousness of the Intifada began to break through. The news was bloody and hard. The death toll was rising each month, and there were many children among the victims. Walking in the Old City, I couldn't help noticing how frequently stores were now shuttered for one strike or another. When shops were open, their owners were glum and taciturn. As the weather got better, skirmishes around Damascus Gate intensified. And sometimes I would find myself lingering nearby, watching the Palestinian youth darting in and out of sight behind walls while military jeeps gave chase, blue lights flashing, disgorging uniformed men clutching weapons. I'd stare, trying to understand what I was seeing. As though what I was seeing was not exactly what it seemed. As though I might penetrate the explicit scenes of violence and suppression to some more arcane truth. As if the fragmentized uprising of a discontented population against a public order they felt no stake in, and the harsh clamp-down by the State against that revolt, must be concealing another story.

Part of what I found confusing was the air of performance that imbued the actions of both sides — the repetitive, iconic gestures of defiance and command that gave the scenes of attack, flight, and capture the feel of archaic drama on a loop tape. Sometimes when you see rocks flying in Jerusalem, you can't help wondering if those very stones had been hurled at someone thousands of years ago.

I had a difficult time grasping the idea that an event can be simultaneously theatrical and real, that when roles are so ancient and reactive, the Furies obey scripts. Perhaps we've become self-justifyingly attached to the idea of there being great depths of complexity to the situation in Jerusalem, when the truth plays out right at the surface.

I listened in on conversations in public places trying to understand what was actually going on. Most of this debate was endlessly repetitive, but I was jolted one day when I heard some NGO type at a café in East Jerusalem say that the Palestinians were rioting not because they didn't have a state but because they didn't have any rights. That line stuck in my mind, trying to find a place in my vision of Jerusalem and failing to integrate.

At the same time I became friendly with a young man named Rafiq, who was in some of my classes at the university, one of very

few Palestinians doing graduate literary studies there. One day he
sat down at the table I'd taken in a café near the library and introduced himself. He remarked on a comment I'd made about Edgar
Allan Poe's "Fall of the House of Usher," which we were reading
then. He'd read Poe intensely for years, he said. But more than
my observation about Poe—whom Scholem named a "poet metaphysician," calling Benjamin's "Theses on the Concept of Justice"
something Poe might have written—Rafiq was curious about why
I was studying at Hebrew University to begin with, and what had
brought me to Jerusalem.

I stumbled through part of the story. He wasn't satisfied. Everything about him was rather intense, actually. He was wiry, jumpy,
long faced, good-looking, but too thin. Up close the ripples in his
cheekbones were so hard drawn it was as if he were being sucked
into a vacuum. His eyes were huge and black. He chain-smoked.
He pushed me for better answers, then very abruptly he receded,
softened—smiled, not quite relaxing, but showing another side,
lighting another cigarette. Now he was talking about his own studies. He'd read all he could to teach himself different subjects. Knew
several languages. But it had been very hard for him to get to the
university. It was very hard for him to continue studying. I didn't
quite follow but didn't want to press too hard. He drew a battered
paperback out of an old briefcase and read the end of Poe's story
aloud to me. I mumbled some cliché about the tale's power. Then
his face turned in profile again; the skin was chipped. He lit another
cigarette and our conversation trailed off. I went back to my book.

We met from time to time after that. Gradually, he began
exposing flashes of his life in the village close to Jerusalem that
he came from. It had become very difficult, he said—the army was
bursting in all the time. He was struggling with military checkpoints and problems with identity papers. But it was beautiful
there, he said. He invited me to visit; his uncle who worked in the
Old City could bring me. But shortly before the appointed date,

some complication arose and he said my visit would have to be postponed. He was noncommittal when I invited him back to my own apartment in West Jerusalem.

Then one day he met me and his face looked ravaged. He began telling me what he'd been through the night before. The story was jumbled and his sentences kept breaking down. But his mother had been shoved by soldiers who'd crashed into the house, and she had fallen to the floor. He'd been hit by a rifle on the back. Why would they do this? The image he painted of the dense little village swarmed by wailing military vehicles came to life. Crackling loudspeakers. Ricocheting lights. Terror and rage kept changing places while he spoke.

I expressed my shock. Sorrow. Shock. Sorrow. Slowly he seemed to calm, fractionally, his eyes cooling.

It began to happen more and more that he would spend the night with a relative in Silwan to avoid the hassles of trying to get in and out of his village. But he missed his family and felt guilty about leaving them alone. "I want to get my degree," he kept saying. "I want to learn. I want to teach. I want to learn." Then Rafiq missed several classes in a row and fell behind. At last he stopped coming to class altogether. After an absence of several weeks, we ran into each other in one of the wide, blank corridors of the campus near the wing of administrative offices. We sat a moment in a big window embrasure. He began explaining that he had to take some time off from his studies — and then just stopped talking. We shook hands. And that was all.

Now, when I read Poe's "House of Usher," everything converges: the university, the village, his eyes, the destruction. "The radiance was that of the full, setting, and blood-red moon, which now shone vividly through that once barely discernible fissure...extending from the roof of the building, in a zigzag direction, to the base. While I gazed, this fissure rapidly widened — there came a fierce breath of the whirlwind..."

But you learn to live with a compromised view, like living in a house with cracked windows you can't afford to replace, and so just keep crisscrossing with tape, until you see only what holds the pane in place. I told myself the Intifada couldn't go on forever. So many Israelis I spoke to wanted peace. Besides, the uprising didn't *really* affect me, except as a mild, gnawing regret that relations weren't better—a feeling like periodically remembering something you keep forgetting to do and then postponing again when memory does come to you.

Three years of knowing Walter Benjamin—"of an attempted and unrealized fellowship with him," as Gerhard put it—had educated him, goading him on and confining him. And now their friendship would either have to pass into history or sublimate into some purer form. Either way, Gerhard decided what he required above all at this point was order.

In pursuit of this grail, Gerhard enlarged his meditations on distance as a moral necessity. Just as he'd argued that one couldn't merge with the landscape without succumbing to pantheistic delusions, Gerhard began formulating a position against even the aspiration to unite with the Divine. In place of immediate presence and union, his evolving theological vision depended on separation and suspension, two principles that he absorbed not only from Jewish religious texts but also from the psychological demands of his relationship with the man he'd sought to mold into his Personal Redeemer. One could have an "absolute relationship" with Benjamin only "from afar" he decided. "Faith itself is a relationship based on a distance," he noted around this time.

Hitherto, Scholem's ideas and observations, inspired and demented alike, fall from his journal and letters in a furious storm. They're like snowflakes—fascinating, intricate crystals that melt in your hand when you try to catch one. But something happened around the time of his twenty-first birthday. Insights began sticking and accumulating. He noted that despite having been labeled an incurable maniac a year earlier, since his military discharge he'd *not* become crazier. The real question was whether, given the chaos in Germany, it would be possible to continue studying there, or whether he would have to become a pioneer in Palestine before being fully spiritually prepared for this vocation. For Germany itself had gone utterly mad, he realized. In 1914 he'd proclaimed the imperative of being revolutionary. Now, it appeared, a revolution was actually beginning in Germany, but it wouldn't climax on a messianic note. "In the days of the Messiah man will no longer quarrel with his fellow but with himself," the mystical Rabbi Israel of Rischin had observed. Self-division didn't always indicate confusion or fraudulence, Gerhard now believed. While disjunctive traits in ordinary individuals signaled hypocrisy, in a truly visionary character they might echo the illusion of contradiction within God Himself. "That ever-flowing fountain [of emanation from which the Torah originates] has different sides, a front and a back; from this stem the differences and the conflicts and the varying conceptions regarding the clean and the unclean," said one Kabbalist.

In a brief spell of harmony near the end of 1918, Gerhard entertained Dora and Walter at the room he'd rented on the edge of a woodland. Over the course of a long evening together, they talked about the Ten Commandments and the Laws of Torah until, at some point, Gerhard felt moved to read them a draft of the essay he'd begun on the Book of Jonah. It was arguably his first important work of biblical criticism, and a kind of gift offering for all Benjamin had taught him.

The Bible story begins with Jonah getting ordered by God to go cry to the people of Nineveh that their wickedness is so terrible it's come up before Him—the warning knock God often gives before He wipes out a place.

Jonah balks at delivering the prophecy. We don't know why at first. He runs off to Jaffa and boards a ship to Tarshish. The ship embarks and a huge storm whips up the sea. The crew realizes this is no ordinary tempest. After casting lots to discover who brought this disaster upon them and discovering that Jonah is somehow to blame, they question him. He confesses. "I'm a Hebrew and I'm afraid of the Lord who made both the sea and the dry land."

The sailors are terrified. "What are we supposed to do with you?" they wail.

"Toss me overboard," he suggests.

The men worry for a minute or two about incurring God's wrath for killing Jonah, but after a quick prayer for mercy, they chuck him into the water.

Once in the deep, instead of drowning, Jonah gets swallowed by a whale. He's inside the whale's belly for three days and nights. He might have resigned himself to death, but he can't bear being trapped inside the dark body of the sea monster. He begins praying to God and making all sorts of promises—including the vow to go off to Nineveh to invoke doom upon that city.

At this, the whale vomits him out, and Jonah trudges off to do God's bidding, shouting around the city, "Another forty days and Nineveh shall be overthrown."

This is where the last act of the story begins, which Scholem's essay focuses on.

After hearing Jonah, the people get the message. They put on mourning clothes and begin fasting while crying to God for mercy. And it works. God repents of the evil He was going to do. He calls off the destruction.

Jonah is incensed. "Oh Lord, was not this my saying when I was still in my own country?" he complains. Jonah tells God this is why he ran away in the first place: He knew God was gracious, slow to anger, and full of love, so He wouldn't carry through on His threat.

In a sulk, he stalks off to the east side of the city to see whether God will now finally keep His word and wreck the place. The sun beats down on Jonah's head as he sits there. God makes a castor oil plant sprout up to shade him, and Jonah is very happy about the plant. The next day, God makes a worm appear who attacks the plant, so that it shrivels up and leaves him in the full blaze again. Jonah faints in the heat and begs to die.

The book ends: "God said to Jonah, 'Art thou so greatly vexed on account of the plant?' And he said 'I am greatly vexed to death.' Then the Lord said, 'Thou art concerned about the castor oil plant…which came up in a night and perished in a night: and should I not be concerned for Nineveh, that great city in which are more than one hundred and twenty thousand persons that cannot discern between their right hand and their left hand; and also much cattle?"

The Book of Jonah is unique, Scholem explained, for being the only work in the prophetic canon that, instead of being comprised of prophecies and petitions, focuses on the prophet's own biography. Through Jonah's life story, the book conveys "the very key to understanding the prophetic idea in general," he commented. With God playing the role of exemplary teacher, and the prophet that of typical student, the narrative became a pedagogical case study in which a person "is taught a lesson about the order of what is just." The profundity of the book lay in its simplicity, Scholem maintained. "One could derive the concept of children's literature from it: *Jonah is a childlike person.*" The book is also comically ironic: "The prophet does not understand prophetism; what he does is essentially politics."

Jonah's great error, in Scholem's estimate, is to confuse the categories of history and prophecy. When he prophesies "another forty days and Nineveh shall be overthrown," Jonah believes he's communicating a fact; from God's perspective, though, Jonah is delivering a warning. Like those historiographers whom Scholem found offensively reductive because they presumed that history unfolded according to rigid laws—Hegel and Marx at their vanguard—Jonah deduces on the basis of Nineveh's past behavior that the city's character is fixed. Hence its annihilation is a cosmic-moral necessity. Appraising the sins of Nineveh, "Jonah takes the standpoint of the law," Scholem writes, while "God takes that of justice." The meaning of justice in its deepest sense is that "judgment is allowed, but the execution of it remains something entirely different." Invoking the imperative of human intervention in fate—against the law of nature—Scholem writes, "Justice is the idea of the historical annihilation of divine judgment." For all his sharp vision of the wrongdoing happening in Nineveh, Jonah appears unable to perceive that the place is also over-spilling with life—contains a multitude of helpless people, not to mention much cattle. What Jonah cannot see when he rages at God about the failure of His promise of destruction to come true is that he, the prophet, is fatally self-absorbed.

Aspects of Jonah's character, in particular his black-and-white perspective on profound moral questions, seem less childlike than adolescent. His sulks and rages against the Divine call to mind, in fact, Gerhard's own youthful outrage at God's careless handling of creation, and his displays of zealous righteousness before Walter and Dora. But here, in this mediated form, Scholem appears able to wrestle with the peril inherent in trying to impose notions of purity on others. He examines the way that failure to project one's own high-minded ideals onto reality can trigger an urge to destroy the real world.

On the deepest level, what Jonah fails to understand is simple: People and societies can change and are extremely hard to create, so even when they're screwed up, don't kill them. Instead, find ways to influence behavior.

The problem Scholem's Jonah faces exemplifies the challenge of asymmetrical warfare. God is the Great Power who can unleash mass death at any moment in response to what He judges to be dangerous wickedness. But to what end? What is an *effective* use of destructive capacity if the objective is to halt evildoing rather than just confirm a sense of nihilistic hopelessness among the survivors? In the realm of the just, God teaches Jonah, the Last Judgment will be forever deferred by the true prophet's message, which must inspire even the genuinely wicked to change their ways. The postponement of judgment becomes a form of distancing that enables the perpetuation of justice. While the Torah allows for the death sentence, it "enacts the idea of deferral" by making the standard of guilt so stringent that execution is all but impossible. Scholem cites as evidence the story of a law court that executed a single death sentence in seventy years and was deemed homicidal by Talmudic commentators.

The burden of proof constraining the court might apply, as well, to the state seeking to justify the execution of military judgment against a general population, even one harboring real evildoers in its midst. From the prophetic perspective, the balance of responsibility shifts from the community pronounced guilty by the state—a community that God sardonically, resignedly, perhaps even affectionately says does not know its right hand from its left—to the state itself that must find the language that will catalyze a change in behavior such that the call for destruction itself becomes anachronistic.

After hearing the essay, Walter and Dora were both stirred. Walter pronounced himself *very* pleased. Dora began eagerly questioning Gerhard about when it was possible to violate the Laws of the Torah. Their spirited discussion continued late into the night.

And then Gerhard was alone once again.

EIGHT

THE WAR between the Great Powers sputtered to a close in November 1918. Germany and Austria collapsed. The Bolshevik Revolution exploded. For a time in Germany, the Spartacans, a radical Socialist party led by Rosa Luxemburg and Karl Liebknecht, Scholem's former pacifist hero, appeared to be sweeping into power. "Our goal is communism, freedom's golden land of anarchy!" the Spartacans declared. On November 9, while machine-gun companies occupied the forecourt of the Potsdam Station and infantry fire echoed across Berlin, the Spartacan revolutionaries, drawn heavily from the disaffected rank and file of the armed forces, seized the palace and the Police Presidency. Soldiers ripped off their cockades and epaulettes. Iron crosses littered the streets like calcified ashes. Two of the city's largest newspapers were commandeered and began printing communistic declarations. The bells of Berlin's illuminated cathedral rang out in celebration of a proletarian victory.

The emperor abdicated and fled to Holland. Within a few days, a variety of political clubs and councils aligned with different left-wing parties butted to the fore of the melee: People began joking there'd soon be a Council of Abdicated Princes. The Workers' and Soldiers' Council posted a big sign in front of Arthur's printing shop: COMMUNAL INSTITUTION! TO BE PROTECTED! Troops with red armbands were planted at the doors. How could Gerhard help smirking at the thought of his father being forced to allow Socialist revolutionaries to secure his business?

Ostensibly the struggle in this first phase of the insurrection was between Spartacans and their allies, who sought the immediate socialization of all means of production under a dictatorship of the proletariat, and the Majority Socialists, who endorsed some kind of democratic process. In reality, things were always more layered and crisscrossed. Recently minted revolutionaries joined the Spartacan occupation of the Reichstag. The place was swarming. In the palace, cigarette butts splotched the carpets, along with dirt and rubbish from the streets. Droves of armed civilians, military veterans, and deserters packed the lobby. Liebknecht took to sleeping in the kaiser's old bed, infuriating the aged palace servants. Outside the seats of power, things seemed to be calming down. "The colossal, world-shaking upheaval has scurried across Berlin's day-to-day life much like an incident in a crime film," the urbane diplomat Count Harry Kessler observed.

The Armistice had barely caught Scholem and Benjamin's attention. The revolution was different—a bit. A general strike in Switzerland coincided with events in Germany, halting the printing presses. But after this was put down by the Swiss military, and word began filtering back about the chaos in Berlin, Gerhard worried that Walter had become so dangerously overwrought that he was making himself sick.

Soon, the two men started debating the Spartacan goal of securing a workers' monopoly on power. Benjamin voiced strong opposition to any kind of dictatorial government, while Scholem argued in favor of a "dictatorship of poverty," which he distinguished from a dictatorship of the proletariat. To Escha Burchardt, a young woman he'd met some months earlier through Zionist circles, he wrote that while the vacuity of the war had always been apparent, the revolution, which unquestionably had a contingent historical justice on its side, at least merited watching. "I take it into my field of vision," he noted, "nothing more than this, though also nothing less."

Before the end of the year, he attempted a fuller reckoning with prospects for the righteous implementation of political power, in an essay on the Bolshevik Revolution. Unlike what he called the pseudorevolution in Germany of 1848, which, with its strong middle-class backing, promulgated the false belief in "progress," the Bolshevik Revolution operated with the knowledge that the messianic kingdom could not be reached through gradual reforms. Its claims to justice arose out of the absolute *injustice* of conditions of life for the poor. The premise of bolshevism, Gerhard proposed, was a magical dictate: "The messianic kingdom can only unfold in the dictatorship of poverty."

But while he defended the principle in conversation with Benjamin, on reflection his approval was qualified. If a dictatorship of poverty is essential for invoking the Messiah, this means that only the impoverished deserve revolutionary power—and, concomitantly, that the poor can never be unjust. Yet if the poor attained power, were they then obliged to maintain their poverty in order to keep justice on their side? Moreover, if the poor *are* the perpetual, de facto guardians of justice, then "Moscow's theory of the firing squad" must be deemed morally valid, since the poor are its executors. This notion turns the idea of divine judgment upside down, Scholem commented. "It kills in the name of a mission." The dichotomy between true justice and judgment he'd explored in his interpretations of the Book of Jonah here found expression in the real-world dilemma of the Russian Revolution. By late 1918, it was apparent to Scholem that the Bolsheviks' determination to seize power not only from autocrats but also from the Divine would result in an unending series of death sentences aimed at preserving transcendent authority over the here and now.

Abruptly, Scholem veered into his theory of how Judaism opposed this structural logic: "Revolution exists where the messianic kingdom is to be established without the teachings," he wrote, referring to Jewish tradition and the Torah. A strictly political revolution would never produce a truly just society since it could only replace one earthly power with another. "For this reason there *can* be *no* revolution for the Jews," he resolved. The teachings superseded the entire framework of worldly politics. Bolshevism was correct in its position on labor but mistaken in believing that it could act simultaneously in the current historical moment *and* "futuristically," by implementing a system of legal judgment that implied its utopian revolutionary aims had already been achieved. For himself, Scholem wrote in the draft of a letter to a friend, the only choice was anarchism. Not because anarchism was ideal but because anarchism, in its resistance to any uniform organization of power, its insistence on maximal autonomy, and its total opposition to the present-day social order, could be considered the ideal precursor to the divine reign. Anarchism, he wrote, was "a theocratic state of mind" that refused the convenience of ethical compromise. "I am, so to speak, too far to the left for today's revo-lution. I am *entirely* beyond this revolution."

Since early youth, Scholem had refused to invest any absolute principle with fixed content, positioning the highest concepts in his spiritual lexicon as directions or channels, not definable prop-ositions. Thus, when he was only seventeen he'd written that "God is at best the aim of deeds we seek to achieve, but not something that is, that exists." Two years later, he asserted that "Torah is not a law, just as Judaism is not a religion. Torah is the transmission of God and divine things." Torah was a path for rediscovering truths that had been written down in holy books but that could no longer be understood. Now, at the end of the First World War, Scholem was intensifying his efforts to frame Zionism along sim-ilar lines. Zionism, he wrote, was the object of his life, a "tradition of a way of life," not a political platform; as such it constituted for him "a movement within Torah." The Zionist life was necessar-ily "very silent" and spoke a "quiet language," he added, invoking his and Benjamin's work on silence as the antidote to the murder-ous chatter of the times. Ultimately, Scholem sought in Zionism a language for simultaneously repudiating the violence engulf-ing Europe *and* for catalyzing solutions to the Continent's social ills that would resonate beyond the Jewish problem. Zion, he'd written earlier, would be built out of all humanity's suffering—it would be nothing other than the common humanity that existed at the dawn of time.

While working on various political-theological tracts, Ger-hard was also yearning for Escha to join him in Switzerland. He'd decided by now that Benjamin was at heart an incorrigible revo-lutionary. This was the essence of everything that stood between them on the critical journey to Jerusalem. The two men got in a fierce argument on a brief walking trip when Benjamin suddenly announced that he saw their ways of life as fundamentally identi-cal. A few years earlier such a declaration would have been thrilling to him; now it struck Scholem as oblivious of his own investment in Jewish tradition. From his perspective, Walter and Dora existed in a dissolute whirlwind while the secret moral order of his own life sustained him. "Religion is the consciousness of the Order of things," he announced.

Though he'd barely met Escha in person, Gerhard had been conducting an expressive correspondence with her throughout his travails. And his efforts now to bring more structure to his inner life involved not only distancing himself from Benjamin but also slowly — with occasional relapses — letting go of his fixation on Grete Bauer and replacing that with this woman who represented perhaps the least stormy character from his student coterie in Germany. He

described Escha as "the type of mother God intended." She floated in his imagination: "very pretty and very large, with eyes like those of a very young girl." She had an absolute directness of being. Gerhard wrote her not even much caring, he confessed, how often she answered but happy to be engulfed in her "wordless silence."

When the two at last were able to spend time together in Switzerland, he kissed her many times, while also telling her that he couldn't have a lover just then. In his view, she wanted everything she could get from him — most of all to have children. She was languishing without children, he wrote in his diary, and that was horrible. One *ought* to love her, he told himself, because she had such a deeply feminine movement about her and movement gave the world order. One night he went to see *Hyena of Lust: The Greatest Sensation of the Year*, a blockbuster film about the white slave trade, and came away despondent that almost all the slave traders were Jews, religious men among them. The image of proletarian Jewish girls being shipped off to Buenos Aires as prostitutes was the epitome of blasphemous Judaism. Escha now embodied in his imagination the holistic Jewish purity that the Benjamins had casually demolished with their expedient falsehoods, material indulgences, and surprising concern with social appearances. In these dark times, a life of justice could be achieved only through renunciation, and while his own notion of renunciation was all-embracing, the Benjamins felt there were objects and attitudes they had a right not to surrender. "Walter and Dora's notion of propriety is catastrophic," he decided.

During the weeks following the initial Spartacan victories, sporadic outbreaks of violence disrupted supplies of basic provisions throughout Germany. "No one commands, no one obeys. Conditions are miserable," Betty Scholem wrote Gerhard. She'd been biting her nails down to the quick. As the Spartacans alarmed and outraged the Scholems by driving around Berlin firing off machine guns, the reactionaries disturbed them no less by issuing propaganda leaflets that blamed all disorder on the Jews.

Everyone clamored for answers about what had been achieved and where things were heading. Although some in the international press reported on massacres taking place across Berlin, others began wondering whether the whole revolution had been exaggerated. Liebknecht, with his pained stare and pince-nez, was caricatured as "a man of declamations and parades" who surrounded himself with machine guns, then shouted for the Berlin populace to mutiny. Reading about the deadly Grand Guignol made Gerhard's commitment to truthful language all the more fierce — which prompted further outbursts against his brother.

Werner had begun working at a Socialist newspaper after the armistice. Gerhard picked up several issues with curiosity. But reading them convinced him that any vestigial hopes he entertained for his brother's party were misplaced. If the Socialists ever got into power, "the shocking baseness" of the paper's language would lead directly to violence, he charged. The workers had trusted the Socialists, and the Socialists had answered that trust with demagoguery. "Because you fed people an impure language, rotten ideology, and self-righteousness…your regime will unavoidably drown itself in a sea of blood," he prophesied. Instead of using language to make people realize what a just future would look like, language was being used to salve pangs of conscience in the present. In his journal, Gerhard delivered a bleak prognosis for the fate of intellectuals under a Socialist regime: Since people who think for the sake of thinking recognize no limits and cannot conform to any group mentality, they would challenge the very premise of economic socialism and have to be murdered.

Relations with his parents mellowed, a little, with time and distance. Betty managed to patch up a functional rapprochement with Arthur, and in the spring Gerhard wrote them to announce that he'd figured out his study plans. He was going to finish his degree in mathematics and also acquire formal training in Jewish studies. With the mathematics degree he could teach in Jerusalem. In light of the ongoing disruption ("constant putsches and riots" was how Betty characterized life in Berlin), this scheme could no longer be considered preposterous. Fluency in Hebrew would enable him to get supplementary work as a translator. He hoped this proposal would strike them as reasonable, he wrote, so that they would bankroll his studies. He didn't intend to tax their generosity forever, he stressed, pointing them to a translation of a Bialik essay he'd recently published in Buber's *Der Jude* as evidence of his stature among people who counted. Arthur grudgingly agreed to sponsor Gerhard's doctorate, noting that he'd passed his son's article straight on to Betty. ("Sorry to say, it's all over my head.")

Gerhard's letter was couched as a frank outline of his academic plans, but he'd been candid only up to a point. For one thing, notwithstanding Germany's problems, Scholem knew that his fixation on moving to Palestine removed all pragmatic justification for the pursuit of a doctorate—in Jewish studies or anything else. There was no university in the country to work at. Indeed, as he later wrote, "The renunciation of ambition was a primary factor in my decision to go to Palestine…Anyone who went over there in those days could not think of a career." There was another tactical omission from the letter as well: Gerhard had decided to focus his thesis on kabbalistic literature. Having now spent years filling notebooks with quotes, translations, and interpretations of the Kabbalah, "the bacillus had taken hold," he admitted. By composing his dissertation on the linguistic theory of the Kabbalah, he felt he would be able to fuse his interests in philosophy, mysticism, and philology in a Judaic key.

He informed Escha that he saw himself developing an astonishing conception of philology, "which should be discussed only with the greatest reverence. Philology is truly a secret science and the only legitimate form of historical science that has existed until now." His investment in this idea reflected the conviction that by penetrating etymological layers down to the origins of specific terms, you could reach an ur-historical truth about concepts, clarifying the nature of their authentically Jewish content along the way.

Benjamin responded enthusiastically to the plan. Gerhard set about enrolling at the University of Munich, where Germany's greatest collection of kabbalistic manuscripts was archived. Benjamin himself was in the final stretch of completing his doctorate. Scholem visited him and Dora on Lake Brienz in June 1919 while he was preparing for his oral examinations. Things were playful and exhilarating with the trio once again. The night after Benjamin sailed victoriously through his tests, they celebrated, trying to outdo each other telling "meaningless-meaningful stories" about Pappelsprapp, a make-believe land invented by Dora. Their high spirits continued through July when, at a belated birthday party for Walter, Gerhard presented him with a copy of *Das deutsche Gaunertum*, the classic work on German criminals, which included a long account of Jewish gangsters—a topic that Jewish historiography had shunned but that Scholem found highly appealing. It seemed a perfect complement to the "Jewish 'upperworld' of mysticism," he felt. "The crooks as God's people—now that would be a movement," he remarked.

Comedy's philosophical possibilities had long fascinated both men. Benjamin argued that only in humor was language able to be truly critical. Through humor's unique "critical magic," the counterfeit substance in literature was disintegrated. The ash left behind by this "heavenly unmasking" was genuine. "We laugh about it." Gerhard, meanwhile, had been convinced since adolescence that Jewish comedy had a singular capacity for piercing the self-deception of the assimilationists. Of two Jewish works of fiction on his parents' shelves, one was a joke book, and he relished its contents as a vital tonic: "Honesty directed against ourselves" was the essence of Jewish humor, he wrote. Nothing so infuriated him as the Jews' tendency to falsify their identity. He declared at one point that just as his commitment to Zionism hinged on its anti-apologetic attitude, so he'd decided to devote himself to investigating Kabbalah because its subject matter "conflicted with the apologetic Jewish historiography of the day." The truth-revealing potency of comedy and Kabbalah were parallel—perhaps even cognate—phenomena: "From Cervantes and Shakespeare to Jean Paul, humor is an essential form of mysticism," he declared. Moreover, comedy's unique type of self-accusation aligned jokes with the principle of divine justice explored in his Jonah essay. For no punitive action followed the accusation in Jewish comedy—there was no execution of judgment. Scholem observed that an age-old Jewish legal principle maintained that someone who accuses himself cannot be condemned. "Laughter is the unending acoustical resonance of adjournment," he avowed.

Just before Scholem was to head back to Germany, his friend Leo Bramson dropped by his room to tell him that Chaim Weizmann, acknowledged leader of world Zionism, was in Berne. He would be delivering a speech to local initiates at the train station that night.

No one could have had a better sense of the basic challenges in store for young Zionists than Weizmann, who'd been a clear-eyed force in the movement from the start. One of eleven children born to an Orthodox timber merchant in a village near Pinsk, he'd started off in cheder, then did such a stunning degree in science and mathematics at the Real Gymnasium in town that he won admission to one of Berlin's finest technical schools. Living in Berlin allowed him to take the measure of the Western Jews' Orientalist fantasies firsthand. After having viewed them as "wild men from the uncivilized East," the Germans came to know the

Russian-Jewish students and "developed a kind of liking for us — or perhaps merely a weakness," Weizmann recalled in his memoir.

From there he moved on to the University of Geneva, where he studied chemistry. Between the two cities, he got involved with Zionism, which he saw as the strongest counterforce to the ethos of assimilation. Weizmann, no less than Scholem, had been inspired by the work of Ahad Ha'am, the early Zionist thinker who'd eloquently condemned the spiritual slavery of so-called emancipated Western Jewry while also criticizing the impatience of those Zionists who wanted to advance pell-mell, without advancing the Jews' inner rehabilitation as an essential prerequisite to their resettlement in Palestine.

Weizmann had always viewed his contemporary Theodor Herzl as fatally impetuous. ("Everything must be done immediately!" Herzl remarked in 1895 of his Zionist plan.) His whole approach was "*simpliste* and doomed to failure," Weizmann argued. He'd never put much faith in the rich Jews Herzl went courting. And Herzl's Zionism was just too abstract. He was "not of the people" and never managed to "grasp the nature of the forces which it harbored," Weizmann contended. To Russian-Jewish realists like himself, Weizmann said Zionism was an organic force, "which had to grow like a plant, had to be watched, watered and nursed, if it was to reach maturity." But in truth he, too, was ready to move precipitously when doing so made tactical sense, even if only for symbolic reasons. The previous summer he'd been in Jerusalem, laying the cornerstone of Hebrew University, which at that point lacked a building plan, financing, faculty, and students, while General Edmund Allenby gazed on incredulously, reminding Weizmann that the war was ongoing. "This will be a great act of faith—faith in the victory which is to come and faith in the future of Palestine," Weizmann explained. At the end of the ceremony they sang "Hatikvah" and "God Save the Queen." Weizmann confessed later that at that moment their hopes for the university "seemed as remote as the catastrophe of the Roman conquest." By the time of his appearance in the Swiss train station in August 1919, Weizmann was counseling fellow Zionists that given their lack of clout relative to the Great Powers, they would have to create their title to the land out of "our wish to go to Palestine."

Weizmann's notion that "ripeness is all" accorded with Scholem's feelings that a premature implementation of Zionist ideals would be disastrous. But in Weizmann's case, the call for patience referred less to concerns about the inner readiness of Zionists themselves than to the imperative of gauging the temperature of global opinion to determine how much pressure could be exerted at each stage to cultivate support from the European nations without stirring Arab resentment. "One has to be careful not to turn the screw too tight. It is slow, it is disagreeable...but I think it would be worse if you had riots in Palestine," he said when attacked for not moving faster.

Weizmann didn't want to rush things, but he was advancing relentlessly toward the goal of a state. His own roots in Russia made the early-twentieth-century pogroms indelible, lashing his conscience to negotiate a Jewish national refuge. Scholem could sympathize with that sense of mission, but not share it. As he later assessed his own motivation to emigrate, "The problem was a personal, not a national, one." He admitted that he didn't know what his position would have been had he "come from among the impoverished Jews of Poland." In his own case, the question of Palestine was, he explained, *"is this the way?"* — meaning the way for himself. The eschewal of political objectives in favor of what we might call self-realization, while immunizing Scholem against strains of Zionism that sought to dispossess the Arabs for nationalist reasons, entailed a degree of sociological solipsism respecting both other Jewish predicaments and Arab concerns about large-scale Jewish immigration. Weizmann, on the other hand, saw himself channeling the will of millions "who had the rope around their neck, who could not live in the hell then called Russia," when he announced that Palestine "would become Zion whether the Sultan wants it, or whether anybody else wants it." This position was simply out of Scholem's geopolitical depth. So far from seeing himself speaking in the voice of the oppressed Jewish masses, Scholem tended throughout his youth to see *himself* oppressed by the Jewish middle classes — speaking *against* the will of the German Jews he knew who wanted to continue basking in the fleshpots of Berlin.

Scholem's daydream of a tiny "band of fanatics" devoted to clandestine theocratic-revolutionary activity could not have been farther removed from the main-stage diplomatic maneuvering of Weizmann, who'd been a principal force behind the Balfour

Declaration, the most unequivocal state endorsement Zionism had ever received. That document, published in November 1917, consisted of a letter from the British foreign secretary, Arthur James Balfour, to Baron Rothschild, expressing his government's favorable view of "the establishment in Palestine of a national home for the Jewish people," and extending the promise to work toward the achievement of that objective, insofar as this could be done without prejudicing "the civil and religious rights of existing non-Jewish communities in Palestine, or the rights and political status enjoyed by Jews in any other country." (On the document's release, Ahad Ha'am, who'd been one of Weizmann's advisers on its wording, noted, "The British Government promised to facilitate the establishment in Palestine of a National Home for the Jewish people, and not, as was suggested, the reconstitution of Palestine as the National Home of the Jewish people.")

Weizmann was often credited with having devised David Lloyd George's war strategy against the Ottomans, which culminated with Allenby's triumphant march into Jerusalem. Just as he'd assisted British war efforts to further his Zionist goals, he'd prevailed over the Zionists' own inner divisions, managing almost single-handedly to reconcile the political Zionists with so-called practical Zionists, who held that the goal of a Jewish homeland could be pursued most effectively by buying and cultivating land in Palestine (creating "facts on the ground") without first negotiating changes to the Jews' political status there.

Weizmann was a colossus, and the young people who'd shown up to hear him at the lecture hall in Berne's train station had high expectations. But an hour after the talk was supposed to begin, Weizmann was still up front whispering with the other nabobs. At Scholem's table, nothing but small talk and silence. He was starting to feel humiliated. The way everyone sat around like bovine peasants appalled him. One person was spooning up ice cream. Another was sipping tea. Maybe Weizmann was spent. Or he'd lost his voice. Who knew? Everyone just kept casting their eyes around the room, "as Jews do," Scholem observed.

A message got slipped into his hands with a few signatories: "What now?" Forty-five minutes later, Scholem announced he was leaving. Give it a minute more, people around him begged. He tried to make up his mind whether to declaim a few sentences in Hebrew about this indignity. Eventually someone asked whether maybe they *should* go. "Excellent," Scholem said, jumping to his feet. Mortified, the guy tried to tug him back down. Heaven forbid, a scandal! Scholem wrenched loose and strode out. No one chased after him. Did anyone even register his departure? He was horrified at himself for having sat there. God, what a debased people! This was supposed to be the time of their redemption. They spoke of noble labor and salvation—then sat around, like yokels in a barn, lapping up refreshments. He didn't have to go searching for some outside villain to explain why they hadn't been saved yet: It was their own psychotically fraudulent Jewish spirit that condemned them to exile. Scholem later discovered that Weizmann had been under the impression that he'd been attending some kind of student drinking party. Still, what kind of Zionist leader refrains from addressing an assembly, even of carousing students?

What got to him, he later wrote, was the way that "Zionists were creating assimilation within Zionism, imitating alien frameworks." This assimilation took various forms, depending on the branch in question. But it was always Jewishly inadequate from Scholem's perspective. The Zionist youth movement cut itself to the pattern of German nationalist youth movements. The Zionist elders (few in number) spoke of labor, salvation, and God knew what else while continuing to waddle through their bourgeois routines, devoid of the Teaching or any serious thought of relocating to Palestine.

Concerning the practical mandate of Zionism's leaders, Scholem was at once hopelessly conflicted—and fundamentally uninterested. His anti-authoritarian streak was the strongest, most consistent political value he ever espoused. Along with the admirable independence of mind his sensitivity nurtured, it also released him from having to bother with real forms of engagement.

Yet Gerhard was aware that by now Zionism itself had become a more credible proposition than ever before. At the Paris Peace Conference, which opened in the winter of 1919, various nationalist movements were appraised with a view to the revision of state borders consequent on colonial power shifts. With the collapse of the Ottoman Empire, the prospect of a Jewish homeland had earned a place in these discussions, alongside the assessment of Arab nationalist interests. Meanwhile, events in Europe after the armistice gave the Jewish cause new urgency. In Poland and Ukraine, pogroms connected with both the Russian civil war and fighting between Soviet Russia and independent Poland resulted in waves of slaughter unseen in the region since the seventeenth century. For these populations, war and mayhem didn't stop at the end of 1918 — or in 1919, or in 1920. The brutality against civilians was at once coolly premeditated and gorily regressive. In February 1919, a brigade of Cossacks entered the town of Proskurov in Ukraine and skewered fifteen hundred Jewish men, women, and children on bayonets, before hacking them to pieces with sabers. The Cossacks' commander had prohibited the use of guns since the sound might alert Jews on one side of town about what was happening on the other. Only after Soviet control of the region was secured in 1921 did bloodshed abate.

One of the arguments against the Zionist cause at the time — put forward by anti-Zionist Jews as well as non-Jews — was that the problem of Jewish human rights had to be addressed at once in the eastern Jews' home countries, without global attention being diverted to the establishment of some remote, inherently problematic new place of refuge. It was this conviction that led thirty-one prominent U.S. Jews (Henry Morgenthau Sr. and Adolph S. Ochs among them) to send a letter to President Wilson in the midst of the Paris negotiations, lobbying against the Zionist proposals.

While they shared the wish to protect Jews from the brutal consequences of their legal vulnerability in Russia and Romania, the solution in their eyes could take the form only of amending that stature with full citizenship. They raised their voices in "protest against the demand of the Zionists for the reorganization of the Jews as a national unit to whom, now or in the future, territorial sovereignty in Palestine shall be committed." For one thing, the number of Jews in the "lands of oppression" was estimated to be between six and ten million — a population that couldn't possibly be absorbed by tiny Palestine. Instead of ending the scourge against communities in the east, "the establishment of a Jewish state will manifestly serve the more violent rulers...as a new justification for additional repressive legislation," they cautioned. Moreover, "Whether the Jews be regarded as a 'race' or as a 'religion,' it is contrary to democratic principles for which the world war was waged to found a nation on either or both of these bases...'The rights of other creeds and races will be respected under Jewish dominance,' is the assurance of Zionism, but the keynotes of democracy are neither condescension nor tolerance, but justice and equality." A segregated nation would, of necessity, become a reactionary one. The letter writers concluded by expressing the hope that Palestine, "once a 'promised land' for the Jews may become a 'land of promise' for all races and creeds, safeguarded by the League of Nations."

Their petition has a noble, sensible ring. And in fact, partly as a result of the peace talks, Jews *would* soon be granted full rights across much of the Continent, including in postrevolutionary Russia, the Ukrainian republic, and the freshly united sovereign Poland. But as a solution to the Jewish problem, civil emancipation proved to be a historical trompe l'oeil. A fire exit that opened onto a brick wall. Within a handful of years, that same liberation would be rescinded, formally or in effect, at almost every place on the map where it had just been granted.

Despite all the ensuing troubles, it's hard not to be moved by the image of the winter scene at the Paris conference, when the little Jewish delegation, led by Chaim Weizmann and Nahum Sokolov, was given an audience at Quai d'Orsay before the Council of Ten, in a state room hung with tapestries of the gods. No body of Jewish representatives had been afforded a hearing of such grand international dimensions since antiquity.

"The Jewish people have been waiting eighteen centuries for this day," Sokolov began. "We claim our historic right to Palestine, to the land of Israel, to the country where we created a civilization that has had so great an influence upon humanity. We were a happy people in Palestine, but since we lost our motherland ours has been a long martyrology, of which I shall spare you an account." "Two thousand years of Jewish suffering" were visible in Sokolov's countenance as he spoke, Weizmann said.

No specific resolution emerged from the meeting, but Weizmann expressed satisfaction to the press, announcing that the historical title of the Jewish people to Palestine and the right of the Jews to reconstitute their national home had been recognized. He clarified that this didn't mean he'd requested a Jewish state, but rather the creation of conditions that would enable large numbers of Jews to settle in Palestine "on a self-supporting basis, to found their own schools, universities and other institutions—in short to establish an administration that will carry out our program and ultimately make Palestine as Jewish as America is American." The mere fact that in the court of world opinion, the Jewish commission to the Peace conference had, without fanfare, or even a gesture toward democratic ratification, become synonymous with a Zionist delegation represented an extraordinary validation of the cause.

Scholem closely followed these developments. He understood, presumably without regret, that one consequence of the war's end was a historic shift in Zionism's power base from Berlin to London. The center would have moved somewhere even without

Weizmann's influence, given Germany's defeat and the fact that many of the country's Zionists had fought for the kaiser and either been killed or lost credibility as enemy nationals. Scholem had to have been glad that the movement was advancing. But what exactly all the changes meant for his personal Zionism was unclear.

Around this time, a politically minded Zionist acquaintance asked Scholem whether he believed Jews thought in objects or concepts. His response was, "neither, nor." Jews think *linguistically*, he opined. Indeed, from the beginning, Scholem's decision to write his thesis on the linguistic roots of the Kabbalah was undertaken partly as a Zionist action. Every text hid a primal scene of inspiration and inscription, the recovery of which might electrify present-day Jewish consciousness, stimulating the people's will to reform, preparing them for the return to the Land that would culminate in the utopian restoration of humanity as such.

These different elements—Hebrew, redemption, Kabbalah, and Zion—all orbited the same circle in his consciousness, interpenetrating and reconfiguring their respective significances. In later years, Scholem recalled his youthful belief that "if there was any prospect of a substantive regeneration of Judaism, of Judaism revealing its latent potential—this could happen only here [in the Land of Israel], through the Jewish person's reencounter with himself, with his people, with his roots." But the long-dreamed-of territorial consummation for his whole quasi-semiotic Zionistic project made it also inherently political. For why should the necessary linguistic rehabilitation of the Jews be supported by the other peoples of Palestine? Particularly when that renewal took place through the medium of Hebrew, the language in which the Bible was written, with all its stirring promises of eternal Jewish property rights to the Land.

Scholem conceived of his Zionism as a cultural initiative to revitalize his own people, not to exercise control over another. But the belief that this reawakening had to transpire in the physical space of Palestine—at the point of origin of Jewish language and Jewish identity alike—trapped him in a kind of time machine. During the eighteen hundred years since the Jews had gone into exile, the Land had begun to speak other tongues.

I don't know when it happened that Anne and I ceased to "play house" in Jerusalem, what the transition moment was when we were no longer effectively cultural-historical tourists and began having to reckon with the idea that we were truly living in the Land. Immersed in Hebrew so much of the day, I know there was a time when I began to feel I was losing my "street English," and this troubled me. I loved the radical concision of Hebrew, which seemed as profoundly economical with words as a desert plant with water drops, but I valued it in counterpoint with the luxuriant abundance of English. I believe the hour of linguistic anxiety came late, however. After a time, the visa we were on as certified Jews in the homeland converted us to full-fledged citizens more or less by default, and this would be a natural point at which to assume we'd really switched over our identity. But I'm sure this official change happened before we'd assimilated on deeper levels. Perhaps the moment when we moved into the house that became our home until we left Jerusalem marked the changeover?

In the summer of 1989, we switched residences within Rehavia to an unusual compound of apartments a few blocks from the prime minister's residence. Conceived as workers' housing under the British Mandate, the two-story buildings faced with cement stucco were built on Bauhaus principles in a spirit of Socialist idealism, with each apartment allotted a little plot of earth for a garden. Upper-story flats like ours had large balconies. The apartment itself was modest but warm, with brown and yellow tiles patterned in rich arabesques that turned gold in sunlight and tea color in shadow. The back side of the buildings formed a wall

against the streets they bordered, and together they enclosed a garden courtyard, edged with tight blasts of hot orange trumpet vine and translucent lemon-satin honeysuckle. In its center was a small rectangle of grass with green benches at either end, one towered over by a great shaggy date palm, framed by clusters of nectarous pink and white oleander. A pomegranate tree dangled its big red-pink fruit like mumpy cheeks. There were countless nooks between the walls and bushes for children to plot schemes in. And we'd had our second child by then, another boy. His birth was so swift and eager, he'd seemed to leap into the world. We named him Tzvi, the Hebrew word for the gazelle in the Song of Songs to whom Solomon's beloved is compared, skipping upon the hills and perched atop a mountain of spices. Waiting for Anne's labor to build the August night he was born, we walked half the city, and the moon washed the sky and the stones with lavish white light, melding them. Everything in life glowed then.

There seemed to be innumerable children in the courtyard for ours to join. An elegant French modern Orthodox family had at least six offspring, kept in line by a commanding, sharply witty matriarch and a brusque, prominent cardiologist father. A musical Argentine family — the father was a doctor, the mother an artist-designer — had several children. A warm Australian family, with whom we became close, had sons almost exactly the same age as ours. Along with all the children were grandchildren. One of the founders of Jerusalem's Biblical Zoo lived in the courtyard. As did a respected elder poet and literature professor, from an old Jerusalem family, father of a rising female novelist. His wife was a painter. A woman who was a retired schoolteacher gave our son Yona a set of silkworms. By now, he was walking. We would often take him down when the heat of day had broken — the way it breaks almost every evening in Jerusalem, like a glass at a wedding — to sit in the shade and watch the little world, which was beautiful, and cloistered as the belly of Leviathan.

What we wished to see as a vibrant microcosm of Jerusalem in its diversity of origins, languages, and generations, its mixed degrees of faith and atheism, its general air of cultured liberalism, I now think by virtue of those same qualities was less microcosm than reliquary of a Jerusalem that had all but disappeared. Even there, the only Palestinians were the lone women who wandered through, peddling their harvest from villages remote to us as outer space, and the street sweepers and trash collectors we glimpsed through the gates.

But in truth, the boundaried nature of our idyll, too, was something we knew before we knew it, without knowing what to do with our knowledge. On our first Memorial Day in Israel, Anne walked outside to a busy intersection to observe the two minutes of silence that would commence with the siren of remembrance. Her eyes filled with tears as she witnessed all the cars stopping, followed by the drivers getting out and standing, like Giacometti sculptures, as the sirens wailed. Then she saw two Arab gardeners weaving their way through the frozen scene, tools balanced over their shoulders.

At first she felt shocked, wanting them to be still also, to at least acknowledge the moment's power. But then she reflected, "Why should they? Why should they want to honor Israel's dead even tacitly?" Even if cooperation and peace were possible, it could never be as "one nation under God," she observed afterward. "How could that be when, moved as I was standing there, I knew that if I were a Palestinian, I, too, would have kept walking?"

I suppose the moment when I was drafted into the Israel Defense Forces *did* change my status, although my profile as an army conscript never seemed entirely real, or even realistic. I was already old enough that it was unlikely — if not quite inconceivable — that I'd be recruited to perform true military service. I'd like to say that I at least undertook a sober, moral self-examination on receiving the IDF papers instructing me to show up for my physical and associated bureaucratic procedures. I'd prefer to record that I interrogated myself whether, in the event that I really was posted to, say, some remote guard outpost (I pictured a high scraggly hilltop with views of old Crusader ruins) where human lives would be placed under my protection, I was prepared to undertake that duty. Frankly, however, what I remember most is my curiosity. What would an army base look like? The sleeping arrangements would be what, exactly? What would be asked of me? I was so staggeringly technically incompetent that the thought of learning how to take apart and put together a gun required its own form of magical thinking. And what would they do to me if I simply couldn't learn? Would I go to jail for sheer ineptitude? Be struck?

How would I respond to being hit by an officer? I abhor conflict, but I've also never found myself able to stop from responding to a physical provocation, no matter how doomed in advance. The more I thought about it, the more likely it seemed that one way or another my military service would end with my being imprisoned by the IDF itself, and this would surely furnish a great deal of material to think and write about. How much paper and how many books would I be allowed in my cell? Would there be censorship? And would I memorize what had been censored, along with psalms and long poems and chess games to keep my brain humming the way Natan Sharansky had in his Soviet cell before he became a right-wing zealot in Israel?

One gloomy winter day I showed up at a large old building not so far from where we lived, with my packet of papers, and stood in line at a table in a bare, fluorescent-lit room where female soldiers were conducting the initial sign-in. I was trying to make a mental note of everything I saw and heard, and soon became aware by how sullen everyone seemed that this was a more serious occasion than I'd been willing to grant. I was in an obliging mood. Yet the unabridged answers and polite smiles I gave did not elicit even nominal good humor. When I was ordered on to the next station in this ritual, I was *ordered*, I realized. Looking again at the regulations on my draft papers as I plodded forward, I felt my brow furrowing. I had no choice but to do what I was told on this day or I'd end up in jail even before having been accepted, which seemed unduly preemptive.

It made me nauseous to feel I *had* no choice but to do what I was doing at that moment, regardless of how innocuous it might be. It made me feel dead. Over the next several hours, as I traipsed from one room to the next, and answered the questions put to me, and submitted whatever body parts I was summoned to exhibit for inspection, the experience became progressively more humiliating. Being forced to be part of a group took me back to the worst experiences of compulsory sports in middle school — the narrowed eyes of bitter gym teachers dangling jockstraps, like rodent parachutes, before the young draftees for some sadistic competition like Fox and Chickens.

I left feeling drained, and beginning to suspect that I might end up a not especially conscientious objector, without even starting basic training. However, after batting around my case for some months during which the prospects of my admission waxed and waned, I received notification that my tour of duty had been placed on indefinite hold for undisclosed reasons, which meant that, outside of the hassle of having to apply to the IDF for permission to travel every time I left the country, I was done.

My army service — my nonarmy service, my daylong bureaucratic runaround — was at least a step in the transition toward grasping that the nature of our personal identification with the society was not altogether discretionary. One degree of affiliation leads naturally to another. In moving to Jerusalem, one sets off a chain reaction, becomes part of the chain. Religiously, culturally and, perhaps, also politically, life in Israel had seemed to offer us an opportunity to be *of* the group but not *in* it, not bound to any particular form of group being. We thought to receive our Jewishness in Jerusalem by selective osmosis.

The moment when we realized we were not just absorbing our group identity vicariously but dispersing our individual identity into the group through the heavy filters of the army, the workplace, the schools — all those structures of institutional psychology we'd slipped through insensibly in America, like walls in a dream — changed our stature. We no longer felt quite like ourselves. But I would also say that the moment when we began to live a more knowingly illusory life was the same in which we began to lose some of our subtler illusions about where we were. And in this sense the process also conveyed a form of release. Or at least changed the terms of the spell.

NINE

IN THE SUMMER OF 1943, an advertisement began running in the *New York Spiritualist Leader*, a mimeographed journal read by those interested in psychic phenomena: "Haunted houses can be UNhaunted through mediums releasing the earthbound spirits — but Dr. Oskar Goldberg (Yale University research man, working from New York City) wants to photograph the apparitions first, by means of ultraviolet rays to PROVE THEIR EXISTENCE, thoroughly scientifically."

A *New Yorker* writer who set out to investigate the notice ascertained that Goldberg was "definitely not a nut," but a German scientist of considerable repute whose immigration to the United States had been sponsored by Albert Einstein, Thomas Mann, and other prominent exiles. After twenty years on the faculty of the University of Munich as a specialist in "Oriental psychology," he was now researching Eastern medicine at Yale. A "round, bald, kindly-looking man" in his late fifties from Berlin, Goldberg's studies had frequently taken him to the East. On one of these trips, he'd become acquainted with a guru in Kashmir who taught him to see ghosts. The only reason for psychic research was "releasing earth-bound ghosts — who are all unhappy," Goldberg said. He'd seen a couple of dozen ghosts over the years and witnessed the handiwork of twice as many poltergeists ("elementals" who hurled furniture about and broke things).

New York seemed unconducive to ghosts. After two years, Goldberg hadn't seen a single specimen — though he'd heard one in a vacant third-floor apartment in the far West Forties who objected to "nosy people" and ordered him to leave. But Goldberg hadn't given up. "Since we live now in a technical culture, we must prove immortality by technical means," he remarked. Hence his camera with special film sensitive to ultraviolet and infrared light. Striking a defensive note, Goldberg announced that whenever the opportunity to photograph a ghost did arise, he would insist on the presence of a team of experts to examine his equipment and remain on hand throughout the procedure. "I do not wish to go to this great trouble and then be termed a swindler," he said.

This unconventional professor roaming through Manhattan in search of spooks had, as the correspondent indicated, a noteworthy history back home in Germany. But it was not quite so benign as the magazine suggested.

It's unclear when Scholem first set eyes on Goldberg, whom he described as "a small, fat man who looked like a stuffed dummy" and "exerted an uncanny magnetic power over the group of Jewish intellectuals who gathered around him." His name had been circulating among circles close to Scholem for years. Ever since 1916 — when Goldberg solicited Buber's help interceding with the Foreign Office to get an exit permit for India, where he hoped to enlist Himalayan sages as a kind of spiritual special-ops force in Germany's war effort — it was obvious that Goldberg sought real influence on the global stage. That project flopped, but in the Weimar ferment Goldberg's star was ascendant.

Ten years Scholem's senior, Goldberg came from a devout family and had not only a deep knowledge of the Bible, which he drew on for numerological speculations, but also great fluency in Hebrew. As a student at Berlin's Friedrich Gymnasium, he'd tutored classmates in Talmud, among them the future philosopher of Jewish thought, Erich Unger, who influenced Benjamin. Later, Goldberg got involved in the Neopathetic Cabaret and rose to become one of its leaders. By the war's end, Goldberg had begun articulating a radical occult theory of Judaism, which emanated a "Luciferian luster" in Scholem's telling. While admirers gathered around him in salons of Munich and Berlin, Goldberg entered into "schizoid twilight states," Scholem wrote, from which emerged audacious revelations about the Torah, which "made him an absolute authority for the initiates."

Goldberg's doctrine was multifaceted, but the core idea was that Judaism had become insipid and impotent since its "Hebraic" heyday as a cult religion: "The god of the nation, who is present and effectual, the 'national god,' representing the metaphysical energies of the people, has been turned into the pallid, abstract, universal, 'good God' who is 'everything' and thus nothing at all," Goldberg wrote in his summary 1925 opus, *The Reality of the Hebrews*. Ritual practices as dictated by the Torah had once consisted of spells for harnessing God's powers. Temple offerings had nurtured His physical body. Reform Judaism represented the complete self-abasement of the Jews whereby, under pretense of "spiritualizing" the religion, they'd substituted prissy morals for cosmic, thaumaturgical energies.

Though Thomas Mann helped Goldberg emigrate, he caricatured him in his novel *Doctor Faustus* as Dr. Chaim Breisacher, a man of "fascinating ugliness," devoted to paradox as he mocked notions of progress. Asserting that "in the genuine religion of a genuine *Volk* such flabby theological concepts as 'sin' and 'punishment' simply did not occur," Breisacher left Munich society ladies "clasping their hands above their heads in a kind of prim jubilation."

Parts of Goldberg's critique of the limp and phony state of contemporary Judaism resonate with Scholem's perspective. Goldberg's disbelief in the category of "the universal," and his faith in the mystical potency of purified, archaic Hebrew as expressed through the Torah, parallel important themes in Scholem's thought. But the material literalism of Goldberg's idea of God—coinciding with his understanding of Jewish practice as a magical technique for attaining earthly power—diverged sharply from Scholem's theology. Goldberg shadowed the margins of Scholem's world in the 1920s, exciting his fury for framing the Bible as a primitive spell manual and haunting him for the ways their projects shared a family resemblance.

Goldberg was not the only charismatic figure to bubble up into public consciousness during the Weimar years, flogging ideas that bore affinities with Scholem's project to reinvigorate Jewish identity, albeit with a poison twist. There was also Walter Moses, the leader of the Blau-Weiss group, one of the nature-inspired youth groups that had formed in the early twentieth century and which, in the postwar years, developed an increasingly overt militarism. Modeling the Blau-Weiss on Italian fascism, Moses required members to subject their individual wills to strict regimentation—swearing oaths of lifelong fidelity to the cause and dressing in uniforms of brown shorts, blue shirts, and low boots as they trained for battle to forge a new, self-determinative Zionism. (The young Leo Strauss, who was a Blau-Weiss member, noted the group's "absolute negation of the sphere of the 'private,'" calling it "pagan-fascist"—only half critically.) At a 1918 youth festival, Moses frightened Buber, who'd hoped to make him an ally, by announcing that everything their fathers considered valuable they viewed as worthless. An "army of permanent preparedness" was in the making, he promised, which would achieve freedom through "unshakeable belief in the victory of power."

Scholem denounced all these developments as the "diabolical" fruit of frustrated authoritarianism. When Goldberg found it impossible to realize his dream of "magical dominance," he sought compensation "through the subjugation and exploitation of human souls," Scholem cautioned a friend. When Moses failed to manufacture an ideology of his own, he deployed what Scholem called "German romanticism in Zionist guise" to induce a "vacuous intoxication of youth for power" that made his decrees appear "beyond good and evil." But Scholem also knew that despite its reliance on what he labeled "unscrupulous mysticism," Blau-Weiss had become one of the most forceful critics of mainstream Zionism. Vowing that those who associated themselves with the emigration-driven Blau-Weiss would be vitalized, while their opponents would be doomed to perish with the bourgeoisie, Moses echoed, more crudely, Scholem's complaints against the assimilationist tendencies of German Zionists. Eventually, Moses even began calling for the establishment of a "culturally creative colony" in Palestine. Sometimes the malignant variants on Scholem's cherished ideals came so tauntingly near his own positions that he may have felt he was jousting in a fun-house hall of mirrors. Years earlier, Buber had begun invoking a new Jewish "primitivism" to reignite the faith; now Scholem was discovering how people's fascination with elemental religiosity could be whipped into a frenzy by those ready to sacrifice all restraints of civilization in pursuit of their own apotheosis.

Germany itself flickered in and out of a "schizoid twilight state" during this era. Ink on the Spartacan posters announcing the great proletarian victory was still glistening when Field Marshal Hindenburg entered Berlin, marshaling troops who remained loyal to the old government and proceeding systematically to crush the uprising. In the middle of January 1919, Liebknecht and Luxemburg were arrested. Luxemburg was flogged unconscious by a mob wielding canes in the Hotel Eden, then shot en route to Moabit prison. Liebknecht was shot in the back by the right-wing paramilitary Freikorps, who were supposed to have been transferring him to the same spot. All the chaos was, Betty Scholem informed Gerhard, "good for the printing business: handbills, proclamations, and placards follow each other in furious succession." She wrote to the sound of machine gun fire: A bullet had just blown through

a spleen on the local butcher's countertop. The clock on top of the nearby Spittel Market took a plug through the dial. Buildings all around were gouged by shells. Everything had changed. Nothing had changed. As the writer Kurt Tucholsky observed that March, "If revolution means merely collapse, then it was one; but no one should expect the ruins to look any different from the old building."

The squashing of the Spartacans did not, in fact, end the revolution. Like a fire that wouldn't extinguish no matter how hard it was stamped on, year after year there were new general strikes, interspersed with fresh clashes and assassinations. What could appear on the streets a repetitive, low-rolling storm revealed lurid flashes of a new order on a pullback view. As the right galvanized toxic hysteria around the menace of global conspirators out for the blood of the *Volk*, the left splintered and floundered. In a period of which even doctrinaire Marxist historians have written that workers were being incited to fight for reasons that grew ever more fantastically confused, as if, according to one, "incantations and imprecations could produce miracles," Scholem found it unsurprising that Goldberg's magical "negation of the bourgeois world" brought the movement close to the era's social-revolutionary groups.

Werner Scholem joined the German Communist party in the fall of 1920, just as it began focusing on internationalization and calibrating how closely to identify with the Russian Bolshevists. He soon built a reputation as one of the party's star orators. But Gerhard was skeptical about how far his acceptance would go, for all his doctrinaire gusto. At one workers' rally he attended, Gerhard looked around at the crowd before Werner mounted the stage and felt instinctive mistrust. "Don't fool yourself," he remarked. "They'll applaud your speech and probably they'll elect you as a deputy at the next election, but behind your back nothing will change." Werner ignored the admonition and bounded off to make his address. The audience was plainly roused. Then Gerhard heard a worker say to the man next to him, "The Jew makes a nice speech." *The Jew.* Not "our comrade," as he would have said of any gentile leader. There was no "brotherhood of man" to rally around.

Instead of reevaluating his politics, Werner was being seduced into justifying "the 'revolutionary necessities' (read: the terror that shrank from nothing)," Gerhard claimed. As with Oskar Goldberg and the Blau-Weiss vision of Zionism, the German revolution became an emblem of counterfeit utopian prospects.

Given the complexities of the different fights Scholem picked — and had thrust upon him — over those last years in Germany, his uncompromising indictment of conservative pieties and revolutionary fantasies alike seems impressive. The determination that he would move to Palestine as soon as he'd completed his doctorate may have given him a critical distance on events at home that honed his moral vision: He already had one foot off the German soil, reaching for the ground of Zion. Further bolstering his self-assurance, he'd launched the historical work he felt most inspired by—and done so, moreover, with institutional endorsement.

Gerhard's arrival in Munich to take up his place at the university had the air of a reunion party. He rented a big room in an apartment near the Victory Arch. In the same building lived a Zionist cousin who was studying Romance languages, and the children's book artist Tom Seidmann-Freud, Sigmund Freud's niece, who lived on cigarettes while creating enchanting illustrations of strange animals cavorting with colorful humanoids. There were always interesting characters around. Escha Burchardt was also enrolled at the University of Munich, and Gerhard's awareness that she'd be on campus was one of the factors tipping the scales toward his studying there. The two began reading Judaism's classic works side by side, beginning with Maimonides' *Guide for the Perplexed*, the medieval Torah scholar's effort to reconcile philosophy and Jewish Law. Soon they were living together.

When not poring over Maimonides, he was "waltzing my way through books of magic," as he told one friend, and attending classes where he flaunted his knowledge of the Jewish canon over his teachers. Rumors were circulating around Munich, he told his parents, that using black arts he could make mice and elephants appear. For the present, however, he could "conjure up only flawless texts." Studying avidly, heading back to Berlin for visits with friends, and boxing his ideological adversaries made for the most fulfilling period of Scholem's life thus far. The scores and debts he scratched off in his final German years released him from the place, as if he himself had been one of Goldberg's earthbound ghosts. More than any relationship, what brought him psychic stability now were his deepening researches into mysticism.

He was creating a "vast foundational philological-philosophical monograph" on an early kabbalistic manuscript, he told Erich Brauer. Kabbalah was almost the only thing he devoted serious thought to, he said. At this time, the entire realm of Jewish mysticism "resembled an overgrown field of ruins, where only very occasionally a learned traveler was surprised or shocked by some bizarre image of the sacred, repellent to rational thought," Scholem recalled. The religious, afraid of Kabbalah's potency and infuriated by its heresies, had abandoned it to collapse and decay. The secular, embarrassed by its weird, primitive visions, never acknowledged it as part of their heritage. But that strange land of Kabbalah saved Gerhard's sanity—partly by allowing him to see how the swirling conceits of nightmares and madness might be elevated into a grand, cosmic tapestry. God has a virtue named "Evil," declared the book Scholem was studying. "It is the 'form of the hand,' and it has many messengers, and the name of all of them is 'Evil, Evil.'...And it is they who plunge the world into guilt."

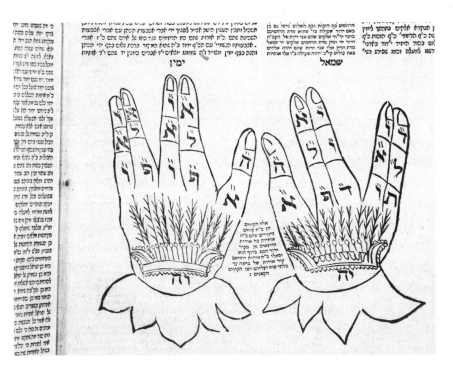

Once again, the shifting patterns of Scholem's relationship with Walter Benjamin shed light on Scholem's inner development. For now their respective predicaments had so altered that Scholem became Benjamin's counselor. In the summer of 1920, Benjamin at long last began preparing for his Jewish studies — at least he'd bought a number of books on Hebrew. Dora reported that he was already making jokes in the language. After what Benjamin called a total, final break with his parents, he and Dora were living in a whimsical little house belonging to Erich Gutkind, a former pupil of Scholem who'd started tutoring Benjamin in the holy tongue. "I have never thought of you more often and more affectionately than during the entire time I remained silent when your beautiful letters... kept your presence alive for me now and as a comfort in the future," Benjamin wrote in a convoluted blandishment, after failing to keep up his side of their correspondence. The deep understanding of his situation that Scholem expressed had persuaded him to start learning Hebrew, Benjamin added, "a decision I would not have dared make on my own."

Scholem believed in Benjamin's resolve, even recognizing the impediments to its fulfillment. He knew that both of them were equally concerned with sacred language and the Kingdom of God, not as the goal of the historical dynamic but, as Benjamin said, as its terminus. It's easy to see why Scholem would have trusted that they were on the same path. Some passages in Benjamin's writing are overtly theological when read in isolation: "Only the Messiah himself completes all history, in the sense that he alone redeems, completes, creates its relation to the messianic," he wrote in one fragment. Scholem cited such pronouncements as proof that those materialist historians who later wanted to claim Benjamin as one of their own were deceitful. But even when Benjamin employed religious terminology, there was usually an intricate

political context for his statements that refashioned their theological implications. Benjamin's politics might not annul his messianic references, but the two play off each other in an unstable
counterpoint that precludes a categorical assertion of where he
stood — reflecting Benjamin's own inability to commit himself
firmly to any one cause.

Soon, anyway, Benjamin's attachment to Hebrew slackened.
The problem of "the job market, as well as current conditions in
general," compelled him to divide his attentions between Hebrew
and the studies that might actually bring him paid work, he confessed to Scholem in early December. He was so broke that he'd
had to leverage his skills at handwriting analysis to make a little
cash. Though he continued to promise that the hour for "an intensive occupation with Judaism" was at hand, nothing happened.
Scholem warned him that the older one got, the more difficult it
became to make such choices, to begin a new spiritual apprenticeship. "Age can ultimately turn the choice into a catastrophe,"
Scholem said. This was true, Benjamin acknowledged, "even if it
is a purifying catastrophe." Still, he resolved that he had to quit
Hebrew altogether until he'd built the foundation for "a more
peaceful future, family support, etc." To this end, he announced
his decision to devote the next two years to what somehow
appeared a more manageable endeavor: "an analysis of the concept of truth." "The only thing left is to add my promise that, after
completing this project, I will truly not allow myself to be detained
by anything that may come up," he concluded, unconvincingly.

Registering Gerhard's disillusionment, Dora wrote him, "Do
not turn away from us. I hope with all my heart that we shall
meet on the common ground of things Jewish, and sooner than
we all think." At his Christmas break, Scholem found that the
couple had once again retreated to Benjamin's parental home in
Grunewald. Walter was having lots of new bookshelves built and
arranging for a piano to be moved in, on which Dora would play

him Mozart, Schubert, and Beethoven. Scholem couldn't understand how this retrenchment had come about. Years later, Benjamin would confess to him in a brokenhearted plea, "Where is
my production plant located? It is located (and on this, too, I do
not harbor the slightest illusions) in Berlin W. [West]...The most
sophisticated civilization and the most 'modern' culture are not
only part of my private comfort; some of them are the very means
of my production." He likened himself to a castaway adrift on a
wreck who scales an already crumbling mast. "But from there he
has a chance to give a signal leading to his rescue."

"Wait for me with your heart," Benjamin said, but Scholem
saw how "at all times other projects prevented him from entering
the world of Judaism," even though, in Scholem's eyes, that world
represented "the crucial literary experience of which he stood in
need to come really into his own." Adding to Scholem's apprehensions, Benjamin now took inspiration from a figure in Oskar
Goldberg's circle as he began defending the justice of proletarian
violence against the state. Erich Unger, Benjamin's political philosopher muse, was no doubt more congenial than Goldberg himself, whose "impure aura" had so repelled Benjamin when they met
that Benjamin couldn't even shake his hand. But Unger, too, railed
against empirical Zionism's efforts to build physical settlements
as a waste of the people's magical energies. When Goldberg's
crowd next began trying to appropriate the Kabbalah into their
necromantic arsenal, and courted Scholem himself as the field's
acknowledged master, Scholem told their chief recruiter that he
considered Goldberg quite simply "a representative of the devil in
our generation."

After Scholem returned to Munich, Benjamin wrote to say
that he felt certain the three of them would yet find a way to work
together, lavishing him with the kinds of compliments Scholem
had pined for a few years earlier: "I could not imagine Dora and
me bound to any other third party in this way, but I am indebted

to you for the direction my life and thought have taken." At the same time, Dora regaled Scholem with her vision for their harmonious reunion on Jewish grounds. "Everything I do is only a fight for the means," she assured him, positioning herself as the key to unlocking Benjamin's Judaic potential. When Scholem visited the couple again in the spring, Benjamin had withdrawn intellectually into the golden age of German letters and their marriage was plainly disintegrating.

Ernst Schoen, a composer who'd studied with Debussy and was the sole friend from Benjamin's youth to have remained close to him, had recently become a fixture in their life. Among his broad circle of acquaintances, Schoen was known not only for his suavity but also for being perpetually available to step out on the town: "a flâneur of charm," according to another friend, Charlotte Wolff, whom Schoen often escorted to Berlin's lesbian clubs, along with Dora. (Though herself a "femme à homme," Dora had a penchant for such places: "These women are authentic," she said of the club ladies.) Wolff herself had been introduced to Dora and Walter through a mutual friend, Jula Cohn, a sculptor known for her petite figure and oversized head, her finesse, freckles, dainty nose, and cynical sense of humor—along with the lorgnette on a long ebony handle through which she peered voraciously at everything around her. In a photo of Schoen and Cohn together, Schoen sits on a fence in a suit, looking like a debonair gangster, alert and unflappable, his legs dangling, his hands folded in his lap, a cigarette jutting from his lips. Cohn is beside him in a long white dress, with her face tilted to the sky, as if she's listening for a sprite. Just as Dora fell for Ernst, Walter grew besotted with Jula.

During Scholem's visit, the Benjamins spoke unabashedly of their conviction that they'd each found the love of their life—and sought his advice about what to do with the fact that they now wanted to marry other people. The absence of apparent jealousy was striking. Benjamin had begun working on a long essay, which he would dedicate to Jula, about *Elective Affinities*, Goethe's tale of two couples who almost nonchalantly switch partners in a manner that mirrored the emotional crisscrossing he and Dora were engaged in. Scholem wrote that he'd never seen the pair so affectingly concerned with each other as they were during this period ("Did Walter pretend, or was he really so much more civilized than most human beings that he could dispense with the capitalism of possessive love?" Wolff wondered. She decided that he could not really "face physical love for any length of time, adding that he resembled the troubadours of the Middle Ages who loved nostalgic love.")

For Dora, despite her euphoria about Schoen, the situation was more of a strain. When she developed a serious pulmonary condition, Benjamin guiltily confessed to Scholem his suspicion that their marital interloping had provoked the illness. From this point on until their final breakup in 1923 — by which time they'd each lost their dream lovers — the two lived mostly apart.

Scholem doesn't record the advice he gave Walter and Dora. But it was sympathetic enough that Dora began turning to him to speak of Walter's obsessive-compulsive tendencies — employing the kind of psychological terminology they'd formerly shunned — and making clear also that the erotic realm was not exactly Walter's forte. The idea may or may not have surprised Gerhard. But given that he didn't scruple to broadcast Benjamin's sexual ethereality in his memoir of their friendship — citing remarks by other female friends, who claimed that for them Walter "had not even existed as a man, that it had never even occurred to them that he had that dimension as well" — it seems plausible that Scholem's sense of his own potency was aggrandized by these disclosures, which would constitute another reversal in the balance of power between them.

Regardless, the mere fact that the Benjamins turned to Scholem for help with their marriage was a swing of the pendulum, considering how they'd formerly accused him of being actionably naïve.

Walter, now solo, began visiting Gerhard and Escha in Munich, finding Escha delightful and taking their hospitality as a nurturing boon in a manner that recalls Gerhard's own early trips to visit Dora and Walter. After buying Klee's painting *Angelus Novus* — that strange wiry man-bird with a giant head, which was to prove so iconic a work for Benjamin that it seemed, friends said, to be a part of his mind — he dropped it off with Gerhard and Escha for a time. The picture's disjunctive geometries bring to mind Wolff's account of the inapt juxtapositions in Benjamin's own appearance then: the "rosy apple-cheeks of a child" along with the "cynical glint in his eyes"; his tense, tight posture and gestures with his sudden enthusiasms; his "spindly legs that gave the sorry impression of atrophied muscles" and nervous habit of pacing that made people feel on edge. Gerhard composed a poem about the painting in honor of Walter's birthday in July 1921: "I am an unsymbolic thing / what I am I mean / you turn the magic ring in vain / there is no sense to me."

Walter eagerly submitted to Gerhard's tutelage that summer, pressing him to expound the commentaries of Talmudic mystics on angelic hymns. With Scholem's scholarly prowess gaining recognition, he now emanated the institutional prestige that persistently eluded Benjamin. At the same time, for all his veneration of Benjamin's genius, Scholem increasingly saw Benjamin's muddled personal affairs as symptoms, not just blows of fate.

In the summer of 1921, Benjamin received news that elated him — the first really exciting professional development of his life. Richard Weissbach, a publisher who'd been putting out Benjamin's translations of Baudelaire's *Fleurs du Mal*, invited him to become editor of a well-regarded literary journal. Benjamin declined, saying he didn't want to take over the mission of any established periodical, so Weissbach made a counterproposal: How would Benjamin like to start his own magazine in which he could do whatever he wanted? It was a dream offer.

Benjamin got in touch with Scholem right away, gushing enthusiasm. He would name the periodical *Angelus Novus*, after Klee's painting. It would serve as an annunciation of "the spirit of its age" and would explore the "fate of the German language," which manifested in "the crisis of Germany poetry." Language would be plumbed to its utmost philosophical depths.

Furthermore, carrying their anarchic principles onto the masthead, Benjamin announced that the journal would proclaim "through the mutual alienness of its contributors how impossible it is in our age to give voice to any communality." Benjamin wanted the debut issue to include polemical statements by Scholem against Martin Buber's "pseudoreligious and pseudorevolutionary" Zionism. He meant to come to Munich immediately to discuss details. "I want to and must speak with you about your collaboration," he wrote. "As far as I can tell, it is a prerequisite for the *success* of this journal." *Angelus Novus* was, Benjamin implied, the lofty project their entire friendship had been preparing for—and it came too late. Scholem's chief reaction on receiving Benjamin's giddy appeal was embarrassment. Benjamin must have known by this point, Scholem felt, that his thoughts were elsewhere. How could Benjamin *imagine* he would thrill to the prospect of collaborating on "a German periodical" dedicated to exploring the German language? "My mind was on quite different things and goals," he wrote afterward.

When Scholem gave a tepid response to the proposal, Benjamin's first reaction seems to have been shock, followed by denial. He became convinced that if he could only address Scholem's specific concerns, everything would get back on track. "Your letter is hesitant," he wrote Scholem, "but my confidence in you must remain all the more unhesitant, because I could hardly have undertaken the project without it." He decided Scholem's objections must have to do with suspicions that the magazine would pander to popular taste. So he bent over backward to prove that the periodical would have no commercial viability whatsoever. Those people who could afford to pay for the publication won't even subscribe to it for free, Benjamin promised.

But Scholem never embraced the undertaking—hardly anyone did. In the end, nothing more was completed than Benjamin's announcement of the journal's impending appearance, a tract that culminates with the assurance that the magazine will be ephemeral—a fair price, he asserts, for "true contemporary relevance." Transience was not to be mourned, Benjamin concludes, in a reflection that came straight from Scholem: "After all, according to the legend in the Talmud, the angels—who are born anew every instant in countless numbers—are created in order to perish and to vanish into the void, once they have sung their hymn in the presence of God."

All that crepuscular Weimar spirit conjuring and utopia mongering—Scholem had his fill of it. How paltry these enchantments seemed while he was stepping deeper into the textual wilderness of the real thing: age-old traditions of Jewish speculation on God's universe.

Scholem's thesis, which focused on the origins of the *Book Bahir*, was warmly received. He was encouraged to take a position as a professor of Jewish studies—remarkable at a time when anti-Semitism on German campuses was becoming flagrant. But it didn't cross his mind to remain. His last year in Germany, he lived between Berlin and Frankfurt, part of the time teaching a well-attended course on the history of Jewish mysticism, part of the time combing through archives. Scholem's most active friendships now involved cultural Zionists like himself, who were preparing to leave Europe: Hugo Bergmann, whom he'd met with Escha in Berne; S. Y. Agnon; and Ernst Simon. He led a reading group on the Zohar's explications of various biblical texts, which attracted some of these figures, along with other humanist intellectuals. Scholem had finally discovered and helped crystallize a sympathetic Zionist cabal.

He and Escha made plans to get married. She immigrated to Palestine before him, as did Bergmann, who'd become director of the Jewish National Library and who conspired with Escha to offer Scholem an invented position as head of the National Library's Hebrew Department, thereby enabling him to outmaneuver British visa restrictions as "a specialist outside the quota."

Scholem didn't know what he would actually do in Palestine, but he knew that he was on his way, while Benjamin seemed to grow only more disoriented. His financial position deteriorated after relations with his parents soured again and the German mark went into free fall. (Betty called the inflation "a million-fold witches' sabbath.") New waves of food rioting along with violent agitations in Bavaria by Hitler's Guards and other nationalist

organizations led the government to declare a state of emergency. In these savage conditions, even cemeteries were ransacked. Thieves formed "storming columns" to strip all monuments and headstones of metal attachments—pilfering everything down to the floral tributes.

As Scholem prepared to depart for Jerusalem in November 1923, Benjamin gave him a parting gift: a scroll with a draft of his essay on German inflation. "The air is so full of phantoms, mirages of a glorious cultural future breaking upon us overnight in spite of all, for everyone is committed to the optical illusions of his isolated standpoint," Benjamin observed. "The people cooped up in this country no longer discern the contours of human personality...a heavy curtain shuts off Germany's sky, and we no longer see the profiles of even the greatest men."

The scroll was addressed "to a happy emigrant." Scholem wrote in his memoir that it mystified him how someone able to write

such words could remain in Germany. His own life was about to take a new direction. Or rather, Scholem corrected himself, "the direction it had been taking for years would only now fully come into its own."

Even though I can't identify the precise transition point when we realized we were truly settling in Jerusalem, I know the moment when we looked backward and realized it had already happened — we'd made a life in our new home. The discovery brimmed with promise, notwithstanding the persistent stumbling of our efforts to assimilate economically. For everything on the cosmic-historical plane of the Land had changed once again, spinning topsy-turvy back into hopefulness. In the second trimester of Anne's third pregnancy, in September 1993, the Oslo Accords were signed in Washington, ending the Intifada. There would be a just peace. Mutual recognition. Autonomy progressing to a full Palestinian state. Of course there were questions and bitter repudiations, from both the Israeli right — many likened Rabin's government to Vichy — and fundamentalist organizations like Hamas. Edward Said called the agreement the Palestinian Versailles, because of what he saw as its irredeemable compromises with core principles in the Palestinian struggle for equality and independence.

But notwithstanding invocations of both symbolic French epicenters of capitulation, the mood among our little vagabond circle in West Jerusalem was magically buoyant. Since many of my friends were Anglo expats who'd arrived with a basic set of Western liberal values, there was another emotion as well: *vindication*. Right when it had begun to seem that the country we'd moved to with such idealistic hopes was becoming mired in bloodshed, good old Jewish fair-mindedness sprang up from the abyss. The State was going to do the right thing. We felt validated again in our choice to live in Israel — grateful for the intensity, beauty, and gravitas of our life in Jerusalem, while America was caught in its usual circus of lunatics and greed: Waco, the Unabomber, the savings and loan crisis.

At the university, teaching was going well, and I was nearing completion of my thesis. Apart from my academic work on Poe, I'd begun writing about the post-exilic prophecy of Zachariah, an early example of apocalyptic literature promising divine reparations for the loss of Jerusalem. (The name Zachariah means "God remembers.") Anne was moved by his invocations of the social justice and peace that would accompany the Jews' return. Since our child was due to be born in the Hebrew month of Shvat, when Zachariah delivered his message to the world, we decided that if we had another boy. we'd name him after the prophet.

Zachariah was born in late January, just before the Jewish holiday of Tu B'shvat, marking the anniversary of God's creation of arboreal species. It's an important holiday in different kabbalistic traditions, especially Isaac Luria's school, which developed a special Tu B'shvat seder, observed by eating thirty different fruits in a particular order, accompanied by readings. "The flow of God's beneficence is called in Kabbalah the Tree of Life — the roots, above in God; the fruit, here below," begins one passage from the Lurianic guide. The Tree of Life, in Scholem's interpretation, "represents the pure, unbroken power of the holy, the diffusion of the divine life through all worlds and the communication of all living things with their divine source." Since the Fall, when the forbidden fruit of the Tree of Knowledge was eaten, the world has been ruled by the mystery of this second tree in which good and evil have their separate places, as do the holy and profane, the living and the dead, the divine and the demonic. With the messianic salvation, the glory of the utopian would again break forth, dissolving these differentiations. True to the idea of the Tree of Life, this redemption was understood as a restoration of the original conditions in Paradise. We gave Zachariah the middle name Ilan — "tree" in Hebrew.

Even Zachariah's birth seemed to partake of the spirit of miraculous renewal. We woke in the middle of the night and rushed to the hospital. He appeared almost before we knew it — the labor a matter of minutes. "Zachariah Prochnik was born this morning at 3 AM, it is now 7," Anne wrote in her journal, "and I feel I should write now before the last gold and crimson traces have worn from his birth as they have from the sky. May his life be filled with happiness and blessing, peace and security — may his birth at the beginning of Shvat, and the reminder of his name, herald peace for Jerusalem, and may he be a man of peace who remembers G_d. I thank G_d for everything, for all our blessings, and feel that in watching the dawn I've seen the world itself reborn."

That was the mood then in those first weeks of new life, when we rolled in the wave of creation. Our life might not have been growing more religious according to the Law, but we felt awakened to some mystical truth. Anne had begun to find fulfillment in painting, beyond what writing offered her, and on the birth announcement she sketched images of the baby tranquilly sleeping above lines from Zachariah's prophecy: "Old men and old women shall yet again dwell in the streets of Jerusalem...and the city shall be full of boys and girls playing in its streets...for there shall be the seed of peace, the vines shall give her fruit, and the ground shall yield its increase, and the heavens shall give their dew."

When I read again the list of people who came to Zachariah's circumcision ceremony, I realize that we'd become part of a Jerusalem community without knowing it. The godfather at the ritual was Adam Yakin, a playwright, puppeteer, and gardener whom I'd come to know after our children began playing together. Unlike most of our friends, Adam came from a Jerusalem family that went back many generations on his father's side; he lived in a few rooms of an old stone compound his great-grandfather had built near

West Jerusalem's open-air market, Mahane Yehuda. His mother emigrated from Holland as a refugee from the Nazis. As a teenager, Adam had written an antiwar play that became something of a national sensation. He learned Arabic and was involved with the founding of the first Jewish-Palestinian school in Jerusalem. Now to earn his meager living, Adam staged children's puppet shows in an old train boxcar. With his luminous gaze, wild wreath of hair, love of nature, and utter detachment from materialism, Adam had struck a friend of ours visiting from Manhattan as the spirit of St. Francis incarnate.

In the first weeks after Zachariah was born, Anne and I walked through Jerusalem's gardens, breathing the smell of stone in the damp winter air and seeing the cyclamens nestling in limestone hollows like soft violet fingernails, registering the imminence of another season, speaking about the growth of our children in the Land. We loved the way they took their Jewishness in with the air they breathed rather than having to define it in opposition to their larger environment. Whatever ambivalences we ourselves might occasionally have been prey to — with one eye forever cast back over our shoulders toward the culture we'd left behind — their identities would be clear and complete.

In the second month of Zachariah's life came Purim, the Jews' ecstatic upside-down holiday, celebrating the time when Haman, an adviser to the Persian king who wished to exterminate the Jews, himself became the subject of the king's deadly wrath, so that the Jews were all saved. Purim calls for the wearing of costumes and the drinking of so much wine that the names of the good and evil characters in the story become indistinguishable. That year, Baruch Goldstein, a Brooklyn-born physician — who often wore a yellow star with the word *Jude* on it, since he felt Israeli democracy was equivalent to Nazi Germany — stepped into Hebron's Cave of the Patriarchs and opened fire on Muslim worshippers, killing 29 and injuring 125, believing he was acting in the spirit of

Purim and hastening the messianic redemption, since each Muslim was a potential murderer of Jews. His family later claimed to have ancestors who were killed by Arabs in Hebron in the massive riots of 1929, and said that their son knew, as did others, that the Arabs were planning a new slaughter of Jews on Purim morning. Goldstein's advocates invoked the Talmudic concept *ha ba l'horgecha, haskem, l'horgo*, which requires a Jew to kill an attacker, even in cases when there is only an intention to attack—reversing the roles of murderer and victim, prophylactically.

Goldstein was treated as a hero by the thousands of mourners who flocked to his grave, many of whom wore the yellow Star of David. One of those who traveled to Goldstein's funeral was Yigal Amir, a law student at Bar Ilan University. He'd been intrigued, he later said, by the idea of how a man whom people thought of "as a doctor, as a noble soul," could "get up and sacrifice his life. This was a man who left a family and martyred himself," Amir marveled.

That day, I went back to the Book of Zachariah, reading the prophecy again. While the part of the prophecy I'd singled out when suggesting to Anne that we give our son his name was about peace in Jerusalem, I recalled that what really had captivated me in the book was its haunting mystical opening: a vision of a man riding on a red horse who comes to stand among myrtle bushes in the glen. A wild image of a man on a beast the color of fire and blood, surging into a vale of fragrant green leaves. "Be not like your fathers, to whom the former prophets cried, saying: Thus says the Lord of hosts: Turn now from your evil ways, and from your evil doings: but they did not hear, or hearken to me," Zachariah said, ventriloquizing God. "Your fathers, where are they? And the prophets, do they live forever?"

I was not aware then of the garbled legends that claimed the prophet Zachariah was stoned to death by the Jews themselves for condemning their evil behavior and predicting the destruction of the Temple. When the Babylonians overran Jerusalem, it was said that the blood of the murdered prophet seethed on the Temple floor. The Jews sought to hide the source of the blood, pretending it was the remains of a sacrifice to God. Yet the blood went on boiling and reeking, acting as a curse upon them, until Nebuzaradan, the captain of Nebuchadnezzar's guards, had slain a million souls to try to appease Zachariah's spirit. I didn't know how the prophet of peace could blur with a specter of vengeance, or how the promises of redemption were tangled with chronicles of vast slaughter.

But we were thrown into sorrow and confusion. And for the first time I read Scholem's words about the demonic vitality brought to Judaism by the Kabbalah with different eyes. For the first time, the intriguing notion of God's own evil aspect became horrifying. What had seemed so enlivening to our bourgeois Jewish experience in America—and so attuned with my initial zestfully orientalizing vision of Jerusalem—lost its luster. Became gray and dark, as the grave of some victim whose death exposes one's own greater negligence.

For a time everything seemed turned inside out again. However, the peace negotiations did not cease, and the blessings in our life were not yet diminished. So we slowly forgot the deaths in the cave of all those men with their faces bent to the earth, and our hopes for the future reascended.

Part II

TEN

RIGHT BEFORE ME, a beautiful woman with a golden ponytail, wearing a scant white leotard and a white plumed tiara, rode a huge white winged horse rearing into the sky. She flung her bare arms over her head. She beamed. The horse, with its golden mane and big fluffy angel wings, was almost vertical now, almost aligning with the high silver pole topped by a tiny fluttering Israeli flag behind her and the elaborate red-and-white needle of an antenna on the roof of a nearby municipal building. Beyond, the sky was blinding blue.

The crowd filling Jerusalem's Safra Square was fantastically colorful. Women on stilts dressed in pink, lime, saffron, and scarlet wove through our midst. Golden hats and sparkly magenta ribbons of hair were everywhere. Clusters of people sheathed face to foot in tight suits of glistening turquoise satin whisked right and left. High up the wall of City Hall, a couple in red and gold performed a daring aerial ballet. There were pirates, Shriners, and glittering princesses galore. Psychedelic balloons and bubbles filled the air. All the bright, prismatic hues that had drained out of certain Jerusalem neighborhoods in recent years seemed to have pooled and splattered here.

In March 2015, I chanced to be in Israel when Purim was being celebrated, and the impending elections dangled overhead the prospect of a new chance for the State. I learned that the rave at the medieval citadel known as David's Tower, just inside Jaffa Gate, was sold out. I didn't hear about the rally for political change in Rabin Square in Tel Aviv until it was too late to attend. But I wandered where I could, and when my puppeteer friend Adam Yakin told me one of his troupes was performing in the square before City Hall, I hurried over.

It took me quite some time to find them in that mass gathering. But there was so much to see that I didn't mind milling about. And the image of that young woman in white on the flying horse against the turquoise sky framed by an Israeli flag and a governmental antenna seemed to symbolize more than I could articulate. I hate a crowd, but the mood here was so happily kaleidoscopic that I was glad to be part of it. "All festivals will one day be abolished, except for Purim which will never be abolished," remarked a rabbi of antiquity whom Scholem cites to illustrate utopian hopes for the messianic era.

When I at last did find Adam, he was helping his players prepare to operate a group of twelve-foot-tall puppets made of fabric scraps, costume jewelry, and papier-mâché. Except for one flashy orange feline, all the puppets represented human figures. I didn't register much about them at first beyond the grotesque exaggeration of their features and their general air of being at once decked out and shabby—dressed up for festivities but still limited to patchwork. The longer I watched Adam moving between the figures, lending a hand as the performers grappled with the bulk and scale of these creations, the more I became aware of how they contrasted with the glitzy, polychromatic splendor of other acts I'd seen—poor cousins, no less impressive but in a more primitive, mysterious key.

They were joined by a motley young marching band playing what sounded like shtetl wedding-feast music. In the swirl of song, the puppets began dancing with intoxicated rapture, undulating and spinning, arms and legs waving in the air. It was only as they danced that I realized what gave the figures their uncanny dimension. With their combination of giant stares and large noses,

their overdone cosmetics and facial expressions that ranged from defiant to deranged — the tatterdemalion extravagance of their clothes, which abounded in old-fashioned floral prints, misshapen hats and shoes, autumnal shades and sudden bursts of gay spring pink — they resembled totemic caricatures of Jewish refugees, exiles or new immigrants arrayed in awkward finery for some rare fete. And despite the twisted, even macabre exaggeration of their demeanor, as they danced they came to life with a vibrancy that gave them a grace all their own.

I could see the crowd watching them become enchanted. And I found myself thinking of one of the most impassioned, furious essays of Scholem's mature years: "Reflections on Modern Jewish Studies." It was published in 1944, but he'd begun contemplating it twenty-three years earlier, when Walter Benjamin solicited the work for his stillborn journal, *Angelus Novus*, and it serves in part as Scholem's ultimate reckoning with his historian predecessors: figures like the Romantic scholars Heinrich Graetz and Abraham Geiger, who'd purported to be creating a rigorously objective, comprehensive approach to the field of Jewish studies, inaugurating a "Science of Judaism."

In the essay, Scholem attributes a corrosive brilliance to these scholars, holding them responsible for nothing less than "the suicide of Judaism." The litany of charges he levels against them reads like the biblical plagues chanted at a Passover seder: "Morose sentimentality," "self-justification," "apologetics," and "trivialization" are among the counts he adduces. (Geiger and Graetz, he noted, also possessed that "sovereign ability which makes for the great historian, to rape the facts for the sake of his construction.") But the greatest source of their guilt—Scholem calls it "the fundamental, original sin which outweighs all the others"—is their "removal of the pointedly irrational and of demonic enthusiasms from Jewish history," for the sake of rendering the past spiritually unobjectionable. The practitioners of the Science of Judaism founded their version of Jewish history on the immaculate virtues of Judaism's martyrs in order to placate the "pride of a generation which did not expect to follow in their footsteps and which awaited the liberal messiah." What this group of deeply learned men achieved under pretense of merely identifying and classifying the constituent elements of Judaism was to take the "awesome giant" of Jewish history—a "great creation, filled with explosive power, compounded of vitality, wickedness and perfection"—and so shrink it that it ultimately "declares itself to be naught." The quintessential expression of this attitude for Scholem appeared in a popular pamphlet that declared, "The Patriarch Jacob was a model citizen of the city." Here, Scholem wrote, "the prince of the nation is seen in the model of a petit bourgeois."

Against this attitude, he continued, his fellow Zionists had sought "to rebuild the entire structure of knowledge in terms of the historical experience of the Jew who lives among his own people and has no other accounts to make than the perception of the problems, the events and the thoughts according to their true being." Secular or sacred, this focus would lead, he wrote, to a revolutionary change in values. "The powerful battles over the soul of the nation between the temporal and the eternal will no longer be hidden away. We will be required to discover the secret of our true stature...In brief: the stones that were rejected by the builders will become the cornerstone. There is no longer a need for castration of the truth, for idyllic recasting of the past, for enlightenment, small-mindedness, and for the adventures of illusions."

Staring at these colossal whirling, fantastical characters at the Purim carnival, who appeared so brazenly idiosyncratic, sublimely mongrel, and infinitely displaced, I felt I was gazing at Scholem's wild giant of Jewish history itself. And there, at the center of Jerusalem, I experienced a jolt of solidarity with Scholem's Zionism — an urge to embrace the unfettered individuality of this identity so often borne in camouflage and self-denial. When Scholem described the essence of his Zionism as a reentry into Jewish history, he meant this equally as an *exit* from Diaspora history—a repudiation at least of its stereotypical mournful demeanor, replacing the attitude of impotent suffering with rambunctious, perilously naked self-expression.

Amid that exuberant crowd aiming their phone cameras every direction and holding up their beautiful wide-eyed children to the dance of the giants, I found myself dreaming back to the Jerusalem Scholem came to in 1923. That year the new British governor, Ronald Storrs, had expressed the hope that "the city of a great soul," as he called it—"battered forty times in its

history"—would one day "be able to create its own future from
the wrecks it contemplates." It was amazing, despite everything,
to see the future wrested from those ruins in less than a century.
Not many years before Scholem's arrival, Karl Baedeker's guide to
Palestine had confined its remarks on Jerusalem's Jewish world to
a sentence: "The dirty Jewish Quarter contains numerous Synagogues, hucksters' booths, and taverns, but offers no object of
interest to the traveller." Damn the sneerers and the slighters, the
anti-Semites and the life deniers. Look around at this panoramic
spectacle now!

That's what I felt, anyway, on Purim morning. I'd spent so
many months—years, actually—weighed down by the tragedy, the
anguish and cruelty, of this story. But for a few hours I shed that
leaden mantle and remembered falling in love with Jerusalem. It
helped, of course, that it was spring. When I walked in the Valley
of the Cross, the grass was so bright green it looked switched on;
rosy clusters of wildflowers poked up from the rough limestone
like children at play. Everywhere, couples were strolling, families
were picnicking, earnest solitary figures were seated on rocks reading books. The idyll was complete, so long as you didn't look for a
Palestinian to share in it.

What must it have been like for Scholem to enter Jerusalem's
dazzling summer in late September 1923, when the dropping tem-
peratures and diminishing light in Germany were already signal-
ing fall's arrival? Looking out at the steep, dramatic hills, striated
with stone necklaces, split with sunbeams, I thought how wide the
sky must have seemed in Palestine after the sooty urban density of
Berlin. And the colors washing and streaking that great sky were
so lavish. God paints with a big brush in this land, I thought.

Then again, the question might be asked: *Did* Scholem in fact
see where he was once he arrived here—really notice it? In the hundreds upon hundreds of pages he wrote from Jerusalem, he barely
makes mention of the natural surroundings. He might be writing

from space, from a black box theater, or — most plausibly — from between old manuscript pages. It's not that Scholem projected over the landscape any particular vision but rather that he often seems to see nothing at all save the archival work before him and the dangers posed by human evils to that grand enterprise. The scope of what he wanted to achieve in his studies of sacred literature make this urge to keep his head down understandable. But that extraordinary concentration on the Book also casts into relief the mystery of his belief that the reading had to transpire in Palestine. He lived in Jerusalem from his library, in the spirit of a famous Mishna: "Rabbi Ya'akov said: One who is walking along the road is studying [Torah], and then interrupts his studies and says, 'How beautiful is this tree! How beautiful is this plowed field!,' the Scripture considers it as if he were guilty of a mortal sin." Even as a young man reacting against Buber's philosophy,

Scholem had rejected the prospect of engaging his environment. "He who 'experiences' a landscape, or his fellow man, or anything else, escapes from the ultimate imperative," Scholem wrote in his diary. "With Experience he'll always remain a German Jew — and never get to Zion." The course of his later life suggests that for Scholem, "getting to Zion" also required looking past the physical setting of Palestine.

Escha was there to greet him when the boat docked in Jaffa. For a while, Hugo Bergmann, Scholem's old Zionist friend from Berlin, put Scholem up at his place. It was a time when there was hardly a shut door in Jerusalem. No one locked up when they went out. There was no fear of thieves, Scholem said, but likely as not when you got home there'd be someone lying in your bed, a friend of friends who'd passed along your house number.

He changed his name from Gerhard to Gershom. It was the name Moses gave his first son with Zipporah in Midian after escaping from Egypt. Moses said, "I have been a *ger* [stranger] in a strange land." But Gershom can also mean "Stranger is his name." And Scholem surely relished this duality. Once a stranger, now home; forever a stranger, by destiny.

Everything moved forward extraordinarily quickly. The Zionist Executive's teachers college had lost its head mathematician to the University of Vienna, and the director of Palestine's Hebrew school system told Gershom he could have the man's place. The Executive had no money to pay him, but he'd get vouchers he could use to purchase staples at a cooperative. Meanwhile, there was the imaginary position dreamed up for Scholem at the National Library. Truth be told, they *did* need a librarian for the Hebrew department, Bergmann informed him. There wasn't actually funding for that job, either, but the hours would leave Gershom time for his kabbalistic studies. He snatched up the offer.

He and Escha were married less than a month after arriving. His parents were pleased. Arthur wrote him with cheery self-aggrandizement that he'd predicted the whole thing. He wished them great joy. Escha came from a good family, which he deemed essential. What's more, she was smart. How exactly they would finance their household on his puny salary — that he didn't know. Don't count on any handouts from your parents. At least don't expect anything from me, he graciously signed off.

They moved into the old Arab house just beyond the walls of Meah She'arim. There was no running water, let alone electric power. But then again, there were no service bills either. They got water from a cistern, and in years when the rains didn't fall, they purchased a hundred donkey loads from an Arab.

At the library, Gershom threw himself into the labor of preparing bibliographies of Jewish literature, notably the first major bibliography of Kabbalah, and began shaping the Dewey decimal system to the requirements of Judaica; his classification became the basis for cataloging Jewish texts around the world. Barely a month after his arrival, Gershom was building a name for himself. His mother wrote him at the start of November that at a big to-do in Berlin, a top Hebrew novelist had called him "the hope of Palestine."

That Scholem could acquire such stature in so brief a time wasn't only testimony to his exceptional gifts and discipline, however. It also serves as a reminder of just how small Jewish Palestine was then. There were fewer than a hundred thousand Jews in the entire country, many of them in Jerusalem where, though Jews made up only slightly more than 10 percent of Palestine's total population, they comprised half of the city's sixty-three thousand residents. The so-called garden suburb neighborhoods outside Jerusalem's Old City were just in the process of being constructed: Rehavia began to be built in 1922. Groundbreakings for other core West Jerusalem neighborhoods, like Quiryat Moshe and Bayit VeGan, were still a year or two off.

In the immediate aftermath of the First World War, the whole of Jerusalem was in a dire state. Food supplies were short. Wells and cisterns were infested with malarial mosquitoes. There was insufficient housing, and ramshackle wooden shops and schools teetered on the verge of collapse. Garbage pickup was sporadic and sewers inadequate. Livestock had not yet been banned from the city's central thoroughfares. Regular bus service didn't begin linking Jewish neighborhoods until the early 1920s. At the beginning of Scholem's life in Palestine, West Jerusalem was a place for the young and strong, but as he never tired of reiterating, "Zionism was essentially a youth movement." And for the young, that rough-and-tumble wildness could make for an adventure with storybook luster.

Nor, even then, were the harsher aspects of life in Jerusalem the whole picture. In the last years of their empire, the Ottomans had begun instituting more reforms than they're typically credited with. Overseas Jewish charities eagerly launched new philanthropic ventures. (A British army joke of the period asked, "What is a Zionist?" "A Zionist is a Jew who is prepared to pay another Jew to go and live in Palestine.") The postwar era inaugurated a period of intense municipal activity to accommodate population growth, improve living conditions, and repair Jerusalem's antiquities. The English military administration began installing networks of iron pipeline connected to reservoirs on high ground at the western side of the city even before the civilian Mandate authorities assumed power. Cultural institutions were opened, making music and literature more generally accessible. Houses, banks, and government buildings were constructed by ambitious architects influenced by the International Style and the Arts and Crafts movement, all faced, according to Mandate stipulations, with Jerusalem's distinctive light peach–gold limestone. Many parks were built. Trees were planted up and down the main roads. In the initial Mandate period, these projects, aimed at sanitization, beautification, and historical restoration, were being launched across the city's Jewish and Arab neighborhoods at a comparable pace.

Leaving aside its deeper historical foundations, the city Scholem came to in 1923 was at once rife with vestiges of a more recent, premodern identity and seething with future-oriented change. These latter, European visions of progress incorporated both incontestable benefits and unmistakable ideological biases. "By 1922," Ronald Storrs wrote in his memoir, the Mandate government had begun to think of introducing grand opera to Jerusalem—"like tapestry, a criterion of higher civilization"—and the

Jews, with their "native genius," soon succeeded in realizing this dream. Storrs observed, "That the Arabs had 'achieved' nothing in Palestine was undeniable." However, he added — on the classic upper-crust English pivot between disdain and fair-mindedness — achievement shouldn't constitute a criterion for the right to live somewhere. And he noted that the Jewish position on immigration — framed as a "return" for their people "on the strength of a Book written two thousand years ago" — carried myriad risks. "The setting-back of the political clock set minds also back into fanaticism, dying and better dead altogether."

Yet Storrs also saw his own work fulfilling a biblical mandate of restoration. "The Psalms of David and a cloud of unseen witnesses" seemed to inspire the labors of his administration, he wrote, which heeded the command, "Build ye the walls of Jerusalem." In these efforts, Storrs recalled, "We put back the fallen stones, the finials, the pinnacles and the battlements." Hundreds of tons of Turkish barrack rubble were cleared from the medieval ramparts. Tons of stolen Roman stonework were returned to their historic locations.

The period of Scholem's arrival was one in which the legendary stones of Jerusalem were in motion. For all the ways the city might have struck a Berliner as backward, in the mid-1920s it was molten, not petrified.

Scholem had his own term for such interludes when migrations of peoples and changing political alliances dissolved the status quo. He called these times the "plastic hours" of history: "Namely, crucial moments when it is possible to act. If you move then, something happens." Although the Zionist movement itself was weak, it was infused with a profound sense of responsibility toward this prospect of radical transformation. And though in his memoir any hint of longing for the past is rare, a note of nostalgic pride flares up when he invokes the young pioneers with their great hospitality and deep sense of historical consciousness — particularly relative to youth activists of the 1960s, for whom, Scholem avowed, history was "even a dirty word." While he was engaged with the "dialectics of continuity and revolt," he said, it would never have occurred to him and his fellows to reject the history of their people wholesale. "With our return to our own history, we, or at least most of us, wanted to change it, but we did not want to deny it. Without this *religio*, this 'tie to the past,' the enterprise was and is hopeless, doomed to failure from the start."

The National Library was located two minutes up the road from his house on the Street of the Prophets. Two minutes down the road was Meah She'arim, always a bastion of Orthodoxy, which perched "like a fortress in the midst of the rocky desert," half a mile beyond the Old City walls. If the library was his workplace, this neighborhood with its secondhand-book dealers was, he wrote, his "playground." Gershom strode back and forth between these worlds, and within little circles of recent arrivals from Central and Eastern Europe who were fast becoming Jewish Palestine's sociocultural elite. Lean and gawky, disruptive and insatiable, he cut a figure moving through Jerusalem that might itself have conjured the demonic giant of Jewish history.

His advocates and close pioneer friends in Jerusalem were likewise formidable: the leading Hebrew poet, Chaim Bialik; the future Nobel Prize–winning novelist S. Y. Agnon; Hugo Bergmann; Judah Magnes; his old friend from Pension Stuck Zalman Rubashov, who would go on to become president of Israel. Eventually there were other German Jews, including Werner Kraft, whom he'd come to know through Benjamin; the educator Ernst Simon; and the writer Ludwig Strauss, who'd been an early perceptive commentator of his work on Lamentations.

These were Scholem's comrades-in-arms, but they were hardly average types. Despite his later gloss, Scholem's letters reveal the extent of his distaste for the broader scene he encountered. Writing to Kraft in December 1924, he commented that as far as the future of the Zionist movement went, he had pledged himself unconditionally "to the sect with apocalyptic views." Too many different worlds came into violent collision in Palestine for the risks of some extreme disaster not to be huge, he argued—and he was referring only to dangers within the Jewish settlement. One English observer of the era noted, "Seldom can any community have been divided among so many factions; and each faction strove to bring up their children according to their own ideology." There were the aggressively anti-Zionist ultra-Orthodox, Central Europeans who spoke Yiddish, transplants from Mediterranean countries who spoke Ladino, Oriental Jews speaking Arabic, and the ardent Zionists who refused to speak to any Jew except in Hebrew and posted signs outside shops forbidding discourse in any other tongue. And then of course within the Zionist camp there were the religiously Orthodox, the anti-Orthodox, the Socialists, the capitalists, the revolutionaries, and numerous variations between. Every statement people made took on the air of a public declaration in this combustion chamber, and whoever was speaking, Scholem reported, was compelled to indulge in theological posturing. "The phenomenon of *primal*, aboriginal (not to be confused with original) Jewish stupidity is quite clearly unknown in the Diaspora," he railed to a friend. "In this apocalyptic place, and only here, you meet the utterly amazing phenomenon of Hebrew-speaking philistines."

But the combination of disarray and stupidity he attributed to the society may also have fostered a sense of its malleability under the right leadership. The group of young men who became Scholem's intimates in the early years were rising into positions of power in the cultural sector—and sometimes the political sphere as well. When he and his friends got together to debate signal questions regarding the renewal of the Jewish people—what kind of existence they could shape for themselves in the historical environment they'd come to, how their life could "be established on firm foundations with or without or in conflict with the Arabs," as he wrote in his memoir — they realized their stature as individuals who might sway the course of the country. "We have not come to the land of our forefathers in order to be conquerors...but in order to upbuild ourselves while keeping faith with a humanistic Judaism," Hugo Bergmann said, quoting a Christian philosopher who argued that "the Land of Israel must and would be a laboratory in which the Jews would solve the problems of cooperative life which plague all humanity." Scholem sometimes felt that his youthful vision of a tiny band of educated, pure-minded Zionists leading the nation was coming to life. And one consequence of this was that the appeal of the more fanatical aspects of the undertaking receded. The feverish mood of the place seemed to temper his own.

But there were other consequences of this plasticity. In his own field, Scholem felt a certain freedom to mold his material to suit his larger agenda of reviving modern Jewry's revolutionary self-consciousness. If kabbalistic practice had once helped reconcile the Jews to exile by contextualizing the people's homelessness within a divine scheme, *knowledge* of the Kabbalah might now help to fuel a creative awakening around the idea of the exile's conclusion — reminding Jews of historical energies and radical spiritual desires they'd repressed for centuries. In this sense, Kabbalah functioned for Scholem on the national plane a bit as the id did for Freud on the personal level: It wasn't that he felt one should unleash such forces unchecked on the world. Scholem didn't tell people to go out and become Kabbalists. But the powers of Jewish mysticism, if simply bottled up inside, distorted and deadened Jewish identity. One had to understand what was happening in the depths of the national self in order to free up its potential for dynamic growth.

The indeterminate face of pre-State Zionism made it tempting for both historians and philologists to look at Judaism's canonical texts through the lens of their own aspirations for the Jews' future in Palestine. Moreover, when it came to Kabbalah, that huge body of commentary and poetry, and poetic commentary, Scholem knew he was the only academic who could claim real fluency.

At first, Scholem did make some effort to further his textual knowledge through dialogue with the living remnant of kabbalistic practitioners, as he obliquely revealed in the opening to "Kabbalah and Myth." Years later, Scholem acknowledged that he himself had been the "young friend" he wrote about in that essay, and he identified the authority he'd approached as a man known as Vilner, an elder of the famous Sephardic Beit-El yeshiva in the Old City. It's not incidental that the Kabbalist he'd at last succeeded in tracking down was an "Oriental Jew": The Kabbalah itself, in Scholem's evolving view, had arisen in the East, from the dust of Oriental antiquity. Vilner was a "remarkable Jew, a shining personality," but the conditions he placed on their relationship—that Scholem ask no questions of his teacher—were, he implied, untenable for someone who sought to maintain standards of scientific integrity. Besides, what was actually left of the living Kabbalah? When he visited Beit-El, Scholem reported being unable to tell whether the place was even functioning as a synagogue. "I had the feeling that I was dealing with a group of *Eretz Yisrael* Jewish-style Yoga practitioners," he declared. Why not just read the writings of the great Kabbalists themselves, then?

Only Scholem's tale of his foiled quest for the living mystical tradition is misleading. A new portrait of Jerusalem's early-twentieth-century kabbalistic landscape has begun to emerge, one that contrasts sharply with the moribund, twilight realm Scholem depicted. Beit-El actually enlarged its operations after 1900 with the building of new study halls and remained an active site of esoteric learning for years after Scholem's arrival, argues the historian Jonatan Meir. While it may have been past its apex, it was hardly defunct: When an earthquake destroyed part of the building in 1928, funds for its reconstruction were immediately forthcoming, and it went on nurturing Kabbalists up through the end of the Second World War. Nor was Beit-El the last refuge of the mystical remnant in Jerusalem: An observer in 1938 reported that there were five hundred Kabbalists in the city regularly engaging in mystical midnight prayers. Another yeshiva, Oz ve-Hadar, opened its doors in 1923 and supported a number of high-profile Kabbalists. Most vibrantly, there was Sha'ar Ha-Shamayim yeshiva, established in 1906 as the new incarnation of Beit-El. It was the outstanding kabbalistic institution of Scholem's era, fostering interchanges between Ashkenazi and Sephardic Kabbalists, offering its students both exoteric and esoteric Torah studies, conducting prayers from a special prayer book based on the work of Isaac Luria, and framing its mission in relation to Jewish settlement in Palestine. A fund-raising document from 1919 stated that "rabbis, elders and men of action" affiliated with the yeshiva sought to "awaken the Gates of Compassion upon the exile of the Divine presence, the destruction of the Temple and the dispersal of God's people in the diaspora." As early as 1907, one of the yeshiva's founders declared that "the exile was prolonged due to the insufficient study of the wisdom of Kabbalah." Shortly after Scholem came to Jerusalem, the yeshiva's leaders warned that present-day Zionism was endangered by its lack of "the soul of the Torah, and of Israel, in the mystery of oneness," which could be accessed through the wisdom of Kabbalah.

Like Scholem, the leaders of Sha'ar Ha-Shamayim believed that the Zionist movement could receive vital nourishment through engagement with kabbalistic texts. But instead of viewing the formal practice of Jewish mysticism as, essentially, a closed project, they positioned Kabbalah as an ongoing endeavor that was energized by ritual observance inside the Holy Land. If fresh insights were still attainable through Lurianic prayers, worshipping with *kavanot* (special intentionality) and various acts of *tikkunim* (cosmic repair), then Kabbalah itself became an unstable, evolving proposition — much like Scholem's vision of Jewish history.

One might assume that Scholem just didn't know of the yeshiva's existence, except that his archived private library includes publications from Sha'ar Ha-Shamayim, many containing scribbled marginalia in Scholem's own handwriting. Among these notes are mentions of conversations he held with other Jerusalem Kabbalists as well.

The inconsistencies don't end there. If the Kabbalist from Beit-El told Scholem that he was only prepared to offer a form of teaching comprised of irrefutable axioms, it was reasonable for Scholem to infer that he was being told: We possess the Truth. You have no role to play beyond passively receiving our Teaching. What difference would it have made, then, had he chosen to decipher the wisdom for himself instead of through documents by Kabbalah's real masters like Luria? But some believe that Scholem mistranslated what Vilner was saying. (Despite his textual proficiency, for many years Scholem's spoken Hebrew was notoriously stilted.) Vilner may have been idiomatically declaring, "I refuse to teach you Kabbalah." As Scholem acknowledged, the idea of a form of Jewish learning in which questions are forbidden sounds bizarre. In fact, it probably doesn't exist. Scholem's secularism may have made him ineligible for induction into the Kabbalah's secrets in the rabbi's eyes. The rejection of Scholem himself, as opposed to the refusal of questions per se, preserves the possibility that Jewish mysticism was still alive in the oral tradition, where truths that could not be tweezered from old manuscripts by solitary researchers continued to be elucidated through dialogue.

In point of fact, a booklet published by Sha'ar Ha-Shamayim in 1924 presented the yeshiva's mission as, precisely, avoiding the dangers of disorientation "due to the powerful, intoxicating aromas" released in the course of kabbalistic studies undertaken without proper guidance. (A late-nineteenth-century mystic likened the person who learns Kabbalah exclusively from books to a blind man in a king's palace who is forced to listen to a description of what must be seen to be appreciated.)

The picture Scholem left behind of twentieth-century kabbalistic Jerusalem suggests a landscape of ghostly ruins where mystical truths were confined to the minds of cranky old men who wouldn't permit cross-examination, and to the pages of forgotten books dumped by widows on secondhand dealers. However, the image of an alien young man stalking the narrow streets of Orthodox quarters where kabbalistic yeshivot were still thriving—full of teachers and students praying all hours of the day and night, seeking forms of mystical union, composing and printing new kabbalistic works—transforms Scholem himself into the spectral figure.

Even Walter Benjamin, writing from Capri, where he was then falling in love with Asja Lacis, the Bolshevist who would galvanize his intrigue with communism, sensed that Scholem was leaving something out of his account of present-day mysticism in Palestine. "You say very little about Safed," Benjamin noted in a 1924 letter. "Isn't there still a school there devoted to the study of the Kabbalah? I imagine all sorts of things about the considerable number of incredible types whom you seem to run into there." But why would Scholem play this game of seek-and-hide with Kabbalah?

For one thing, a living tradition might prove uncontainable as an object of study: too fluid, disparate, and volatile. How could Scholem make Kabbalah *his*, if it was already dynamically connected to Jewish life in Palestine? Yet Sha'ar Ha-Shamayim maintained close relations with Rabbi Isaac Kook, who became the first Ashkenazi chief rabbi of Mandate-era Palestine. The yeshiva's members conducted prayers at sacred sites all around Jerusalem at the behest of wealthy patrons. Mystical ceremonies were staged to promote spiritual healing among the broader populace. During the Second World War, one of the yeshiva's founders brought together prominent Kabbalists for a rite involving the public cursing of Nazi leaders, which was thought to have triggered the Third Reich's collapse. What other rituals might Scholem have missed? Just as he kept his eyes in his books, away from Jerusalem's blossoming trees, is it possible the ceremonies that he described as having passed into history in fact persisted — such as the "sacred marriage" rite once held in the fields of Jerusalem, at which the divine exile was suspended and the promise of salvation blazed. The Kabbalists of Jerusalem, dressed in white, walked from the city into open fields, which in anticipation of the arrival of the Shekinah, God's feminine aspect, were transformed into a "holy apple orchard." They went to meet their banished lover, singing, "Go, my beloved, to meet the Bride/Let us receive the face of the

Sabbath." Indeed, this mystical hymn continues to be sung today in the regular Friday night synagogue service.

Given the current face of religion in the world, perhaps a linear model of religious faith, in which one phase succeeds the next, from animal sacrifice to verbal prayer and so on, should be replaced by one of endless branching, in which different permutations of belief continue to unfold simultaneously, like the interlacing limbs of the sacred fruit tree itself.

If Kabbalah was still efflorescing when Scholem arrived, he couldn't circumscribe it according to the overarching interpretation he sought to impose—which included the thesis that, after refracting melancholic themes of exile for centuries, the Kabbalah itself in some fashion had now morphed into the Zionist experiment. Where the scholars of the Wissenschaft des Jüdentums, in Scholem's account, sought only to give a "decent burial" to Judaism, one might say that Scholem himself sought to mummify the Kabbalah, so that it could be worshipped as a murdered deity, long entombed in the ruins of European history, now reincarnated free of the body of wearisome material practices in Palestine. To create the vital colossus of Jewish history Scholem celebrated in his approach to Kabbalah, he had to shrink and suppress other dimensions of the people's lived experience. One way to make a giant is to cut off the legs of everyone around him.

Finally, in considering why Scholem held back from engaging with the living Kabbalah in Palestine, it must be remembered that on a more mundane level, he was an immigrant looking to make his way in a tough new society where the very absence of established traditions could harden the conservative tendencies within institutions. Scholem was already proposing to make Jewish mysticism a respectable field of inquiry. Had word gotten around that he was also consorting with living Kabbalists, it would have been professional suicide.

Scholem came to Jerusalem already formulating his synthetic

narrative of Kabbalah set in the elegiac key of exile, which illuminated that experience even as it cast others into darkness. And
what he saw that belied his vision he contrived not to see. In the
Zohar, Scholem observed, the Shekinah is described as "'the beautiful virgin who has no eyes,' that is to say, who has lost her eyes
from weeping in exile." Scholem's identity as "Gershom"—the
stranger from the strange land, forever in exile from Orthodox tradition, from the ideal of Zion, and from his birthplace alike—resonates with that image. Scholem notes that the literal meaning
of that metaphor referred to a virgin "upon whom no eyes are
directed"—the virgin whom no one sees. It seems a prophetic
etymology, fusing blindness to disappearance, foretelling the day
when the virgin whose lamentations obscure the living world herself becomes invisible.

I was reaching the end of the expansive first part of my thesis,
thank God. We were teetering ever closer to the financial abyss,
and this submission would help secure my future at the university.
The process of composition had grown more difficult. My adviser's idea of criticism struck me as numbingly bland. Furthermore,
though I could fake it, I didn't really feel like myself when writing
in a theoretical academic key. And this problem interlocked with a
larger, goading awareness of how much was happening around me
that the frame of a scholarly thesis couldn't encompass.

   The only respite from my increasing alienation came through
my one truly commanding literature professor, a man who'd developed a grand theory of the transmission of culture from Homer to
Milton, Kant, and beyond. Silver haired, intensely concentrated,
with a brow so high and bright it was like an ever-waxing moon,
his eyes stared beyond his students from behind thin wire spectacles as fixedly as I imagined Walter Benjamin's had done. From the
right angle, with his faintly pink-tinged skin, he even *looked* a little

like Benjamin, if only Benjamin had lived two more decades. In his richly allusive discourse, and the august modulations of his voice that somehow seemed to swell into faintness—rising to the edge of utterability itself—I heard echoes of the tradition of Benjamin and Scholem.

Though he had a reputation for being frosty and intimidating, he responded thoughtfully to my reflections on his lectures and occasionally surveyed my academic trajectory. "Just get your doctorate," he told me. "Think of it as your passport, and just get the degree." I knew he was right and kept diligently working. But it didn't stop troubling me that this process of getting my passport should make me feel increasingly exiled from myself.

The peace process continued to lurch forward, jerking to a halt now and then after violent incidents, like a car with a shift driven by someone who'd never handled a clutch. The atmosphere was fraught but labile, shot through with fresh lines of hope. You could see the right becoming more hysterical, but that was unsurprising. The propaganda posters plastered to the walls and poles of Jerusalem multiplied and grew scarier: doubling the faces of Rabin and Arafat, masks switching places with skulls, leering caricatures aiming guns at the spectator.

Ten minutes from where we lived was a big supermarket, and with three small children and an apartment too small to store much in, I found myself having to run out to the Supersol all the time. I preferred to go of an evening, when the sun's burn had gone and the breeze raced electric. The walk took me through Tzarfat Square, the meeting-point of a handful of big streets near the prime minister's residence. At some point, the right began staging regular demonstrations at the site. They blocked traffic and made a lot of noise, beating saucepans and shouting, shaking flags and signs demonizing Rabin. I'd stop for a few minutes and watch the mob protest. It wasn't only bearded men. There were numbers of women. Many youths. A few smaller kids. Families here and there.

Some demonstrators were very serious; others were euphoric. But the mood overall seemed flush with conviction. Eventually, the security forces began to break up these protests. One evening when I crossed the square, a big knot of people stood at its center chanting in place, ringed by police. By the time I returned from the supermarket with my heavy bags, the scene had deteriorated into aggressive scuffling, a few figures stomach down on the pavement being manacled.

The next night when I happened by, the crowd had swollen to fill the whole intersection and their voices were louder and wilder, as if they themselves were screaming forth the dark wind. Police arrived in great trucks. Everything immediately became chaos. Chants turned to howls. People were rushing every which way in blackness cut by scythes of artificial light, water jets impaling buckling figures. The scene had no axis. Until I saw the horses: giant black mounts charging into the midst of the mass, wheeling and rearing back, their riders in helmets and face shields, wielding truncheons, swinging down into the demonstrators. I remember one long white banner bearing a grotesque cartoon of Rabin flashing like lightning as two protestors waved it, then crumpling into a broken accordion as they collapsed. I remember a heavyset middle-age woman wearing a hat stuck with a sparkly brooch plopping down on the pavement, legs jutting out before her, yelling curses. And I remember the eyes of those horses, wide and dark, their hooves lifting higher, the muscles on their dark flanks twisting and glistening.

The violence the government was willing to unleash against this mob startled me. These armored figures on the backs of huge steeds weren't discriminating as they meted out blows. They were sending a message, just as they had sent one to the Palestinian protesters during the Intifada. It was obvious that, as with the Palestinians, the message would not only be ignored but would inflame resistance — that the calculated application of brutality against demonstrators would give the retaliation a more reckless edge when it came.

I felt shaken, and viscerally sympathetic to those hurt and afraid. But I also felt an eerie tingle. Every large protest I'd seen in the United States had involved some demand that government listen to the people — by addressing social injustices, by not building nuclear plants. Those crowds insisted that the government could no longer treat one demographic or another as if it were invisible. But in Jerusalem the protesters were declaring their intention to behave as if the government itself did not exist. "Rabin has stolen the Land from the Zionists and is surrendering it to the Arabs," they shrieked. Rabin was a traitor. A murderer. A terrorist collaborator. The note I heard that night was not *The government must listen to us* but rather, *We do not recognize this government. This state is not the State of Israel. We are the Jewish nation.* And the harder the police tried to break them, the louder they shouted, the more pots they pounded, until I felt I was listening to a mass Purim ceremony where the participants were blotting out the name of Haman.

That night I started composing a poem that I couldn't stop writing. And when I finally submitted my chapters on Poe and the history of psychoanalytic criticism, meant to serve as my passport to academia, I knew that instead of making a travel document, I'd created a scrapbook of a trip off the map. What could I say to Anne if there was bad news from the university? She'd been searching for a teaching job herself for a while now, to no avail.

Word finally came from my adviser; there was no reprieve. What I'd done needed many more references, she said. (No, not those esoteric references to what I was experiencing in Jerusalem filtered through Poe's words that I'd tried to weave in.) What I'd written didn't have the right *voice* for academic work, I was told. I had to go back to the beginning and redo everything, she said. I felt humiliated, then enraged.

But as I cut through the open land beneath campus, striding down the long winding road back from Mount Scopus to Rehavia, I began to feel lighter, then liberated. On that walk from East to West Jerusalem, the voices that for months had been swirling in my mind swelled in volume, and I didn't have to suppress them any longer. I'd be free now to create a mosaic work, constellating the characters I'd met here against the haunting scenes of this natural world, engaging questions about religion, and why we were here, and why we felt so guiltily remote from the lives of the Palestinians around us. It would end with the birth of our second son, Tzvi, shortly before the Gulf War began. I remembered that white night when Anne and I walked hand in hand outside the hospital through the white stones of Jerusalem and everything seemed purified, as if before a sacrifice...

I burst into the apartment in a state of giddy exaltation to tell Anne what had happened: that I was going to concentrate now on my fiction, and try to do more freelance journalism, and let my thesis take the time it would, and I was going to be so much less melancholy and constricted and...I could not contain my ebullience.

"How are we going to survive?" Anne asked.

"Well, I'll work. I'll work different jobs and —"

"How are we going to survive?"

"I'll work. I'll borrow —"

"We have so much debt. We're so overdrawn already. We can't go on this way." She was shaking.

There was a torchlit procession through the streets of Jerusalem that night, another antigovernment action. And when we tried to resume our conversation after the boys were in bed, while I floundered for words and could find none, while she stared without speaking, the banging and shouting came nearer and nearer, rattling the panes, casting weird shadows. There was nothing to say. But we stayed. Until the children were woken and came in fear of the clamor to where we sat without moving in silence. Crying as if wrenched from a bad dream, rather than into a nightmare.

ELEVEN

THE NEWS beamed round the world: On April 1, 1925, all roads in Palestine led to the top of Mount Scopus, where, in a magnificent stone amphitheater, Lord Balfour would dedicate Hebrew University. Special trains had been chugging into Jerusalem from all over the country since dawn. Motor vehicles of every variety rumbled and snorted up the long pathway that climbed to the summit. Slopes were black with pedestrians trudging and scrambling. Gershom Scholem was part of this pilgrimage. More than seven thousand Jews attended the university's opening, which the press called "the cultural climax of the Jewish homeland movement."

The establishing of such an institution was first suggested in 1897 by Hermann Zvi Schapira, a Lithuanian-born rabbi and mathematics professor in Heidelberg, who envisioned Jewish theology and the sciences being taught in tandem — in German — at this Palestine institution. As early as the Second Zionist Congress in 1902, however, Chaim Weizmann was arguing that the university should be "a nursery fostering the living Jewish national language." It would furnish the homeland project "not only with a moral, scientific and cultural base, but also an economic one." Cultural activity radiating out from the center formed by the university would expand in tandem with the country's technical development, while the sheer concentration of Jewish youth in Jerusalem, combined with the institution's replenishing effect on the Jewish spirit, would foster public acceptance of the "moral right of ownership over our homeland."

Together with Judah Magnes, Weizmann developed a conceptual blueprint of the project, and the university's cornerstone — actually twelve stones, one for each biblical tribe — was laid in July 1918. Committees for hiring faculty and fund-raising were created, drawing on the support of prestigious figures from the realms of finance and the sciences: Baron Edmund de Rothschild, Paul Ehrlich, Felix Warburg, and Albert Einstein among them. Ahad Ha'am played the role of elevated moral guide throughout, despite his faltering health.

Deep challenges, external and internal, existed from the start and mounted as the university neared completion, but these did not dim the glow of its ideals for Judah Magnes, to whom Weizmann had effectively ceded leadership of the project by the early 1920s. Scholem met Magnes right after his arrival in Palestine. He found this "American radical" to be an exceptional personality, of "great charm and complexity," whose high-minded vision for the university, infused with orphic notions of Jewish humanism, resonated with Scholem's own dreams. Neither the university — nor, indeed, the homeland — signified in Magnes's view the Jews' withdrawal from the world and its great problems, but rather the establishment of a unique laboratory in which experiments for redeeming both could be conducted. Men and women of every race, religion, and nationality would be encouraged to study at the university, and even the question of what Judaism consisted in, which would be the focus of the Institute of Jewish Studies, should be approached as a matter relevant to everyone. Magnes proposed that the university's mission would be, "Not here Judaism, there humanity, but rather fusion of the two into a harmonious whole, an enriched, enlarged Judaism, an enriched and enlarged humanity." At the peak of Mount Scopus, it would serve as a vantage point from which to look out at humanity, "unblindered by

a civilization that seems doomed to destruction by reason of its bondage to its machinery and its material achievement."

No wonder Gershom felt swept up in the excitement that spring day. So many Jews felt the event's galvanic pull that authorities were obliged to begin turning people back at the wall surrounding the institute, which was situated, evocatively, at the spot where Titus stationed his troops when he laid siege to Jerusalem — a point from which you could also see where the Jews first entered the Promised Land. The amphitheater, facing east toward the rugged desert wilderness and the Dead Sea, rich in biblical associations, hadn't been completed yet. But even at this stage, it held twenty-five hundred people. Speakers would orate from a rickety wooden platform suspended over an abyss. Students brought homespun mats and goatskins to sit on; dignitaries were handed cushions. Those who couldn't get a good view and were agile enough scampered up the surrounding trees.

In the eyes of many Jews seeking entry, Balfour's presence at the event meant more even than the university's opening itself. His 1917 declaration was still viewed as the outstanding international gesture of support for the Jewish homeland. Hawkers plying the grounds of Mount Scopus did a brisk trade in Balfour chocolates, Balfour photographs, Balfour biscuits, and Balfour meatballs. Following a long-winded prayer by Isaac Kook, the Ashkenazi grand rabbi, Weizmann opened the ceremonies to respectful applause. But when the seventy-seven-year-old Balfour rose to his feet, the entire assembly rose with him, giving a standing ovation that went on and on.

Balfour declared that the gathering marked "a great epoch in the history of a people who made this little land of Palestine the centre of great religions, whose intellectual and moral destiny is from a national point of view reviving and who will look back to this day we are celebrating as one of the great milestones in their future career." Whereas for hundreds of years, the Jewish people had been scattered, its culture "the separate efforts of separate individuals," they would now at last be able to concentrate their "peculiar national genius in a common task." Balfour made a special appeal to the Arabs, urging them to remember the Dark Ages: "When Western civilization appeared almost extinct and smothered under barbaric influences, it was the Jews and Arabs together who gave the first sparks of light which illuminated that gloomy period." Why couldn't they now cooperate, to make this university a place from which "all sections of the population of Palestine may draw intellectual and spiritual advantage?"

Scholem never forgot the sight of the splendid-looking Balfour in the amphitheater that day, framed by the setting sun, "delivering his eulogy of the Jewish people, its achievements in the past, and its hopes for the future." And the ardent reception Balfour met with must have been deeply gratifying to the aging statesman himself who, with his stolid demeanor, deep-set eyes, crisp mustache, and genial air, struck admirers as the archetype of a gentleman.

Yet this view was not universal. When, against the pleas of the police, Balfour was escorted by Governor Storrs on a visit to the Church of the Holy Sepulchre, their entire route through the Old City's steep, narrow streets was mobbed with stern, silent onlookers. Storrs greeted some of these mute figures, who returned his salutations, and Balfour assumed the salutations were directed at him. At the church doors, his entourage deftly evaded a menacing throng.

It was only after he left Palestine and went on to Damascus that Balfour was compelled to register that his presence evoked not only adulation and discreet respect but also mortal fury. Massive bloody riots broke out, and had his train not been expeditiously diverted to a secret destination, Balfour might have been ripped to pieces. His tour of the Holy Land ended unceremoniously with him bobbing for two days on a liner in Beirut harbor, shielded from a hostile shore by the continual orbiting of a French torpedo destroyer.

Despite his heroic stature among Zionists, Balfour had a different reputation even back home in England, where some saw him as fatally self-absorbed, "spinsterish and architectural…a very beautiful object to look at, and at the same time a frustrated and perverse nature," in the words of one contemporary. "Nothing matters very much and few things matter at all," Balfour liked to say. Was he even aware before sailing from England that numerous warnings had been issued by the Arab Executive forecasting serious disturbances if the Jews gave any kind of ovation in his honor? Dozens of abusive telegrams addressed to Balfour were quietly destroyed by his minions at Government House before he laid eyes on them. The Arabs called a strike when Balfour reached Palestine. Students walked out of their classrooms. Jerusalem's shops were shuttered; an endless succession of bars and padlocks made the city feel evacuated. Houses were draped in mourning. Arabs wore black rosettes. Even unsympathetic journalists acknowledged that the protests unfolded in a spirit of sorrow, not rage, demonstrating the scope of grief over what was happening to the country in consequence of the Jewish homeland movement — refuting claims that discontent was confined to small parties of agitators.

In fact, Balfour's 1925 visit prompted what was probably the largest peaceable action of civil protest yet mounted by Arabs in Palestine. Storrs said that Balfour's visit "put the clock of reconciliation back by at least a year." Magnes, for his part, was livid. Before the ceremony at Mount Scopus, he'd written in his journal that Balfour's presence would turn the university into a "political

Esh-Shoura Newspaper
CAIRO, EGYPT

TO LORD BELFOUR

WHATFOR HAVE YOU COME TO MY COUNTRY?

HAVE YOU COME TO SEE THE MISFORTUNE AND MISERY, THAT HAVE BEFALLEN MY COUNTRYMEN THROUGH YOU?

HAVE YOU COME TO WITNESS THE PROCESS OF EXTINCTION AMONGST THE NATIVES OF PALESTINE WHICH IS THE HAND WORK OF YOUR OMINOUS DECLARATION?

HAVE YOU COME TO ASCERTAIN WHETHER THE DESTRUCTION OF MY COUNTRY HAS BEEN COMPLETED?

HAVE YOU COME TO HURRY MY COUNTRY'S DISASTER WHICH IS AN INEVITABLE ISSUE TO YOUR PROMISE?

HAVE YOU COME TO ENJOY THE SIGHT OF "ROME IN 'FLAMES'?

I WOULD HAVE YOUR LORDSHIP KNOW THAT YOU HAVE BECOME THE IMPERSONIFICATION OF INJUSTICE, THE BLACK SPECTRE, THE EVERLASTING SYMBOL OF MISFORTUNE IN PALESTINE.

«ASH-SHOURA»

instrument" that would badly damage relations with Arabs, the Muslim world and, indeed, the entire Near East. Opening the university "under the shadow of guns," the Jews would now be seen as "the tool of imperialism"—all to gratify the Zionists leaders who wished to make an "advertisement of Palestine."

Afterward, he wrote Ahad Ha'am despondently: "It was to have been expected that the University of all enterprises would be that agency which upon the high plane of pure scholarship, would in the course of time, bring about a spiritual reconciliation between the two most gifted races of Semitic stock. But the University has become the instrument of the very reverse."

It might be supposed that the Arabs overreacted to Balfour's symbolic presence, detracting from the university's mission on behalf of all peoples of Palestine. Except that *everything* was overwhelmingly symbolic at this juncture, since almost nothing tangible existed. Magnes himself felt uneasy about the opening, quite apart from Balfour's invitation, since, as he wrote Ha'am, "We have, unfortunately, very little to open, and I was fearful lest we create the false impression that we already had a University when we really have not." In addition to the Institute of Jewish Studies, the campus then consisted of only two small departments for scientific research.

Moreover, it was precisely *as* a symbol that the university had been championed by Weizmann, among others, who contended that the nationalist incentive was the reason why a Jewish university had to be established inside Palestine. In truth, there were as many uncertainties about the future identity of the institution as there were about the nature of the Zionist project itself, manifesting in overlapping practical and theoretical debates. Should the university serve as a research institute, promoting the achievements of an elite scholarly cadre in a core set of disciplines that Zionists had a vested interest in advancing in Palestine? Or should it be launched as a full-curriculum university for Jewish students regardless of their Zionist affiliation? If the latter, would its mission focus on providing a general Jewishly inflected education for all those young people whose educational opportunities were contracting on the Continent due to anti-Semitism and economic hardship? Or, as Weizmann first argued, should the university serve as the engine for a greater revitalization of Jewish culture?

Scholem saw the necessity of combining research with pedagogy for economic reasons, but even with more funding it was unclear that many qualified academics could be lured to this remote environment. What should the university's relationship to the Diaspora be? Some of its most important sponsors, including Rothschild and Warburg, opposed the university's Zionist mission, worrying that it would make the institute provincial. Religious interests balked at the whole premise of a secular bastion. "If the world could be saved by universities, Germany would have been the Messiah of the 20th Century," declared one American Reform rabbi about the opening on Mount Scopus. He opposed the project as an expression of "secular nationalism." That criticism was mild compared to the ultra-Orthodox line which, as Scholem learned in Meah She'arim, viewed all Zionist undertakings as Satanic and saw in the new university only cause to issue "fresh maledictive proclamations."

With such extreme dissension among the Jews themselves, can the Arabs be blamed for putting the worst possible construction on the university's mission?

It was an increasingly volatile time. Jewish immigration to Palestine was soaring: Between 1922 and 1927, the European influx almost doubled, from 83,000 to 150,000. The year of the university's opening marked the height of the wave, with more than 34,000 new arrivals. The population surge coincided with the rise of an affluent middle class in Palestine, which sought to catalyze opportunities for free private enterprise that contravened the Socialist tendencies of the Zionist Executive. It was Scholem's German bête noire of godless materialism, recrudescent in Jerusalem—only here it was often the German Zionists who formed the bulwark against commercial zeal. Around the time of the university's opening, Scholem wrote Benjamin about his apprehensions surrounding "the effects of intense capitalist colonization."

Compounding these forebodings, the same month that saw the festivities on Mount Scopus, Vladimir Jabotinsky founded his Revisionist party in Paris, intended to signal a return to Herzl's action-oriented political Zionism, which had been sacrificed to the Olympian pretentions of Weizmann's cohort. "Dr. Weizmann merely wanted research institutes in which scientists would work and strive to win the Nobel Prize, and not a school in which students would study," Jabotinsky charged after the university's founding.

While some recent scholarship about Jabotinsky has stressed his tactical brilliance and poignant psychological complexity, his platform was crude and incendiary, and its legacy thrives. Jabotinsky insisted on the revival of plans for a powerful Jewish militia in Palestine, demanded that the land on both sides of the Jordan River be considered part of Palestine, and emphasized the principle that Zionism was a political movement promoting mass settlement to establish a Jewish majority. He scorned the cooperative policies advocated by the German Zionist leadership and incited mob actions to achieve political gain. He was virulently anti-Socialist and anti-agrarian, mocking the Zionist "culture of the cow" that believed it could turn Palestine Jewish one farm at a time. He opposed territorial compromise and—perhaps most damningly in Scholem's eyes—sought to make the Jewish presence in Palestine a populist, vigorously mercantile middle-class heaven. In 1926, Jabotinsky wrote an inspirational film script for the Jewish National Fund in which the protagonist's great dream was to open a perfume factory that would achieve prosperity through global exports of the magic scent "Balm of Gilead." Even had Jabotinsky's means not been anathema, the Revisionist image of a successful Jewish settlement in Palestine was Scholem's worst nightmare.

When Jabotinsky announced the Revisionist platform at the Fourteenth Zionist Congress in the summer of 1925, Weizmann recoiled. "Palestine is not Rhodesia," he exclaimed, reminding Jabotinsky that the six hundred thousand Arabs had as much right to the land as the Jews had to a national home. "We must accept Palestine as it is, with its sand and rocks, its Arabs and its Jews," he said. "Anything else would be a deception." But of course Palestine "as it is" was always a factor of aggressive fantasizing about what Palestine might eventually become, as Weizmann knew from two decades of diplomatic maneuvering for the homeland. In 1925, the Revisionists garnered only 2 percent of the delegates to the congress; four years later they were Zionism's third-largest party. "No more gallant officer, no more charming and cultivated companion could have been imagined than Vladimir Jabotinsky," Governor

Storrs observed, adding, "I can imagine no man who, if allowed his extreme logical way, would more certainly than this Arch Revisionist have involved Palestine, and perhaps Syria too, in battle and sudden death." Storrs conceded that Jabotinsky had at least served the purpose of making the mainstream Zionist position appear eminently moderate.

In the spring of 1925, Arthur Ruppin, a German-born Zionist leader who helped launch the kibbutz movement, began holding discussions with other Jewish intellectuals who hoped to reach some kind of rapprochement with the Arabs. Magnes became part of these talks, as did Scholem. The first political essay Scholem wrote in Jerusalem arose out of these conversations: a forceful condemnation of Revisionist propaganda agitating for the restoration of the Jewish legion. Accumulating weapons and promulgating fear and mistrust do not deter but rather incite war, the manifesto proclaimed. Magnes and Bergmann were among its six signatories, who together promised to struggle against militarism and nationalist bravado.

Ruppin's group started outlining the framework for what it labeled "a bi-national Palestinian community." That August at the Fourteenth Zionist Congress in Vienna, Ruppin declared, "Palestine will be a state of two nations. Gentlemen, this is a fact, a fact which many of you have not sufficiently realized." The blunt assurance of Ruppin's prognosis did not make it more congenial to the main body of the congress, where Jabotinsky grabbed the attention. His belligerence perhaps appeared less paranoid in light of the fact that the congress had been preceded by two days of bloody anti-Semitic riots in the Austrian capital, during which thousands of men rampaged through the streets, calling for an uprising by "Christian Vienna" and instigating "Jew hunts" to expel the Jewish populace. There were mass stonings of taxicabs, streetcars, and restaurants, with many severe injuries and more than $4 million worth of damage. It was hardly an atmosphere to make Jews feel

sanguine about their local identity. When the early Zionist movement swerved alarmingly right, violent European anti-Semitism
loomed in the rear, waving the black flags that sent Jews over
the edge.

It soon became apparent that the binational proposal Scholem
was helping to develop would pose as much of a challenge to
Weizmann's Zionist faction as it did to the Revisionists. Scholem
wrote bitterly to Ernst Simon in September: "You know that I
came to Palestine without many illusions. After two years, I can
now assure you that I unfortunately have even fewer than before."
Zionism, he continued, "abdicated long ago; the only question the
Zionist should now ask is where he really belongs."

Scholem's assessment of the Zionist position could hardly
have been bleaker. Yet his professional outlook grew steadily more
promising. He developed a proposal for a ten-year program to
gather, analyze, and publish a comprehensive array of mystical
texts, through which he aimed to uncover the history of Kabbalah's evolution from generation to generation, along with evidence
for whether it constituted an intramural Jewish development or
was driven by outside influences. When he informed Chaim Bialik
of his plan, Bialik responded euphorically, "You are the man who
will find, at the end of your labors, the lost key to the locked gate
of the temple of Kabbalah." He vowed to bring Scholem's project
before the board of Hebrew University.

Soon thereafter, the search committee for the Institute of Jewish Studies began to assess Scholem's eligibility for a professorship
in the philosophy department. Magnes thought the idea of a chair
in Jewish mysticism highly peculiar and wonderfully appropriate.
It was a big help that the young scholar who'd dug deepest in the
field was already in Jerusalem so that the university wouldn't incur
relocation fees. Though he had various backers outside the scholarly world, the recommendation that clinched Scholem's appointment came, to his amusement, from Immanuel Löw, one of the

last survivors of the Wissenschaft des Jüdentums school, a bota-
nist who'd written a tome on *The Flora of the Jews* and who once
happened to read two pages by Scholem about the bisexuality of
palm trees in kabbalistic literature. "Such a man can be relied on,"
Löw promised.

Scholem was granted the further honor of delivering one of the
institute's inaugural public lectures, in November 1925. He chose
to speak about the Zohar—specifically the question of whether
Rabbi Moses de León, who died at the beginning of the fourteenth
century in Spain, was the Zohar's author, or whether its origins lay
much farther back in time, perhaps with the second-century Rabbi
Shimon Bar Yochai, to whom Moses de León himself attributed
the work.

Scholem launched with an attack on the historian Heinrich
Graetz, who claimed that Moses de León had perpetrated one
of the most successful and reprehensible forgeries in history. He
tried to dismantle Graetz's main piece of evidence: a manuscript
purportedly containing statements by Moses de León's wife and
daughter, who swore that he'd never had any ancient text resembling the Zohar in his possession. Everything he wrote came from
his heart and his head, they said. When the pair saw him scribbling
without any manuscript before him, they asked why he pretended
he was working from some source other than his own brain. "I'm
only doing this to make some money," he confessed.

Scholem attacked the document from different angles—least
edifyingly, by refuting the statements of the wife and daughter on
the basis of their being women and therefore unreliable witnesses
according to Jewish Law. He went on to critique the widely held
assumption that Moses de León decided to make his move into
pseudepigraphy—the spurious attribution of authorship—when
he realized that nobody was paying any attention to his books.
Scholem pointed out that unlike the vast majority of Kabbalists
at the time, this man *never* laid claim to authorship of his books,

always citing earlier mystical midrashim as his sources. "Moses
de León avows that all the works he has penned have been transmitted to him alone as an esoteric revelation concealed from the
eyes of the multitude," Scholem wrote. Though a definitive answer
couldn't be given, the available philological clues indicated that
"right of primacy belongs to the Zohar," he concluded.

The lecture made neither an especially persuasive argument
against Graetz's position nor a strong case for Moses de León's
credibility. But still, Scholem developed his argument with vehe-
ment bravado, and from a position of textual fluency that no one
in his audience could match. Insofar as Scholem's opening lecture
at the Institute of Jewish Studies blasted the stale truisms of the
last generation of Jewish historians — showing why even the foundational texts of Kabbalah needed to be reexamined without interpretative bias in a spirit of genuine scientific inquiry — it was an
impressive performance, predicated on the idea of returning to an
earlier model of visionary authority.

Ten years later, however, Scholem reversed his position. Having
now had time to immerse himself in details of the text, he declared
Moses de León to be the author of every part of the Zohar, which
"contains no layers of ancient mysticism." In a subsequent lecture
delivered in English in New York, he elaborated the reasons that
Graetz had been right all along.

A decade of hard study with a wealth of new sources might easily lead a young scholar to revise former opinions. But matters are
more complicated. For one thing, Scholem was working with the
same sources in his earlier and later assessments. More provocatively, he'd begun staking out a strong position on pseudepigraphy long before he wrote the lecture. In 1919, Scholem declared in
his diary, "with virtually no exceptions kabbalistic literature is a
forgery. The idea of pseudepigraphy belongs to one of the most
profound problems of history." He observed that Walter Benjamin called such falsification "a legitimate historical idea." In 1920,

Scholem scathingly reviewed a book by a German author that defended the antiquity of the Kabbalah in general, and the Zohar in particular, challenging its claims on philological grounds, among others: "It is simply not true that the language of the Zohar is identical with that of the Jerusalem Talmud." Scholem had discovered additional arguments against the work's antiquity in other early writings.

Was Scholem's speech at the institute itself a great fraud aimed at saving the reputation of one of Judaism's most brazen literary impostors? If so, was this his way of getting back at Graetz and his gang of "erudite liquidators"? Or was the deceit perpetrated out of fear that he himself might one day be accused of sharing Moses de León's tendencies to play dice with history?

Certainly it wasn't going to bolster Scholem's argument that Jewish mysticism was a legitimate scholarly discipline if the work viewed as the closest thing to a Bible for Kabbalists had been written a thousand years after it was ostensibly composed — by a struggling author in Spain whose own wife and daughter called him a liar. In Palestine, as was becoming ever more apparent, historical primacy translated into contemporary power.

Still, it's startling that he elected to downplay his own skepticism in his debut appearance at an institute that aspired to bring unprecedented scientific rigor to the task of Jewish self-understanding. Once again, the question of Hebrew University's identity as symbol of the past and adumbration of the future is thrown into relief. Given that at the age of twenty-two, Scholem was sufficiently well versed in the history of Kabbalah to question the time line and authenticity of the entire canon, his 1925 speech endorsing the view that the Zohar just couldn't be Moses de León's work appears oddly literal minded.

But another interpretation of Scholem's talk is possible, in which the conservatism of his defense is less indicative of faith in the tradition's historical integrity than of his own psychophilosophical vulnerability. Having at last arrived in the country he'd been yearning for since early youth, and finding the experience profoundly unsettling, what could he hold on to save the purity of the texts that had brought him there? In his autobiography, Scholem described how his earliest experience of studying the Talmud kindled his intellect and imagination by virtue of "the power of a tradition thousands of years old." The duration of historical time itself conferred authenticity. Perhaps the savagery of Scholem's attack against those who considered the Kabbalah itself something like a counterfeit version of Judaism reflected his desperate need to believe that in the temporal depths of his beloved manuscripts, the spiritual realm in which he'd found his life's calling remained intact.

In early adolescence, Scholem's riposte to Buber and the lesser lights of the Neopathetic Cabaret had been to elevate historically mediated knowledge as a counterpoint to the faddish embrace of pure present-day being. Later, he would write that "revelation will come to unfold its infinite meaning (which cannot be confined to the unique event of revelation) only in its constant relationship to history, the arena in which tradition unfolds." Philology was the practice that gave content to the principle of spiritualized time.

Scholem's notion of philology, as the scholar Andreas Kilcher has proposed, was steeped in the term's root meaning: "love of words." Imagine a gleaming stone, glimpsed through layers of clear sea, then being slowly drawn up from the water, passing colorfully through different spectra of light into the air, where it fast loses its magical glow. The process of philological exploration for Scholem was the reverse: taking dry words from ancient texts and plunging them back down through waves of time until they regained their mystical luster, at last reaching a depth where they shone with God's own light. In 1920, in a review of a book of kabbalistic poetry, Scholem wrote, "I do believe that deep philology can have a mystic function if it fosters, accompanies and evokes the changes of time in its works."

Just as in its root definition "Kabbalah" means "tradition and reception" — the process of transmission — philology could be understood as the medium in which transmission became perceptible. "In their critical work historians must expect to suddenly appear as restorers," Scholem wrote. If philology involved both rendering transmission legible and *embodying* transmission as it resuscitated the past, then philology itself became Kabbalah.

But this messianic redemptive process could operate only in a realm with deep, collective roots. If all you were transmitting into the present was one renegade medieval rabbi's fantastical visions cooked up in private from an unhappy home, if you could never lose sight of the human-psychological in your pursuit of the historical divine, the whole process of transmission became less one of forging revelatory links between generations than a shabby business of rewriting history to escape the here and now.

Although in 1919 Scholem had dutifully recorded Benjamin's comment that falsification was a legitimate historical category, he wasn't yet able to assimilate the concept. And in Palestine, with everything up for grabs (the meaning of the university, the nature of the Jewish settlement, the purpose of Zionism), if even the old texts defining his vocation were latter-day forgeries, how could he help experiencing vertigo? In this new country, where history was already being invoked right and left as a political tool, a foreshortened past meant a truncated future.

Anyone, Scholem declared in a later essay, unable to accept "the principle of Torah from heaven," anyone who "does not share the firm faith of our forebears, whether he is engaged in other paths toward faith, or whether his path has become clouded by history and historical criticism...," may be objectively considered a religious anarchist." But if the collapse of religious authority made everyone religious anarchists, the acceptance of pseudepigraphy in the tradition he'd hoped would restore Jewish authenticity on new grounds threatened to make politics and religion alike the domain of pretenders and nihilists.

When she'd all but given up hope, Anne suddenly got offered a teaching position at a new experimental religious girls' school for the arts. It was just in time. We'd crashed against our overdraft limit and begun bouncing rent checks. Though I'd vowed to keep working on my thesis, I'd lost all investment in the project and sensed that the administration was quietly scaling back my course load. Though I'd promised to find other work to close the gap between our life and our means, I'd gotten nowhere beyond scanning job requests for technical writers by Tel Aviv software firms, and feeling a sense of preemptive defeat so bitter that it seemed to recuse me from actually having to apply for employment. At one point I interviewed at a nonprofit engaged in human rights work with new immigrants, but the organization could pay someone for only a few hours a week. Through a connection made by a cousin, I began writing promotional material for a network of progressive foster homes, but the organization had no funds allocated for the work, and I couldn't bring myself to take what little they might spare. I found some private students to tutor. I taught English to exhausted workers at the mammoth Angel Bakery. I cobbled together what I could, but what I'd cobbled barely made the sole of one shoe.

Anne was excited, but also scared, about the new job. It had the potential to be the school of her dreams — one that would allow her to become the teacher she'd always wanted to be, melding faith and art while molding young minds in Jerusalem. But disciplining students had always been hard for her, and expectations were high at this school, which had to prove its legitimacy to a resistant Orthodox community. Indeed, a school of this nature would never even have been attempted for boys — their minds would obviously be consecrated to Torah. It was grotesque that these girls were being given the chance to study art only because they were restricted by gender from learning what ostensibly mattered most. But we tried to keep in mind that from a broader perspective, the boys' loss was the greater.

The director who interviewed Anne made it clear that she would be required to dress appropriately, which meant not just long skirts and sleeves but also head covering. We reminded ourselves that other places of employment required other kinds of alien costuming, whether a stiff suit or a skimpy halter top. The school really *might* be her dream job, whatever she was wearing, and anyway, we were dead broke.

Things started out rocky. But the director took a liking to Anne and helped mentor her teaching. She got along with the girls and enjoyed introducing them to the literature and artworks that had been inspiring her own burgeoning painting. By the second term, she'd built some rapport with them, and everything began to feel like things might work out after all. Then one warm day when she didn't have class, we went to the center of town together to run an errand. As we walked along, Anne spotted one of her students and started to greet her. Then she saw the student's eyes running up and down her in shock. It took a moment to realize that the girl was absorbing Anne's immodest dress: jeans and a T-shirt. There was an awkward moment of interaction between us before we walked our separate ways.

Anne fretted that she could lose her job if the student reported her. "It's not limited to school," she told me. "We have to be more careful." The idea that having to follow the religious dress code "for work" meant observing it in public, too, had somehow failed to register until that moment.

I didn't think further of the encounter until a few weeks later when we were taking a Sabbath walk, with the boys in their usual sartorial free-for-all, and me yarmulke-less. Suddenly Anne exclaimed under her breath; the next moment she was awkwardly introducing me to another student and her family.

"They're going to report me," she said when they'd left.

"No," I said, without conviction.

"They will."

"Well, you'll find another job. In a secular school."

"There weren't any jobs in secular schools."

The boys stared at us anxiously.

Words came into my head and popped loudly and meaninglessly, like balloons at a children's party.

"We need the money," she said. "And I like the school. Why are you always so resistant to even being a little observant?"

"We've been through this."

"You make it impossible for us to even be the least bit traditional. I'm going to get fired."

We returned home, and again nothing happened. But in the next month two girls were suspended for violating the Sabbath. And we both felt, superstitiously, that if we were caught in our secular underwear a third time, our luck would run out. And so a situation evolved whereby we gradually became more and more careful when we left the door of our apartment to ensure that our clothes and behavior comported with Orthodox dictates. On the Sabbath, we became, indeed, exactingly observant, at least to casual observers. Anne wore big hats or sparkly head wraps. I took care not to wander outside without my dark yarmulke. The boys were stuffed into button-down shirts. Suddenly, it became clear that, while we might have worked through the issue of how far we were willing to go with our personal religious identification early on, we had not worked through how far we were willing to go toward revealing our religious laxity.

Or rather, once again, the answer seemed to be "not very." Not so far that we would risk a salary at a moment when economic pressures were dire. In the eyes of the outside world, we were assimilating to Jerusalem's religious world—that *was* our group identity, whatever we might privately believe. Anyway, the whole issue of "belief" in Judaism is tricky: What is clearly mandated is the performance of certain actions. It didn't matter that our conformity was largely limited to dress and what we ate in public; this practice had a larger symbolic value within the community, even if for us it was a means to an end. And so increasingly we were living two lives: one hidden within the walls of our apartment, which bore hardly any traces of religious identity, and another, religiously traditional one, on the streets beyond the secret garden of the courtyard.

I didn't like the dichotomy, but there's always a certain frisson in living a double life. So we tried to manage our strategic duplicity, shutting out thoughts of how our outward conformity might be projecting a larger, more uniform message about Israel to the world. And this was, in its own way, a form of regional assimilation as well. How many people in the Middle East are living these kinds of dualities—secretly lenient inside, devout out of doors? Instead of the ice we'd been sliding on cracking all the way through, we ourselves split in two.

Meanwhile, I cut myself off more and more from the heterogeneity of the city, without even realizing I was doing so: spending less time in the Old City, not finding occasion even to wander through East Jerusalem. My life out of the home was mostly conducted through the university, where my serious students now were almost all new Russian immigrants in the humanities faculty, for whom Israel would prove but a way station.

And while the doubleness of our day-to-day existence was not very onerous, the question of what exactly we did believe—what exactly we were doing in Jerusalem—was rekindled between us. For while it wasn't exactly that we no longer believed the same thing, our individual senses of responsibility toward enacting whatever belief we did retain popped out of alignment. Anne asked repeatedly why I had to make such a big deal of doing just a little more religiously than we did, when I said I still felt attached to Judaism. And I would ask again and again whether she really wanted to assume even some lighter model yoke of the Law, given the status of women, for one thing. And she would remind me of things I might do to lighten the yoke of her status as a woman, quite apart from religious obligation. And point out how I actually made things harder for her, by virtue of defying the expectations of observance that were part of her job — our main source of income, she added. What was more, she now said, since the boys naturally had no wish to go to synagogue or perform any home rituals, she felt that I allied myself with them against her.

Which was true, if not exactly deliberately so, at least not in the way that she meant. But I tried to remind her of how incapable she, too, had felt of really carrying out the dictates of the Law. And she would acknowledge that, while saying this didn't mean she felt at peace with how we'd stopped even trying. We've been through this and through this, I reminded her. I still feel thwarted every holiday, she reminded me — and I don't really know why it should be so threatening to keep the Sabbath once a week, for God's sake. And maybe even if we've been through these questions before, that doesn't mean we ever resolved them. Because to really resolve them would mean we'd given up on Judaism.

Or become totally Orthodox, I said. And I'd try to reiterate the argument we used to make: that the Sabbath, in its essence, was largely observed by the whole of West Jerusalem, and so by us, by default. So far as I was concerned, we got as much as we wanted — the slowdown of time, the reduction of consumer opportunities, the drop in car traffic and profusion of quiet — just by walking the streets and reading at home. As for synagogues themselves, well, on the high holidays, or those rare Friday evenings when we both felt moved to hear the prayers sung and to join in where we could, there were countless options—from the colorful young Reform congregation near the train station, to the seventeenth-century synagogue transported stone by stone from a town between Venice and Padua, where services were sung in Italian and Hebrew, to the large nearby Orthodox synagogue favored by French families, which had its own stylishly dignified inflection, and so on. We were not alone in Jerusalem in keeping our engagement with the religion spontaneous, I insisted, but keeping it nonetheless, and trusting in doing so that the connection was yet more authentic than what we'd known from our temple experience in New York.

Well, I feel the urge to go to shul more than you do, she replied, so it's not my caprice; it's my acquiescence. And maybe there's just something half-assed and false about that pick-and-choose, make-your-own version of Judaism, she added. Maybe deciding what you will and will not do, when and where you want, has got nothing whatsoever to do with whatever being a believing Jew means—and you tell me you still believe in God, she reminded me. I do still believe in God, I said, several times in a row. Like Dorothy in her ruby slippers saying there's no place like home. Knowing as I said so that the belief increasingly seemed void of determinable content as some gobbledy-gook version of the grand mystical Ein Sof.

And I thought of one friend at the university—an American, a brilliant Miltonist who'd been president of a Marxist group at his Ivy League school, and then at some point had begun returning to the religion. He was the opposite of an enthusiast: rigorously analytic in all areas of thought. Over the early years of our acquaintance, he moved from modern Orthodoxy to absolute ultra-Orthodoxy. This made complete sense to me: If you take any of it seriously, how can you draw the line anywhere? This drive to follow the pure letter of the Law—a drive that can never be realized—comes, over time, to cannibalize all other drives, I said. Freud postulated that Judaism, having begun with a ban on making an image of God, developed into a religion of "drive renunciation." In fact, he maintained, drive renunciations, and the associated ethical rules, constitute "the earliest beginnings of a moral and social order"—the foundational gesture of the collective. And perhaps the collective that began in this way ultimately finds it can survive and continue to grow only by multiplying that original renunciation—extending restrictions through space and time, the same way that certain branches of Christianity hold that original sin unoriginally recycles through each generation. For Freud, the ball starts rolling in response to guilty feelings about killing the father—a suppression of hostility toward God Himself—which offers an inexhaustible font of resentment, so that the "commandments must be made ever harsher, ever more meticulous, and at the same time ever more petty." But the source of unassuageable guilt may equally arise simply from killing natural urges—from murdering nature itself, a process that, once begun, by definition has no natural conclusion.

So yes, I hover ambivalently before even the first step of consistent observance, I allowed. I could see no way out of the cascading sequence of commandments, subscribing to a domino theory of religious Judaism. "If you start lighting candles Friday evening, what's to prevent you ending up crosshatched in phylacteries with a tiny box on your brow every morning?" I asked.

And Anne said that was ridiculous. Dramatic and childish. As though accepting the value of tradition meant annulling all power of discretion. And I asked her what she really wanted by way of a religious life. And she said she didn't know, but had lost patience with my tendency to invoke Freud or some other Central European pessimist to justify laziness when all she was asking for was a little more thoughtful observance in our home—which could make our outward lives in Jerusalem more harmonious and also be aesthetically gracious in a manner we both once aspired to. We always thought we had to keep advancing toward a greater spirituality in our life somehow, she reminded me. We used to believe that was vital for who we are. It used not to be so hard for us to do more than we do now, and get something out of it, she cried. That's true, I said, trying to soothe her. "We've moved backward," she cried. And I knew she was right. Without seeing any way forward. Or indeed either side of us.

And though we didn't fall into an out-and-out fight then, the abiding question of what our faith was left a hollowed-out place in our home where the light didn't switch on anymore and I felt guilty but wouldn't change, and the sight of the religious in Jerusalem left me more and more estranged, less and less certain that I believed *anything* they believed, and wondering what I was doing then in their midst, pretending to be like them, uncertain even in my own heart what I did believe and beginning to secretly ask myself whether — if I'd really stopped believing altogether in formal Judaism, having moved either beyond or behind whatever faith I once possessed — that meant I could no longer say what we were doing in Israel. For the first time a little voice crept into the back of my mind whispering that our move to Jerusalem might have been a mistake. And all these complexities were only compounded by the way questions of our economic and spiritual existence now snarled together, more and more loudly, like two dogs on one chain.

Once again, in my free hours I tried to find some solace rereading essays by Scholem that helped bring me to Israel, trying to recover what I'd felt then. In the Zohar, and in certain kabbalistic texts that grew out of this work, there arose an idea of two manifestations of Torah. These corresponded with the two sacred trees: the Tree of Knowledge of good and evil, and the Tree of Life, "the tree of freedom, symbolic of an age when the dualism of good and evil was not yet (or no longer) conceivable," Scholem wrote. All the restrictive aspects of Torah were connected with the Tree of Knowledge, which was the historical Torah, while the Tree of Life represented the Torah's utopian aspect. The second tablets, which were created after Moses broke the first set in wrathful despair on seeing his people worship the golden calf, were derived from the Tree of Knowledge, but the first tablets had inscribed "a revelation of the Torah in keeping with the original state of man…This was a truly spiritual Torah, bestowed upon a world in which Revelation and Redemption coincided, in which there was no need to hold the powers of uncleanness and death in check by prohibitions." The second tablets, by contrast, were identified with exile, which becomes almost synonymous with sin in some kabbalistic works, because "the exile of the Shekinah, which began in principle with the fall, took on its full meaning with the historical exile of the Jewish people."

But now we're in Jerusalem, I said to Anne, finally. We're here in Zion, I noted. Now, in fact, we've returned, so why can't we live as though the utopian Torah has been restored? *Here we are today at this place in this moment*, I said. *Aren't we?*

And she stared at me. I go every day and stand in front of a group of religious girls, dressed up like a religious woman, pretending to be part of their community, trying to help them grow in their creativity. Which I keep telling them has something to do with being true to yourself. And I feel like a total hypocrite. I *live* this every day. And you're telling me to act as though we exist in the age of the utopian Torah so you can avoid doing anything halachically just because you find it a drag. You're trying to make the case for some higher, self-created faith that has no basis in the Torah, or even in the actual Kabbalah—which always attaches to its utopian imagery the reminder that now, in our fallen world, every single law still applies. You're trying to use Gershom Scholem to avoid making a real life in Jerusalem.

Or so I imagined her speaking as she stared at me then. But in fact she just stared and stared at me, until at last one of us walked out of the room. And then it was morning. And then it was night again.

TWELVE

IN THE SPRING OF 1927, Gershom Scholem went to England, where he cloistered himself in the amber majesty of Oxford's Bodleian Library and read manuscripts about the greatest false messiah in Jewish history. The gist of the story was already known to him.

Sabbatai Sevi, born in Smyrna in 1626 to an affluent family, was still a young man when his strange behaviors—his swings between euphoria and melancholy, the novel twists he gave to ancient law—provoked the censure of local rabbis. Along with the anger he caused, however, Sabbatai's voice was reputed to be transcendently beautiful; when he sang hymns, listeners were enraptured. In time, Sabbatai was effectively cast out of Smyrna. He lived for a while in Jerusalem, then Cairo, where, in 1664, he married a woman named Sarah who'd been orphaned as a girl by the Chmielnicki massacres in Poland. Soon afterward, he met a brilliant, eccentric young scholar known as Nathan of Gaza, who told him that his sadness reflected his mission as the messiah. Thereafter, Nathan became the chief prophet and spokesperson for Sabbatai's movement.

By the summer of 1665, reports of the sublime revolution Sabbatai had ignited were circulating beyond the Levant, throughout much of Europe. Fervent expectations among the Jews disrupted the course of trade across the Ottoman Empire. The gift of prophecy swept over multitudes in the wake of Sabbatai's preaching. Entire communities in Poland and elsewhere on the Continent shut down their mundane affairs as they prepared to depart from their homes to join their brethren in the Holy Land.

In February 1666, Sabbatai was arrested by the Ottoman authorities as he sailed into Constantinople — partly because of the disturbance he'd caused to business and governance and partly at the instigation of rabbis who condemned what they saw as Sabbatai's heretical teachings. For seven months, Sabbatai's followers visited the fortress in Gallipoli where he was locked, becoming progressively more excited by hopes that redemption was imminent. But late that summer, one of the visitors, a preacher from Poland, Rabbi Nehemiah Kohen, challenged Sabbatai's mission: He announced that he himself was the Jews' long-awaited redeemer.

Kohen didn't actually deny Sabbatai's messiahship; rather, he framed the struggle for salvation now under way as the work of two messiahs. There was the messiah of the House of Joseph, whose title he claimed, and whose mission was in large part martial, concerned with revenge and reconquest of lost Jewish lands. Sabbatai was, Kohen said, the messiah of the House of David, the final executor of redemption. The tasks of these two messiahs necessarily unfolded sequentially, with the work of the messiah of the House of Joseph preparing for the advent of the messiah of the House of David. According to Kohen, therefore, Sabbatai Sevi could not launch his messiahship until his own mission was complete, which meant that Sabbatai's activities hitherto had been fraudulent.

Lacking even the erratic learning that had allowed Sabbatai to master the Zohar and certain Talmudic treatises in his youth, Kohen's prophecies were grounded only in popular apocalyptic tracts. But his relentless, stubborn literalism made him a formidable adversary. Refusing to relinquish his claims on the messianic crown, Kohen denounced Sabbatai to the Turkish authorities, accusing him of inciting sedition against the sultan and committing sexual transgressions.

As a result, Sabbatai was brought before the sultan in the northern capital city of the empire, Adrianople, and told by the grand vizier that if he was indeed the messiah, it was obvious he would have no difficulty performing miracles, which the sultan looked forward to witnessing. The greatest archers of the empire had been assembled to conduct the demonstration, Sabbatai was told. They would now proceed to encircle Sabbatai and shoot arrows into every part of him. The court was prepared to be amazed when the arrows bounced off the messiah's flesh, leaving him unscathed.

Given the choice between apostasy and execution, Sabbatai "donned the turban," in the contemporary phrase for conversion to Islam, and took the name Mehmet van Effendi. Adopted by the sultan's court in his new identity, Sabbatai was given a sinecure among the palace gatekeepers. He became a favorite of the sultan's powerful mother, Hatice Thuran—herself a Ukrainian Christian who had been kidnapped as a girl by Ottoman armies and now served as a zealous promoter of the Muslim faith. Sabbatai's wife, Sarah, who joined him in Adrianople, also converted. She was now known as Fatima Cadin.

Sabbatai continued preaching, disseminating an increasingly unpredictable message, sometimes pressing other Jews to convert, other times encouraging them to understand his own conversion mystically, as a prologue to the consummation of his messianic kingship. Eventually, amid reports that he'd resumed certain Jewish practices and was secretly fraternizing with Sufis, Sabbatai was exiled far from the center of the empire, to Dulcigno in modern-day Montenegro, where he died several years later. Nathan continued writing intricate treatises, yet only rarely addressed the community directly. In his last extant letter before dying in 1680, he bitterly deplored the divisive quarrels that had ruined the people's hopes for redemption, signing himself—in a complex double wordplay on his middle name Benjamin—"the little child, Wolf of the Wilderness."

But the Sabbatian faith did not vanish with the messiah's apostasy or the prophet's death; rather, it inspired an underground mystical movement that remained active in various guises up until the First World War. Scholem was captivated by the theological ingenuity that enabled believers to withstand the crisis of the messiah's conversion to Islam. Indeed, the radical tensions of this whole drama — at once so politically reckless and metaphysically fertile — arguably became the catalyst to the greatest works of Scholem's career.

Working in Oxford that summer, he became fascinated by the writings of Abraham Cardozo, scion of a crypto-Jewish Marrano family in Spain, who reconverted to Judaism in Venice in 1648. Cardozo's embrace of the Sabbatian movement, as Scholem saw it, bore the direct imprint of Marrano thought. Indeed, for Cardozo, Scholem later wrote, "The apostasy of the Messiah represented a kind of highest justification of the apostasy of the Spanish Marranos in 1391 and 1492." Cardozo understood that Sabbatai's actions had precipitated a crisis in Jewish tradition. The rupture could not be repaired by blotting out Sabbatai's memory; it required that the tradition itself be reinterpreted to embrace his apostasy.

To achieve this, Cardozo drew on strands of Kabbalah concerned with the division between the Tree of Knowledge and the Tree of Life — between a world subjected to the Law in its current form and a world of primordial harmony in which those commandments did not apply. Like other theologians of the movement who were contemporaries of Sabbatai and had direct personal experience of his spiritual leadership, Cardozo did not doubt the necessity of Sabbatai's personal descent into the sphere of darkness. He likened the situation of Torah in the age of exile to the predicament of a person who has fallen from a high roof into a deep well, suffering injuries all over his body that require medications and cures to heal. The laws were the equivalent of a physician's prescriptions for the individual patient. But with the advent of the Redeemer, all marks of injury vanished, as if the fall itself had been reversed. The Redeemer "has the power of restoring all worlds because he himself is the first Adam [in his messianic reincarnation]," Cardozo wrote.

So far from glossing over Sabbatai's apostasy, Cardozo made it the central act in his career. He joined Nathan of Gaza in proposing that the messiah was compelled to enter the realm of the *kelipot* (husks or bark) — the realm given over to the materialist forces of evil — because only the Redeemer, the holiest of men, could rescue the last imprisoned sparks of divinity scattered there. Once these had been reclaimed, the Kingdom of Evil would dissolve of its own accord, since that divine residue alone had sustained it. Thus it was precisely by taking the turban that Sabbatai Sevi could perform the mission God had assigned him. "It is ordained that the King Messiah don the garments of a Marrano and so go unrecognized by his fellow Jews," Cardozo wrote. "In a word, it is ordained that he become a Marrano like me." Both men had sought to resolve the conflict between the exterior and interior worlds by attaching themselves on the outside to an unredeemed realm, but on the inside to a mystical, messianic Judaism.

In expressing the notion that Sabbatai had to camouflage himself as a Muslim, just as members of his entire sect had to pretend they were Christian, Cardozo's deeper concern emerged: What could the Jewish people as a whole extrapolate from Sabbatai's actions regarding their obligations? The commandments were understood mystically as steps that would encourage the Messiah's arrival with his mission to redeem the world. What became of Jewish Law now that the Messiah had already walked among them, and what could be expected to transpire when Sabbatai returned from his journey? Noting that the Sabbatians confronted the same problem that the first generation of Christians encountered after Jesus's death, when the transfiguration of the world predicated on the Messiah's appearance was not manifest to everyone, Scholem argued that the Sabbatians came up with their own solution to the problem. Whereas St. Paul had proclaimed the end of the Law, Cardozo said the Law was infinite and plastic: It could remold its decrees to match changed historical circumstances. The present thus marked a fresh phase of the tradition, not its abrogation. As one theologian phrased the matter, "The Days of the Messiah represent the religious and political consummation of the national history and, however idealized, still belong to the world in which we live."

Cardozo explained how the tradition could accommodate such a transformation by reframing the difference between the written and the oral Torahs. Whereas conventionally those rabbinical commentaries on Scripture and Law that comprise the oral Torah were understood as strict translations of God's words that merely elaborated the terms of their practical fulfillment, he proposed that the written Torah had no fixed application. Instead, it was understood as "pure revelation," Scholem wrote, which made it a fundamentally mystical document that took on different guises for different ages. Some Kabbalists believed that the actual letters of the Torah combined in new patterns for Adam, for Noah, for the Jewish people at Sinai, and so on. Everything became historically contingent.

Reflecting on Sabbatai's behavior even before the apostasy, Cardozo observed that at moments Sabbatai's actions clearly went beyond the way of life endorsed by tradition. Sabbatai stood "at the boundary between the validity of the old law and the coming into view of a new level of the Torah's fulfillment," Scholem wrote. His individual behavior thus foreshadowed a larger shift in obligations that would eventually affect the whole people. With the world cleansed of every blemish and restored to its original state, the existing commandments would become obsolete. This process had begun with Sabbatai's arrival. However, until he returned from the darkness, the transition would be ongoing, so the Torah of the Tree of Life remained an abstraction for most people—a matter to contemplate, not act upon.

This intermediate phase in which humanity now existed was hardly cause for rejoicing. "Induced by a historical event, the conception of the Messiah suffers a dialectical ruin," Scholem wrote. "His mission takes on a destructive and paradoxical quality which must come into full effect before the positive part of the redemption becomes visible." Indeed, Scholem declared, the figure of the Messiah himself now assumed "a sinister character." One had to recognize "the abyss which yawns between the figure of the Messiah who died for his cause upon the Cross and this figure who became an apostate and played his role in this disguise." Nonetheless, that "ambiguous and treacherous twilight figure also exercised a seductive fascination."

Scholem hypothesized that the extraordinary degree "of contradiction, of duplicity and duality" that formed the Marrano religious sensibility had made this community singularly receptive to the Sabbatian movement. Not only did Marranos share the radically paradoxical vision of the Sabbatians, Scholem contended that without "the unique psychology of these reconverts to Judaism," the new theology could never have prospered. The doubleness and alienation of the Marranos' experience enabled them to grasp the theological dialectic of the Sabbatians and contribute to its earthly fruition.

Scholem's account of the Marranos' psychological dualities resonates with his own youthful self-portrait as an esoteric "reconvert" to Judaism among the assimilationist German Jews. Extending the analogy, since Scholem positioned Zionism as the latest link in the kabbalistic chain, we might infer that he thought the doubleness of Jewish life in Germany shaped the mentality that allowed Zionism to flourish. The volatile paradoxes of the Zionist movement in Palestine may also have struck Scholem as consonant with the post-apostatical Sabbatian faith.

Indeed, just months before his sojourn in Oxford, Scholem wrote one of the most profound letters of his career, a meditation on the Hebrew language. "The land is a volcano, and it hosts the language," this epistle to Franz Rosenzweig began. The purpose of "updating" Hebrew had been to secularize the language so that it would become the tongue of everyday discourse. But what had been achieved instead was the production of a "ghostly language," a kind of Esperanto only superficially adapted to the mundane business of Palestine. Hidden within this instrumental discourse were all the religious words from ancient texts which, like Luria's sparks, still carried intact their original divine charge. The disjunction between utilitarian Hebrew and the language's titanic capacities presented a greater threat to the Zionist enterprise than that posed by the Arab people about which one heard so much, Scholem argued. For the children growing up in the Land would have no other language than Hebrew, which they would receive in its full, sacred dimensionality, notwithstanding the pragmatic intentions of those Zionist leaders who'd so blindly revived the ancient tongue. "Will not the religious power latent therein one day break out against its speakers?" Scholem asked. "This Hebrew language is pregnant with catastrophe; it cannot remain in its present state—nor will it remain there."

Nowhere does Scholem's contradictory attitude toward the apocalyptic intervention in history emerge more clearly than when he states that despite Hebrew's present-day trivialization, at times "the holiness of our language leaps out and speaks to us from within its spectral degradation." After all, these words "were not created arbitrarily and out of nothing, but were taken from the good old lexicon," and were hence "filled to the brim with explosive meaning." Nouns live a life of their own, Scholem argued. "Were it not so—woe to our children, who have been abandoned to emptiness."

What initially appeared to be a warning about the eruptive forces concealed in Hebrew twists at the end into horror at the void that must prevail in its absence. "God cannot remain silent in a language in which He has been evoked thousands of times to return to our life," Scholem maintained. "The inevitable revolution of a language in which His voice is again heard—that is the only subject not discussed here in the land, because those who renewed the Hebrew language did not believe in the Day of Judgment which they set up for us through their deeds." A transformative catastrophe is inevitable because of the potency of Hebrew, itself now a Marrano tongue, passing as the Jewish vernacular in Palestine.

Bursting with the fruits of his Sabbatian research, Scholem went to Paris, where he planned to explore certain manuscripts at the Bibliothèque Nationale — and to see Walter Benjamin, whom he'd been missing acutely as his vision of Zionism darkened. Benjamin was initially ambivalent about the reunion, oppressed by the thought of having to deal with Scholem's "rather ostentatious self-assurance," as he wrote. But in the event, he and Scholem, along with Escha, bandied about the city evening after evening, strolling the boulevards and frequenting cafés around Montparnasse, reveling in a summer spell that conjured old times together.

Benjamin appeared to be in an unusually placid state of mind, but when Scholem and Escha visited his flat in the Hôtel du Midi, they found it barren and squalid. With Dora only rarely present, and a new French lover already spurning him, loneliness shadowed Benjamin. Scholem characterized him as someone "whose harmonious view of the world was shattered," and whose impulse toward a metaphysical world vision "had fallen in a state of dialectic disintegration."

Perhaps it's not coincidence that the description echoes Scholem's account of how, after Sabbatai Sevi's apostasy, "the conception of the Messiah suffers a dialectical ruin." Scholem regarded Benjamin's newfound Communist allegiances as an apostasy equivalent to Sabbatai's donning of the turban; he may have felt himself to be in the role of the oracular Nathan of Gaza to Benjamin's Sabbatai Sevi.

Scholem's brother Werner's recent experiences with the German Communist party could only have heightened his misgivings about Benjamin's political inclinations. After having become one of the party's most outspoken representatives, by 1926 Werner had been expelled, "along with the others who refused to bow to the dictates from Moscow," Betty Scholem wrote Gershom, adding that "the boy has a real cross to bear." (It may have been a relief that Arthur couldn't weigh in on this "cross" of Werner's—their father had died two years before, leaving no valuable objects other than two gold watches, one for the pocket and one for the wrist. Pick which you want, Betty told Gershom. Werner will take the other. "He doesn't care which." So much for Arthur's legacy.)

In Scholem's view, Benjamin's ideological future hung in the balance that summer, with surrealism and communism occupying one side of the scales and Hebrew and Jewish studies the other. Clearly an intense "fermentation" was taking place inside him. Scholem wrote that by comparison, "I was bound to appear as the more secure person, a man who had been guided by a more accurately functioning compass in his absorption in Jewish studies." Seeking to steer Benjamin upon a complementary path, he introduced him to Judah Magnes, who was in Paris at the same time, in the hope that Magnes might select Benjamin as a scholar for the School of Humanities he was planning to open at Hebrew University.

The meeting went well. Benjamin eloquently recounted—or deftly ad-libbed—the story of how his work as a translator had awakened him to his Jewish identity, which he expected to resolve philosophically through "immersion in Hebrew." He told Magnes that he responded positively to the "reconstruction work" going on in Eretz Yisrael, even if he hadn't associated himself with political Zionism, and he proposed coming to Jerusalem for a year to dedicate himself exclusively to Hebrew studies. This would give him the opportunity to determine whether he could ever hope to communicate effectively as a scholar in that language.

Scholem was astonished by the unprecedented firmness with which Benjamin voiced enthusiasm for the project of Jewish renewal in Palestine. Magnes, for his part, was stirred by Benjamin's obvious brilliance and political radicalism. The two men vowed to stay in touch while Magnes considered the practicalities of Benjamin's offer. Benjamin afterward told Scholem that he saw the conversation as a possible turning point in his life.

Earlier on that trip, following Scholem's passionate exposition of Cardozo, the two men had sat at Café Le Dôme with the writer Franz Hessel, discussing whether Judaism was "still alive as a heritage or an experience, even as something constantly evolving, or did it exist only as an object of cognition?" For a long time now Benjamin had been speaking about wanting "to leave the purely theoretical sphere," a project that seemed to him "humanly possible" only through either "religious or political observance." It was still plausible, Scholem concluded, that the former would claim his commitment after all. (The back-and-forth with Magnes hummed along buoyantly for months. Benjamin's plans to come to Jerusalem grew more and more specific. Finally Magnes forwarded to Benjamin the whole of the stipend he'd promised him for studying Hebrew in Palestine — which Benjamin proceeded to live off in Berlin and Paris. The Jerusalem plan unraveled, leaving Scholem humiliated and Magnes hurt.)

No less surprising than Benjamin's "vibrant avowal of the chances of rebirth for the Jewish people and Judaism" was his refusal to discuss his developing political ideas. On this point, Benjamin told Scholem only that he couldn't imagine his "radical-revolutionary perspectives" being in conflict with the approach he'd taken hitherto, "albeit in dialectical transformation." But on August 23 — the date on which Nicola Sacco and Bartolomeo Vanzetti were to be executed — huge demonstrations were organized in Paris by the French Communist and Socialist parties to protest the sentence, and Benjamin suddenly announced that it would be "unthinkable not to be present for these events."

For the first time in Scholem's experience, Benjamin dressed himself in pointedly grubby clothes and knotted a red necktie around his throat. The scene when they arrived was volatile, with more than a thousand demonstrators expressing their outrage, calling for justice and boycotts on all American products. Police were out in force, charging into the crowd on horseback, wielding truncheons. The protest turned into a riot. Hundreds were injured. Smashed glass, mirrors, and crockery scaled the pavement. Benjamin and Scholem barely managed to elude the cops, nipping off just in time to a café on a side street. Benjamin was feverishly excited. The image of his old friend, exemplar of delicate elegance, arrayed in his scruffy costume, sweaty and bright-eyed above a flaming red necktie—gulping down quantities of wine while his mind swam with visions of the sublime revolution—inscribed itself in Scholem's mind. Recalling the moment years later, he employed language reminiscent of that he used to describe Sabbatai Sevi in the flush of messianic illumination: "his face shining with a great radiance." The comparison was perhaps made more vivid for Scholem by his own identification with the prophet, which had supplanted youthful fantasies of himself as the Redeemer.

When Scholem got back to Jerusalem in the early fall, the idealistic Zionist project in Palestine seemed to be foundering. The great wave of immigration that had swelled the Jewish population since his arrival—the Fourth Aliyah, drawn mainly from Eastern Europe—had subsided. Professionally, these new residents had been, for the most part, small business owners and middlemen. ("Capitalists without capital," an observer quipped.) Shops opened all over Tel Aviv, until there was one store for every five families. Huge amounts of money poured into the construction of new, taller buildings throughout the Jewish settlement. Warsaw's latest fashions were showcased behind the fresh plate glass of Tel Aviv, Haifa and, to a lesser extent, Jerusalem. Little investment went into manufacturing, still less into agriculture. Scholem and his crowd were increasingly appalled by the replication of the urban, petit-bourgeois societies they'd fled.

But before the end of 1927, the real estate bubble burst. Building dropped off. Unemployment spiraled. Workers clamored for bread, and the tide of immigration receded. Nearly twice as many Jews left Palestine that year as arrived. On the one hand, rough economic times strengthened the hand of the labor-oriented strands of the Zionist government. The engines of investment wheeled from land speculation to citrus growing and other ventures with tangible yields. On the other hand, the Revisionists blamed economic hardship on the mealy-mouthed apologetics of Weizmann and his gang. Everything that was going wrong underscored the imperative of getting the English to ratify the Jews' role as their partner in colonialist enterprise.

Socialist coddling had to stop. Merchants were the ones who brought progress to society, Jabotinsky argued. Money needed to be channeled from Labor's pet projects, like the kibbutzim, to shopkeepers and artisans. By accepting the hard reality that building required private capital, and private capital would flow only where there was potential for profit, opportunity would expand throughout Palestine, triggering new Jewish immigration, ultimately establishing the demographic majority necessary to create a Jewish state. And because people were hungry, the appeal of brute force and decisive action, regardless of consequences, grew in tandem with the Socialist tendencies that sought to enfranchise workers and defuse political conflict between Jews and other stakeholders in Palestine. Whatever the most viable economic policy for Jewish settlement might be, it was clear that current lines of development would exacerbate tensions with the Arabs. As Governor Storrs noted, where the Zionists viewed their movement as an idealistic cause built on sacrifice, the Arabs viewed the project as "entirely materialistic, nationalist, acquisitive, and non-religious." True, the financial circumstances of some Arab farmers and landowners had been improved by higher market prices, but Storrs asked, "Was it altogether dishonorable for Arabs to sigh for

a less advanced, but a traditional, an Arab civilization?" Arab leaders took pains to remind the Mandate government that there was considerable evidence disputing the thesis that Zionist measures for economic reinvigoration trickled down to Arab populations. Nor were the dynamics of development always one way. More than 750,000 olive trees were planted in Palestine between 1925 and 1928, almost entirely by Arab cultivators. Jewish agricultural interests had largely disdained olive growing; labor was too expensive to make it pay. But as other businesses collapsed, that industry was reappraised. Mandate policies encouraged Jewish settlement on land for the purposes of olive cultivation, "including State lands and waste lands not required for public purposes." Such guidance was regarded by Arabs "as Englishmen would regard instructions from a German conqueror for the settlement and development of the Duchy of Cornwall, of our Downs, commons and golf-courses, not by Germans, but by Italians 'returning' as Roman legionaries," the chief Mandate representative acknowledged. Scholem cautioned in 1928 that the Zionists were making a grave mistake by trading on stereotypes about the "ignorant Fellah," when in fact the fellahin were profoundly interested in the education of their children and political issues. The Arabs would achieve autonomy by their own actions before long, and the Zionists would do well to remember that their moral title to the land rested on a commitment to true parity, he maintained.

The circle that Arthur Ruppin had organized in 1925 to discuss Arab-Jewish relations (formally launched thereafter as the Brit Shalom [Covenant of Peace] movement), stepped up activities in the latter half of the 1920s. Scholem was attached to its radical core. Although Brit Shalom was not technically a political organization, but rather a group dedicated to trying to talk through the problem of coexistence, statements issued by them were published in influential periodicals and played a de facto political role in Zionist debates. Though it was a small movement—at its largest, it boasted only a hundred members—some participants were figures of international influence, including Martin Buber, who led the German chapter. As Hugo Bergmann, another of the group's founders, later wrote, Brit Shalom represented "the last flicker of the humanist nationalist flame, at a historical moment when nationalism became among all the nations an anti-humanist moment." One can sympathize with the urge to get nationalism right after it had gone so horribly wrong at its point of origin, but could you really reset that European experiment somewhere else, in someone else's homeland, where nationalism had no deep roots? Scholem was not alone in coming to believe over time that the entire Zionist project, in both its positive and negative guises, had catalyzed the development of Arab nationalist movements that replicated just those paradigms Brit Shalom had hoped to transcend in Palestine.

Be that as it may, part of Brit Shalom's attraction was that it offered a high-minded intellectual fellowship difficult to come by in the broader society. Many of the movement's members knew one another from professional circles at Hebrew University, and the Old World–style cafés where German-speaking immigrants congregated. The dream of a utopian marriage between Jewish and Arab cultures was partly fueled by a rude reawakening to the mutually alienated affections between Eastern and Western Jews, an incompatibility borne home by differences over how to secure the Jewish settlement's survival that were far removed from the hothouse dialogue "across the aisle" once savored in Berlin and Prague.

Certainly many Brit Shalom participants were more interested in trying to work out the nature of Zionism by addressing the Arab problem than they were interested in the Arabs themselves. Almost none of the members knew Arabic, and the first reported instance of a Muslim even speaking at a Brit Shalom meeting didn't occur until 1930, five years after the organization's founding.

The contradictions cut deeper. While the movement's catchphrase, "Neither to dominate nor be dominated," has the ring of higher justice, the commitment to absolute political equality with the Arabs was presumptuous at a time when Jews were still less than 20 percent of Palestine's overall population. Even some Brit Shalom sympathizers viewed the contingent as hopelessly detached from realities in Palestine. The publisher Salman Schocken, who'd provided material support to Brit Shalom leaders, wondered whether dreamy academics whose knowledge of the Arab people was derived primarily from books and chats with their gardeners were equipped to negotiate a political solution between these two peoples whose attachment to the Land was so fiercely antagonistic.

Still, Brit Shalom was at least *trying* to think about what form Arab-Jewish cooperation might take, rather than attempting to ignore the Arabs' existence — or just to grab what they could of Palestine before the gate slammed closed. The movement wasn't coming at the Arab-Jewish problem by way of an armed Jewish legion, as the Revisionists proposed, or by banking on the Jews' access to representatives of the Great Powers. Brit Shalom not only recognized the justice of Arab claims to the Land; it also worked to articulate detailed programs for honoring these while also accommodating Jewish hopes for cultural-historical rejuvenation in Palestine. Looked at from today's ideal-gutted perspective, some of the proposals seem impressively thoughtful.

After Scholem's return from Paris, when the entire Zionist project appeared precarious, he redoubled his efforts on behalf of Brit Shalom, writing essays and taking part in public debates at which he lambasted the Revisionist agenda. The organization gave Scholem a platform from which to articulate a greater anti-bourgeois polemic. Benjamin gleaned this early on, when Scholem charged him essentially with hypocrisy for playing the enflamed revolutionary from the comfort of his West Berlin home. "If I were in Palestine, it is quite possible that things would look completely different," Benjamin acknowledged. "Your position on the Arab question proves that there are totally different methods of unambiguously differentiating yourself from the bourgeoisie there than there are here."

It appeared more politically credible to attack the Revisionists for aligning Zionist interests with British imperialism at the expense of relations with Palestine's indigenous population than to fulminate vaguely against their petty middle-class ambitions. Going after those entrepreneurial tendencies head-on might also have risked identifying Scholem too closely with the Socialist cause, which he saw pointing ultimately toward the muddy palette of the universal. Throughout his first years in Palestine,

Scholem strove to sustain a tricky double standard: supporting the Labor party's efforts on behalf of land nationalization and other measures to promote a classless Jewish society against the private-capital-fueled economic vision of the Revisionists, while not extrapolating from that model to champion a larger human collective. You can be truly universal only on a local canvas, he suggested — at least until the real Messiah arrives.

The rationale behind Scholem's involvement with Brit Shalom was thus bound up with his aspirations for the ideal manifestation of Zionism, not with a sense of fellowship with the Arabs — even in the form of the Buberesque Oriental brotherhood he'd championed as a teenager. In his early years in Palestine, Scholem did occasionally attend salons hosted by Arab intellectuals, but these interactions left no known fingerprints on his intellectual development. And in later years, Scholem acknowledged that there was always a certain theatricality — a doubleness — at work in his Brit Shalom activities. His membership in the group "was for 'external' purposes," he told an interviewer. "'Domestically,' I was something else."

Indeed, on the domestic front things were becoming progressively more comfortable — even, dare one say, a trifle bourgeois. His university appointment was extended by three years. When Benjamin received Scholem's bibliography of kabbalistic manuscripts, he wrote him, "You have now occupied the actual fortresses of philology, the footnotes, with your name, and from now on you can let your thoughts prosper and be nourished with all assurance in the vineyards and fields of what is printed in capitals." And along with these enormous labor-intensive research works, Scholem had begun publishing tracts that took a more historical-analytical approach, such as a small book exploring the relationship between Kabbalah and alchemy.

To achieve all this, while still performing the duties of his library day job, he had to devote his home life as well to his vocation. "I have long since become wedded to my room," he wrote a friend. The prodigious quantity of texts he worked his way through as both reader and author left little time for marital nest building. There were six cats at home, but no prospect of children. Escha had her own job at the library, and the intimacies domestic life still afforded were sometimes double-edged. "Rest assured that this man, your son, mercilessly exploits me and I'm not happy about it," Escha wrote her mother-in-law, only half joking. "It occurred to me long ago that, in his mind, a woman exists to serve," she remarked.

The long tab of Gershom's requests to his mother indicates that he still considered her at his disposal as well, finally driving Betty to strike. "You can buy your own filing cabinet, instead of constantly nagging me for one. I bought two *sausages* for you today with my last penny," she protested. "I've done nothing but respond to your screams, to the point that it brings tears to my eyes." But still books, ties, towels, money, marzipan, chocolate, goose fat, and more sausages were bundled into the mail for Gershom.

In return, he regaled her with anecdotes about the absurdity of life in the homeland and defused her anxieties about rising tensions between Arabs and Jews then making German newspaper headlines. "You are a shrewd woman, and I hope you won't think that we're all slaughtering one another," he assured her.

A week later, Arab-Jewish violence exploded.

We were cut off from the sea. Word had it that the entire highway, from Jerusalem to Tel Aviv, was being shut down to secure President Clinton's motorcade as he traveled from Ben Gurion Airport up hill to the City of Peace. The measure seemed extreme. But who knew? There were plenty of crazies on both sides who'd gladly pop the leader of the free world. When a friend suggested we walk up to the gateway of Jerusalem to watch Clinton's entrance into the city, I thought: *Why not?* I felt I *should* be turning up at more public events to demonstrate my support of the Palestinian-Jewish peace process, although I'd found somewhat disappointing, or even disconcerting, the fact that there'd seemed to be virtually, or literally, no Palestinians at the demonstrations I did go to.

We made our way toward the edge of the city where the highway whirled up from the fertile plains past pine groves studded with the rusted shells of military vehicles memorializing the War of Independence. As we came nearer to where the white buildings ended and the earth spread beneath Jerusalem in harsh, beautiful declivities, seasonally copper and green — shot through with sunbeams, like St. Sebastian with arrows — crowds grew denser, swelling by the roadside to dizzying magnitude. I'd known that large numbers would turn up for the president's arrival but not that I'd be witnessing what felt like a mustering of the entire population. Nothing I'd seen since coming to Jerusalem approached the size of this gathering. Certainly none of the peace demonstrations I'd witnessed came close.

There was another thing that began to impress itself on me as we pushed deeper into the multitude. There were a few people with signs advocating peace between Israel and the Palestinians, but from where I stood a greater number held up American flags and posters expressing love for the U.S.A. Here and there I saw people waving photos of Clinton. The mood in the crowd was festively jubilant. The snatches of conversation I overheard were all Clinton this and Clinton that, interspersed with good-humored jocularity about family members who'd managed to move to America. The names Brooklyn, Queens, New Jersey, L.A., and Florida were being tossed through the air like candies at a bar mitzvah.

When the first black vehicles came into sight, everyone began shouting, whooping, and clapping, their faces flushed with joy, chanting the president's name. His car was rising into view. I was shoved from behind. "CLINNNTTONNN!!!" And suddenly there he was, clear as day in his black SUV. For three seconds I saw him: a glimpse of pink flesh, like a giant Christmas ham, at the car window. His hand waving to the droves with the automatic regularity of a metronome, his big face bobbing with the slowness of a Macy's Thanksgiving Day balloon.

Stumbling in retreat, I tried to remember what it was exactly Clinton had done for this country that would lead to his being treated as a liberator. America of course gave millions of dollars every year to Israel, but I didn't really think this was about gratitude for the country's defense budget. Nor did the mass euphoria seem to have been driven by conviction that the president had brought peace at last to this violence-torn land by helping to develop the Oslo Accords. It was more that Clinton seemed to symbolize fulfillment of the crowd's earthly desires—physically embodying the land of plenty. Less liberator than messiah of redemptive materialism.

And I remember feeling vertigo as I at last left the masses behind. If what all these fellow citizens wanted was America's inflated abundance—if *that* was the Israeli vision of salvation—what was I doing here? If that condition was what the society was heading for, why not be back there in Cockaigne where I came from?

Of course this moment was not the first to provoke those kinds of doubts. Locals often asked Anne and me why on earth we moved from America to Israel. What's wrong with you? They'd be smiling and good-humored, but the question was always there, and always, along with the irony, serious. Its repetition didn't make answering easier. Rather the reverse. I hemmed, and smiled back, but I hated the question, all the more because I felt I could once have answered it.

For several years already there'd been signs that penetrated even our shady Rehavia cocoon of the ways Israeli consumer society was in the ascendancy—signs especially troubling to us because of how they seemed bound up with the agenda of the

Labor party, which we supported as the dominant engine of the peace process, and which not so many years back had been practically Socialist. You couldn't feel exactly nostalgic for all those bureaucratic hassles still in place when we first came to the country: the exorbitant taxes on bringing back foreign goods when you traveled, the currency restrictions, and so on. But these burdens had been vestiges of a nationalized economy. Now momentum was building toward a wholly privatized state. And the people who would reap the spoils of this process more often than not were men from tight circles in the upper ranks of the Israel Defense Forces. Industries and utilities that had been at least nominally owned by the public became the property of retired generals, who fought solo — Scarface-style — for their knockoff versions of the American dream.

The image of Clinton blessing the masses at the threshold of Jerusalem crystallized something I'd been sensing for a while: The America we'd left behind was coming to meet us. Running and leaping in Air Jordans. Perched cowboy style atop a caravan of big brand chain stores already dumping product across the country. Bearing glad tidings of the good life, gleaming in the generic countenances of sleek models on billboards and screens, cooking and pirouetting amid leisure-time reveries. But to critique this development, in a country that had for so long suffered real deprivation and war upon war, risked aligning one with the ultra-Orthodox, the settler zealots, or other subscribers to apocalyptic agendas.

Of course it didn't help that we watched the boom while ourselves becoming more economically hopeless. Early in 1995, our landlords announced they were going to raise the rent. Even at the current level, we never made the payment without adding to our burden of debt. We started looking for a new place and couldn't believe how much the market had ratcheted up over recent years. Where would we move? What could we do? We looked at all the construction and renovation happening across the city, our eyes growing narrower and narrower, green slits of envy flecked with political righteousness. How did other people manage?

Well, I knew how my friend Dave did it. Dave, who'd tried to sell us a little house at one point that was somehow bound up with a larger development project he was trying to finagle. Dave was fun. We'd met my first day in the new immigrant absorption center. He was a New Yorker, the Upper West Side by way of Midwood and Deal. Used to go to consultations with Schneerson, where he saw the rebbe's blue eyes light up and start spinning. "I'm telling you, *mannn*, the rebbe's eyes were *sparking*." Dave was chatting up the tired ladies taking aliyah applications, and making everyone crack up. He was trading Israeli real estate before he arrived and soon began building a huge villa for himself in the German Colony, which he filled with excellent bibelots from his freewheeling travels in previous lives. Jeweled carvings from Morocco. Gorgeous temple doorways from Thailand. We took off together sometimes late at night in his fast car to Tel Aviv to hear jazz. We sat in dark clubs, snapping and smoking. We watched the Knicks on his satellite TV before anyone else got the games and ate at some excellent restaurants hidden away in parts of the city I'd never been to before and could never find again the next day. He was a blast. And a reactionary, chauvinistic bastard. It was obvious how Dave made his life work — he was a hustler with a gift for slipping the noose. All we wanted was a little apartment where we could live with our hundred children and five cats and two parakeets, and he tried to snooker us! All we wanted was to live without always feeling the knife at our throat! The fire at our back. The reaper at our door. What could we do?

I finally dragged myself through a few interviews with young software firms advertising for technical writers. I got a couple of little contract jobs, but nothing sustained. After getting back from Tel Aviv one night, Anne announced to me she'd just found out that Hebrew University was threatening to take us to court over a leftover tuition bill. The whole reason she'd gone to the university was in the hopes of being able to earn more income.

I told her I would make more money. And she said it wasn't about making *more* money. It was about making *enough* money. No more of these on-and-off gigs. We were shouting, and the parakeet in the window was rattling the cage, and the black cat's tail beneath it was switching right, left, right, left, just waiting the moment when the door would swing open and it could wreak carnage. Which came. Feathers. Blood. And the children in shock again.

We cut back further and further on spending. Our ideas about what to do ranged wider and wilder. Maybe we should take a year away from Israel. Yes! We talked for days about where to go and finally one night we had a revelation: Russia! Yes. We loved Russian literature to death. We would go to Russia for a year and study the language and the culture and the art. And then we would…what? We dreamed of living a life simple yet not impoverished. And Anne cried to me about how everyone around us seemed to be just wildly seeking malls, and how could a minuscule four-room apartment cost $500,000 and all the roads were now jammed with cars driven by drivers jabbering on cell phones. "This is not what attracted me to live here!" she wailed. And I said people were ignoring the larger realities of this region, of being where they were in this flush of Western-style consumerism. It could all come tumbling down any second, I prophesied.

But I don't know what I actually believed. In my mind's eye, I just kept seeing the enormous, glowing American president-redeemer, waving from the window of his black chariot, bringing the message of delivery from that faraway never-never land from which we'd come, and where our old life remained, always promising to be different next time. And also exactly the same.

THIRTEEN

EARLY FRIDAY AFTERNOON on August 23, 1929, Gershom Scholem was at home when he got word that a gang of Arabs with clubs and knives was rampaging through Meah She'arim. Two minutes from where he lived, Jews and Mandate police officers carrying pistols were guarding distraught crowds that were milling between the weary gray buildings filled with trembling religious families. Arab attackers had just been repulsed. But riots that began at the

Wailing Wall were now spreading all over Jerusalem. Long lines of the Orthodox could be seen evacuating the Old City, carrying little children and giant sacks filled with their earthly possessions. Soon news was pouring in of escalating violence across the country. Jews were forming armed defense leagues.

At nightfall, the bloodshed was raging. Cars racing back from the university on Mount Scopus were being peppered with rifle fire. There were reports of a massacre at the rabbinical college in Hebron. Local police were overwhelmed. Petah Tikva, home of the settlement's richest orange groves, was at risk of total destruction. The British were roaring around town in armored vehicles. Then English planes started flying across Palestine, machine-gunning

groups of Arabs who appeared to be mustering. More troops were being flown in from Egypt, and British warships were speeding from Malta to Jaffa. Before long, the world press was reporting scores dead and countless wounded. In Hebron, fifty children were said to have been slaughtered in one fell swoop, with survivors soaking themselves in the blood of dead friends and lying still to fool the mob. Jerusalem was under martial law. It was the worst outbreak of violence between the two peoples in the history of modern Palestine, with more than 130 casualties on each side.

But what on earth had just taken place?

The immediate cause of the riots was apparent. In the grand Middle Eastern tradition, faith served as the accelerant for a fire lit by mundane power worshippers. However, problems at the Wall had been smoldering for years. At this time, the site consisted of a narrow alley bordered on one side by the monumental blocks that once supported Herod's temple platform. But that isolated foundation wall was the epicenter of Jewish lamentation. Abraham Halevi, a disciple of Isaac Luria, had seen the Shekinah herself at the Wailing Wall in Jerusalem, appearing as a woman dressed in black and weeping for the husband of her youth. There were myriad other mystical notions, which made the Wall out to be the meeting point between heaven and earth, where the two spheres exchanged energies. One tradition pictured God standing in perpetual vigil behind the Wall, peeping through its crevices, seeing but unseen. The Wall could be understood as the ultimate marker of absence or loss—*and* the manifestation of the promise that all external reality was an illusion, since in truth "nothing separated the father from the son." The Wall, observers said, was "never desolate." Always, day and night, there were people praying, kissing the stones, using candles to smoke prayers onto its surface, shrieking, tearing their clothing, pulling their hair, mourning. Yet the whole place, from a legal standpoint, belonged to the Muslims.

Scholem acknowledged this—almost everyone did. Trouble

began at the fork between law and convention, where traditions felt threatened by the enforcement of technical possession. Years earlier, elderly "professional wailers" began showing up at the Wall, looking for charity. Less devout Jews started hiring these old men to lament for them. Out of pity for the old men so exerting themselves, benches were installed on which they could rest. Muslims protested that the alley, which provided the only route to some of their prayer houses, would be blocked by any permanent structures. What about chairs, then? No. Chairs would lead to wooden benches, Muslim leaders said. Wooden benches would become iron benches. Iron benches would become stone benches. Stone benches would prompt calls for walls and a roof, to provide shelter against sun, rain, and cold. Before long the Jews would insist the whole site was their land. The Arabs went to the British; the British went to the League of Nations. Finally it was agreed as a stopgap measure to let elderly wailers carry in one-legged chairs strapped to their backs. But tensions were not defused by this measure.

Some months before the Day of Atonement in 1928, the Jews tried to erect a partition to separate male and female worshippers. Again the Muslims saw in this structure Jewish designs on the whole property. After appeals to the Mandate authorities, the government instructed the Jews to remove the partition before Yom Kippur. They didn't comply. Mandate soldiers burst onto the site on Yom Kippur itself to tear down the wooden partition. The Jews begged for ten minutes to finish their prayers. The British didn't oblige. A struggle ensued and the police began beating worshippers with whips and clubs — outraging Jews the world over for violating the holiest day of the year.

In the subsequent turmoil, Muslim leaders charged that Jews were now making their move to occupy the "Noble Sanctuary." Fears were exacerbated as Jewish representatives began trying to buy buildings near the Wall in hopes of creating a larger plaza to accommodate the growing numbers of worshippers. The grand mufti's cohort appealed to King George. Next, the chief rabbis of Palestine wrote the sovereign, denying any plot to rebuild Solomon's Temple and beseeching him to use his influence to obtain rights for them to hold unrestricted services at the Wall.

Around the time King George began pondering these petitions, the Muslims completed a new structure directly on top of the site; the Jews demanded the Mandate remove it. But the Mandate government reiterated that Jews had right of access only to the pavement. The Jews protested to London. The Arabs declared plans to form a world association to protect the rights of their holy places, giving special attention to the Wall. The Zionist Executive tried to intercede, issuing a statement "recognizing unreservedly the inviolability of the Muslim holy places."

Arabs threw stones at Jewish worshippers and dumped refuse on the stones where they prayed. Revisionists issued statements confirming the Arabs' worst fears about Zionist intentions. The next summer, tensions reached new heights around the August holy day of Tisha b'Av, commemorating the destruction of the Temple. Rumors began circulating in the Old City and villages that the Jews planned to sanctify the date by destroying the Mosque of Omar and laying the foundations of the Third Temple.

Ten thousand Jews came to the Wall to read the Book of Lamentations under police guard; some two thousand young men, mostly from Jabotinsky's youth group Betar, showed up to help with security. They marched to the Wall waving blue-and-white flags symbolizing Revisionist aspirations for a Jewish state. They wore brown shirts, which many people assumed were modeled on Fascist uniforms, though Betar's leaders said they were only evoking the hues of Palestine's sands. Their crisp dress and clean-shaven chins anyway made a sharp contrast with the heavy beards, black clothes, striped prayer shawls, and pious head covering of the religious. While they marched, the young men chanted: "To sacrifice all for the Western Wall!"

Police blocked off major passageways to the Wall. Crowds of Arabs who were more or less confined on the mosque site became increasingly enraged as the day went on. After dark, when most worshippers had dispersed, a mob said to number in the thousands rushed down into the alley. They destroyed sacred objects, burned prayer books, removed all seating, and injured those in their path. Late that night, a young Jewish man playing ball was stabbed to death.

Much of the city had already gone indoors to bed at the hour of the killing. But people became aware of what had happened because of the shrieks of the mother echoing through the streets as she followed her son's body to the hospital. Revisionist youth gathered at the building shouting "Shame on the government!" and turned the subsequent funeral procession into a call for vengeance. The police tried to quell the mounting fury, further provoking the mourners. When clashes ensued, the police began beating the marchers, including the pallbearers. After the burial, during which speeches blasted the government, the Jews protested that not a single Arab had been beaten when the Wall was violated a few days before, while twenty-eight Jewish mourners had been savagely clubbed at the funeral. If we can't be equally blessed, at least let us be equally abused! Jabotinsky, who denied responsibility for organizing the march, praised the action: "The argument that the Arabs should not have been stirred up, is a heritage of the ghetto." Muslim leaders meanwhile began issuing calls admonishing believers throughout Palestine to protect their shrines from imminent Jewish attack. The rioters who came within steps of Scholem's door were among the waves of Arabs responding haphazardly to such exhortations.

For months afterward, a British commission gathered testimonies with the aim of apportioning blame and determining compensations. In Scholem's eyes, the whole process was a mistake, serving merely to allow Arabs and Jews to hurl accusations at each other week after week, ingraining their mutual abomination. The persistent miscalculations of the English in Palestine outraged him. He was incensed when Werner scribbled on a letter from Betty, "Warm regards to the servant of British imperialism."

Apart from the roster of specific charges, Arab representatives stated that the English had been deceiving them since first taking over administration of Palestine, promising them their own country and failing to deliver it, declining to enforce Mandate provisions that Jewish immigration be facilitated only insofar as it didn't prejudice the rights of other inhabitants of the land. Instead, the British had allowed the Jews with their far greater financial resources to purchase all the best lands in the country from Arabs, whose miserable economic plight—partly caused by Mandate taxes—gave them no choice but to accept the best price offered. For fourteen years, the Arabs' representative told the commission, Arab grievances had risen like water in a glass. The violence in Jerusalem marked the moment when that glass overflowed.

From the Jewish perspective, meanwhile, the British had failed to uphold their primary obligation to safeguard the lives and property of all Palestine's residents. By confiscating Jewish arms on top of neglecting their policing responsibilities, the English turned the most vulnerable individuals into sitting ducks. As Scholem wrote to his mother, the killings made the Arabs look dreadful in the eyes of the world, since they hadn't even assaulted the Zionists, but instead murdered scholars, students, women, and children.

Still, the commission rejected almost all Zionist claims about British misgovernance. As one authority remarked, "There seems to be a considerable body of opinion, against a considerable body of evidence." On a deeper level, the British also decided that Arab fears of Jewish immigration could no longer be ignored. A policy paper was issued, declaring that no land remained available for Jewish colonization and placing stringent limits on the numbers of Jews who could enter Palestine. But Arab leaders would not publicly support the document because it refrained from endorsing Arab nationalist aspirations, and the new immigration quotas were anyway mostly rescinded some months later. For right-leaning factions, this revisal did not annul suspicions that the English were no longer committed to the Balfour Declaration.

No one was satisfied with British efforts to manage the two peoples' demands for security and autonomy — which only expanded in the wake of the August events. On many levels, the riots strengthened pan-Arab sentiment, with Palestine becoming a rallying point for wide-ranging nationalist ambitions. Islamic organizations in Egypt raised money for Arab victims of the violence and called for solidarity with Palestine Arabs. Egypt's fledgling Muslim Brotherhood strengthened its links with the Palestine Arab leadership. There were solidarity strikes in Syria, while in Iraq anti-British nationalism galvanized around the plight of Palestine under Mandate control.

As the Arabs forged a greater regional unity in response to the suffering of their brethren in Palestine, the riots encouraged an opposite tendency in Zionism. The movement turned inward, reorienting from the Diaspora to the Yishuv, the Jewish settlement in Palestine. The role of Diaspora Jewry became increasingly confined to transferring capital to Eretz Yisrael. In a memorandum titled "Fortification" written in 1929, Ben-Gurion argued that the lessons of the August events were "expanded immigration, particularly of young people, increased mobilization of financial resources, land settlement, Hebrew labor in the Jewish economic sector, and upgrading the settlement defensive capability."

Concurrently with what historians have characterized as the respective centrifugal and centripetal movements of the two peoples resulting from the Wailing Wall events, talks between Arab and Jewish leaders about coexistence dropped off. Rolling Arab strikes and Jewish boycotts of Arab goods, and Jewish strikes and

Arab boycotts perpetuated resentment and fears, as did sporadic violence. Arabs were accused of poisoning grapes sold to Jews; Jews were charged with pouring gasoline on Arab grapes to make them unsellable.

Between the grotesque rope-a-dope bloodshed, the destruction of the fruit of the earth, the religious terror, the economic terror, the toxic mistrust, regional alliances and tensions, Islamic fundamentalist support of Palestine Arabs, political moves by Jews among global power brokers, and ill-conceived international interventions pleasing nobody, one might be forgiven for supposing that time has stood still in Palestine since the summer of 1929.

This uncanny sense of suspension resonates with the mystical allusions on display even in official proceedings examining the debacle. During summary remarks by the Arab counsel to the British Commission, testimony veered directly into the realm of messianic dialectics to which Scholem dedicated much of his career. The counsel reminded the commission of the hour when the grand mufti was brought to the witness stand to defend his inflammatory cries of alarm before the riots. He reiterated his belief that the Jews had the intention of rebuilding Solomon's Temple on the site of the Mosque of Omar. As evidence, the mufti cited a statement by Chief Rabbi Yitzhak Kook, who had said that while Jewish aspirations were spiritual, nevertheless the Jews were forever awaiting the earthly coming of the Messiah, when the Temple indeed would be rebuilt. Who was to say when the Jews would decide the moment of His arrival had come? And who could deny that many people wished to hasten His appearance? One might say that by this logic, the Messiah's reinstatement of Jewish sovereignty at the expense of the Muslims could be interrupted only before it began — that is to say, before His appearance was recognized by the Jews themselves.

Whatever one thinks of the mufti's argument, it's clear that imputations of ignorance didn't adequately explain the incitement or its consequences. Indeed, up to a point, the more erudite one was regarding each side's theological claims, the more likely one might be to run amok. At Scholem's ultra-elite level, where contradictory positions could be juggled in a spirit of gamesmanship, the urge to violence might no doubt be sublimated. Anyone bent on finding license to do *anything* except meditate and recite liturgical petitions on the strength of classic kabbalistic texts would be guilty of shearing off subtleties. "Precisely understood, there is nothing concrete which can be accomplished by the unredeemed," Scholem wrote. "This makes for the greatness of Messianism, but also for its constitutional weakness. Jewish so-called Existenz possesses a tension that never finds true release; it never burns itself out. And when in our history it does discharge, then it is foolishly decried (or, one might say, unmasked) as 'pseudo-Messianism.'"

Foolishly condemned or righteously revealed? Pseudo-Messianism? Or "pseudo-Messianism," in skeptical quotation marks?

Scholem was happy to have it all ways at once. But at that level of philosophical pretzeling, who could follow him — other, perhaps, than Walter Benjamin?

In the aftermath of the violence, it was clear that Brit Shalom would face broad criticism for continuing to promote rational compromise. Even the official publication of the Labor party now accused Brit Shalom representatives of being "atomized, individualized, confined to their small groups." They were people who "feared everything associated with the masses." But, as Gershom reminded his mother, bellicosity was in the Scholem blood, and initially he saw the challenge before him as just one more in the long line of fights he'd been waging his whole life: with Arthur, the archbourgeois hypocrite; with Werner, the self-deceiving Socialist apologist; with Buber and the Neopathetic crowd who thumbed their noses at history; with Oskar Goldberg, that weird Hebraic enchanter of bored German-Jewish salonistas; with the Blau-Weiss gang of prancing thugs — he'd gone into the ring with them all and come out righteously energized. But somewhere along the way, Scholem began to realize this battle was different.

At first, he plunged into the breach, writing essays and participating in public debates. Hugo Bergmann observed that Brit Shalom was now more active than ever before, and "the soul of this activity is Scholem." He joined Brit Shalom's call to reprieve all the Arabs sentenced to death by the British for their role in the riots. And he railed against those who charged that Brit Shalom made Jewish settlement out to be a charitable act by the Arabs. Brit Shalom had always credited the Jews with a *right* to exist in the Land. Their platform insisted on the two people's equality. Indeed, Brit Shalom was the most truly realistic organization, he insisted, because its participants understood that another people existed in Palestine. The struggle to defend Brit Shalom's honor and denounce the stupidity of their opponents' policies felt hard yet rewarding. But indications of how far Scholem and his comrades were out of step with popular opinion kept accumulating. When Menachem Ussishkin, a Russian-born Labor Zionist who became head of the Jewish National Fund, said the entire organization was tainted by a pathological criminal mind-set inseparable from its members' German roots, he gave voice to a broader suspicion that Brit Shalom represented a throwback to the Old World perspective Zionism was invented to escape. The young son of Arthur Ruppin, Brit Shalom's founder, came to him one day, announcing, "There should only be Jews and Hebrew spoken in Palestine." Ruppin asked what the Arabs should do. They should move to Arabia, came the answer. "He told me that a child at school told him he should be ashamed that his father belonged to Brit Shalom," Ruppin wrote later. If they were losing their own children, how could they hope to fight chauvinism in the country at large?

Scholem tried to hold firm. "Zionism never ceased to rely on the most exalted principles of morality," he argued. "Why should these principles be revoked when they are no longer comfortable for us?" But at some point he seemed to realize that such moralistic pronouncements were beginning to sound almost quaintly mandarin in the new atmosphere of raw hatred. His optimism finally crumbled. In May 1930, Scholem wrote Buber an extraordinary letter in which he described the Zionist perspective becoming divorced from reality. The problem was not the political dilemma regarding the Arabs, he explained. It was the physiognomy of Zionism itself, which appeared to be hardening into a definite and hideous form. The torture of this recognition almost surpassed endurance. Scholem and his comrades always felt it would be intolerable to discover the cause had failed without their having been fully engaged. Well, now the decisive hour was upon them, and their utter disillusionment left little hope that anything could be salvaged. Such historic hours do not repeat. The interpretation

of Zionism for which they'd fought their whole lives would be useless if one day it were revealed that "the face of Zionism, even that
which is only turned inward, should prove to be that of a Medusa."
As the movement became more set in its features, it would freeze
the Zionists themselves, Scholem suggested.

All his idealism was wrapped up in the idea of history's malleability, but history as a Zionist project seemed to be calcifying
before his eyes — as though the stone of Jerusalem had gotten into
their veins. "If a definite and fixed image of Zionism becomes historical in our time, where shall we stand and how will it be possible
to have discussions that will proceed no longer on the basis of a
living power but from the magical double of a stage peopled by
ghosts?" he asked. The lifeless stone of Jerusalem now faced them
in the mirror; the Wall stared back from the looking glass. When
they cast their eyes up to God, the Zionist Medusa threatened to
petrify heaven itself.

In this darkening atmosphere, Scholem was approached by
representatives of the Zionist Executive, who were preparing a
dossier seeking to persuade a British commission of age-old Jewish religious ties to the Wailing Wall. Having learned of Scholem's
expertise in mysticism, they asked him to submit a full list of kabbalistic sources attesting to Jewish spiritual investment in the site.
Scholem refused to put his scholarly knowledge at the service of
their political mission, and for this principled demurral he himself
was now personally savaged in the press. He didn't quit fighting,
but he began to sound winded — as though the idea were dawn-
ing on him that he might actually lose. In June 1930, he completed
"Encounter with Zion and the World," a monumentally bleak
poem that surveyed his journey from Berlin to Jerusalem and concluded with the lines: "The dream twists into violence, / and once
again we stand outside / and Zion is without form or sense."

Yet one aspect of the decision to be in Palestine appeared more
enlightened with time: the decision *not* to be in Germany. In the

federal election of September 1930, the Nazis won more than six million votes, ballooning from being the smallest to the second-largest party. Betty Scholem assured her son that stories of a Jewish panic were inflated, while tales of fat Jews escaping over the border to Switzerland with their moneybags were simply lies. But by the time Betty and Scholem's older brother Erich came to visit him in the spring of 1931, matters were more dire. She told Gershom she'd heard twelve million Germans were now living off the state, a third of them unemployed, the rest pensioners and war invalids. By contrast, life in Jerusalem appeared enviably prosperous. New creature comforts were popping up all over the city: Escha and Gershom had installed a bathroom inside their apartment! There were fresh cafés, cabarets, a cinema and theater to attend. Neither Betty nor Erich could get over how beautiful the city was. She mocked the questioners back home who pictured Palestine as a sort of "Hottentot kraal."

But what did this congenial Jerusalem life of modern plumbing and whipped cream have to do with Scholem's image of the sublime Zionist imperative? The summer of 1931 marked the climax of this phase of Zionism's self-definition. Jabotinsky's influence had been steadily rising since the Wailing Wall events, while the power of Weizmann, who'd been derided as "weak, near-sighted, bewildered" by Revisionists in the wake of the riots, declined. At the Seventeenth Zionist Congress, held in Basel in July 1931, Weizmann had decided beforehand not to stand for reelection. In the gathering's inaugural address, he gave a long, spirited defense of his legacy — highlighting his efforts to foster Arab-Jewish relations even while maintaining a strong claim on Palestine. "We on our part contemplate no political domination. But they must also remember that we on our side shall never submit to any political domination," he said. He reconjured the dream of two races, living in cooperative harmony: Together the Jews and Arabs could establish "a belt of flourishing countries stretching from the

Mediterranean to the Indian ocean…Surely this is an ideal worthy of an ancient race." But the audience wasn't in the mood for old Orientalist pieties.

Jabotinsky's address, delivered two days after Weizmann's, focused on attacking the mainstream Zionists' relationship to the British, and bluntly articulating the *Endziel*, the final objective of Zionism, to wild applause. He scorned the Mandate's efforts to secure Arab-Jewish understanding. He spoke of the necessity of creating a Jewish majority in Palestine. "A National Home is a country in which the people whose National home it is, constitute the majority of the population," he said — but this was not the ultimate aim of Zionism. "One million Jews would suffice today to create a majority in Palestine," he observed. "This, however, is not the limit of our hopes. We want a Home for all the suffering Jews, and nobody can predict how many Jews there will be who will suffer during the next few generations." While "the immediate aim of the practical Zionist effort must be the creation of a majority," that was only the first step in a process that would eventually require Jewish settlement on both sides of the Jordan River. In a rhetorical passion, Jabotinsky clutched both lapels of his big dark jacket; his hair made a little black duster swept to the side of his skull, his lips thrust outward. Rather than blaming the world for Zionism's policy failures, Jabotinsky proposed that the Zionists adopt the terms of the Yom Kippur liturgy and confess, "I have sinned, I have betrayed," then roll up their sleeves and set about rejuvenating the movement's original grand program.

The audience was elated. In a press interview, Weizmann issued a response that might have come straight out of the Brit Shalom playbook: "I have no sympathy or understanding for the demand for a Jewish majority. A majority does not necessarily guarantee security. A majority is not required for the development of Jewish civilisation and culture." The congress devolved into name-calling, with Brit Shalom supporters comparing the Revisionists to Hitler's supporters in Germany, and the Revisionists calling Brit Shalom Communists. Ultimately, the Revisionists submitted their formal resolution defining Zionism's objective as a Jewish state with a Jewish majority on both sides of the River Jordan. When the resolution was defeated, fistfights broke out in the back of the hall. A squad of young Revisionists stormed to the front of the room and tore down the Zionist flag. Jabotinsky raced to the stand, waving his delegate's card high in the air. "This is no longer a Zionist congress!" he cried. Then he tore the card to bits and flung the fragments of poster board into the faces of Labor delegates. His enemies lunged for him. Revisionist youth locked together in a chain to shield their leader. Pandemonium ensued. Suddenly, Jabotinsky leaped onto a table. "Revisionists Out!" he yelled, whereupon his followers hoisted him onto their shoulders and marched from the hall.

Thenceforward, Jabotinsky turned to the question of whether the Revisionist union should launch an entirely independent Zionist entity.

As word began filtering back to Jerusalem of what was happening in Basel, Scholem and his friends in Brit Shalom were mortified. Their shock was heightened by the conviction that they themselves were the uprising's true targets. Weren't they the ones who'd demanded that Zionism clarify its stance on the great issues confronting the movement—among which the question of how to situate themselves with respect to the Arabs loomed as paramount?

Jabotinsky's resolution on Zionism's final objective had been intended to consummate what Scholem called the "fantastic agitation" aimed at their ranks since 1929. Moreover, Scholem was convinced the only reason Jabotinsky's resolution hadn't passed in Basel was strategic calculation on Labor's part that the manifesto would invite bad publicity. "It was not their heartfelt belief but, rather, their political acumen and anxiety about the fate of the Zionist enterprise that spoke from the mouths of the majority of those opposed to the declaration," he wrote in an essay.

In a letter to Benjamin, Scholem dissected the debacle. His own conception of Zionism had always involved "a religious-mystical quest for the regeneration of Judaism," he wrote, while empirical Zionism was based on "an impossible and provocative distortion of an alleged political 'solution to the Jewish Question.'" Despite the differing viewpoints, Scholem maintained, until two years ago it had been possible for someone like himself to pursue his vision within the framework of this organization that "God knows, originally had nothing to do with Englishmen or Arabs." Personally, he didn't believe that a "solution to the Jewish Question" even existed insofar as that implied "normalization" of the Jewish people, "and I certainly do not think that this question can be solved in Palestine in such a sense. I have always realized that Palestine is necessary, and that was enough, no matter what was expected of the event here; no Zionist program bound our hands here," Scholem declared axiomatically, and inscrutably.

Now, at last, the rise of reactionary forces in Zionism, which came to a head at the congress, had forced him to confront the "radical split" between his own ideas and those of the movement's majority, precipitating an acute crisis. A "fantastically reactionary resolution" had been passed against Magnes and teachers of the university like himself "carrying the banner of Ahad Ha'am." Even though, Scholem continued, the elements "that are about to accomplish the wrecking of Zionism certainly can be identified, who knows whether you will understand me when I say that Zionism has triumphed itself to death. It has anticipated its victories in the intellectual realm and thereby has lost the power to win them in the physical realm." Long before they ever got to Palestine, Scholem recounted, "we lost our forces in a field on which we never intended to fight. When Zionism prevailed in Berlin—

which means in a vacuum, from the point of view of our task — it no longer could be victorious in Jerusalem."

The pristine Zionism he and his cadre dreamed up in the void of Germany was already theoretically complete by the time it hit the stony ground of Palestine. Thus it was impervious to the place itself, infertile. "It turned out that the historical task of Zionism simply was quite different from the one it posed itself," Scholem wearily acknowledged. In consequence, all those high-minded phrases articulated by Ahad Ha'am's followers, rather than being deployed to nurture a true, idealistic community, had simply been appropriated by the reactionaries as tools for promoting their own disastrous agenda. "For years the despair of the victor has been the real demonism of Zionism; this is perhaps the most important world-historical example of the mysterious laws according to which propaganda (the substance of our defeat) works," Scholem lamented.

Whereas to Buber, Scholem had expressed fear that Zionism might petrify in a definite form that would prove a Medusa, to Benjamin he was suggesting that Zionism's metaphysical form had been fixed long before by Scholem's own circle in Germany. The root problem wasn't the Revisionists at all. It was the liberal revolutionary poets of Zionism, whose imaginations had so outstripped reality that their unrealized visions could easily be repackaged as cheap intoxicants for the masses. "The mountains of articles in which the intelligentsia documented our victory in the visible realm before it had been decided in the invisible realm — that is, the regeneration of language — are the true Wailing Wall of the new Zion," Scholem wrote, confessing that "we ourselves have invoked the forces of destruction." They ought to have continued developing their community in its "legitimate concealment," cultivating their secret, transcendent values away from the public forum. Alas, "the encounter with Sleeping Beauty took place in the presence of too many paying spectators for it to have ended with an embrace," he declared. "Zionism disregarded the night and shifted the procreation that ought to have meant everything to it to a world market where there was too much sunlight and the covetousness of the living degenerated into a prostitution of the last remnants of our youth."

The whore and the marketplace, the night and the procreative embrace — at its climax, the letter mashes the history of Zionism with a Brothers Grimm–style sexual nightmare. Woken too soon, the frozen maiden Sleeping Beauty transforms into the paralyzing harpy Medusa. "Between London and Moscow we strayed into the desert of Araby on our way to Zion, and our own hubris blocked the path that leads to our people," Scholem concluded.

For all its metaphorical extravagance, Scholem's argument crystallizes around one point: The Revisionists maintained that the purpose of Zionism was to alleviate the suffering of Eastern European Jews through the refuge of Palestine, while his own contingent of Berlinese Zionists had struggled for a loftier, esoteric revival of the Jewish spirit through language. And though Labor had not yet fully subscribed to Jabotinsky's program, its party leaders could not disregard the core Revisionist demand for rescue and relief.

Indeed, Scholem himself was discomfited by the problem of where Europe's increasingly beleaguered Jews were supposed to go. The crisis in the German banking sector that summer, caused by huge foreign debt and the withdrawal of credit lines after the U.S. stock market collapse, threatened to erase his family's fortune. In August, his mother wrote him that it seemed definite she would be unable to maintain a home of her own. "You must bear in mind that we have *nothing*," she warned him. Part of the reason Jabotinsky felt so dangerous was that Scholem knew his diagnosis of the European state of affairs was not altogether mistaken, especially for the Ostjuden who formed his base of support. Unlike most of Scholem's former foes with their abstract cosmic gripes, the problem Jabotinsky set out to solve was deadly real. And the

way he fought — dirty and relentless — claimed its license from a mass hunger for survival that could not be reasoned away, philosophically or judicially.

After the congress of 1931, Scholem realized that the Revisionists might have the power not only to dismiss Brit Shalom's platform but also to redefine Zionism itself as a movement to which Brit Shalom's members could not belong. His illusions had been mostly smashed before. But that summer Scholem grasped that he might be forcibly exiled from the very movement to which he'd devoted his life — the movement created to end the Jews' exile.

The wave of suicide bombings struck, and each blast echoed through Jerusalem — from shop to shop, from car radios and apartment windows, from the expressions of sad rage and fatalism in face after face, in snatches of dialogue and glimpses on screens of Orthodox men gathering each minute body fragment from the pavement, the dirt, stalks, and branches, so that they could be buried together, to ensure the perfect bodily resurrection of the dead.

In late January 1995, a bombing at a road juncture in the center of the country killed nineteen soldiers, and when Anne came home from teaching that day she spoke of what it was like to be among the young girls after one of these events, the way they were mesmerized by newspaper images of the carnage, huddled in the halls crying and comforting one another. The girls had known some of the soldiers killed this time. They'd known soldiers killed and abducted before. They all went to the funerals, to the shivas and synagogues. They grew up in a rolling wave of tragedies while awaiting their own army service. This whole year seemed to have been characterized by these hideous incidents; teaching was often impossible. It must be so stressful for the girls, Anne observed. And yet their solidarity was intensely moving. Profound, even. Now and then we'd watch some American pop culture trinket, and the irresponsibility of those lives in a vacuum seemed to carry tragedy as a pathogen, if not a felt symptom.

At some point that year, life turned to glass. We stopped trying to think through anything. We knew our existence wasn't sustainable, but we felt transparent to the world. The light and blackness of Jerusalem streamed through us, and it was unclear what might shatter this glazed state of being. In one way, it seemed now as though we could be here forever. In another, for the same reason, we were already spectral. Sometimes the sense of deferment, of being preserved as we were like encased specimens, was beautiful. Other times the suspension felt eerie.

I found a job through the Jewish Agency as a kind of social worker–counselor helping troubled youth, many of them recent immigrants to Israel, at a halfway home in a working-class neighborhood on the edge of Jerusalem. I worked with only a few kids.

They were older adolescents, still palpitating with hope despite the suffering that had made the homes they were born into around the world unlivable. Thank God they'd been given refuge in Jerusalem when they had nowhere else to go. The political question of their right to be here moved me to wish them peace.

It had been so long since I'd imagined myself working in some therapeutic capacity not so different from the one I now found myself in that I didn't even register at first that I'd come full circle. Here I was in Jerusalem actually performing the service I'd dreamed of doing when I began studying all those years earlier in the little drab building on the slope beneath the Israel Museum above the Valley of the Cross. There was one young man from South Africa to whom I felt particularly attached. He was pale, with freckles like the flakes of wet snow that speckled the bare hills that winter. He strained so hard to quell his fears, to overcome his mind's twists and walls. I took him around the city to help him find work, to cope with bureaucracies, to explore possibilities for further schooling, to try to start him on the way to a new chapter. The work felt substantial, yet so remote from the place time had brought me that I could barely recognize myself in the role. I'd come back to where I began. Only I was no longer there.

I hadn't succeeded in making this work a foundation for living. The job couldn't begin to sustain us. And I knew my heart lay irrevocably in language, my soul in the book. "All we have left is the productivity of one who is going down and knows it," Scholem wrote in the penultimate lines of his 1931 letter to Benjamin. "It is the productivity in which I have buried myself for years for, after all, where should the miracle of immortality be concealed if not here?"

In my free time, I began to wander the city again, but now I was often with one friend or another. I'd come to know a young poet at the university, and we'd walk the paths that thread the summit of Mount Scopus, gazing out toward the desert and the Dead Sea, ending in the enchanted shade of the botanical garden, where we found a stone bench by trickling water facing a copse of trees whose deep red limbs resembled a fountain of frozen blood.

She was of Romanian descent. Both her parents had been in concentration camps as children. She suffered from nightmares conjured by the scraps she knew of her mother and father's experiences—terrifying, hypnotizing visions of evil. And I saw that there was no escaping the camps inside her, even though they'd come into her through the memories of others. Sometimes she would speak of her parents' journey to Palestine: the miracles and hardship of their passage when other routes of escape were barred. "What could they do?" she asked, in a voice like the water falling in that dark shade. "What would have happened if they couldn't have come here? They would have died. Died again, after they were liberated from the camps."

And she spoke with bitterness about the suicide bombings. How can the Palestinians try to kill us after what we've been through? When we're trying to make peace with them? When Rabin is offering them a state of their own? My parents came as close as my fingers to the chambers. And they want to take this country away from us? The world blames us for everything. We're supposed to trust the Europeans? They would be happy if this time we got killed off for good. Let the Arabs finish us. They'd thank them.

The water rippled behind us and the sun stabbed the leaves in long needles. Time stopped harder and harder.

And sometimes I walked with a former student from Kiev whose family had only recently arrived in Israel. She spoke of how her parents had been blocked from all hope of advancement in Soviet Russia. And when they finally decided they had to emigrate, the cruelties inflicted on them grew until her father was broken. He gave up everything. What was everything? I asked. Her eyes stared at mine until I realized she was not seeing me, not seeing anything but the everything lost to them.

"Life and death both," she said, turning away.

How could her family have been denied the right to find refuge here any more than the parents of my Romanian friend? This country should never have been conceived as the solution to the Jewish problem. But the doors backward shut long ago. The keys have been lost. And all the clean lines of liberal skepticism about this hard little state in "the desert of Araby" tangle on the European problem of endemic inhospitality to races that wander. While the grief of the Palestinians and the Jews revolves on a circle through space, like figures on a medieval clock tower enacting a morality play when the hour is struck. And the hour keeps striking. Over and over. Until repetition itself becomes confused with morality, and the passage of time becomes a marker of stasis.

On the first Sabbath in November, Anne and I walked with the children through neighborhood after neighborhood after a long lunch with religious friends. In the middle of the afternoon, everything was still and beautiful. A neighbor had pressed us to attend a peace demonstration scheduled for that evening in Tel Aviv, but the prospect of the late night with the children, with school and work the next day, dissuaded us.

When we got home, Anne read a strange story — an inconceivable story, but allegedly a true one — given her by the principal of the school where she taught. It told of a woman who'd saved someone's life in a concentration camp, but "gave" this mitzvah as a gift to a rabbi, who was afraid to undergo an operation for fear he would die without a mitzvah to redeem him. Her son was with her in the waiting room when the rabbi underwent the operation, and he made a drawing of the room while they sat there, including the clock and calendar that hung on the wall. The woman lived exactly thirteen more years after that night. Then she died at the precise time shown on the clock in the drawing, and on the same day as her son had inscribed — for the year at the top of the calendar he had drawn was thirteen years in the future from that on which he made the drawing, though he'd been unaware of this detail when his hand moved the pen.

A copy of this drawing was included in the envelope with the narrative, and we stared at the picture, which had the slightly feverish warp of rooms in a Van Gogh. And we remembered suddenly that just before leaving America we'd seen the deed of purchase of my grandparents' grave site — the grave the red fox led me to in Boston. They'd bought the plot on November 26, 1948 — the birthday of our first son, transposed to the year of the birth of Israel. We felt suffused with a sense of the uncanny in a manner we'd not felt since moving to Jerusalem. In this way, also, we'd come full circle, to the beginning of our Zionism where magic and idealism commingled.

That night, I watched Rossellini's film *Germany, Year Zero*. At the film's end, after the terrible suicide of the child, I flicked off the tape and turned to the state television channel. There were talking heads, and a tiny box in the corner of the screen depicting the peace rally we'd elected not to go to. It was some kind of special report; then I saw that Rabin had been shot.

I called Anne, and we stood in shock as they replayed footage of Rabin speaking that night about the promise of peace, turning away at last from violence. He was already dead then. God forgive us, we said.

Two days later, Rabin's funeral was held. We walked down from Rehavia into Sachar Park, a route we must have walked a thousand times since coming to Jerusalem. Now an endless line of people snaked up from the valley through the trees toward the Knesset. We stood in the rose garden beneath the building with friends, watching that line of humanity moving slowly toward the body lying in state. Everywhere around us, people were saying Rabin was a great man, a great man, may his soul rest in peace.

One of our friends asked if we ever wanted to return to America.

Anne turned to her in horror. "No. *No.* Especially not in times like this." As she spoke of feeling a sense of community, of identification with the people, someone not far from us in the line collapsed weeping, and the snake broke apart and transformed into a ring around her crumpled figure.

That night we couldn't sleep. We talked and talked inside the thick stone walls about the way our souls felt bound up with the place, despite our yearning sometimes for respite. We'd feel in exile if we ever left, Anne said.

And I said something about how even here we sometimes felt estranged. And she said perhaps this feeling of estrangement here is the longing for the Messiah.

In my mind, I saw the mourners on the path winding through the garden, waiting to pay their farewells to what was already gone.

FOURTEEN

IN 1933, Escha and Gershom finished building a home of their own in Jerusalem. After ten years, they'd finally staked their claim on property in the city. If they only had some money, they'd be quite comfortable, Scholem acknowledged in a letter to Benjamin. Benjamin by then had fled Germany and was dipping his toes in the experience of exile at a small peasant's house in Ibiza, set amid fig trees behind a windmill with broken sails.

Scholem and Escha planted carnations out front of the house, which she had to water continuously since the heavens refused to do their job in Jerusalem. Out back extended a rather bleak stone desert. But eventually they'd plant some cyclamen, and the shrubs that began to grow and blossom charmed Gershom in a manner nature rarely did. Everything took on a fantastical shape, so warped and bowed that it seemed imbued with strange grace.

Hugo Bergmann had, after all, invested in the building with them, and resided there for a time with his wife, Else. They made space for refugees and family members passing through as well. When a young cousin of Escha's who lived nearby turned twenty-four, Escha and Gershom baked the cake and organized festivities, inviting youthful colleagues so she wouldn't feel out of place on her first birthday away from her parents. Among the guests Gershom asked were students, including Fanya Freud, Sigmund Freud's cousin, a "cat-like young thing who some day will be able to describe herself as the world's first professionally trained female kabbalist," Gershom informed his mother.

When they weren't hosting proper little entertainments in a manner befitting their status as senior representatives of Jerusalem's nascent academic community, they often attended dinners connected with the university where, at the start of the 1933 fall semester, Gershom was appointed a full professor: Betty burst into tears of joy when his visiting card with the title "Dr. Scholem" fell out of his announcement letter. The evening before the Scholems' tenth wedding anniversary that October, the couple went to hear *Rigoletto* — a new opera production was opening every week in the country. This one would be performed at the Zion Cinema downtown, nearby which a roller coaster would soon be erected. Once it was finished, you could hear the riders yelling all the way to Rehavia, Scholem reported. Betty was appalled at the vulgarity of this addition to the city. It was lamentable that Jerusalem was rushing "to adopt the worst parts of the West and of America," she wrote. It always lifted her spirits to tell herself that on visits to Palestine she'd at least had a glimpse of the authentic Orient.

Her spirits needed cheering badly now. Werner had been rearrested, along with other former members of the Communist party, in the aftermath of the burning of the Reichstag in February 1933. He'd managed to secure his release in early March, using his legal training to draft statements to the police that proved he'd had no association with Communists for years. The family arranged to spirit him over the border to a cousin in Switzerland once he got out of jail. But Werner hung about Berlin, encouraged by his adroit handling of the Nazi bureaucracy to believe that it might still be possible for him to get his law degree and earn his livelihood representing the persecuted, a calling that promised to be a boom business under Germany's new chancellor.

It was a wretched miscalculation — so delusional in Gershom's view that it provoked almost as much anger as sorrow. Werner was arrested once again in April, along with his wife, Emmy, and Betty collapsed in terror. This time, they were locked up without any pretense to legal proceeding. Weeks later, they hadn't even been interrogated. When Emmy was finally brought before the court at the end of May, she learned that they'd both been charged with high treason in support of Communist activities. Werner wrote Betty letter after letter, begging her to visit and to find him a competent lawyer. But she couldn't get permission to see him, and every lawyer the family approached was frightened to take on Werner's case. The only result of all Werner's desperate petitions (he sometimes wrote his mother three times a day, eight pages scribbled with his erratic handwriting) was that the warden limited his correspondence to one letter a week.

In October, Gershom himself got a letter from "Prisoner 1660" in the Moabit penitentiary offering congratulations on his university appointment: Gershom had managed to make something of himself because he'd stopped trying to become someone in Germany, Werner wrote. Now he'd be fine so long as the Arabs didn't kill him — which didn't seem likely at present, though it might well happen at some point. For his own part, Werner went on, he was a double target: as a Jew and a former delegate to the Reichstag. His six years of legal training had proved utterly worthless. But he'd predicted that exactly this would happen when they spoke on his last visit to Germany, Werner reminded Gershom. Everyone called him a "pessimist" then. Well, it turned out that so far from being a pessimist, he'd been wearing rose-tinted glasses. "*Nemini parcetur*," he wrote — no one will be spared. He signed himself, "Your brother, Job."

Werner's case stagnated for months. When Betty finally received a pass to visit him in March 1934, she found her miserable child weeping in his cell. "Where's Emmy?" he kept asking. He'd heard nothing from his wife since her sudden release a few weeks earlier. On getting out, Emmy promptly fled Germany with their two daughters, which made Werner's case even more suspect in the eyes of the authorities.

In April, the prison secretaries informed Werner that a letter from Emmy had been received in which she assured him that she wanted to remain faithful. But they couldn't actually give him the letter since the only man able to authorize the release of correspondence from outside Germany was on Easter holiday. Werner burst into hysterics.

Betty was present at the time and watched in horror as her son shrieked at the officers and called them inhuman. He screamed until his voice was gone. She was amazed he wasn't dragged off during the outburst. Instead, the officers began howling back at him. The whole scene was ghastly. She'd hoped that confirmation of Emmy's being safe would stabilize him, but instead he became worse, because now he was terrified that she might cheat on him.

The Germans had succeeded in breaking Werner, Gershom realized. He suspected that this time his brother's fate was sealed.

After two years' imprisonment, Werner was at last given a hearing before the People's Court; following four days of secret deliberations, he was acquitted. He was immediately placed under protective custody, whereupon he disappeared from the face of the earth — presumably, the family knew, into a concentration camp. Little wonder that Kafka — specifically *The Trial* — became ever more a touchstone in Scholem's thought. "Kafka's world is a world of revelation," he wrote Benjamin, "but of revelation seen...from the perspective in which it is returned to its own nothingness."

The disjunctive character of Scholem's life magnified through the 1930s. During the first half of the decade, within his immediate circumference, life became cozier, more sociable, and professionally fruitful. He'd embarked on his carefully planned multiyear project to write a comprehensive history and philological analysis of all Jewish mysticism. He'd begun sketching out the summary of his Kabbalah studies that would turn into the revolutionary series of lectures he delivered in 1938 in New York. He was actively engaged in shaping the larger discipline of religious studies at Hebrew University, and was becoming recognized as one of the foremost scholars in Palestine.

The Jewish community itself appeared surprisingly robust in 1933. One English visitor, the usually caustic travel writer Robert Byron, reported that year how refreshing it was to find a country "with a prosperous cultivation and a prodigiously expanding revenue, with the germ of an indigenous modern culture in the form of painters, musicians, and architects." Scholem fretted that the country might not be able to absorb the sudden influx of gifted intellectuals. "One recent ship alone had fourteen architects and engineers on board, and before long we will be receiving doctors from municipal hospitals, professors, and lawyers," he wrote Benjamin in March.

With revenues strong, Jerusalem's municipal council embarked on a five-year beautification program. Sanitation was to be improved in accordance with "the sentimental and religious values of the Holy City," even as Germany was turning into an abattoir. "More blood is spilled than the newspapers use printers' ink to report on it," Joseph Roth remarked early in Hitler's chancellorship. By April, hundreds of immigrants from Germany were arriving on every ship to Jaffa, carrying with them "a harrowing picture of medieval events," Scholem recorded. He and Escha were besieged with telegrams from family and friends begging for advice and practical help. Everywhere on the streets, all that anyone was thinking or talking about was how to get their loved ones out of this new hell.

Increasingly, Scholem's letters were layered with references to the Jews' expulsion from Spain in 1492, which for him signified the catastrophe that led to the merging of the apocalyptic and messianic elements of Judaism with the traditions of Kabbalah. "The last age became as important as the first...the 'beginning' and the 'end' were linked together," he wrote. Events since Hitler took power provided deep insights into Jewish history, he observed to one correspondent. They differed from those of the fifteenth century only morally: There hadn't been "'national Spanish Jews' who still licked the boots that trampled them."

In June he told Benjamin that everywhere he went now he bumped into acquaintances from Germany, and the extraordinary thing was that many of them still didn't grasp the disaster's scope. On one occasion Scholem got into conversation with an affluent lady who so flabbergasted him with her naïveté that he ended up reducing her to tears by his merciless analysis of the dreamworld German Jews inhabited. He would never have imagined, he wrote, that the day would come when he would gain a reputation for radical chauvinism, but this was no doubt "the just revenge of the *genius loci.* Our old thesis, that Zionism shows superior insight in the diagnosis of the Jewish condition but has a tragic weakness as a therapy, will probably be uncannily reconfirmed, in view of the unfolding events," Scholem observed.

In August 1935, Scholem marveled at reports that there were now five thousand new arrivals a month, and the number of Jews in the country had doubled over the past three years. Along with questions about how so many people could be assimilated—and apprehensions about what would happen once the Mandate authorities decided it was time to choke off the tide—Scholem understood that the implications of what was happening in Europe for Hebrew University were colossal. Among the new refugees, there would surely be serious scholars who otherwise might never have considered moving to Jerusalem. Indeed, for the Yishuv as a whole, the massive increase in the Jewish population meant an expansion of political muscle—as well as money. Each year from 1933 onward, the number of Jews entering Palestine who brought with them a substantial sum of capital rose. Customs dues filled the coffers of the government. Imports and exports both grew by approximately 300 percent between 1931 and 1935. Land prices sky-rocketed again. Jabotinsky's fantasy of a Jewish majority might still be years off, but world events had contrived to so enlarge the Jews' presence that the settlement felt solid and tough.

This newfound stability further diminished the sway of those seeking to reorient Zionism's priorities in line with a transnational moral mission. Brit Shalom fizzled in these years. At one of the group's final meetings in 1935, Martin Buber remarked that the organization had become like "yeast seeking dough"—its members no longer had any field of action to operate in. Scholem by this point had nearly written off the prospects for overt intervention on the political stage. The growing power of the Jewish settlement coincided with a mounting dissonance between the external face of Zionism and his Platonic ideal so extreme as to qualify almost as an inversion. Whatever exactly Scholem's Zionism consisted in was the opposite of how the movement presented itself to the world. As he wrote Benjamin after the havoc of the Basel congress, "Our existence, our sad immortality, which Zionism had come along to stabilize in an unshakeable way, once again has been assured temporally—for the next two generations, but at a most horrendous price."

Though everyone knew nothing had been solved, on the surface, relations with the Arabs were quieter. There was a brief spate of Arab rioting in the fall of 1933—directed mostly at the British—but compared to 1929 it was minor. Still, even the staunchly Zionist British Jew Norman Bentwich acknowledged of this era, "The indefiniteness of the Jewish inflow, and the apprehension that within a short time the Jews would have a majority, gave a permanent handle to Arab nationalist agitation. It was also a weakness that the Jews could not follow a policy of 'sacred altruism.' Their socialism was national socialism."

But the breakdown in relations between the Arabs and Jews was something Scholem concerned himself with less now. It made more of an impression on him when Chaim Arlosoroff, an old comrade from his Zionist youth group days in Berlin and a Labor leader in Palestine, was assassinated while walking with his wife on the beach in Tel Aviv—apparently by Revisionist fanatics. Police raids and arrests took place all over the country, hunting for evidence of an extremist Jewish underground. The Revisionists organized protests in consequence, calling the investigation a blood libel motivated by political opportunism. The crack-up in relations between the different Jewish camps seemed irreparable.

Before the end of 1933, Scholem completed a poem titled "Media in Vita," which began on a note about lost faith, recalling his 1931 poem on the encounter between Zionism and the world, then took a revealing twist: "I am uncannily attracted/by the darkness of this defeat; /...I'm not fighting for any 'cause,'/all I'm fighting for now is me,/I stand the loneliest of guards,/it takes courage to see what I see." Though his verse style harkens back to the stiff rhythms of nineteenth-century German poetry, the voice carries the oracular lone wolf, fuck-you lucidity of Bob Dylan. Embracing the alienation to which fate has consigned him, Scholem concludes, "I could perhaps put on a disguise/but the world decides everything else."

The poem brings to mind a remark by Franz Rosenzweig about Scholem: "One cannot catechize him at all. I have never seen anything like it among Western Jews. He is perhaps the only one there is who has actually returned home. But he has returned home alone."

In the 1930s, Scholem allowed his vision of the Zionist collective to slip into a kind of mystical shadow. Distancing himself from the struggle to conquer opinion on the visible stage, he made his battle for Zionism's identity a subterranean, occult endeavor, which could be conducted from the isolation of his study. In another poem he sent Benjamin that year (inside a copy

of Kafka's *The Trial*), Scholem wrote of humanity's confinement
in the "enchanted kingdom of illusions." At a time when God
has been utterly disavowed, He could be experienced solely in His
negation, Scholem wrote. Only by recognizing this could "a teaching" come into remembrance that cracked the illusion.

The tradition of making a spiritual virtue of real-world failure
is, of course, a trope. And the Land itself, in some strains of Kabbalah, had long ago fractured into a double state where the divorce
between reality and appearance assumed a religious character.
Writing of the "model of a renewed humanity and of a renewed
kingdom of David" that represented the legacy of Messianic utopianism, Scholem observed that "it always retains that fascinating vitality to which no historical reality can do justice and which
in times of darkness and persecution counterpoises the fulfilled
image of wholeness to the piecemeal, wretched reality which was
available to the Jew. Thus the images of the New Jerusalem that
float before the eyes of the apocalyptists always contain more than
was ever present in the old one, and the renewal of the world is
simply more than its restoration."

This strategy—of effectively ceding the explicit field of battle, then recasting what occurred there to proclaim an esoteric
victory—was one Scholem increasingly deployed in interpreting
Walter Benjamin's own character. As it became clear that Benjamin would never embark on his long-promised course of intense
Jewish studies, and was in fact irresistibly drawn to Marxist
thought, Scholem began envisioning him as a kind of cryptodi-
vine: "a theologian marooned in the realm of the profane," as he
would later describe him. Benjamin, too, had been forced to wear
a mask—whatever he himself said. "Indeed, the peculiar self-
willedness of Benjamin's materialism derives from the discrepancy
between his real mode of thought and the materialist one he has
ostensibly adopted," Scholem declared.

In 1932, while still in Ibiza, Benjamin wrote an essay in which he described walking into a countryside where age-old pathways used by farmers, their families, and herds converged. As weariness conquers the walker, he loses control of his feet, becoming aware "that his imagination had made itself independent of him and, poised against the broad slope that paralleled his path in the distance, had begun to operate on him of its accord. Does imagination shift rocks and hilltops?" Benjamin asked. "Or does it just touch them with its breath? Does it leave no stone unturned, or does it leave everything as it was?" In answer, Benjamin noted that the Hasidim have a saying about the world to come: "Everything there will be arranged just as it is with us. The room we have now will be just the same in the world to come; where our child lies sleeping, it will sleep in the world to come. The clothes we are wearing we shall also wear in the next world. Everything will be the same as here — only a little bit different." Applying the proverb to his observation about imagination, Benjamin wrote, "It merely draws a veil over the distance. Everything remains just as it is, but the veil flutters and everything changes imperceptibly beneath it."

Scholem recognized the saying as one he'd shared with Benjamin. He knew with certainty that he was the one who'd brought this intriguing saying into circulation because — as he gleefully announced at one point — he himself made it up. The idea constituted one of his first reflections on the nature of Kabbalah. "I learned from this what honors one can garner for oneself with an apocryphal sentence," he wrote in a footnote, where he exposed Ernst Bloch as the latest author to unwittingly canonize this invented fragment of tradition.

Perhaps the "slight adjustment" characterizing the next world consists just in the capacity to perceive the same scene we already exist in differently — as the eternal realm. "Things change, and trade places; nothing remains and nothing disappears," Benjamin wrote. If he'd rightly interpreted Scholem's fable, this world becomes the world to come when imagination subtly reconfigures

our view of the horizon. The veil flutters and everything underneath metamorphoses, perhaps because we now see the folds of
that material along with the vanishing point. By injecting his
apocryphal sentence into tradition, Scholem had himself performed a kind of messianic trick — "slightly adjusting" the present by subverting our thinking about this world's relation to the
world to come.

If Buber, according to Scholem, made the mistake of discount-
ing history, his own realization was that he could elevate history
into an absolute — but then, through the lyric molding of his textual commentary, make history conform to the contours of his
own vision. The stone from which history was made was as real
as the mass of manuscripts to which he dedicated his life. But
the idol carved from that block was his own creation. This idea
hides the secret to his anarchic theology, which crystallized in the
mayhem of the mid-1930s. As he wrote in his verses on Kafka, with
the loss of Scriptural authority the great deception of the world
was consummated. Then again, as he argued later, the basic technique he employed had always been the characteristic form of Jewish truth seeking: "Not system but *commentary* is the legitimate
form through which truth is approached," he wrote. Tradition as
a living force reveals that "what had originally been believed to
be consistent, unified and self-enclosed now becomes diversified,
multifold, and full of contradictions."

In 1935, Scholem's efforts to bring Walter Benjamin to Jerusalem almost came together, for the umpteenth time. That February, Scholem extended a very specific invitation, hoping thereby
to overcome the resistances that had thwarted looser overtures in
the past. He was planning, he wrote Benjamin, to withdraw from
the world from July until November to write a volume on Kabbalah that would run between five hundred and a thousand pages

and provide a "concise exposition of the last 15 years of study." He encouraged Benjamin to come visit before or after this labor. If Escha's health permitted—she'd been suffering from sciatica and gallbladder problems—they would be delighted to host him in their flat. They also had friends nearby whose apartments would offer more seclusion and comfort. If he stayed for a month or two, he would spend nothing on board or lodging. Escha added a cajoling note of her own: "Of course, the voyage itself would probably be more interesting than agreeable, since you would surely have to make it on an emigrant ship populated by restless Jews. But once you are here, I can almost promise you rest and comfort."

Benjamin eventually replied. He would certainly come but would be obliged to defer the trip until winter; there were colleagues whom he needed to confer with before they too emigrated. Scholem replied with disappointment; Benjamin's commitments were especially unfortunate, given that it seemed in no way certain "that you will really be in a position to travel in winter." There were simply too many unknowns in the current climate for him to feel sanguine. The next month, Scholem wrote Benjamin again, to say that hosting him that winter would not, after all, be convenient: "This has as much to do with family matters, which do not lend themselves to detailed description, as with my possible absorption in work on the book until it is completed."

After this letter, Scholem's correspondence dropped off precipitously, to the point where Benjamin himself began protesting. In December, Scholem reported that Escha had gone to Tiberius for an extended period to recover her health. She'd been fired from the library, but her whole position there had become uncongenial anyway since Bergmann had left to become rector of Hebrew University. The difficulty of maintaining two households, with Escha up north on top of the loss of her income, were "fatal" he wrote, and their plans for eventually honoring the invitation they'd extended to Benjamin had been "drastically affected."

That was the last letter Scholem sent Benjamin until the following April, when he abruptly revealed that he'd just gotten a divorce. "Separating from Escha caused very great inward and external difficulties in my personal life," he wrote. "As a friend who has been through a similar experience, you don't need a description of just how great." Since Scholem was the one who'd filed for divorce, the material implications of the settlement could be devastating to him if she remained single thereafter. But, he added, not very cryptically, "If Bergmann were to succeed in getting his divorce (which, however, is exceedingly problematic), then she would remarry."

Exactly what happened is unclear, though friends later said that Escha and Hugo had begun an affair even before Scholem's arrival in Palestine. It's plausible. Scholem never made much time for Escha, and he was away from home enough that logistics of a liaison would have been undemanding. Nor does it strain credulity to suppose that Scholem would have been too absorbed in his own work even when around to register an intimacy happening under his nose. This wasn't only a matter of ego. He was also, in his own way, touchingly naïve and trusting.

Matters may also, however, have been more complicated. Before the end of 1936, he wrote Benjamin to announce that the change of address on his letterhead provided "the most succinct expression of some of the changes my life has undergone." He now lived at 28 Abarbanel Road while Escha remained in their former home. "She herself has since been transformed into a Frau Bergmann," he explained. "Moreover, in order to give other news its due right away, I should say that I was recently married again, to a young woman from the depths of the Sarmatian forests by the name of [Fanya] Freud" — his former student.

Was the rapidity of his own remarriage an indication that there'd been some preexisting liaison with his ex-pupil? Or did he merely want to restore as quickly as possible a conventional domestic arrangement once it became clear that Escha's long-term

affair had created an irresolvable breach in their marriage? Either way, he never expressed any rancor toward Bergmann—or, for that matter, Escha. Despite his lament for the months lost to the divorce, the transposition from Escha to Fanya seems to have been almost seamless. He'd moved just a few blocks away in Rehavia from where he'd been living before. Soon he and Fanya were designing their own flat in the building, in which, as had been the case in the house he shared with Escha, his library would be the centerpiece. Everything was the same as it had been before, only a little bit different.

The interlude of relative quiet with the Arabs also ended. Riots that began in April 1936 at first seemed to be repeating the Wailing

Wall events. But this time the violence didn't end in a few days or a few weeks; it continued for three years until the eve of the Second World War. Arab fatalities may have exceeded five thousand, while several hundred Jews were killed. The similarities between the 1929 riots and the uprising of the 1930s were at once profound and deceptive.

In the summer of 1936, when Scholem's divorce was still raw and Jerusalem had been in a state of siege for three months—at a time when Scholem himself had been enlisted to spend several hours on guard duty each evening from the roof of a building at the edge of Rehavia, when Arab snipers were killing Jews through the windows of their own homes, including Scholem's colleague, the Arabist Levi Billig, who was gunned down at his desk while reading the Bible—Scholem completed the most important essay he'd yet written—quite possibly the single greatest essay of his career. He titled the work, which considers the fate of the Sabbatian movement in the wake of Sabbatai Sevi's apostasy, "Redemption Through Sin." Scholem had described the work in progress to Benjamin as a study of religious nihilism, though he meant by this also that it constituted an analysis of the contortions of faith people will undertake to avoid nihilism in the face of defeat on the main stage of history. "Here we find ourselves standing before a blank wall, not only of misunderstanding, but often of an actual refusal to understand," Scholem wrote of the so-called heretical Sabbatianism that evolved after the messiah's conversion to Islam.

At the beginning of the essay, Scholem draws explicit parallels between the psychological situation of his subject and the "times of Jewish national rebirth" he and his readers were living through. Scholem was writing the history of an idealistic belief system that had essentially died without becoming defunct—while continuing, indeed, to walk the face of the earth with explosive power. In its contemporary echoes, "Redemption Through Sin" reflected on Zionism as a zombie morality play.

I found myself returning urgently to this work in the wake of Rabin's assassination. The more that emerged about events leading up to the murder, the more this period also seemed riddled with scenes of an almost fantastical, ghoulish nature.

We'd celebrated when we heard about the vote in parliament the day after Yom Kippur in 1995, to approve the second phase of the Oslo Accords that would end twenty-eight years of Israeli occupation. The ratification had been expected, but still there was something liberating in the news that the withdrawal would now actually commence. We knew that the debates in the Knesset had been protracted and bitter. That was unsurprising.

But only later did I read detailed reports of those Knesset proceedings. While settlers and ultra-Orthodox agitators mobbed the building, Benjamin Netanyahu, the leader of the opposition, delivered a speech decrying the terms of the international agreement. "You, Mr. Prime Minister, have said that the Bible is not our land registry," he bellowed. "A man should not give up his country and his home with that kind of ease and joy. Only one who feels like an invader and thief behaves in such a fashion...How can a nation that does not recognize its right, a nation that has lost the dream, continue to defend itself and struggle for existence?" He knew Rabin wasn't listening, but he also knew that tens of thousands of right-wing supporters would hear his words as a summons to battle.

The night after that debate, demonstrators gathered in huge numbers with torches in Zion Square in Jerusalem. I'd run out to the store on an errand, and from the edge of Independence Park I could hear the crowd roaring and the harsh crackling voices of politicians reverberating from loudspeakers. The previous year I might have wanted to go downtown to see for myself what was happening, but now my instinct was to stay far away. So I learned only afterward about the cries of "Nazis! and "*Judenrat!*"

that had rippled through the throng. And about the burning of
Rabin's portrait. And the circulation of a handbill depicting the
prime minister's head superimposed over a Gestapo uniform.
Only afterward did I read about Netanyahu's speech, the culminating address of the night. He spoke standing before a huge banner,
painted with the words OUR FATE TO BE DECIDED BY A VOTE
OF JEWS ALONE. "This government has a non-Zionist majority!" Netanyahu thundered. "This government rests on five Arab
deputies who are identified with the PLO!" He invoked a remark
of Rabin's, in which the prime minister had said there were only
four hundred Jews in Hebron, some of whom were to be evacuated
under the terms of the peace settlement. " I tell you it's not only
four hundred Jews in Hebron, it's four thousand years of history
that ties us to this land," Netanyahu went on. "You say the Bible is
not a property deed. But I say the opposite — the Bible is our mandate, the Bible is our deed." A chorus of support arose from amid
the crowd: "In blood and fire we will do away with Rabin!"

Torches were hurled at the police monitoring the demonstration. Chants of "Bibi! Bibi!" alternated with choruses of "Nazi!
Nazi!" as images of Rabin with his head at the center of a bull's-eye
framed by the word "Traitor!" in Hebrew and English were bran-
dished aloft. Later that evening, as a torchlit procession marched
to the Knesset, Rabin's car passed by, and a number of protestors,
mistakenly believing he was inside, began smashing the doors and
windows with fists and sticks, ripping off the hood ornament and
gloating afterward that they could get to the man just as they'd
gotten to the symbol.

I heard *something* about this demonstration, but there were so
many demonstrations then. And they were all rabid and bloodcur-
dling. I'd stopped paying much attention. I made the mistake of
reading repetition as rerun rather than a transfixed determination.
Only long after Rabin was dead did I realize how Netanyahu had
always been there, placing himself at exactly the right spot relative

to the firestorm to whip up the flames without getting singed, always preserving plausible deniability for the worst excesses committed by the followers he goaded. Netanyahu, with that stentorian, commanding voice—the orotund angry bull baritone that could slip when expedient into stately English, the almost Kissinger-deep registers carefully modulated to make the breasts of conservatives swell with a sense of their own vigilant machismo while sending psychopaths into a frenzy—proved himself the most dangerous kind of politician: He has the courage of his lack of convictions.

Over time, reports of overtly mystical events preceding the assassination began to surface. On the evening of Yom Kippur, right in front of Rabin's official residence a few blocks from our apartment, a group of men stood in a circle draped in prayer shawls chanting softly. We passed Rabin's home that night, since it lay on the route to the synagogue we attended on high holy days; and if I caught a glimpse of the men then, I thought nothing of them, since almost every man we saw was draped in white and many people were murmuring prayers. But it later emerged that these men were uttering what they understood to be a kabbalistic curse, the *Pulsa da-Nura*, Lashes of Fire. At its climax, the leader raised his gaze to the prime minister's residence and chanted, "I deliver to you, the angels of wrath and ire, Yitzhak, the son of Rosa Rabin, that you may smother him and the specter of him." "Put to death the cursed Yitzhak, son of Rosa Rabin, as quickly as possible because of his hatred for the Chosen People," chorused all the men together. And then the leader cried at the top of his voice, "May you be *damned, damned, damned!*" The medieval legend surrounding this curse declares that its recipient will die within thirty days. And to the group's satisfaction and awe, exactly thirty days later, Rabin was murdered.

Yigal Amir, Rabin's assassin, performed mystical rites just before pulling the trigger. As Rabin stood above him on the stage singing "Song of Peace," Amir waited in the darkness, practicing the esoteric art of Geomatria, which involves meditating on Hebrew letters

from passages of Scripture and manipulating their order to prophe-
size. Concentrating on lines from Genesis, in which God promises
the descendants of Abraham the land from the river of Egypt to
the great river, the river of Euphrates—a passage that includes the
line "a smoking fire pot and a flaming torch passed between these
pieces"—Amir found that by sliding forward one letter from each
word to join the following word, the words "a flaming torch passed
between" transformed into "fire, fire, there is evil in Rabin." And
then Amir knew his bullet would strike home. He would be able to
save the Jewish people from the man against whom influential rabbis had passed a *din rodef*, a legal judgment authorizing believers to
kill the condemned individual as a "pursuer" who has endangered
the life or belongings of another Jew.

The Geomatria and the kabbalistic curse might have been
fringe phenomena. (The *din rodef* was not—it comes straight from
the Mishna.) But even so, what did it mean if aspects of that mysticism I'd found so beguiling were being used to promulgate evil—
were capable, as a practice, of inciting murder?

The more I read, the more clear it became that an extraordinary number of people had foreseen this assassination—in fear
and yearning, logically and kabbalistically, from the right and the
left—among them numerous powerful figures. And after he was
dead, many voices were raised blaming Rabin himself for having
created an atmosphere in which such violence became inevitable.

Sometimes in the first weeks after the assassination there was
a feeling that the boil had been lanced, the nation would now
surely draw together in mourning this death for which we must
all feel a measure of complicity. Some because they had prayed for
Rabin's elimination. Some, like Anne and myself, because of heed-
lessness to what this political moment required. We knew we had
failed to be as vigilant in our support of the peace as we might
have been. We hadn't understood what it would take to realize
that dream, having assumed that once the plan was agreed upon,

and the democratically elected majority in the Knesset had ratified the accord, it was effectively a fait accompli. We did not recognize that it was the dawn of another plastic hour in which anything might transpire.

What if we had gone to the rally in Tel Aviv that night with our friends from the courtyard? What if one of our children had dashed from our guard into the crowd and, as we broke through the masses of people in desperate search, the focus of everyone on the stage had been diffracted for a moment, and in this dispersal of attention all the configurations that so perfectly aligned for Amir's deed were rearranged in ways that prevented him getting his aim? What if just the addition of our family, along with all those others who *almost* came that night, had been enough to change the dynamic in a cascading sequence of slight adjustments such that Rabin survived to this day?

Impossible? Grandiose fantasy? More so than the notion that mystically rearranged biblical verses could confirm the feasibility of Rabin's murder in the eyes of the man who then proceeded to commit the killing? (What if Amir had not been able to find that Hebrew alphabet-soup validation? Might even that have been enough so that, shaken, he bungled his plan?) More so than the idea that through a series of impossibly careless oversights and malignant flukes of fate, one unimpressive little man, who'd earned a reputation during his army service in Gaza for seizing children who violated the curfew and for malevolently ripping down laundry strung between houses with his rifle, could get inside the security perimeter and assassinate the prime minister? And if any fantasy about what might have been different had our family been at that peace rally is too far-fetched, yet, still, *we might have been there.* Tens of thousands of others almost came. And if everyone who almost appeared in support of some cause dear to their hearts had not let some trivial concern trump their sense of moral responsibility, how can we say what the world would look like today? I think of a letter Betty Scholem wrote her son in April 1933. For the past couple of years, she said, she'd been able just to accept what was taking place in Germany, but now her equanimity had broken. "I cannot digest what is happening—and I refuse to do so. I'm completely speechless. I simply can't imagine that there are not 10,000 or 1,000 upright Christians who refuse to go along by raising their voice in protest." What would have happened had there been ten thousand then? And where are those ten thousand now?

For several months after the assassination, we were, anyway, dominated by a sense of solidarity—with the country and with each other. We were tender with everyone and turned again to the question of what our Zionism—what *Judaism*—ultimately consisted in. And in this spirit I read, and reread, Scholem's essay on religious nihilism.

FIFTEEN

"REDEMPTION THROUGH SIN" traces the final theological recalibration performed by the Sabbatians after their messiah abandoned his people's faith and adopted a whole new belief system. Having made the argument that the messiah's "descent" — most starkly expressed in his conversion — was a divine mission to salvage the last embers of holiness from the point of greatest darkness, the Sabbatians were inspired to reinterpret an old rabbinic concept, *mitzvah ha-ba'ah ba-averah* — mitzvah that comes from transgression. When it was invoked in the Talmud, the phrase referred censoriously to the execution of a commandment with the help of some illicitly procured element. (For instance, if one has stolen a measure of wheat and has grown, kneaded, and baked it for challah, the blessing one recites over it would be a blasphemy.) The Sabbatians, however, ingeniously read the phrase literally and positively, as "a commandment which is *fulfilled* by means of a sin." As Scholem writes, "Once it could be claimed that the Messiah's apostasy was in no way a transgression, but was rather a fulfillment of the commandment of God...the entire question of the continued validity of the Law had reached a critical stage."

By the early 1930s, when Scholem had started to grapple with the recognition that Zionism might not simply fail to realize its ideal form but could mutate into a monstrous caricature of that vision, the power of Sabbatai's story as a historical model for what he was living through grew beyond measure. The essence of the

Sabbatians' conviction, he said, "can be summarized in a sentence: it is inconceivable that all of God's people should inwardly err, and so, if their vital experience is contradicted by the facts, it is the facts that stand in need of explanation." He proceeds to cite the words of one believer some thirty years after Sabbatai donned the turban: "'The Holy One, blessed be He, does not ensnare even the animals of the righteous, much less the righteous themselves, to say nothing of so terribly deceiving an entire people...And how is it possible that all of Israel be deceived unless this be part of some great divine plan?'"

Although it was an exaggeration to suggest that "all of Israel" had been swept up in the messianic movement, it's nonetheless true that staggering numbers of individuals from different socio-economic classes, including highly educated rabbis, along with entire Jewish communities throughout Europe and the Levant, did become intoxicated by the conviction that salvation was upon them during Sabbatai's heyday. When his conversion appeared to make a mockery of their sublime experience, many of the messiah's followers, helped by the theosophical acrobatics of Cardozo and Nathan of Gaza, instead adjusted their interpretation of history. And the consciousness thereby engendered "was directly opposed to the outlook of ghetto Jewry as a whole, of which the 'believers' themselves formed a part." In consequence of their dissident position, the Sabbatians "of necessity tended to become innovators and rebels," Scholem writes. "Herein lay the psychological basis of that spirit of revolt which so infuriated the champions of orthodoxy." In a dramatic reclamation of the renegade apostles, changing them from fools to heroes — or perhaps heroic fools — Scholem states, "A new type of Jew had appeared for whom the world of exile and Diaspora Judaism was partly or wholly abolished and who uncompromisingly believed that a 'restored world,' whose laws and practices he was commanded to obey, was in the process of coming into being."

Scholem's words suggest deep parallels between Sabbatai's followers and the followers of Zionism. They, too, had maintained
a state of consciousness that dissolved the reality of exile, while
cherishing a tenacious faith that, in their return to Zion, a renewal
of the people was initiated that would ultimately give birth to a
restored world — notwithstanding history's judgment against
the project's credibility. Like Sabbatai's adherents, the Jews who
embraced Zionism came from every conceivable background: rich,
poor, learned, uneducated, Western, Eastern. And ultimately the
Zionists as well reached a critical mass too great for their project
to simply be abandoned in response to betrayals by forces within
and outside their ranks.

When Scholem recounts how, in mystical, heterodox guise,
"Sabbatianism assumed different and changing forms: it splintered into many sects, so that even from the polemical writings
against it we learn that the 'heretics' quarreled among themselves
over practically everything," his description evokes the disagree-
ment on core articles of Zionist faith that began fragmenting the
movement into antagonistic factions from the start, and grew progressively more rancorous with time. The open fault line Scholem
describes eventually breaking the Sabbatians in two may give
insight into what he envisioned having happened to Zionism in
the aftermath of the Wailing Wall riots, the Seventeenth Congress,
and Hitler's assumption of power.

The key division within Sabbatianism can be understood as
the culmination of a three-part process. First, the medieval Lurianic school of Kabbalah had developed a new myth of the Messiah, which, in Scholem's interpretation, allegorized the Jewish
experience of exile. By concentrating on the spiritual aspect of
redemption far more than its outward realization, Luria's disciples "gradually converted it into a symbol of purely spiritual processes." The messianic hopes they nurtured "were not put to the
test of the actual crucible of history."

There is intellectual beauty to Scholem's reading of the Lurianic Kabbalah, which bore parallels to pre-State Diaspora Zionism. But for him, the imperative of the Jews' "return to history,"
with all its attendant responsibilities, required something beyond
contemplative epiphanies. Not content with cognitive Zionism,
he pursued a living commitment to the creation of a new Jewish
society—at the physical point in space with the greatest historical
resonance for the Jewish people.

In Scholem's arc of the Kabbalah's evolution, Sabbatai Sevi's
arrival marked the moment when Luria's vision of the Redeemer
entered the "crucible of history." The spread of popular belief
in Sabbatai's messiahship made the sense of inner freedom and,
indeed, of the world's restoration that had been fostered by the
Lurianic perspective "become an immediate reality for thousands."

For all the difficulties of Scholem's initial period in Palestine,
he continued to feel himself invested there with a spiritually elevated mission: to catalyze the Jewish people's collective renewal.
"The people who came to Palestine between 1923 and 1933 had
made up their minds that they wanted to live among Jews and not
in a ghetto," Scholem asserted. "They wanted to be free men and
women and work for the renaissance of the Jewish people. These
people—and I was one of them—regarded themselves as the *vanguard* of the Jewish people."

The political side of Zionism alienated him from the beginning. But it was not clear then that political Zionism would
become the dominant factor shaping Jewish settlement activity
in Palestine. The period of Sabbatai's apostasy might be likened
in Scholem's schema to the phase between 1929 and 1931 when it
became obvious not only that cultural Zionism and political Zionism were irremediably at odds but also that events had conspired
to make the "heretical" political face of the movement outwardly
determinative of Zionism's identity.

And yet once Scholem had gotten over his initial shock, this paradigm shift did not challenge his inner Zionist belief. It only compelled him to accept that the divergence between appearance and reality might persist until the era of redemption. "The great historical disappointment experienced by the Sabbatian had instilled in him the paradoxical conviction that he and his like were privy to a secret whose time had not yet come to be generally revealed," Scholem wrote. "Hidden in the 'believer's' soul was a precious jewel, the pearl of Messianic freedom, which shone forth from its chamber of chambers to pierce the opaqueness of evil and materiality." The person who shared in this secret was "a free man by power of his own personal experience."

The creed of "heretical" Sabbatianism remained ambiguous until the debate over whether Sabbatai's behavior should be considered a model for the people at large or a unique lapse drove different factions to codify their doctrinal positions, which ultimately fissured the movement. The "moderate Sabbatians"—such as Nathan of Gaza and Abraham Cardozo, with whom Scholem clearly identified—held that Sabbatai's strange actions, and his conversion in particular, were never intended to inspire mass imitation. Instead of advocating sacrilegious action, these leaders developed revolutionary theological concepts to explicate Sabbatai's doubleness. Their perspectives were radical but remained in the realm of ideas. The moderate Sabbatians effectively promulgated a two-tier class system of religious access: In the "upper class" stood the Messiah and the inner circle of prophets who interpreted his actions. Then there was everyone else, whose mission was, for the present, largely confined to receiving illumination from the elect.

These Sabbatians might be compared to the cultural Zionists who moved to Palestine with the intention of being part of a broad Jewish regeneration but did not believe most other Jews were spiritually prepared for the territorial actualization of their ideals. As early as 1916, Scholem had scribbled feverishly in his journal about the prospects of bringing together a small band of young

Zionists who were "inwardly governed by Zion and for whom Zion has become absolutely religious (admittedly, what I'm saying here is how I'd like to be myself)." This "New Fraternity" would be like Isaac Luria's circle of Kabbalists in Safed, who sparked a revolution in the life of the whole Jewish people. "If news came of a group of a few young Jews who have turned up in the Land of Israel to make Zion the central point of their religious (and every other) vision and to lead—in silence and the highest acuteness of mind—a life of sacrifice and devotion...is there the slightest doubt that, together with some other young Jews, I would at once venture forth to the Land of Israel to start a new life pregnant with the future, even if we had to crawl on all fours to get there?"

The problem, he discovered—as the Sabbatians had found some 250 years earlier—was that others were not necessarily content to let the hyperdedicated, pure-minded few dictate the course of the people's renewal. Although the moderate Sabbatians tried to quarantine the concept of "strange holiness" from the wider public, the line they drew around it only seemed to encourage transgression. "The more ardent 'believer' found himself becoming increasingly restive," Scholem wrote. "And soon the cry was heard: Let us surrender ourselves as he did! Let us descend together to the abyss before it shuts again! Let us cram the maw of impurity with the power of holiness until it bursts from within." Such emotions, wrote Scholem, provided the psychological background for a "great nihilistic conflagration," in which the instincts of anarchy and lawlessness that lie buried in everyone broke free in the form of radical Sabbatianism. Suddenly, an "aura of holiness" enveloped the most extreme profanities. The violation of Torah now became its fulfillment.

Approaching the period in which Scholem was composing his essay, the line of analogy to the messianic heresy swirls into more labyrinthine patterns, entangling both personal and national elements. Sabbatianism revealed the potential for a more dangerous order of transgression after Sabbatai's own death, when certain leaders felt empowered to push the most iconoclastic speculations of the movement to their utmost conclusion. Not only niceties of ritual but also the fundamental laws of the Bible no longer applied. In Scholem's account, at that moment the "Gordian knot binding the soul of the exilic Jew had been cut and a vertigo that ultimately was to be his undoing seized the newly liberated individual: genuine desires for a reconsecration of life mingled indiscriminately with all kinds of destructive and libidinal forces." This new stage, comprising a chaotic democratization of desires, marked the point at which Sabbatian nihilism became "a mass movement rather than the concern of a few isolated Jewish scholars."

Scholem's own quixotic, vanguard-driven model of the Zionist movement became subsumed in 1933. "Hitler came to power and everything changed," he said in an interview. The Jews coming to Palestine were no longer idealistic seekers but desperate refugees. He took to quoting Ben-Gurion's blunt formulation: "Those Jews we hoped for are dead." He also began claiming that, with the arrival of more recent waves of exiles, social problems such as rape and organized crime, "which never existed before in Jewish history," were suddenly flourishing. This, of course, was historically inaccurate — he himself had given Benjamin a book documenting Jewish criminality in Berlin. But Scholem exaggerated the Jews' former purity to make a point about the corruption of Zionism occasioned by the changed nature of the settlement in Palestine — for which he held Hitler responsible. In so doing, he evoked the mingling of destructive and life forces that accompanied the birth of Sabbatian nihilism.

The problem of Eros could well have been viscerally present to him while he was writing "Redemption Through Sin," in light of the sexual transgressions — whatever they were — that contributed to the breakup with Escha. Questions of Zionism and sexuality had always been problematic for Scholem. Back in 1919, questioning Buber's teachings, he had rather primly asserted that "the life of Jewish youth has been undermined by promiscuity on all levels." Similarly, the radical Sabbatians were rapturously devoted to "sacred sin": "It would be pointless to deny that the sexual element in this outburst was very strong," Scholem wrote, noting that in rabbinical excommunications dating from the eighteenth century, the offspring of this sect were "automatically considered bastards."

In the essay's final section, the orgiastic proclivities of the radicals are linked to the drive for a new Jewish national existence through the person of the most extreme latter-day incarnation of Sabbatai's legacy, Jacob Frank, whom Scholem calls "one of the most frightening phenomena in the whole of Jewish history." Born in Ukraine in 1721, Frank started life as a dealer in cloth and gems but became a religious figure, attracting a multitude of believers.

"My desire is to lead you toward Life," Frank told his followers. But because a towering edifice of laws, customs, and religions stood in the way of Life, he would be able to guide humanity to that goal only by way of destruction. "Wherever Adam trod a city was built, but where I set foot all will be destroyed, for I came into this world only to destroy and to annihilate. But what I build, will last forever," Frank promised. *Everyone* had to descend together to the very bottom of the abyss in order for everyone to rise again. "The place that we are going to tolerates no laws," Frank stated, "for all that comes from the side of Death, whereas we are bound for Life."

Startling imagery accompanied Frank's theological pronouncements. Esau — traditionally representative of Israel's evil adversaries — is identified with the place of the Good God to which people must travel. Rachel is now the true Messiah, and also the "holy serpent" guarding the garden of paradise. Lascivious sexual rites and mass baptisms are prescribed as steps toward a salvation transcending all existing faiths. Frank's believers were enjoined to become mystical soldiers, adding that "soldiers are not allowed to have a religion." During Frank's lifetime, this call for disciples to form a military legion that could execute his commands was intended literally, Scholem maintains.

Scholem portrays Frank as an appalling "strongman," who encouraged his followers "to drain the cup of desolation and destruction to the lees until the last bit of holiness had been made a mockery." But having delivered this damning brief, Scholem then yanks his condemnation of Frank inside out. Frank remained a figure of vitalizing potency, Scholem argues, even given the perversion of faith that he sanctioned. He had, after all, fought to establish a zone of settlement for his followers in Eastern Galicia where they could organize their community life as they saw fit. While this effort was partly an expression of Frank's personal lust for power, it was also, Scholem argues, evidence of his followers' desire for territorial and economic autonomy. "For all the negativism of his teachings, they nonetheless constituted a genuine creed of life." Scholem admits that every accusation leveled by Jewish historians against Frank is true—but adds that these sins don't negate the significance of his achievements for the dialectical progress of Jewish history.

The theology Frank cultivated from the loam of Sabbatianism was not original as a body of thought, according to Scholem, but it testified to Frank's brilliance at inventing new, revelatory symbols—precisely the contribution to Judaism that Scholem commends most evocatively in Kabbalah as such. Frank's recorded sayings are colored by a "vigor and imagination" so pronounced that Scholem declares himself unable to comprehend how a sensitive individual could read them without emotion. In his depiction, Frank comes across as a mystical poet, whose vision transformed features of the real world. For all that Scholem affirms the dangerous, even pathological nature of Frank's character and writings, the repulsion he feels plainly coexists with awe. He admires Frank's intrepidness. He seems captivated by the "extraordinary spectacle

of a powerful and tyrannical soul" living in the middle of the eighteenth century—the era of the Enlightenment—who'd succeeded
in immersing himself in a mythological realm of his own creation.

The essay's sensational juxtaposition of the demonic and
deplorable with the moral and sublime marks the birth of
Scholem's mature style. Almost all his great works thenceforth
bear traces of this intoxicating compound: the rousing depiction of theological passion offset by a cool note of historical cau-
tion—with the latter never quite neutralizing the former.

In truth, even the most shocking aspects of Frank's doctrine—
such as his assertion that he came "only to destroy" in pursuit of
life—correspond to abiding features of Scholem's own thought.
In 1914, he described the impression made on him by the work
of a pioneering theorist of the Wandervogel who'd articulated
the movement's infinite yearning for Romanticism and "enormous lust for destruction." Much later, Scholem wrote approv-
ingly that for Benjamin, destruction represented a positive and
noble power—even a form of redemption. And in 1975, when
he was nearly eighty years old, Scholem stated, "I have never
stopped believing that the element of destruction, with all the
potential nihilism in it, has always been also the basis of positive
Utopian hope."

The longing for a shattering rupture that would free them
from the claustrophobic mausoleum of prewar European culture
was a common feature among Scholem's peers. But that general
yearning for some apocalyptic intervention was heightened in very
particular ways by the conditions of life in Palestine. After the Seventeenth Congress, Scholem had experienced moral despair about
the state of Zionism. But by 1936, the threat posed by outside
forces to the Zionist project could no longer be philosophically
reformulated as an intra-Jewish spiritual agon. With the world
going to hell, Scholem's reactions began to twist over themselves
into willfully double-edged arguments.

At the opening phase of the conflict, during which Scholem was writing "Redemption Through Sin," Jewish militias were mostly restrained from acts of counterterror, their leaders trusting that the British would gain control of the situation, and that having refrained from tit-for-tat bloodshed, the Jews would occupy stronger ground in the diplomatic resolution of events. But it was clear that this self-discipline might crumble at any time. Practically every young person had been drafted into one self-defense unit or another to protect against opportunistic raids. University life was almost shut down. In the consuming turmoil, Scholem had no "inner life" to report on, he told Benjamin. A curfew imposed by the Mandate continued for months. Even indoors, behind thick walls, he and Fanya were unable the block out the sound of incessant fire-fights. The murderous atmosphere in Palestine coincided with a steadily deteriorating situation in Germany. On the personal front, the Scholem family's struggle to secure Werner's release from the concentration camp had been frustrated just when his prospects appeared hopeful again. Gershom actually managed to get Werner a certificate for travel to Palestine—whereupon negotiations collapsed. Werner was to die in 1940, in Buchenwald, at the age of forty-five.

With Irgun, the Revisionists' defense league, agitating for a more ruthless policy of retaliation, the temptation to wrest control of Jewish destiny at any price was everywhere in the air that summer. In this climate it's no wonder that Frank's "creed of life" blazed up tantalizingly for Scholem, and in his rendering, the political aspirations of Frank's life appear to deliberately echo the career of Vladimir Jabotinsky. As scholars have noted, descriptions of the "soldiers" or Jewish "legion" Frank sought to establish evoke the Jewish legion Jabotinsky fought to create. When Scholem labeled Frank a "strongman," he knew that for Jabotinsky this notion represented a heroic archetype: the counterpart to the weak, sickly character of the typical exilic Jew.

Beyond such terminological parallels, Jabotinsky's reputation for possessing the "imagination of an artist"—affirmed by the ambitious novels he wrote in which expressions of irreconcilable good and evil abound—aligns his character with what Scholem calls the "hidden poetic impulse" in Frank, "which appears all the more surprising in the light of his customary savagery." Most of all, Jabotinsky's fundamental position that anything was permitted that would help place the Jews on the path to life—embodied for him in the creation of a Jewish state—chimes with Frank's valorization of Life before everything, even when this principle necessitated acts of violence. "We subordinate all human efforts, individual or collective, social, religious, etc., to the jealous primacy of the State idea," Jabotinsky wrote. The path to the Jewish state dominated his agenda because of his apocalyptic vision of the Jews' impending fate in Europe—a conviction of the ascendancy there of a "Ruler of Death" as absolute as Frank's cosmic dictator. Scholem would never have come out in support of Jabotinsky. But in the oblique analogy with Frank, what we might view as Scholem's "Miltonic problem," becomes apparent. Like Satan in *Paradise Lost*, this flamboyantly destructive figure is portrayed in such a way as to make him magnetic.

Frank died in 1790, by which time, Scholem notes, "the hopes he had entertained of abolishing all laws and conventions took on very real historical significance." The French Revolution had occurred, which gave new context to Frank's Sabbatian subversive notions. For the "believers," Scholem contends, the revolution at once corroborated their nihilist outlook and indicated a divine intercession on their behalf. More than this, he suggests that the conditioning of Frankist faith may have inspired some of the "believers" to help bring the French Revolution to fruition, which involved, at least theoretically, the Jews' liberation from the ghetto. Frank's nephews were active in high insurrectionary circles in Paris and Strasbourg. In such circumstances, Scholem claimed, "apocalyptic ideas mingle freely with the political theories of the Revolution, which were also intended, after all, to lead to a 'political and spiritual liberation'"—a phrase in vogue among prominent Frankists.

Ultimately, this role as riders on the storm of modernity—the vanguard of historical forces that would one day emancipate the Jews—extended beyond the French Revolution. Frank's followers were believers; but, Scholem argued, their spiritual and intellectual descendants could be found among the skeptics and secular intellectuals of today, as well as among leaders of Reform Judaism. At the essay's extraordinary conclusion, he writes: "Those who had survived the ruin were now open to any alternative or wind of change; and so, their 'mad visions' behind them, they turned their energies and hidden desires for a more positive life to assimilation and the Haskalah"—toward the Enlightenment. Frank's movement thus enabled the Jews to take the first step toward entering history—a passage that Zionism was now consummating.

With Jabotinsky hovering in the background as he described Frank's legacy, Scholem may have been anticipating the damage yet to come at the hands of the Revisionists, and have seen this potential inferno as an inevitable prelude to the next stage of the Jews' salvation. Was he already imagining what might rise dialectically from the wreckage left behind by this latest "accursed sect"?

Might we in turn be able to look beyond today's neo-Revisionism to another notion of redemption than that implied by the state, achieved through another kind of sin than that enacted through destruction?

Scholem wrote "Redemption Through Sin" in Hebrew, in order to "remain free of apologetic inhibitions," he told Benjamin. Presumably he wished to convey his concern that flashing a light on this lurid historical interlude would risk making the Jews look bad among people predisposed to malign them—a danger he was always sensitive to. But Scholem must have also been considering the ramifications of publishing this work in the ancestral tongue, in Palestine, where it would be read by Jews seeking to free themselves from the tradition of passive martyrdom that had defined their history in Europe—at a moment when that history's ugliest patterns seemed to be repeating. He must have known that his vital portrait of Joseph Frank, while it might leave conservative Orthodox thinkers blushing, could be read very differently by Zionists inclined to a revolutionary negation of everything standing in the way of their own "political and spiritual liberation." If Scholem worried that composing the essay in German might have made him temper his exposition with remorse, wasn't he also revealing that in Hebrew he felt free to make his portrait of the Sabbatian movement as much a rehabilitation as a cautionary tale—an incandescent flare illuminating the long night of the 1930s with a radically unapologetic Jewish "creed of life"?

Ten years earlier, he'd published his essay on the apocalyptic dangers of the Hebrew language revival. Now Scholem himself had written a work filled with citations from the most explosive Hebrew texts, riddled with fragments of biblical phraseology. "One day the language will turn against its own speakers—and there are moments when it does so even now," he'd warned in 1926. "Will we then have a youth who will be able to hold fast against the rebellion of a holy tongue?"

Did Scholem wonder how "Redemption Through Sin" would be read by the young in Palestine in 1936? At the university, he'd now graduated to become their guide: one of Zionism's elders. Perhaps he only pretended to be frightened by the fire he was lighting to destroy Jewish pieties of the older generation, when in fact he knew he was kindling the pyre before another idol, around which his students were already massing, flames dancing in their eyes.

At some point that fall, the counterterror began. A Jewish underground had formed, to which some of Scholem's idealistic pupils
were pledging themselves. Now, along with helter-skelter killings of Jews, Arabs began to be picked off at random around the
country. Explosives were tossed into buses. Cafés were attacked.
Punitive police posts were established in many neighborhoods,
including Rehavia, where twenty additional Mandate policemen
were stationed close to Scholem's apartment. Bombs planted
by both sides, against each other and the British, became more
mechanically effective. At the same time, violence reverted to
archaic hand-to-hand struggles. On one occasion, seventy Arabs
and Jews, all members of the same construction team, fell on one
another, pounding and hammering with fists and stones, until
exactly one Arab and one Jew lay dead, whereupon the injured
remainder limped away from the unfinished ruin.

Yet the existing Jewish settlement and the ongoing flood of European immigration kept rising. Roads around Jerusalem might have been made perilous by Arab shells. The state of siege might continue far into the future. But there would be a future in Palestine. At dusk, even then, there were days when, from the vantage point of Mount Scopus, the world became "a wilderness inhabited by infinite colors," as Scholem's old friend S. Y. Agnon observed. Agnon sometimes walked down from Scholem's university fiefdom into Jerusalem as light illuminated one scene and swallowed another. "Dirt and rock take shape, as do shrubs and grass, fragrant grass which, along with thorns, briars, and wild brush, fills the arid land with its good smell as the day dims," he wrote. "Each step bestows peace, each breath cures, taking in the scent of field grass, a remnant of summer, born of the early rains." Suddenly, the lights switched on "and the whole city glowed."

When Scholem thought back now on his family in Germany — how they'd mocked him in his youth for his Zionism — he felt the old rage. They'd jeered at the notion that he would abandon a supremely cultured nation for a desert of thorns, vipers, and scorpions. When his mother told her friends that he'd become a lecturer at Hebrew University, some professed amazement that the language even still existed outside of old synagogue sanctuaries. When his father's friends had gathered in their patriotic trade associations to bask in the glory of their bourgeois success, bursting polished buttons on their ceremonial vests, wreathed in the haze of cigars aimed like stubby cannons at an enemy in retreat, they demanded every Jew bless God daily for the privilege of living in Germany. Now those men were all dead or transformed into wanderers.

Reinhold got papers to go with his family to Australia. Erich made the decision to follow him as soon as possible. Though Betty was enamored of Jerusalem, her doctor warned her against the climate, and she plainly felt that Gershom might not be the most nurturing son, for all the intensity of their bond. She began reconciling herself, with shame and anguish, to the impossibility of freeing Werner. In time she made arrangements to join her sons in New South Wales, where she spent her remaining years, navigating their depressive exhaustion as they learned to pump gas and run a general store — and eagerly begging Gershom for details about his kabbalistic researches, while pining to be with him to witness his professional glories.

Early in 1937, Gershom got a despairing letter from Benjamin in which his old friend expressed doubt that they would ever see each other again. He tried to cling to the image of their reunion, he told Scholem, "like that of the leaves of trees that are far apart and meet in a storm." When Scholem wrote back offering him the use of a spare room, Benjamin replied with pathos: "I must confess that I can only fix my gaze upon it as if through a frosted windowpane."

By now Scholem had lost patience with the elegiac key of ineffectual yearnings. He was caught up in excitement over prospects for a new partition of Palestine, tied to a British Royal Commission report that made the creation of a Jewish state more plausible than ever. While personally, he told Benjamin, he would have preferred "joint Arab-Jewish sovereignty in the whole of Palestine," that opportunity was unlikely to arise. Meanwhile, it was undeniably true that historically these latest events represented "a watershed for the place of Jews in the world." Scholem's aversion to political Zionism was increasingly tempered with a measure of realpolitik. In assessing the conflicting strands of thought about what should happen in Palestine, he cited the old Jewish adage, "Nothing is cooked as kosher as it's eaten."

So far from placing him in bad repute with world Jewry, the publication of "Redemption Through Sin" helped launch Scholem on his way to international renown. The Jewish Institute of Religion in New York invited him to deliver a lecture series on mysticism after the essay appeared. And these talks, in which he surveyed the history of his scholarship in a discipline that was itself nothing less than "the attempt to discover the hidden life behind the external shapes of reality," further elevated his stature. Judging by the exhilarated American response, he seems to have proved the thesis of his lectures: The effort "to make visible that abyss in which the symbolic nature of all that exists reveals itself...is as important for us today as it was for those ancient mystics."

Our sense of magical solidarity with the Land and the people dissipated like smoke after an explosion. And when we could see again, the fine cracks in our domestic existence resurfaced. The idea that cropped up in conversation between Anne and me every so often that perhaps a "break" of a year or so from Israel might be advisable became serious. I said, it could be that we'd be able to come back and live differently, on a kibbutz or in some outer Jerusalem neighborhood. But we seemed unable to make this kind of economical move from where we were now without some rupture in our existence.

And Anne said, I know we've lived other phases of our life in other places very completely, I just never thought this one would end. And I said I wasn't — *we* weren't — talking about ending but of interrupting in order to begin again. Because the sense of belonging, of connecting we've felt here, despite everything — she said. And I said again I wasn't talking about ending. What exactly will we do, though? she asked. What exactly are we doing? I countered. Oh, God help us, she said.

I'm not talking about *moving away from Israel forever*, I said, as though the idea were an unspeakable blasphemy, as if there were no frisson to enunciating those words that left them sparkling, hissing, in the air between us, depositing a sudden tingly sense of shame. Everything had begun to feel strange, she said. She had been in the rose garden with Zach, she went on, and seen the cyclamen beginning to sprout from the crannies of rock. And I remembered how I used to take so much joy in them, and now even the plants feel unavailable to us. All the little natural pleasures that the city offers seemed to carry a price tag we can't afford. And I wondered whether this sense might be an inkling of what the dispossessed Palestinian would feel. That estrangement from what came through the stone with the seasons, and had once brought delight as belonging to the nature of life, not the realm of possessions.

But I didn't say this. I told myself that nothing happening to us signaled an eclipse of our Judaism, but that there were times for recession, even concealment. Not a hiding of the face of our Jewishness, but a focus on its inward expression, when the face turned toward the world had grown too distorted. The imperative of Judaism changed with the historical calendar, since there was no fixed content to begin, let alone end with. Wasn't that a point Scholem made over and over? Not that I was likening the prospect of a temporary return to America to Sabbatai Sevi's descent into the abyss, I laughed, unconvincingly.

On Sunday, February 25, 1996, there was a suicide bus bombing at six forty in the morning. We heard it, without knowing what we heard. The blast came at the entrance to Jerusalem. And then, for a time, the bombings seemed to be happening constantly, following one another in such quick succession that there was hardly a division between one period of mourning and the next. We heard the profoundly hollow report again, as if the bomb were punching a hole in the sky for the dead to be sucked into. They punctured the air, but they came from below. To us the explosions seemed to come out of the ground, appearing out of nowhere. We speak of alien life-forms. These were alien death-forms.

Yet still, while it was hard to feel optimistic about the peace process after the assassination, the framework had been put in place, hadn't it? When Shimon Peres became prime minister in the wake of Rabin's death, we felt that as a stencil pattern elder statesman, who'd been in the defense forces and political establishment through so many phases of the country's history, he'd know how to muster the national will to consummate the agreement. Though we weren't convinced Labor was the answer. We'd registered the way that as the fantasy of peace ballooned, Labor's billboards and TV advertising became ever more dizzily consumerist. As if the stabilization of Arab-Jewish relations were meant only to authorize the insanity of Western-style materialism, Anne said. But the right was unspeakable, God knew. Even if it no longer seemed quite true to say that Labor was left.

On the streets, more and more there were murmurings about responding to the bombings with acts of counterterror. "The Arabs must learn Jewish blood doesn't come cheap," was a refrain we heard repeatedly, in one form or another: from the young Sephardi vendors on Gaza Street handing us violently sweet yellow musket-ball passion fruit, and on the trembling lips of old Ashkenazi men shaking their gray heads and black hats, shuffling their way home from shul.

Anne and I hardly realized how the Palestinians had almost ceased to exist in our conversations. We heard people right in the courtyard say, "They'll never stop hating us. There's no point giving back more territory. Look what happened when we began making peace!" And we might have disagreed, might have even raised a counterargument, but still we said "they" and "them" as though they were just a great wall of suffering, suicidal, murderous not-*us*-ness; not men, women, children, not themselves a wildly variegated panoply of "I," "you," and "we."

Hamas doesn't believe in the peace process, we gathered, with no real notion what belief in the negotiations actually meant, let alone what the beliefs of Hamas did in fact consist in. We had no clue about the intensity of in-fighting transpiring between Hamas and Fatah, or the place of smaller factions like Islamic Jihad in that conflict, let alone the reasons for this splintering jigsaw across the Green Line. We didn't comprehend the role played by years of financial support Israel had facilitated to Islamic organizations in the hopes of weakening Arafat. Or of the brutality with which Arafat was now responding to the challenges Hamas posed to the PLO, whether through terror that brought down pressure from Israel and the international arbiters of peace against his organization or through moves within Gaza to capitalize on the popularity of their social welfare system by expanding the scope of political activity.

Above all, if someone outside had asked us about the status of the economy in Gaza we would no doubt have sighed that it was bad, but we had no notion of the catastrophic severity of the poverty in which hundreds of thousands of people lived, day after day, year after year. When the troubles of Gaza came up, which was infrequently, it was generally labeled one of those *very complex issues* for which Israel bore limited responsibility at best since it was *an inherited problem*. As if Israel were the Gazans' insurance company, refusing payment for a preexisting health condition. As if the persistence of a problem over time divided responsibility for the present between the past and future, while recusing those living now.

I suppose if we considered them at all, we fell into the common assumption that the closures Israel had imposed on movement from the Strip had begun as a response to suicide attacks, in hopes of containing further events, neglecting to consider the longer history of their imposition back to the Gulf War, and without ever grasping the damage this loss of work wreaked upon the economy. And so we didn't follow why the services offered by fundamentalist organizations grew more literally and symbolically resonant, in a void that "responsible players" on both the Palestinian and Jewish sides virtually ignored out of some admixture of negligence and impotence.

And so in May 1994, when much of Gaza was granted self-rule, we could not fathom why, as the journalist Amira Hass has written, for this people who played so large a part in Israel's glittering development boom, the glimpse of autonomy was at best double-edged. "Who better than a nation of construction workers could understand the injustice of the restrictions on building and development in their own territory?" Hass asked. "And who could better understand that the frenzy of construction in the Strip that so impressed the entire world was only a belated and partial compensation for years of non-development? For twenty-seven years one community had watched daily how their neighbors lived as a free people in their own country." This watching does not translate into bliss when the first gestures of redress, barbed with sharp qualifications, start to manifest.

We could not begin to apprehend all the ways, at once subtler and more brazen, that natural rhythms of existence in Gaza had been disrupted. The curfews that in some cases were enforced every evening for years, which meant the broiling afternoon hours, when people in this region typically rested indoors, became a period to wander the coals of the streets, since through the cool night when these places could actually be enjoyed, the populace was immured. The compulsion men felt to sleep in modest clothing regardless of the heat, so that if soldiers burst in they'd be less vulnerable to humiliation. The resistance to allowing children to play outside even in daytime, for fear they would be shot by mistake, or in spite. All the waking nightmares of Gaza. At best, we gleaned dimly through a dark glass the contours of the larger, unnatural death cycle: a period of restraint on both sides, an out-of-sync assassination of some wanted terrorist provoking another suicide attack, provoking Fatah to act at once harshly and ambivalently, provoking Israel to impose yet more severe collective punishment.

Agnon, who lived through the Mandate constraints on Jerusalem in the mid-1930s, observed, "There are two aspects to the curfew: it locks in and releases. Jews are locked in, forbidden to leave home; triggers are released, spewing rounds of terror and death."

And so it was with the curfew in Gaza: shutting in and unleashing. Before he signed the Oslo Accords in 1994, Rabin notoriously remarked, "If only Gaza would sink into the sea." This is the tenor of mildly genocidal magical thinking in which the region is steeped. Israelis sometimes say "Go to Gaza" as a way of saying "Go to hell." Anne and I could not understand that in this spirit the suicide bombings might be understood as "Gaza going to Jerusalem."

And so, knowing as little as we did, even had there been a framework within which we might have spoken to Palestinians, we wouldn't have been able to understand the context of what was being said. But there was no context in which to speak to Palestinians, even if we'd understood more than we did.

We were sick all the time that winter and spring — the whole family. A roiling flood of ear infections, parasites, and chronic inflammations, signs of possibly fatal conditions leading to test after test, as if the irreconcilable antimonies of our existence were erupting through our bodies to the surface of our flesh, in unexplained rashes and mysterious lesions. As if our flesh were the land, and we were breaking out in the stigmata of our own virulent ambivalences to being trapped inside ourselves.

And now when I did take a walk in the Old City, what I saw was the disease and disabilities. All the people hobbling on sticks because their legs no longer carried them. All the people missing one eye threading the crooked lanes and stairways, the dark covered markets and refuse-strewn alleys. Not blind, but deprived of dimensional sight.

The movement toward our taking a little break from Israel gained momentum month by month. What would we do in America? I would work! I would get into some kind of MFA program. We would work. We would make enough money to get out of debt, and

then, on the firmer footing of real employment, we would return.
In one year. Or a maximum of three. I'm not sure when the time
away expanded from twelve months to an outer limit of thirty-six.
But we were only being realistic, I argued, in acknowledging that
it would take an enormous effort to wrest our life from Jerusalem
and get it over to the United States with three little children, and
ripping it back up that side of the world again to return in one
year might just be overwhelming.

In mid-May, Anne and I had our first rabid, savage out-and-out
fight. I don't recall what set it off, but it might have been a message from my parents in which they wrote how happy they were
to think that we were "coming home." Anne exploded that she
couldn't deal with thinking of the move in those terms: that she
did not think of America as home. Do you really think of here as
home right now, I might have asked her, when you're constantly
going on about how you hate the new consumerism of the place
and bemoan the loss of purity that we at least thought we'd found
when we came here? When you're as miserable as I am? Maybe
nowhere is home for me, she did say. And I did say that it seemed
to me artificial to put a fixed time frame on our return to Jerusalem. First we said one year, I reminded her. Now we say three.
Why not two, four, five, or six years? How can we say in advance
what it will take to renew our life, our sense of identification with
Judaism? Which has become so darkened here. And she did say
to me, What are you saying to me? What are you saying to me?
And I did say, I just mean I think it should be more open-ended.
It should take as long as it takes, whatever that may mean. And
she did cry out and her hand went over her mouth and her white
skin went ashen and I felt her horror dancing up my own spine,
but I couldn't stop. I'm just saying, I started again. And then we
were screaming about the collapse of our Judaism and our failure
to give our children a peaceful home rich in meaning. And then
we were screaming about what each of us hadn't done or been,

how we'd each failed to be who the other had begun believing in, when our love began again here, and then came undone so completely we believed nothing. And then she looked at me and her eyes didn't see. For the first time, we don't want the same thing, she said, and my own eyes saw nothing but that I had to get out of here, wherever we were, whatever our life had become or might never have been. And the politics and the religion and the philosophy and the family and the children and the Palestinians and the Jews all played musical chairs around a vanishing table, until the last chair burst into flame and we were hurtling through a black vacuum away and away from each other.

There were a few days of not really speaking. Then a few days of restitching and repenting. And I said, I just mean I don't know. I just mean I don't want to feel that we know and then have to break that arbitrary self-imposed deadline. I just want to feel we can recover our sense of what gives our life meaning. I just don't want to short-circuit that by then feeling we have to turn right around and come back when we're still broke and on the brink of everything because of something we said for no reason. But maybe it will be just a few months, I added. Maybe we'll just…we'll get there and we'll have had enough, I insisted. And I meant it, and she knew that I did, and she nodded and she knew what I meant.

Look, I said, it could be that all the reasons we came — the need to immerse ourselves in a more Jewish existence on every level to strengthen it, it could be that now it's important to spend a little time in the opposite condition, to draw on our own resources a little more, rather than just having Jewishness supplied by default. Maybe it would be good for us if it were to become a more inward phenomenon, to have to manifest in contrast to the surrounding society? It might strengthen our conviction, I found myself saying, unsure whether I really believed this or whether it was another fine morsel of sophistry. We've achieved one level of identification with Judaism, I said. But what happens now if we take away the

armature of the surrounding environment? How would our Judaism fare then? I spoke as if our religion were a bike from which we
needed to remove the training wheels. Or an endurance test that
we needed to keep making more strenuous in order to gain further benefit from. But even if what I was saying was not altogether
untrue, I knew I, too, dreamed of an easier life. If not spiritually,
physically. If not intellectually, emotionally.

I made willfully contradictory argument after argument suggesting that the very thing that once drew us was now what we
needed to renounce.

And then the elections took place, and in June Bibi Netanyahu
became Israel's first directly elected prime minister. I remember the
shock on the left that this man who had, at the very least, played
a role in the events that climaxed in Rabin's death, had become
the country's leader. I remember seeing a woman fall down on the
sidewalk in Rehavia, just across Gaza Street, outside the courtyard
where we lived, that doubled the image fixed in my mind of the
woman collapsing in the line of mourners outside the Knesset
after Rabin was killed. As though Netanyahu's election were a second, equivalent catastrophe, or perhaps the real trauma.

And that summer, Anne and I, battered and afraid, began taking the first steps to actually leave.

SIXTEEN

AT THE END OF OCTOBER 1937, not long after the university had opened for its fall semester, while police stations were being ransacked, buses sprayed with bullets, trains dynamited, and children shot inside their homes by gunmen firing at windows—just as the annual Hadassah convention was opening in Atlantic City, at which the esteemed Dr. Joachim Prinz from Berlin predicted the total extinction of Jews in Germany within ten years, and the

Mandate government was announcing new political restrictions on immigration to Palestine — Scholem sat down to write a letter. It was, he said "a candid word about my true intentions in studying Kabbalah," and it was addressed to the publisher Salman Z. Schocken, in honor of his sixtieth birthday, which chanced to fall just over a month before the milestone of Scholem's own fortieth birthday. The document was plainly a reckoning with his life's work at the middle of the journey.

Scholem began by declaring that he himself had never become a Kabbalist. The decision to enter this field followed three years of invigorating thought, 1916 to 1918, the period in which he came to know Walter Benjamin. These years had decided the course of his life, Scholem wrote, bringing him to a confluence of rational skepticism and "intuitive affirmation of those mystical theses that lie on the narrow boundary between religion and nihilism."

The figure who embodied this mystical boundary line for him was not, he confessed, Moses de León, or Isaac Luria, or Sabbatai Sevi. It was Franz Kafka. In Kafka's writings, Scholem claimed, he had discovered a secularized, contemporary version of "the feeling of a Kabbalistic world." Kafka's achievement in this respect was so striking that Scholem now viewed his work as "possessing an almost canonical halo."

Earlier in his youth, he added, the book that had held a "magical influence" over him was a work by Franz Molitor, a freethinking nineteenth-century Christian theologian who was fluent in Jewish religious texts and involved with esoteric Jewish circles in Frankfurt. Molitor proposed that the Jewish Kabbalah represented that part of the tradition "which had preserved, in relative purity, those ultimate truths of primeval religion which tend to become more and more revealed with the progress of history." Though he lacked all sense of historical context, Scholem wrote, Molitor identified "a place in which the hidden life of Judaism had once dwelled, to which I attached myself in my meditations."

Scholem had anyway never thought to write the history of Kabbalah, he asserted. He sought to parse the underlying cosmological principles of the field, its metaphysics. And he was drawn to this goal by the barrenness of what people called "the philosophy of Judaism." The figures he associated with that term — Saadiah Ga'on, Maimonides, and Hermann Cohen ranking high on the list — riled him because they seemed bent only on establishing "antitheses to myth and pantheism" in order to invalidate those systems.

It wasn't hard to prove that myth and pantheism were incorrect, Scholem retorted. The important fact was that, although mistaken, they did contain real substance. With regard to Kabbalah, Scholem felt that for all its conceptual deformities, it possessed a higher level — "a realm of associations," touching the essence of human experience. He identified with the thirteenth-century Jewish mystic who'd expostulated against a supporter of the lofty rationalists: "You ought to know that these philosophers whose wisdom you are praising, end where we begin." Writing at a catastrophic historical juncture, the imperative of allowing lived experience to impinge on higher thought appeared evident to Scholem. True enough, he granted, approaching Kabbalah from the "obtuse Enlightenment standard" Jewish scholars typically adopted, the key to actually comprehending this subject was missing. Still, in the very first kabbalistic manuscripts he read, "there seemed to flash forth a way of thinking that…had not yet found a home."

It's a curious conceit, this notion of a vagabond form of thought — as if Kabbalah itself were in exile, and Scholem had been chosen to create a homeland for that vast, wandering body of speculative commentary. But after proposing that the key to truly understanding the Kabbalah might be lost, he conjectures that perhaps it's not a key that's lacking at all, but bravery — "the courage to risk the descent into the abyss that might one day swallow us up. That, and the daring to penetrate beyond the symbolic plane and to break through the wall of history."

Addressing Schocken the same year "Redemption Through Sin" was published, Scholem's use of the phrase "descent into the abyss" surely alludes to Sabbatai Sevi's journey. But for what possible reason would the "scientific" scholar conceive of himself performing some version of the false messiah's mission? Suddenly it's no longer a "way of thinking" that's wandering on an epic search, but Scholem himself. What is the abyss here? How can history be likened to a wall that must be breached?

He dilates on his theme by announcing that the mountain "does not need a key at all; it is only the misty wall of history that surrounds it that must be penetrated." It's possible, he adds, that history is only an illusion; but if so, the illusion is necessary since without it temporal reality cannot be pierced to reach the core of matters. "Through the unique perspective of philological criticism, there has been reflected to contemporary man...that mystical totality of Truth whose existence disappears specifically because of its being thrust upon historical time." Time disperses truth the way a prism diffracts light. Philology reverses this dispersal, regathering the sparks of truth into one radiance. History itself must then be the abyss, albeit a vertical abyss, molded from clouds. "Would I remain stuck in the mist, suffering a professorial death, so to speak?" Scholem asks. While striving to reach ultimate truths, would he lose himself in the dust of old manuscripts? He concludes the letter by affirming that his work is sustained in the present, as it was at the outset, by the paradox just outlined, "and in anticipation of being answered from the mountain, through that slight, almost invisible motion of history, allowing the truth to break through from what is called development."

Between the mountain, the mist, and the bold discarding of the key to plunge through history into Truth, Scholem's account itself reads more like a parable by Kafka than an account of a research project's genesis; and perhaps more like a fairy tale than Kafka. Still, what exactly is the courage that permits one to enter the abyss? If his "true intention" in studying Kabbalah was to furnish a home for a system of thought, what did this naturalization entail?

Early in his intellectual career, Scholem had identified two strands of Jewish messianic thinking: the restorative and the revolutionary. The latter is associated with the apocalypse and a utopian rebirth, with its most sweeping expression found in Sabbatianism. Of the restorative strain, Maimonides was the most consequential theologian. That thirteenth-century paragon of rational Judaism, whose influence through the ages on Jewish philosophy is incalculable, might be considered Scholem's ultimate foil. In Scholem's estimation, Maimonides' work was aimed at nothing less than "the liquidation of apocalypticism in Jewish Messianism. It was deeply suspicious of that anarchic element," he wrote, "perhaps on account of a fear of the eruption of antinomian trains of thought, which apocalypticism, in fact, could easily produce."

But the extremity of this anti-apocalyptic agenda compromised its value as "a truthful representation of the historical reality of Judaism," which was scored with convulsive dispossessions, including those transpiring at the time Scholem wrote Schocken. The "home" Scholem found for kabbalistic thinking was, indeed, the vast caravan of Jewish history—exilic and Zionist. (Sometimes, he also inverted this dynamic: "The historical experience of the Jewish people merged indistinguishably with the mystical vision of a world in which the holy was locked in desperate struggle with the satanic," he wrote, hinting that Kabbalah became the dwelling place of Jewish history.) Almost every feature of Maimonides' redeemed world could be achieved by Orthodox observance, without messianic intervention. The only real difference for Maimonides was that, after redemption, humanity would have unlimited time to study Scripture. Maimonides' version of redemption is a monastic scholar's paradise.

After the Middle Ages, Scholem notes, "to the extent that the rationalism of the Jewish and European Enlightenment subjected the Messianic idea to an ever advancing secularization, it freed itself of the restorative element," in favor of new strains of utopianism consistent with reason. "Messianism became tied up with the idea of the eternal progress and infinite task of humanity perfecting itself," he wrote. In Scholem's view, Maimonides permitted the messianic idea's historical context to be "superseded by a purely universalistic interpretation." Thus, Maimonides became the grand precursor of all those assimilationist tendencies that found expression in Scholem's own time, both in the German patriotism of his father and the international communism of his brother Werner.

"Since the end of the individual life leads it anyhow to the threshold of the longed-for final state—which in reality is not a future world but an eternal present, the immanent logic of Maimonides' general position does not in the least require an effort to bring about the end of world history in order for man to fulfill his task," Scholem wrote. Maimonides had eliminated "the dramatic element, which lent apocalypticism so much vitality." We might see this subsuming of human agency to the dictates of a divine scheme recast in the prescriptive laws of history articulated by doctrinaire Communists—along with the liberal-bourgeois formula of historical progress espoused by German nationalists. In both cases, the role of the individual is largely confined to swelling an already irreversible tide.

Messianism was linked to Maimonides' system only via his "highly presumptuous identification of the contemplative life with the knowledge of God demanded by the prophets," Scholem maintained. Before Maimonides, it was understood that the prophets enjoined mankind to an *active* moral life.

Yet for all that he bemoaned Maimonides' denial of Judaism's particularist energies, Scholem was awed by the way Maimonides had reconfigured the canon to fit his own theoretical priorities.

Reflecting on how Maimonides neutralized the lure of redemptive catastrophe, Scholem praises the "simplicity and decisiveness" with which Maimonides "pulls back from this realm and tries to forbid it to everyone else." Despite Maimonides' valorization of a calm, gradualist historical order, Scholem remarked that Maimonides was concerned not with historical continuity but rather with "gaining the acceptance of a new concept of the redemption which is formed from a selection of congenial elements." More than any other figure, Maimonides persuaded Scholem of the power to shape cultural identity that might be wielded by a fearless textual interpreter. Scholem accuses Maimonides not of inventing material but of breaking apart the tradition and juxtaposing choice fragments with foreign elements, such as the writings of Aristotle, and thereby creating a kind of dialectical mosaic that recalls Benjamin's methodology, along with that of other radical collagists.

Scholem positions himself as the anti-Maimonides, appropriating Maimonides' own audacious tactics to replenish the tradition his predecessor had ossified. In place of the Aristotelian enlightenment, Scholem jams the metaphysics of Kafka and the thesis of a Christian theologian-redactor onto the cosmological preface of his own great *de*-codification of the Kabbalah. And where Maimonides projected a model of beatific quiescence based on communal submission to Law, Scholem's Kabbalah envisions the movement toward messianic transcendence as seismic and self-willed. "The Messiah will come as soon as the most unbridled individualism of faith becomes possible—when there is no one to destroy this possibility and no one to suffer its destruction; hence the graves will open themselves," Kafka had prophesied.

Of course, every great scholar casts a strong interpretative light on the tradition. What every great scholar does *not* do, as Scholem contends that Maimonides did with Aristotle—and he himself certainly did with Kafka and Molitor—is graft heterogeneous work onto the canon and then treat these elements as a key to the tradition being examined.

So what *was* Scholem "candidly" telling Schocken he was doing as he sat in his new Rehavia apartment, preparing to go to New York at the invitation of the Jewish Institute of Religion? If it's true that what sustained him then, as at the beginning, was the "anticipation of being answered from the mountain" of Truth, it's legitimate to surmise that he was awaiting a new Revelation. But this Revelation was somehow to come from within, from the metaphysical scholar's own imagination musing freely on the old, dethroned Scriptures. And Benjamin had passed him the key to this subtle reframing that imperceptibly changed everything.

In his American lectures, Scholem returned numerous times to the idea of pseudepigraphy, which Benjamin had first made him take seriously almost two decades earlier. Scholem now felt confident enough about his own stature to ascribe two motivations to the practice, one psychological and the other historic. "The psychological stimulus emanates from modesty and the feeling that a Kabbalist who had been vouchsafed the gift of inspiration should shun ostentation," he wrote, while the other impulse arose from "the search for historic continuity and the sanctification of authority" that would enable a writer to influence his contemporaries. Either way, he saw no cause for moral condemnation. "The Quest for Truth knows of adventures that are all its own, and in a vast number of cases has arrayed itself in pseudepigraphic garb," Scholem argued. "The further a man progresses along his own road in this Quest for Truth, the more he might become convinced that his own road must have already been trodden by others, ages before him."

On his way to America in mid-February 1938, Scholem was able to stop off in Paris for a few days to see Benjamin. More than ten years had passed since they last met, and the lithe, ethereal young intellectual aristocrat was gone. Benjamin had grown heavy. Slipshod. His mustache was bushy and his hair was riven with gray. He suffered from an enlarged heart. At forty-five, Benjamin had grown old.

Every step weighed on Benjamin now. Despite having migrated to Paris, he explained, he could not seal himself off from the plight of Jews in Germany. Jerusalem was violent, but dynamic. In Paris, life was steeped in twilight angst. Benjamin shambled between friends while trying to expedite his French naturalization. But everything took endless time — and plenty of money, both of which he lacked. "Male impotence: the key figure of solitude," he wrote, in his evolving work on Baudelaire and the city.

Instead of the intellectual symposium the pair had previously enjoyed, the men clashed in harsh arguments, always reverting to Benjamin's Marxist tendencies, which were now openly on display. Their debates included "downright dramatic moments relating to Benjamin's own feelings," Scholem recalled. Given that Scholem attacked Benjamin's institutional affiliations, new essays, and friends, it's unsurprising that Benjamin felt provoked. They argued about Bertolt Brecht, in whose work, Scholem asserted, there was no delight in infinity: "Everything boils down to only the revolutionary manipulation in the finite."

"What matters is not infinity but the elimination of magic," Benjamin riposted.

This incensed Scholem. The eradication of magic from language — squeezing ideas into the airless mold of a materialistic perspective — was in total conflict with everything Benjamin had achieved in his brilliant youthful exegeses on language — mystical speculations that Benjamin continued to elaborate in what Scholem considered his best writing.

Benjamin countered that his Marxism was "not dogmatic but heuristic and experimental in nature."

Scholem nonetheless attacked Benjamin's treatise "The Work of Art in the Age of Mechanical Reproduction," accusing Benjamin of having displayed there a kind of theoretical schizophrenia whereby the first part of his essay was "packed with exciting discoveries and illuminations," while the second part presented an "enchantingly wrongheaded philosophy of film" — invoking Charlie Chaplin to frame cinema as the one truly revolutionary utopian art form. Benjamin insisted that his transposition of theological notions they'd worked on together into a Marxist framework "was in fact meritorious, because in that sphere they could become more active, at least in our time, than in the sphere originally suited to them." But Scholem refused to acknowledge any connection between the approaches. The first part of that essay rested on "a purely metaphysical concept taken over from the mystical tradition," he argued. Presumably, what Scholem refers to is Benjamin's disquisition on the nature of authenticity in art objects, which reflects the aura they possess. "The presence of the original is the prerequisite to the concept of authenticity," Benjamin had written. He develops the implications of this idea for an era when art can be reproduced ad infinitum in a manner that accords with theological speculations on how the original Revelation is carried forward through time. Benjamin observed that "the authenticity of a thing is the essence of all that is transmissible from its beginning, ranging from its substantive duration to its testimony to the history which it has experienced." The historical testimony was jeopardized when its substantive duration no longer mattered, Benjamin said. "And what is really jeopardized when the historical testimony is affected is the authority of the object," he concluded. Scholem might easily have heard echoes here of their conversations about kabbalistic perspectives on the transmission of God's word through the ages. But Scholem was maddened by what he saw as the "pseudo-Marxist context" in which Benjamin was situating the concept of aura. And he bluntly told Benjamin as much.

"The philosophical bond between the two parts of my study that you miss will be supplied by the revolution more effectively than by me," Benjamin fired back.

Scholem was dumbfounded. "Someone who did not believe in *that* revolution hardly could make any response to this statement," he later remarked. He might have been silenced as well by an eerie sense of déjà vu. For Benjamin's words mirrored the response of his poor imprisoned brother when they'd fought as teenagers about politics and Werner finally shouted that the revolution would solve everything. The familial, psychological resonance of the scene may have dulled his sensitivity to the nuances of Benjamin's position. What Benjamin himself rather delightedly called his "Janus face" struck Scholem as a ruinous ambiguity that would inevitably corrupt the morality of his insights. "Self-deception can lead too easily to suicide, and the honor of revolutionary orthodoxy would, God knows, be too high a price to pay for yours," he'd warned seven years earlier. Benjamin's admission now that he felt an enduring affection for France, despite its anti-Semitism, and that he declined to think of England or America, let alone Palestine, as an alternative, conveyed a mood of surrender. "I'm no longer capable of adapting," Benjamin told Scholem helplessly.

Scholem felt that he'd seen all this coming — Benjamin's undoing in Europe — with the certitude of a biblical prophet foretelling the destruction of a decadent city. Scholem could watch this man he loved teetering on the brink of the *wrong abyss* and couldn't wrench him back, couldn't break through the slow-motion nightmare in which vertigo and gravity were conspiring to rip Benjamin from his long fingers.

The only moment when they seemed in real accord was when Benjamin voiced his yearning to be free of all obligations for at least two years to work on Kafka. Considering that Schocken was about to publish an edition of Kafka's work, Benjamin wondered whether Scholem might persuade him to sponsor this project. Given the chance to write such a book, Benjamin promised, he would come to Palestine immediately.

Scholem suggested that Benjamin use a recently published biography of Kafka as an occasion for making this overture. The exchange prompted Benjamin to write a long letter in June suggesting that at a time when truth had lost all consistency, Kafka had not clung to his private convictions as most had done, but rather had "sacrificed truth for the sake of clinging to transmissibility, to its aggadic element." (Aggadah is the part of Jewish tradition commonly defined as "that which is not halakha" — not Law with its binary enumeration of the permitted and the forbidden, but rather the exploration of meaning and values, often through illustrative tales.) Yet in their misery and beauty, Kafka's writings were in fact something more than parables, Benjamin continued. "They do not modestly lie at the feet of doctrine, as aggadah lies at the feet of halakha. When they have crouched down, they unexpectedly raise a mighty paw against it."

The letter is dazzling—a pinnacle in the epistolary afterlife of their friendship. But when Scholem excitedly forwarded it to Schocken, Schocken responded with exasperation. He mocked Benjamin's writing and turned on Scholem, lecturing him about why it was inconceivable he would support such a writer. The publisher concluded, Scholem said, that "Benjamin was something like a bogeyman of my own invention."

Before Scholem could pass on the bad news, he heard from Benjamin that the institute of the sociologist-philosopher Max Horkheimer—his only dependable source of funding for years—was probably going bankrupt. "To sink below this level again would be hard for me to bear," Benjamin wrote in March 1939. "For this the charms exerted on me by this world are too weak and the prizes of posterity too uncertain." Scholem took seriously this not very veiled threat. Already once before, seven years earlier in a hotel in Nice, Benjamin had come close to killing himself. He'd written Scholem then about the "disintegration constantly threatening my thought" due to a welter of contingencies and lamented the fact that although some of his works had perhaps amounted to "small-scale victories, they are offset by large-scale defeats." Though Scholem discovered this only later, Benjamin went so far on that occasion as to write farewell letters to friends and to draw up a will leaving Scholem all his manuscripts. It was unclear what had precipitated the crisis. (Scholem felt it had less to do with the worsening political situation—the Prussian state had just undergone a coup d'état by an archreactionary—or even his financial travails than with the rejection of his marriage proposal to Olga Parem, a ravishing German-Russian who told Scholem that when Benjamin laughed, "a whole world opened up.") It was also unclear what had stopped Benjamin's hand at the last hour. But Scholem felt that the possibility of suicide accompanied Benjamin throughout his later years, perhaps linking the prospect, consciously or not, with the larger predicament of Jewish culture in Europe. The "rather odd fellow" Benjamin told Scholem he planned to join in Nice and share "a festive glass" with might well have been Death.

On receiving Benjamin's ominous letter, in which he'd mentioned once again the possibility of traveling to Palestine if he could be assured of material assistance since he'd become fatally economically isolated in France, Scholem scrambled into action to raise funds for Benjamin among the handful of people in Jerusalem who might be able to finance such a trip. In the event, despite Benjamin's fears, the institute didn't cancel his stipend. However, any solace that reprieve brought was short-lived.

The moment war was declared, Benjamin was interned as an enemy alien, first in Paris, at a site where he slept on a stone bench layered with straw grown putrid from spilled gobs of the cheap liver pâté that served as their main nutriment, then in a bleak camp outside Nevers, where he strove to continue his work in morbidly circumscribed circumstances. He organized a course "for advanced students," asking an admission fee of three Gauloises or one button. Later, he tried to launch a literary journal "naturally on the highest niveau," which would show the authorities just whom they'd locked up as enemies of France. Editorial meetings were held in his quarters, a sort of lean-to at the base of a circular staircase that overhung his patch of straw, where the staff crouched, sipping contraband schnapps from thimbles. The first issue was to contain an article on "The Emergence of a Society from Nothingness," which would detail the sociological history of the camp, from "the groundbreaking for the latrine to the cultural superstructure we were about to create with this journal," one of its would-be contributors recorded of the project.

A young man who'd become a kind of attendant upon Benjamin made a curtain out of a piece of old burlap for his quarters, so that, an observer wrote, like "a holy man in his cave," Benjamin could withdraw from the gaze of others. At some point during his internment, Benjamin invented the phrase "the proletarianization of the Jew." Evenings he would stand at the barbed wire, pondering the sheep grazing on the other side. "Just to sit once more on the terrace of a café and twiddle my thumbs — that's all I wish for," he said.

After his release, he returned to Paris, nearly destitute, continuing to write while his health degenerated. Alluding in one letter to their "fiery disputations" about Marxism, Benjamin assured Scholem that there was no longer any need for such contretemps. Scholem took this to mean he was returning intellectually to the metaphysical frontier where he belonged. The physical separation between them was inconsequential now, Benjamin wrote. "Perhaps it is even proper to have a small ocean between us when the moment comes to fall into each other's arms *spiritualiter.*"

Scholem lost track of him in the winter of 1940, never getting a response to a lengthy attack he'd sent off against Horkheimer's essay "The Jews and Europe." There, Scholem had written that Horkheimer didn't bother to address the true question for people like themselves — what it would literally mean when they were "deprived of this soil, after terrible demoralizations and strategies of annihilation." The Jews interested Horkheimer "not as Jews but only from the standpoint of the fate of the economic category that they represent for him — as 'agents of circulation.' Nor did he ask for Europe: what would a Europe actually look like after the elimination of the Jews?"

Scholem waited in suspense for Benjamin's response to what he viewed as an "explosive" disquisition in defense of the "unallegorizable Jew." But it was more than a year before his anxious queries to Theodor Adorno and Hannah Arendt received a dependable answer. I wonder if he thought back then on his last parting from Benjamin in Paris — striding off through the winter crowd to the station platform, while weary, stooped Benjamin sank into the darkness behind.

After the fall of France in the summer of 1940, Benjamin fled south to the Pyrenees, and then, in September, tried to escape the country with friends, crawling on all fours over the rugged terrain above Port Bou, Spain. Heart disease made his advance impossibly slow. Yet he finally arrived, weeping and pleading with the others at Port Bou's police station for Spanish entry stamps. They were refused, and this would have meant the camps for him, had he not been carrying a large dose of morphine.

There are no times of "greater creativity in the public realm of mysticism, than times of historical crisis," Scholem once observed. And he concluded the published version of his 1938 New York

lectures by expressing faith that "the great cataclysm" then "stirring the Jewish people more deeply than in the entire history of Exile" was destined to reveal nothing less than a new mystical course for them. Reflecting long afterward on the talks and what made him devote his life to the subject they'd surveyed, Scholem mused, "I suppose that I considered Kabbalah as one of the possibilities for Jewish survival in history, that gave a dimension of depth to those who decided to remain Jews."

Benjamin had pressed Scholem to turn these addresses into a book, remarking in his final contribution to their exchange, "Every line we succeed in publishing today — no matter how uncertain the future to which we entrust it — is a victory wrenched from the powers of darkness." The lectures did appear in print, in expanded form in 1941, and were dedicated to Benjamin: "The friend of a lifetime whose genius united the insight of the Metaphysician, the interpretative power of the Critic and the erudition of the Scholar." This volume laid the foundation for Scholem's international eminence. Hannah Arendt contended that Scholem's work "actually changes the whole picture of Jewish history." She welcomed his revelations of how much the Jews qua Jews had contributed "to the formation of modern man." By identifying the uniquely Jewish elements in the alloy of modernism, Scholem's discoveries were "more likely to reconcile Jewish history with the history of Europe than all apologetic attempts which try to prove the impossible, that is, the identity between Jews and other nations, or which attempt to demonstrate something essentially inhuman, namely the passivity and thus the irresponsibility of the Jewish people as a whole," Arendt wrote in a review. Scholem had proved that despite their messianic expectations, the people had *not* just lived a life of deferral. "The religious Jew became a protagonist in the drama of the World; he manipulated the strings behind the scenes." Where Jews could not participate directly, they imagined themselves affecting history's course by the force of their analytic perspective.

"The new interpretation of the Law was based on the new doctrine of the 'hidden God,'" Arendt wrote. In her essay, the hidden God is something like the Freudian unconscious of Creation itself, which removes the sharp division between God and Man, placing them instead in dynamic relation.

Unlike many of his Central European intellectual peers, Scholem found America to be "a most attractive country." It was true you needed sufficient funds to get along, but really that was not so different from anywhere else, even if in America the need may have been a little more pronounced. The air was freer in America, that was certain. And the intellectual atmosphere was on a higher level than what Europeans generally assumed. There was "probably no atmosphere in the world that is not preserved in some corners in a city like New York," he wrote. He enjoyed himself. And in his acknowledgments he thanked all those who had shown him friendship and goodwill during his sojourn in America for having made him "feel at home in the great desert of New York." He knew he'd be back.

We began telling people we were leaving, beginning with the easier outer ring: our loose cast of employers, child care givers, family physicians, landlords, and so on. Among close friends I told only my puppeteer friend Adam, because I knew he wouldn't be judgmental.

"So you'll go. You'll see what happens. Maybe you'll stay. Maybe you'll come back. You'll see."

I nodded, grateful beyond words for his calm understanding. Maybe we'd exaggerated how other friends would respond.

We started with the Australian family in the courtyard who had three sons roughly our children's age.

We explained how the decision was a long, long time coming. How desperately we'd struggled to make our life in Jerusalem work economically. How much we'd hoped and kept hoping, and still hoped, as we were fully resolved to come back if — or rather, *once* — we got our life on firmer footing. And it had been so hard to make the decision, and we would miss them more than...

They exploded. Shock. Rage. We'd said nothing! *Nothing!* They'd never imagined —

You never imagined, but you've heard us saying for years —

Everyone says those things in Israel all the time! You made the decision to leave without even once letting us know how desperate things were for you! There were a million ways we would have tried to help you! I could have let you stay for a while in my mother's old flat if you couldn't pay rent. I could have helped you find work. Have you thought about what this will be like for your children? You make a decision of this magnitude and you don't even open the door a crack to the family you've been closest to since all your children were born? How could you?

That was the beginning.

Some friends burst into tears when we told them; others turned away. Some hugged us, shaking and dissolving, saying they knew just how we felt. Some felt terribly hurt; others looked like they'd just learned of a death. Of someone they loved being found murdered by terrorists! Some wouldn't speak to us; others wouldn't release us. Some asked how we could be so selfish. Some said they'd always seen it coming; others said never in a million years would they have imagined us doing this. Some predicted we would destroy our children; others said we were going to save our boys by preserving them from army service. Some friends said we were no friends; others said we were traitors. Someone we didn't know so well said, "You were converts weren't you?" with a kind of sickly smile that suggested a knowledge of God on high, choosing and leaving unchosen at birth, with an all-seeing eye.

Then there were weeks of excruciating farewell parties. At schools and friends' apartments. Silent. Clumsy. Overhearty and weepy.

Anne and I spoke all the time about how much the whole process of taking leave of Jerusalem seemed like preparing to die. And we became overrun with death fears. One night Anne became obsessed with how clearly she could see the bone of her arm through her skin. It was right there on the surface! One day that bone will be "fertilizer for daffodils," she marveled, staring.

We became overwhelmed by logistics: banking and insurance and all the utilities to disconnect; issues with the teachers' unions and special state taxes and my army deferment and address changes; school transcripts and new overdraft approvals. And suddenly we were all sick all the time again, throwing up and coughing. Riddled with croup and weird skin ailments.

We lived with a perpetual feeling of pulling stitches out of our flesh, of ripping ourselves out of a densely woven fabric, of tearing and wrenching and slashing and rending, leaving severed nerve ends loose in space. Wondering whether they would ever one day knit again or whether this sense of fragmenting would persist.

Anne said she felt frightened all the time. And I tried to defuse the terror, hardening and cradling simultaneously out of a sense of how easy it would be simply to share it, so that we both became helpless.

Friends from New York came to visit us not long before we departed. We clung to them as a reminder that there was life outside Israel to which we would soon be returning; this move wasn't only about ending.

The last night of their visit, we drove to Tel Aviv for dinner by the sea. On the way home, a strange, disembodied mood settled over Anne and me. We spoke later of having felt as cut off from everything as two atoms hurtling through space. Anne looked at the lit windows in the towers of Tel Aviv and said something about the little people moving against the panes, and all the little lives inside the cars rushing by us. And the blackness as we lifted away from the plains became seamless.

Over the car radio news came of a terrorist attack. It was at first unclear where it had happened. Suddenly streams of police and military vehicles, wailing, blue lights flashing, were racing toward us, descending from Jerusalem. Then we heard that the attack happened just beyond the Beit Shemesh junction, moments before we'd reached it. A couple had been killed at almost the instant we passed. A small child in the back survived. And there was a two-year-old at home, we learned later.

"Who will take care of the children?" Anne asked, gazing wide-eyed at ours. The next morning she got a call from her school. The woman who'd been killed was the older sister of one of her students! So much for the existential fantasy of all the little isolated worlds inside cars and apartments. In Israel, nothing is separated from anything, we cried. Even while the Palestinians who'd committed the deed, from the village of Surif, twenty-five miles away, seemed an alien species.

The weather turned broiling. Anne went to the funeral. Right-wing settlers turned out in force. Everyone was rocking and wailing. Anne's student threw herself on her sister's grave and lay there sobbing, while her family and classmates stood above her, racking the air with their misery.

All the shock and sorrow. All the loss and solidarity. *Enough. Enough.* How grotesque it seemed then to imagine we'd been, or could ever be, alone here. We were alone only in our determination not to be there. And we thought of the wicked son on the night of the seder, who asks, "What does all this mean to you?" Not to *him*, but to them — the community of which he denies he's a member.

The hot spell continued. We began selling everything. Most of our furniture we'd found on the street. We still sold it. Tables. Bed frame. Chairs. Bookshelves. Everything. Carpets. Clothes. We'd try to sort through what we had, get a little way, then just dump the whole lot. Word began to get around that the corpse of our life was there for the picking. A young religious couple showed up and bought almost every large object we had. Yeshiva boys came to haul them away. The apartment was filling with people wearing black velvet yarmulkes and white shirts, or big hats and long dresses. Take it. Take that, too. It's free. We don't want it. Take everything. Take the floor and the walls and the ceiling. Take our arms and our eyes and our feelings. Take us, too, and leave us in a corner of your room, we'll lie there unmoving until the Messiah's redeeming.

The heat grew relentless. Our bright, stifling apartment was stripped like bones. The children jumped, crowing on the mattresses. Books and papers were strewn everywhere, dustballs and cats and a funeral pyre of suitcases. We lived like that for weeks on end. "I feel like a snake sloughing off my skin," Anne said. "Shouldn't we have stuck it out? Shouldn't we have held on through thick and thin? Like in a marriage?"

Our last Sabbath in Jerusalem, we were overcome with panic and despair. "I know we have to do this," Anne said, "but I can foresee *nothing.*" And still she saw more than I could see then. More than I allowed myself to face, anyway.

Adam came over the last day and we talked about this and that, the world and the universe.

There was last packing and more last packing to do. We turned into two clockwork automatons, working separate quadrants of the rooms in perfect synchrony, mechanically gathering and dividing every last shard of the life we'd built there.

The last night, the wind blew wild. Neither of us could sleep. I went out onto our balcony at some ungodly hour. All the branches of all the trees in the courtyard were waving up and down — dark arms of admonition, expelling us from the garden.

"At midnight God enters Paradise to rejoice with the righteous," says the Zohar. "All the trees in Paradise burst into hymns.

A wind rises from the north, a spark flies from the power of the north, the fire in God, which is the fire of the power of judgment."

And then we were gone. Clutching the children. Clutching each other, we were blown into the air forty thousand feet above the earth and cast through the sky to America.

SEVENTEEN

FLICKERS OF HIS CHARACTER in the final years emerge from reminiscences. Everyone speaks of the books. They so dominated the rooms of Scholem's modest apartment that people felt engulfed in the volumes. Rich brown and gold, black, green, cream, and maroon. When Harold Bloom described Scholem's bookcases to me, he said he'd never seen anything like them. In his memory, shelves ran along the ceilings as well as the walls, until he reconsidered the problem of gravity.

Some people also speak of how, in almost every room, one shelf on one case was always left bare. No one knows with certainty the reason for this. Perhaps it was intended as a larger symbol of absence: of God, or the dead. Or of the dead God, or silence. But there are also those who say these shelves were kept vacant only so that when his wife began complaining that there wasn't space for another book in their home, he could point to one and say, "What are you talking about? Here's a whole shelf empty."

In 1937, he published a monograph listing all the volumes he desired to add to his collection—a negative catalog—and titled it *Alu L'Shalom*, which means "Ascend in Peace" and also "Come to Scholem"—the kind of double entendre he delighted in. But this particular work came to haunt him, since once book dealers got hold of it, they jacked up the prices of every item on his wish list. He bequeathed most of his kabbalistic collection to the Jewish National Library, and these twenty-five thousand books and manuscripts became a nest egg repository of mysticism, kept in its own special chamber within the main library.

Everyone who met him talks of his prodigious memory and the snap of his wit. The way he would conjure a dizzying array of texts in elucidating a single point or inveighing against one opponent. The impression he conveyed of having forgotten nothing he'd ever read, and of there being nothing he hadn't read.

He liked black humor and playing the provocateur. He told one visitor that on a summer day when he was doing research at the Jewish Theological Seminary Library in Manhattan, he'd gotten too hot, so he just stripped off all his clothes and sat there naked reading kabbalistic manuscripts all day. When Cynthia Ozick met Scholem, he regaled her with this drollery: "A man is invited to a social event taking place several weeks in the future which, however, he most emphatically doesn't wish to attend. So he pulls out his little black appointment book, looks into it, and apologizes, 'Oh, I'm so sorry, but I have a funeral on that day.'"

Acid. Old World. A little hammy.

When Rabbi Herbert Weiner, the American popularizer of Jewish mysticism, came to call, he brought up a barbed remark by Martin Buber: "Scholem is a great scholar; he has made a science out of the Kabbalah." "Buber's glory and fame are assured," Scholem replied, "but he certainly has a talent for making cloudy anything clear."

He had a "great talent for faux pas," observed Hans Jonas, the historian of Gnosticism. "He could say and do the most impossible things. And if you called him on something, he would either deny it — 'Oh, I never said that' — or he would claim, 'That was supposed to be a joke.'"

Something else that comes through the remembrances is Scholem's avid curiosity, which flared undimmed in his later years. He attributed his precocious recognition of his vocation to this quality. When Ozick first visited Scholem, he immediately made a remark about a short story of hers. "How could this be that this grand master should have read a story of mine, concerned, of all things, with Yiddish poetry?" she wondered. "But he simply knew everything about everyone, everywhere."

This was not just a matter of scholarly diligence; Scholem also relished being completely in the know, with that voracious hunger not to be cut out of anything the youngest child in a big family may be prone to. Insight, information, intrigue — he craved it all. The sense he gave of being continually stimulated by gobbling up the universe may have contributed to another feature of his character Ozick discerned: "the capacity to make one's life a surprise, even to oneself — to create the content of one's own mind, to turn out to be something entirely unexpected." By knowing so much beyond himself, he made himself bottomless — unknowable.

Everyone speaks of the intimidating power of his presence, "like a warrior ready for battle," said Elie Wiesel. "I learned not to disagree with him," Harold Bloom remarked. In Scholem's company, "I was a listener," Ozick noted. She described Scholem's gift for assigning a task—in her case, to do some research for him at the New York Public Library—and making this conferral of trust appear a high privilege. "That was a deeply affecting obeisance," she said.

When he felt crossed by someone, personally or ideologically, he wielded his blade without mercy. The mere mention of Philip Roth could make him see red. The lowest of the self-hating low, he pronounced him. In *Portnoy's Complaint*, Roth "revels in obscenity," Scholem wrote; he'd succeeded in writing "just the book that anti-Semites have been waiting for." George Steiner was one of those who came away from Scholem's apartment feeling stung by his bitter superiority. Steiner had tried to press Scholem to say flat out whether he really believed in God. But Scholem would not deign to answer. "The very question was chilled into impertinence," Steiner recalled. "Thus I am left with the remembrance of an ironic agnostic, to whom all but a handful of other human beings were a disappointment, and who had found God, when he tested the concept, enigmatically ineffective."

Steiner's reaction might have been prompted by an intuition that Scholem felt a particular contempt for *him*, which made Steiner want to generalize the master's judgment. For in Scholem's eyes, Steiner exemplified that disastrous Jewish propensity for believing in beatific categories of universalist ideals without regard for the particularist canvas on which history is actually played out—a cavalier jettisoning of the real, which Scholem saw as a displacement of solipsism. "I have no argument with a Jewish intellectual who gives priority to his personal emotional complexes, over the problem of *historic responsibility*," Scholem commented, apropos of Steiner. "A person who gives priority to his own private, personal troubles, and indulges himself in the creative opportunities of alienation—should go where he likes, and live to the best of his understanding."

Everyone speaks of Scholem's idiosyncrasies. Bloom said Scholem had a habit he'd never encountered before of speaking about himself in the third person. "'So and so says such and such,' Scholem would comment. "But Scholem says…"

The self-objectification is suggestive on multiple levels.

The scholar Anson Rabinbach told me, "Scholem had one weakness. But it was a big weakness: chocolate."

Though obviously he meant to be funny, the subject of Scholem and chocolates is so ubiquitous in recollections of those who spent time with him that it merits a moment's thought. After all, he began gorging on chocolates by the side of his reclining mother, from her secret cache, when he tucked her in for a nap.

Ozick recalls Scholem pushing chocolates on her, which she surmised had been left by his last visitor, even as she passed a gift box on to him that she'd carefully chosen, since he was also notorious "for knowing which chocolates will do and which won't." "Why am I being bribed?" Scholem demanded. He was, Ozick said, "a very lofty elf with bold elfin ears and an antic elfin glee advertising tricks and enigmas."

The image of Scholem continuously giving himself the little jolt of another sweet as he engaged his audiences in flights of dialectics is, at the least, consonant with the impression of perpetual high animation he projected. And if the consumption also reawakened the flavor of deep maternal intimacies, his "big weakness" may have been all the more enveloping.

There are, anyway, consistencies of affect and effect in Scholem's latter-day company, but once we turn to the substance of what he was saying, matters remained as they had been: paradox upon paradox, only more so at the end. So much so that people who knew him, whether they were bowled over with awe, infuriated, or both, often conclude, with an air of defeat, that Scholem was just a maze of contradictions. When he directly addressed the relationship between messianism and politics, Scholem always staunchly denounced the whole business — remarking, for example, to an interviewer in 1980 his total opposition to what settlers were doing in the West Bank. "They use biblical verses for political purposes. Whenever messianism is introduced into politics, it becomes a very dangerous business. It can only lead to disaster," he said.

At the same time, as Moshe Idel recounted, a number — "not one, not two, but many, *many* — of Scholem's best students became right wing, or right of the right." And this was not coincidence. The galvanic allure of the messianic-apocalyptic dimension in Judaism he wrote about was stronger than the politically chaste, reflexive critiques he delivered. Idel estimates that fully half of Scholem's oeuvre explored messianism. Moreover, since Scholem went on to become president of the prestigious Israel Academy — quite possibly the most powerful president the institution ever had — and beyond the academy became the center of a kind of personality cult, his influence as a charismatic leader in his own right, even apart from the specific content of his writings, was considerable. He didn't intend to motivate those of his students who became reactionary, Idel told me. "But inadvertently, the forces you release, the vitality, you can't always tell what will become of them." And Scholem was not naïve. He had, after all, felt inside himself those same forces some of the students went into the territories to actualize. "Yes, Scholem is all those radical settlers in the West Bank," Anson Rabinbach said with a sigh. "But he's *also* all the left-wingers in the Tel Aviv cafés bemoaning the entire state of affairs while sipping their drinks."

Indeed, the formidable Israeli literary critic Baruch Kurzweil, himself an observant Jew, charged Scholem in the 1950s and '60s with infecting an entire community of Israeli intellectuals with nihilism. For all that Scholem accused Steiner of neurotic selfishness masquerading as numinous cosmopolitanism, Kurzweil saw Scholem's negation of the rabbinic tradition as being carried out only "for the Self, for individualistic anarchism." Kurzweil took seriously the judgment Scholem passed on himself in one essay: "We came as rebels and found ourselves to be heirs." Thus, Kurzweil argued, Scholem was merely continuing the process of burying Judaism that had been begun by his "Science of Judaism" nemeses. While pretending to be an objective investigator of Jewish studies, he'd transformed Benjamin's angel of history from the herald of the apocalypse to "the most respectable representative of Judaism to the whole wide world," Kurzweil wrote. After years of battling desperately against what he saw as the titanic, dangerous power Scholem wielded—while himself being steadfastly denied an academic post at Hebrew University—Kurzweil killed himself in 1972.

For all Scholem's enthusiasts on Mount Scopus, he gained a reputation as a despotic, even demonic taskmaster. It was horrible to be his student, some felt. One highly gifted pupil fled "the Scholem school" to begin an independent academic career.

Another suffered expulsion for failing to keep a confidence—and then killed himself. Ultimately, the three disciples whom Scholem considered closest to being intellectual peers—Joseph Weiss, George Lichtheim, and Peter Szondi—all committed suicide. The reasons were disparate, but the net effect was a failure to have transmitted his teachings to the pupils he cared most about.

He despaired of Zionism. He missed Walter Benjamin. On learning that Benjamin had taken his own life, Scholem told a friend, "I'll never recover from this terrible blow." He'd lived in a spiral of bloody cataclysms since adolescence. "The mystery of human life is deeper than that of the apocalypse—unless the apocalypse is just another word for the mystery of human life," he'd reflected back in 1916. Germany appeared in his eyes then as "a dark pit of wickedness," responsible for the "funeral of Europe." Yet the Holocaust exposed the inadequacy of even Scholem's harshest judgment against German character. The country "was a vacuum in which we would choke," he'd realized in his youth. But as for Hitler and the Jews' extermination, "*none of us thought of that*," he later wrote.

In 1946, he was sent on a mission to Europe by the university for the purpose of assessing the fate of Jewish book collections expropriated by the Nazis. All the books whose owners were dead or missing should be held in Jerusalem at the Jewish National Library, Magnes argued, until the moment came—if the moment ever did come—when a rightful heir emerged from the ashes. Scholem spent months traveling the Continent, and the scale of destruction he encountered was beyond imagination. Conversations he held with people inside and outside the camps touched the depths of him. In Frankfurt, he found that the whole of the city library's Hebraica collection, among the most important in Europe, had been incinerated in an air raid. The Jewish collection in Munich had vanished without a trace. Everywhere, the damage from aerial bombardments was greater than he'd anticipated.

In Prague, he sat for hours in his hotel room staring numbly at the catalog of thirty thousand works that had been transported from the ashes of Theresienstadt to that city. One day he went to the city's old Jewish cemetery, wandering alone through the graves until he broke down weeping.

When he returned to Jerusalem, Scholem sank into a depression that left him paralyzed for a year.

And yet. That insatiable curiosity, the appetite for play, the perverse, impish aura remained. In one dark moment shortly before the War of Independence, Scholem wrote his ex-wife Escha and his old friend Hugo Bergmann that he lived in despair and could act only out of despair. But he *did* act. The Labor party had just won a major victory; the great struggle for a state would come after Passover, he predicted. Who knew what direction the Jews would take now? Great surprises were always possible, he insisted.

His students had given him a "mountain of marzipan" for his birthday!

"Only he who can change is master of the future," he once observed. For all that he wrote about the importance of maintaining scholarly distance, there's something about the way Scholem took positions that suggests identification, incorporation, even transmutation. One of the rare characterizations of himself Scholem endorsed came from his protégé Joseph Weiss, who described Scholem's methodology as bearing a resemblance to the way certain medieval artists smuggled their own portraits into crowd scenes. Scholem's esotericism, Weiss wrote, was a type of camouflage. "With his thick tomes and his philological research, he has apparently turned the figure of the metaphysician into that of a scholar. But his metaphysics reveals itself through concealment; it is camouflaged utterly to the point of imperceptibility within sentences and half-sentences tucked away within 'pure' scholarly analyses, or in the form of a strange adjective."

To Herbert Weiner, Scholem remarked of his personal feelings on Kabbalah: "I will tell you a secret." He and Fanya glanced at each other then, as if savoring "the moment of teasing disclosure," Weiner recalled. "It is all written down," Scholem continued, "but only in the form of incidental remarks—hints, scattered through my writings."

The sense of Scholem's *diffusion*, across scraps and fragments, in massive crowd scenes and giant texts, suggests not just a personality enamored of philosophical paradox but also a personality composed of an abundance of irresolvable aspects. Where Benjamin, in Scholem's eyes, had doomed himself through self-deceiving ambiguity, Scholem exhibited unrepentant multiplicity. Weiner reports that this impression carried into Scholem's physical comportment. He gave "the appearance of continuous disjointed motion. Even when he is sitting behind a desk and delivering a lecture, there is a perpetual writhing of hands, arms, and legs. His facial grimaces are a completely uninhibited expression of his outer and inner environment."

But, Weiner continued, "Professor Scholem is fully aware and even delighted at the consternation his physical appearance may arouse." More than literal derangement, he detected in Scholem's self-presentation a wild staging of craziness. When Weiner commented on the discrepancy between Scholem's appearance and what students expected from a teacher of mysticism, Scholem leaned back "and raised his eyes in mock apprehension. 'Maybe I ought to roll my eyes more,'" he remarked. They both laughed. Then Scholem lunged forward, reached into the box of chocolates on his desk, snatched three, flung two in his mouth, and laid one aside in reserve.

This instinct for performance may have a bearing on the puzzle of Scholem's core identity. Cynthia Ozick told me of visiting Scholem at his home on Abarbanel Road, passing under the leafy arch covering the entrance and entering the apartment. "The first thing you see is this painting," she said, "and it's a picture of a *clown*. And the face of the clown is uncanny. It resembles *Gershom Scholem*. I was caught by it. And that was the first thing he said that astounded me: 'I have it there because it represents me.'"

In the course of conversation over lunch, Ozick posed to Scholem the primary question she'd come with: Was there a "shadow-Scholem"? Did "the scholar of Kabbalah possess a hidden self, as Kabbalah speaks of hidden 'true' God?"

Scholem immediately shot back, "The scholar is never the whole man." And then he walked to a table littered with documents, picked up a piece of paper, and brought it to Ozick: a newspaper cutting titled "A Friendship and Its Flaws," George Steiner's essay on Scholem and Benjamin's collected letters. "Perhaps you will find the shadow-Scholem *here*," Scholem said.

"This must be one of the saddest books in the world," the review begins. "It tells the story of an intimate friendship between two masters of the spirit and of language; but of a friendship

flawed, even in the subtlest motions of mutual trust and mutual need, by misunderstanding, by subterranean intimations of jealousy, by irremediable frictions of sensibility." Steiner continues, "Scholem is that rare being: an ecstatic rigorist, a man possessed by the merciless authority of the truth and of moral absolutes." It was a remarkable gesture to pass this essay off as a response to the question of his occult character — a gesture Ozick pronounced "tantalizingly wily as a Delphic oracle."

At lunch, Fanya, who'd been pondering Ozick's question, suddenly announced, "I know what the shadow is. It is a joke and it is not a joke." Ozick begged her to reveal what Fanya called Scholem's "great secret." But Fanya said she would disclose it only when she was a hundred years old.

Scholem, meanwhile reveled in the riddling game of this scene. "What is 'information'?" he teased Ozick. "Nothing at all. Use your judgment. Use your imagination."

Ozick marveled that it was as if Scholem didn't mind being invented. They turned to the subject of the "theater of the self."

"I call myself a metaphysical clown," Scholem remarked. "A clown hides himself in theater."

Did Walter Benjamin ever hide himself that way? Ozick asked.

"Benjamin never played theater," Scholem said.

"How much of Professor Scholem is theater?" Ozick inquired.

"Ask Mrs. Scholem," Scholem said.

"One hundred percent," Fanya replied.

Ozick was seated opposite Scholem. There were bookcases to the right and left of her. At some point in their talk, he abruptly made a big, sweeping motion with his hand across what Ozick called an "endless shelf" of books. *"These are all Benjamin,"* Scholem said.

She remembers seeing Benjamin's name on volume after volume after volume. "That sweep of the hand was a really thrilling moment," she said. "A summary of — who knows what." Scholem

was equally definitive when, later in the conversation, he labeled the Jews "a self-destructive people." "Without the arm gesture — a sweeping, complete, definitive pronouncement," Ozick said.

The clown, the hand fanning across the shelf of Benjamin's books, the judgment "The Jewish people is a self-destructive people" — together these clues may help unlock the secret of Scholem's psychological survival after the losses he suffered of beliefs and beloved individuals.

Scholem fretted for decades over the disaster that seemed inevitably to ensue from trying to materialize one's ideals. The time was always premature for Zionist action from an ideal, philosophical standpoint. But what he called the "unspeakable horror" of the years between 1933 and 1945 submerged the question of ideals beneath the imperative of survival. One consequence was that Scholem's residual tolerance for the notion of progressive politics as an abstract good was finished, even though his position on specific issues might still be liberal. (For example, after the '67 War, Scholem was among the first of a group of Hebrew University professors to sign a petition urging the government to immediately return the whole of the West Bank.)

He no longer cared whether people considered him reactionary, he told Hannah Arendt in 1946, after she'd written an essay lambasting Zionist nationalism that infuriated him. The very categories of reactionary and progressive had become hopelessly muddled. The world has revealed itself to be "exclusively reactionary" he declared. Arendt didn't need to tell *him*, of all people, that for Zionism, this reality had "created a situation full of despair, doubt, and compromise." But the reason for this failure was "precisely because it takes place on earth and not on the moon," he told her. "The Zionist movement shares this dialectical experience of the Real (and all its catastrophic possibilities) with all other movements that have taken it upon themselves to change something in the real world." Scholem's lifelong immersion in the

Kabbalah's mythology had given him a vivid conception of evil as a positive presence rather than a mere deficit of the good—and as a presence, moreover, that was profoundly enmeshed in the overall workings of Creation.

Arendt and Scholem fell out over the publication of her *Eichmann in Jerusalem*. Scholem could not forgive what he interpreted as Arendt's facile judgment of those Jews who'd collaborated with Nazi authorities in conditions that defied all known human experience. "We are asked, it appears, to confess that the Jews, too, had their 'share' in these acts of genocide," Scholem wrote. Arendt had betrayed a deficit of love for the Jewish people, he maintained. She had lost her understanding of "radical evil."

Arendt firmly rejected most of Scholem's charges, insisting that she'd never thought of herself as anything other than a member of the Jewish people. But she also admitted that she'd never loved them. "I have never in my life 'loved' any people or collective," she said. "The only kind of love I know and believe in is the love of persons." Even before the trial, she'd had enough of Scholem's sectarian love affair with *Am Yisrael*, which she saw as a mask for megalomaniacal egoism. Moreover, Arendt wrote, Scholem had misunderstood her use of the idea of evil's banality; she'd meant by this not that it was innocuous, but that evil existed now only on the surface, spread like a fungus, and in the absence of depth lacked those demonic dimensions Scholem wished to impute to it.

Arendt's interest lay in the political-structural dynamics that enable people to avoid a sense of personal responsibility for egregious behaviors, while Scholem was more concerned with the engines of individual passion. Of the whole pack of Nazi functionaries, he wrote, "The gentlemen enjoyed their evil so long as there was something to enjoy. One behaves differently after the party is over, of course." He faults Arendt for failing to reckon with the sheer juicy thrill of lording it over the helpless. This wasn't a matter of simple sadism; it was about the rapture of feeling oneself a god.

Scholem would never have disagreed that the Nazis created an extraordinary bureaucratic machine to make the slaughter as efficient as possible. But rather than ascribing Hitler's success to blank functionaries plodding their way through the murder of millions, Scholem saw him as having tapped people's ecstatic drives to destroy anything impeding the realization of their deified ideals. And this was about something more than surfaces — *was* deep, in a Freudian and theological sense. Even if the individuals who committed the atrocities were, as Arendt proposed, "average people, neither good nor evil by nature," the radical evil in their individual natures had been activated. Scholem was no more interested than Arendt in fixing perpetrators or victims with an intractable nature. But where she said "neither good nor evil," he might have said, "*both* good *and* evil." The shift is subtle but carries massive implications, linking individual psychology with the kabbalistic conception of the universe.

The Jewish people's self-destructiveness was, in Scholem's view, a factor of their radical idealism, either in the guise adopted by his brother Werner — which he loosely associated with the positions of people like Arendt and Steiner — or for generations beforehand, in the religious form that deferred action in expectation of the Messiah. The difference between the two was that in its religious matrix, idealism was not an intellectual fad but an agent for the transmission of identity through time.

In "Memory and Utopia," a 1946 lecture addressed to youth movement leaders, Scholem argued that the Holocaust had thrown into high relief the question of Jewish continuity. "Today, following the great disaster which has befallen our people…the revolution finds itself in a vacuum from the national viewpoint; the nation is no longer the great reservoir assuring the continuity of that against which we rebel." The Holocaust foiled dialectics: You can't react against an absence.

Jewish religious sensibility created a potent future-oriented utopianism. However, that focus on the future at the expense of the present was partly responsible for the Jews' vulnerability to the agenda of their murderers. Zionism rebelled against religious indifference to national historical potential. But the movement needed to hold on to radical utopian hope—which meant acknowledging that the past "is still with us, it still has a small opening to the present, or even into the future or the redemption."

To experience something other than world-swallowing vertigo in the encounter with a tradition that culminated so catastrophically, even a secular movement must engage creatively with religious consciousness. There are always possibilities for "discovering new symbols from the past which have been forgotten or to which no one paid attention," Scholem wrote. "We are interested in history because therein are hidden the small experiences of the human race, in the same way as there is hidden therein the dynamic light of future. Within the historical failures, there is still concealed a power that can seek its correction." Ultimately, "the Jewish memory of history is a religious memory."

As a religious enterprise, history in remembrance became a catalyst for the reversal of fate. "At every hour, so long as religion constitutes a living force within him, man is about to bring about the revolution of redemption, and is even called to bring it about," Scholem said. In place of gradual construction over time appears the ever-present possibility of immediate redemption. Scholem replaces a paralyzing vision of the world gone to hell with revolutionary expectancy. Everything is absolutely dark now, he seems to say. And everything can change the next moment. There is no hope of gradual relief. There is only hope of salvation. "It is precisely the lack of transition between history and the redemption which is always stressed by the prophets and the apocalypsists," Scholem remarked. Their ideas of history "have nothing to do with modern conceptions of development or progress."

"In his final years he was very hopeless," Fanya Freud recalled, as a widow. "He said that now the only thing that remained was hope."

As time passed, Scholem reflected not only on Benjamin's published writing but also on their epistolary relationship. Within this correspondence that might conceal the "shadow-Scholem," the most philosophically charged discussions concerned Kafka. Steiner considered this dialogue "one of the supreme acts of literary-moral intelligence and response in modern times."

The long letter Benjamin wrote in the summer of 1938, intended to be his calling card to Schocken, in which he discussed sacrificing truth for the sake of transmissibility, included the proposition that in Kafka's work it was no longer possible to speak of wisdom: "Only the products of its decay remain."

Benjamin identified two such products. The first assumes a melancholic perspective: "the rumor about the true things (a sort of theology passed on by whispers dealing with matters discredited and obsolete)." But the second product is the predisposition to folly, which is more psychologically ambiguous. Here the substance of wisdom has been squandered, but not wisdom's "attractiveness and assurance, which rumor invariably lacks." Folly has preserved, as it were, the confident beauty of wisdom. Kafka was certain of two things, Benjamin said: "First, that someone must be a fool if he is to help; second, that only a fool's help is real help." The only lingering question was whether such help could do human beings any good.

Benjamin added that it was important not to lose sight of the fact that the figure of Kafka, "in its purity and its peculiar beauty...is the figure of a failure." Once he was positive that he would eventually fail, "everything worked out for him en route as in a dream." Benjamin might well have been meditating here also on his own downward trajectory as an indigent exile.

Scholem responded to the letter in terms that evoke his relationship to Zionism as an idealistic project. He told Benjamin that the approach he'd taken was "exceptionally worthwhile and promising," noting only that Kafka's failure should not be seen as unexpected since "the simple truth [is] that the failure was the object of endeavors that, if they were to succeed, would be bound to fail." Kafka the commentator "does indeed have Holy Scriptures, but he has lost them. Thus the question is: What can he comment upon?"

Perhaps Scholem had forgotten that Benjamin addressed exactly this question years earlier when, in the course of interpreting *The Castle*, he wrote Scholem that the question of whether the Scriptures were lost or indecipherable came down to the same thing: "Without the key that belongs to it, the Scripture is not Scripture, but life…It is in the attempt to metamorphosize life into Scripture that I perceive the meaning of 'reversal' which so many of Kafka's parables endeavor to bring about."

The notion of life being changed into Scripture is enchanting, but enigmatic. And when Benjamin first suggested that only a fool's help was real, Scholem did not respond. However, after 1945, the possibility of braving the apocalypse in the costume of folly may have reoccurred to him.

In fact, Benjamin's assertiveness on this point—his attempt to conscript Scholem specifically—went farther: He actually assigned Scholem a mission. In the final passage Benjamin wrote in their long exchange about Kafka—just a year before he took his own life—Benjamin declared: "More and more, the essential feature in Kafka seems to me to be humor." Kafka was, he said, "a man whose fate it was to keep stumbling upon people who made humor their profession: clowns." He went on, "I think the key to Kafka's work is likely to fall into the hands of the person who *is able to extract the comic aspects from Jewish theology.* Has there been such a man? Or would you be man enough to be that man."

Was Scholem's prominently displayed portrait of a clown, a

clown who bore an uncanny resemblance to Scholem himself, his own esoteric signal that he'd accepted Benjamin's challenge? The clown might be seen as figuring midway on the spectrum between the demon and the redeemer. The fool-trickster represents a "third path" to survival, distinct from either innocent utopianism or violent pragmatism.

In his long letter about Kafka, Benjamin noted that the figure of folly lies at the heart of that author's favorites, including Don Quixote. Benjamin, too, was fascinated by the figure of Quixote, observing that his representation in Cervantes' masterpiece taught us "how spiritual greatness, the boldness, the helpfulness of one of the noblest men…are completely devoid of counsel, and do not contain the slightest scintilla of wisdom."

Cervantes built his epic around the idea that Quixote's self-image as a paragon of active chivalric virtue was a romantic fantasy. But Kafka makes the radical suggestion that Quixote himself doesn't exist. In Kafka's schema, Sancho Panza fashioned Don Quixote in his imagination, after having devoured numerous romances and chivalric tales. Quixote represented Sancho Panza's own demon, Kafka postulated, which he'd successfully externalized and so made into a comic spectacle. Thus Quixote "set out in perfect freedom on the maddest exploits, which, however, for the lack of a preordained object, which should have been Sancho Panza himself, harmed nobody. A free man, Sancho Panza philosophically followed Don Quixote on his crusades, perhaps out of a sense of responsibility, and had of them a great and edifying entertainment to the end of his days."

Just as Scholem seemed to Ozick not to mind being invented, perhaps he navigated his grief over the doomed, quixotic crusades of Benjamin by coming to envision them as a way of diverting his own demon. Hadn't Benjamin already appeared in Schocken's eyes to be "something like a bogeyman" of Scholem's invention? Sancho Panza, the clown, becomes Quixote, the holy fool's creator.

Moreover, in his capacity as poetic dreamer able to concoct an "edifying entertainment," Panza revealed the scintilla of wisdom Quixote lacked.

The clown in this vision is an allegorical archetype for the imaginative artist.

Of all the places in his vast body of writings where Scholem may have concealed his personal take on Kabbalah, I suspect that his essay "Religious Authority and Mysticism" hides the mother lode. The divine aspect of a sacred text does not manifest in any particular content, Scholem argues. Rather—in language that mirrors his descriptions of the molten character of Jewish history and identity—Scholem writes that the holiness of these writings resides in their capacity for metamorphosis. Put another way, he continues, "The absolute word is as such meaningless, but it is *pregnant* with meaning…Mystical exegesis, this *new* revelation imparted to the mystic, has the character of a key. The key itself may be lost, but an immense desire to look for it remains alive."

This principle, Scholem contends, informed the perspective of Jewish mystics in antiquity. Observing that one of these figures left an impressive formulation of the issue seventeen centuries ago, Scholem quotes lines which, he says, "date from the height of the Talmudic era" and are cited by Origen, the early Christian theologian: "The Holy Scriptures are like a large house with many, many rooms... Outside each door lies a key—but it is not the right one. To find the right keys that will open the doors—that is the great and arduous task."

Only here's the hitch: No Talmudic-era scholar says any such thing. Not until the Middle Ages does an even remotely analogous metaphor of lost keys appear—and it is from a nonrabbinic source. Given Scholem's obsessive philological scrupulousness, it seems unlikely that he didn't investigate Origen's parable himself and come to recognize its half-invented, psuedepigraphic character. (It's also suggestive that he frames the story between two mentions of Kafka, the writer of fiction.)

Whereas in 1937, the metaphor Scholem crafted to represent the search for truth—the effort to penetrate the mist-shrouded mountain of God's Revelation—carried the aura of romantic legend, this parable sounds closer to slapstick. The large house of Scriptures, with many rooms and doors, before each of which has been carefully laid the wrong key, might be a grand hotel in a Marx Brothers film.

The fact that Scholem has taken a story that is itself a fraud to make his point suggests that everything now has become a product of madcap invention. But under these circumstances, he asks, how can the authority of a text still be recognized? Well, the mystic regards "literal meaning as simply nonexistent or as valid only for a limited time. It is *replaced* by a mystical interpretation." There is no one "right key" because the locks keep changing. The key is the power of make-believe. Here, indeed, Scholem has extracted "the comic aspects from Jewish theology."

At the close of this passage, Scholem writes about Paul reading the Old Testament "against the grain": "The incredible violence with which he did so shows not only how incompatible his experience was with the meaning of the old books, but also how determined he was to preserve, if only by purely mystical exegeses, his bond with the sacred text...The literal meaning is preserved but merely as the gate through which the mystic passes, a gate, however, which he opens up to himself over and over again." Scholem cites the Zohar's gloss on God's words to Abraham: *Lekh lekha.* For this Kabbalist, Scholem notes, the command encompasses not only the literal sense — "Get thee out," instructing Abraham that he must go out into the world — but should also be read with mystical literalness: "'Go to thee,' that is to thine own self."

After Scholem's death, Fanya declared, "Everything that he did in his life in Israel derived from a search for himself." That all-consuming search for and song of the individual self resonates with the great themes of the New World, where Scholem's work found such a rapt audience. ("*Amerika* is one large clown act," Benjamin remarked to Scholem of Kafka's novel.) And Walt Whitman himself — quintessential American bard of the self, whom a contemporary reviewing *Leaves of Grass* described as having "the vigor and suppleness of a clown at a funeral" — became an unexpected beacon for Scholem in his final years.

Recent scholarship has examined Scholem's disillusionment with Zionism in the context of his lasting German intellectual concerns, which arguably became more manifest in later years. Important German academics have joined in this reclamation.

Scholem was scheduled to spend 1982, the year that he died, working in Berlin, which makes this notion of Scholem undertaking a psychological rebound to his origins at the end particularly inviting. Certainly it's true that most of the prominent figures with whom he was mentally in conversation — Benjamin, Ernst Bloch, Franz Rosenzweig, and so on — were German-speaking Central Europeans. And he sought fresh exchanges with a new generation of scholars there. But it would be a mistake to push too far the view of Scholem finding a siren call in the prospect of a return to Germany, whether as a moral guide to the young or as an intellectually ageless disciple of Germany's surviving cultural patrimony. When considering German-Jewish relations after the war, Scholem acidly remarked, "After having been murdered as Jews, the Jews have now been nominated to the status of Germans, in a kind of posthumous triumph; to emphasize their Jewishness would be a concession to anti-Semitism." If Scholem was still searching for himself at the end, I think he sought something new, not a re-embrace of the alien homeland he'd so abominated in his youth.

American readers often found in Scholem a catalyst to humanist faith, sometimes even striving to position him as a guru. "Scholem filled the gap very nicely for Jews who wanted to rededicate themselves to Judaism," Moshe Idel told me. "There was a vacuum in the United States at the time Scholem's writings began to be known there. Scholem's Judaism was antinomian — it was anti-establishment — perfect." And of course I recognize myself among those hovering in the expectant void.

For some Americans, both Idel and Bloom noted, what Scholem wrote *became* Judaism. And when Idel reread the kabbalistic texts from which Scholem made his interpretations and suggested that perhaps all the focus on desolation and the history of exile Scholem found in these works had more to do with his own melancholic Central European milieu than with what the Kabbalists themselves actually said — when he questioned the whole notion of a grand synthetic narrative as illuminating of Kabbalah — there were important American scholars who simply refused to hear it.

Nonetheless, the intellectual pilgrims who came down Abarbanel Road — for whom Scholem's apartment became an essential station on their journey to Jerusalem — often took away something that proved intellectually fertile, even if that bequeathal had an element of fantasy. Scholem spoke enthusiastically of the visit paid to him by Allen Ginsberg in the early 1960s: "A likeable fellow. Genuine. Strange, mad, but genuine."

Fanya asked Ginsberg point-blank: "Why don't you come live here?"

Ginsberg looked at the Scholems. "Me? Your great ideal is to build a new Bronx here. All my life I've been running away from the Bronx, and here I come to the Jewish State and find that the whole big ideal of the Zionists is to build a giant Bronx here. If I have to go back to the Bronx, I may as well stay in the original one."

Ginsberg, for his part, spoke of his deep admiration for Scholem and his work. In his journal during that trip to the Holy Land, he wrote of "Gershom Scholem wrapping his hand under his knee. The gossip that is not written down. The arguments over Arabia & Egypt. 'Where's Ethel?' Honk Honk out the window, waltz on the radio, the return of the universe to itself. Kosmos the magician is born!" In "Howl," Ginsberg riffs off the idea of "bop kabbalah because the cosmos instinctively vibrated at their feet in Kansas." Later, Ginsberg met with Scholem in Paris, where Scholem helped enumerate all the names of the Aeons, emanations of God described in different Gnostic systems, "from Sophia on down to the Garden of Eden," for Ginsberg to use in "Plutonian Ode" — a mystical screed against atomic warfare that Scholem, with his horror at humanity's capacity for technological self-destruction, would surely have been sympathetic to.

For those who want it, there's the image of an elderly Gerhard Scholem mournfully groping his way back through the ghostly ruins of his memory palace in Berlin. I prefer the image of a lanky,

zingy Scholem, the senior cosmic magician, hunched alongside
Allen Ginsberg in a Paris café, hand under his knee, popping chocolates while Ginsberg smokes hashish, doing the bop Kabbalah to
a lyric stream of Gnostic names, charting the spectrum between
material and immaterial, the sensible to the noumenal, in a move-
able Bronx feast of mischievous Jewish dreams.

One subject that would have featured in Scholem's conversations with Ginsberg was Walt Whitman, whom Ginsberg called his
"ultimate American mentor." Whitman's name crops up repeatedly in late remarks by Scholem as an intriguing alternative path.
On one such occasion, Scholem had turned to the subject of
technology, which increasingly concerned him. "The uninhibited
optimism inherent in the expectation that the application of scientific, progressive discoveries directed to the mastery of nature
(the so-called technological revolution) would also solve problems of values is completely unfounded," he declared. While such
knowledge might be able to expose and organize hidden facts, "it
cannot establish values." Scholem contrasted this revolution with
the Kabbalists' achievement, observing of the latter, "It was clear
to them that what we would call *technology* could not be the last
word; that if technology wishes to survive, it must reveal a symbolic dimension. What makes the *kabbalah* interesting is its power
to transmute things into symbols."

Critical to this achievement was the Kabbalists' success at
developing a symbolic key to experience that transcended the
private individual's perspective. The question was whether, in
present-day secular reality, this broad symbolic dimension could
be reactivated. Whitman's writing, Scholem believed, carried some
of this deprivatized symbolic potential: "Walt Whitman revealed
in an utterly naturalistic world what Kabbalists and other mystics
revealed in their world."

At the end, when Scholem speculated about what might save
humanity from itself, the natural world that had been so fiercely

shut out from his consciousness for virtually the whole of his life slipped back into his thinking, transmuted by poetry into the cipher for a new mystical sensibility.

On a day in late March 2015, when snow fell in big, sloppy flakes, I visited Harold Bloom in New Haven. He was unwell, and it was clear that our conversation would need to be brief. But within moments Bloom began speaking of conversations he and Scholem had held about Walt Whitman. "He was haunted by Whitman," Bloom said, and reached for a book of essays about Scholem on his table. On the flyleaf at the back was a handwritten chart in black ink titled "Scholemian WALT (Hermetic.) Whitmanian quasi-Sefirotic Diagram."

"You see we worked on this together," Bloom remarked.

My eyes scanned down the page. There were ten entries, corresponding to the ten emanations of God in the classic kabbalistic Tree of Life. The first read: "Androgyone Poetic Will/Keter/Ayin." *Keter* means "crown"; *ayin* means "nothingness" in the kabbalistic sense, which also equals infinitude. Together they represent the two highest points in the kabbalistic diagram of the *sefiroth*. So in some way, this pinnacle was being equated with the "Androgyne Poetic Will."

I went down through the names: "Female Understanding, Mother's womb / Bina ... Androgyne, Beauty, Sun, Green Leaves of Grass / Tiferet Rahamim ..."

The key to the specifics of this diagram has been lost. But what Scholem was doing, Bloom said, was working to determine how Whitman's themes and imagery might be aligned with core principles of the Kabbalah. In an effort that seems itself as much mystical as intellectual, Scholem was trying to ascertain whether Whitman, in his own pantheistic mysticism, might have arrived at conceptual paradigms parallel with the Kabbalists by "reading" the Scripture of the Cosmos—by exerting his "Androgyne Poetic Will" to display the symbolic dimension of Nature.

His decline was sudden and mysterious: inexplicable abdominal pain, weakness, and a loss of powers of concentration that no one could diagnose. "There must be something basically wrong with the functioning of my organism," he wrote a friend late in January 1982. Yet the doctors had ruled out any possibility of serious illness, and it might still happen, he insisted, that all his pains would vanish as suddenly as they'd appeared. Perhaps he would get to Europe in the spring, he wrote the director of the institute in Berlin where he'd intended to base himself. He asked for patience, since it would be pointless for him to arrive too fatigued to carry out the work he'd outlined on the creation of a new book. Three weeks later he was dead.

Hans Jonas, a former colleague at Hebrew University, wrote Fanya after Scholem's death, offering testimony that others echoed: "For me, he was the essence of Jerusalem," Jonas recalled. "[T]he electric high tension of each exchange, the lightning-quick statements and rebuttals, the inexhaustible originality, the tireless curiosity, the ever fresh interest, the aggressiveness joined with a generous recognition of his foe, a supreme self-confidence along with an open-handed kindness, humor in seriousness and seriousness in humor, humor amid a passion for knowing and naming; and in all this the palpably dark, uncanny, agitated depths behind the blinding brightness of the intellect." In his own final years, Jonas spoke movingly of how in Jerusalem he and Scholem would meet almost every Friday night to read poetry together: poems they'd written themselves and poems they loved by others. The memory of reading verse aloud with Scholem remained absolutely vivid to him when much else had faded.

"What we learn from creation and revelation, the word of God, is infinitely liable to interpretation," Scholem wrote. "Its radiation or sounds, which we catch, are not so much communications as appeals." What we receive is not the word, "but the tradition behind the word, its communication and revelation in time," which is "eventually delivered in a soft, panting whisper." In times like our own, when the tradition falls silent, the question of what might emerge from the "great crisis of language" must be posed "by those who still believe that they can hear the echo of the vanished word of the creation in the immanence of the world. This is a question to which, in our times, only the poets presumably have the answer." For the poets, he concluded, had a link with the masters of Kabbalah, even when they rejected its theological formulations: "This link is their belief in language as an absolute, which is as if constantly flung open by dialectics. It is their belief in the mystery of language which has become audible."

Poetry glittered in Scholem's thought like stars in the black skull of the night. Along with his recovery of Jewish mysticism, Scholem can be credited with pushing intellectual history and scholarly metaphysics toward a kind of lyric sublime. And this convergence too constitutes a form of Kabbalah, which in the Bible means not just tradition and reception but also correspondence and opposition — the state of being face-to-face, which might prefigure destruction or some new generative union.

At first, disorientation saved us. We scrambled around the East Coast for months in our motley, vagabond autonomy trying to find work, until a friend in New York — the one city we'd sworn never to return to — got in touch with someone he knew in publicity, who hired me just like that.

Anne's mother had an apartment, which we rented from her, a glass aerie way downtown across from the World Trade Center. And as soon as we moved in, we began molting our Judaism like birds shedding feathers in spring. When I think back on that period in Manhattan, I see long tables laid end to end, like a sequence of fallen dominoes. Long tables flickering with candles and faces bearing more cheekbone angles than finely cut gems, eyes gleaming to help light the fuse and the wicks at all ends. Bright drinks in big glasses. After years thinking about the meaning of cosmopolitanism in our times, I found myself drinking bubble-gum-pink Cosmopolitans in bars on the Lower East Side, until the ceiling pinwheeled when my head tilted. After years trying to build a substantive life in Israel, I discovered that the American PR firm I worked for had been hired to serve as Israel's publicist. It was absurd, and I got that. But understanding the absurdity of it all wasn't enough to forestall our own little tragedy.

Anne found solace from my extravagant neglect of the economy of our home life with the International Committee of the Fourth International, an old-school Trotskyist-Marxist organization, which had its own occupying activities, leafleting, educating, and protesting. I was with her three-quarters of the way, but that last stretch, where politics felt like a faith with its own orthodox pieties, lay beyond me. And that last stretch emotionally was everything. Meanwhile, she could travel all the way with me socially, hosting big dinners in our see-through aerie that guests all enjoyed. But they made her miserable. Why should she continue?

When Anne and I were able to speak about what was happening to us — that slow ripping apart of the inner seam of our life together — the subject of Israel and our former friends was almost too painful to bear. But I do remember one time when we talked about our last night in Jerusalem, and we remembered our sleeplessness. I recalled going out on the balcony and watching all those heavy boughs that cloistered the courtyard waving in the wind. And Anne spoke of how she'd lain there by herself, savoring the sense of connectedness the country bestowed. "Sometimes I feel so alone when I'm with you now," she said.

And that was the moment when I knew we could not continue. I could not bear to bring a greater isolation to her than literal solitude.

We tried to do what we could do to spare the children the worst of our separation. So we came to the decision to cycle in and out of the apartment by turn, sleeping nomadically, where we could, when we were not with the children for the duration of what we considered a trial period. We dreaded the conversation with them, but when we sat down with them in early September, our eldest son, then twelve years old, broke in to assure us that it came as no surprise to any of them. They had seen this coming. How could we have imagined they might miss what had been so long unraveling just because there'd been so few fights? We gushed about how their lives wouldn't change, that their home would be stable. We would be with them equally, and we loved them equally, and their foundation was as solid as the building we lived in.

A few days later, the planes struck the towers. The glass front of our building was blown in. Much of the building was filled with ash. Our youngest son's elementary school had been in the shadow of the towers; when the first one collapsed he ran into the smoke cloud with all his fellow classmates, fleeing north when no one knew what was happening except that disaster had fallen. The terror we experienced trying to find out where the children were was the worst of our lives — *was* terror. And that night when we were all reunited, my youngest son refused to be washed. He was a gentle boy, but he would not let us clean the smoke and ash from his body, no matter what we said.

I later told this to someone in Israel. Her eyes filled with tears. "He knew," she said.

"Knew what?"

"He knew the smoke was people."

The attack and its aftermath might have brought us together again, but instead that jagged displacement completed our separation.

Sometime thereafter, an old friend sang for his supper at some cool New York dinner party by telling the story of the dissolution of our marriage. "It was the damnedest thing," he said. "It was like the two of them, by the time they got to America, had completely internalized the Jewish-Palestinian conflict and enacted it in their breakup." In his telling, I had held the real power, and exercised it rationally and selfishly. But Anne still had the ability to throw emotional bombs out of nowhere, to take revenge and make mayhem. "At the end of the day, the two of them, with the help of some bystanders, managed to pretty well destroy each other," my friend concluded, pleased with his comparison. "You see what I'm saying? They played the Jews and Palestinians. And now neither of them has anywhere to live."

For all the analogy's flaws, it still gave me pause. But what did it matter? Our family as a family was born in Jerusalem, and as it turned out could not survive its uprooting from that city. The story as a story had ended. If we did not quite forget Jerusalem, we repented of our Zionism and lost our way back into Judaism.

Yet this is only one ending. And there is more than one story.

EIGHTEEN

FOR MANY YEARS after I went away I felt too heartbroken to return. Memories of the city would come back to me, and my failure to have made a life there, my failure to forget Jerusalem, would make my right hand forget its cunning and my tongue cleave to the roof of my mouth. The thoughts that swelled within me were salt-weighed as the Dead Sea. The failure of those who ruled the city to make a refuge for the dispossessed; and the failure of those who were denied the city to stay their hand from bloodshed; and the failure of those who sold the city, and its inhabitants, and hills, and olive groves to see the emptiness they left; and the failure of all who love and fear Jerusalem to turn the city from its darkening course — all these sank my spirits so deep I could not find the will to travel back there. "I share the traditional view that even if we wish to be a nation like all the nations, we will not succeed," Scholem once remarked. "And if we succeed — that will be the end of us." Well, here we are.

But I came to think that melancholy despair was no response to the problem of Jerusalem. It's true the situation is almost hopeless from a purely rational perspective. Today it's possible to say that, just as Scholem pronounced the Jews to be "a self-destructive people," Israel is a self-destructive State. The more it becomes a world-alienating fortress regime, the more likely Israel is to usher in a new apocalypse. Looked at coldly, the crisis, one might say, is upon us.

But the defeat of reasonable expectations for progress, as Scholem came to believe, does not annul the possibilities of irrational hope, which history has rewarded disproportionately in the Holy Land, in the midst of all the punishing disappointments. It was in Gaza that the young scholar Nathan, longing for renewal, was shown a place to dig beneath the floor of the synagogue that revealed a cave in which he found a book that transformed him into a prophet. It was in Gaza that Nathan began to devote himself to kabbalistic studies and told Sabbatai he was the Messiah come to liberate Jerusalem and save the world.

Just as, Scholem argued, the concept of "a purified and rational Judaism" promulgated by the Science of Judaism cohort didn't relate to Jewish experience through the miseries of exile, the purified and rational hopes of Jews in early twentieth-century Berlin couldn't anticipate the actual founding of a Jewish state. "Three things come unawares," said a third-century Talmudist, "the Messiah, a found article, and a scorpion."

In Scholem's theology, this paradigm does not lead us to quietism, but enjoins us to do everything possible to prepare for redemption as if it might arrive the next instant, while recognizing that rationally it's impossible for salvation to come at all. After the '67 War, in a speech insisting that the imperative of pursuing coexistence with the Arabs was a task that the Jews were bound to revive every day, regardless of how often their overtures were rejected, Scholem evoked the alchemists of ancient times who sat in secret chambers where they strove year after year to discover the powers that transform one element into another. "The great enterprise of the land of Israel in which the Jews have proven themselves, casting off one form and taking on another, is also a great experiment in human alchemy, one which shall in the future change hatred and animosity to understanding and respect. To friendship — that is our hope!" he cried.

And perhaps today the unleashing of irrational energies to such shocking, unpredictable, transformative, largely but not exclusively destructive effect across much of the Middle East signals that this time qualifies as one of those interludes Scholem characterized as history's "plastic hours" — "crucial moments when it is possible to act. If you move then, something happens."

After a period of time almost exactly matching the span of years I'd lived there, I at last went back to Jerusalem. My only plan was to walk the city again and visit with a few friends. Though my stay would be for only a few days, I was so overwrought about returning that I was pulled aside by Israeli security and interrogated at great length. I couldn't give a clear answer about why I was traveling or even who I was. I was shaking and sweating and making such a stammering hash of every question that when I was finally waved through, it appeared to be on the assumption that whatever I might have been up to, no one so pathetic could pose a serious threat to anyone other than himself.

I came to Israel from Vienna, where I'd been researching my father's escape from Europe. From the polished blackness of Freud's city, I landed at Ben Gurion after midnight, and a friend drove me up to Jerusalem. It was spring. Limestone façades turned to blocks of moonlight. As we wound through the city's narrow streets, the sight of all the lush, green-leaved trees and blue and purple flowering shrubs amazed me. I opened my window and breathed in that mountain air I'd forgotten. And when I got out of the car, I was engulfed in jasmine.

"My God," I kept saying. "I can't believe how beautiful it is. I'd forgotten how *beautiful* Jerusalem is." I'd remembered so many things about the city — the violence and sorrow administered with the strict periodicity of lamentation in Orthodox ritual. But I'd forgotten the nature of the place.

The particolored petals, the birds and smells elated me. I

recalled one of Kafka's parables: "We are sinful not merely because we have eaten of the Tree of Knowledge, but also because we have not yet eaten of the Tree of Life. The state in which we find ourselves is sinful, quite independent of guilt."

I remember standing one morning before the Dome of the Rock, gazing at all the steeples and minarets that stud the landscape like launch pads of ancient rocket flights. I thought that this was theology's Cape Canaveral—where humanity's most famous souls shot off into orbit. As I lingered, the *taing, taing, chahhmm* of church bells layered with rooster crows arose from somewhere below. All at once I was witness to a major disturbance. Bursts of little umber, white, and black birds lifted off the walls, stones, and grass blades, like handfuls of herbs flung into the inverted blue bowl of sky. They were twittering frenetically. At the same instant, a pair of swifts, dark wings spread wide, swept down from who knows where to the stones the sparrows had been occupying. Lavender-tinged laughing doves burring the ledge of a Saracenic drinking fountain came off their perches with a terrific flickering of wings. Powdery yellow great-tits danced in the dust at the base of an Aleppo pine.

The sparrows wove back and forth. Darting down long roller currents of air into the center of things, then shooting up again to treetops, whirling, plunging once more across the mosque's aquamarine tiles scribbled with bravura contrails of calligraphy. The heap of Jerusalem's domes, spires, crucifixes, and satellite dishes pixilated with dark angels of every dimension—and such a din! Where were they all going? What had so excited them? I wheeled about like a madman to watch, while the lonely human figures scattered around the site—men walking with bent heads, fingering strings of beads; soldiers resting their palms on the barrels of black rifles appeared like attendants on the real drama.

I felt there was some secret hidden in the scene, but I didn't know what to make of it beyond the sense that I'd been captivated.

And so began a series of returns to Jerusalem, during which I
sought to understand what kept compelling me to return. At one
point, I, too, went in quest of the present-day Kabbalists of Jerusalem, seeking some insight beyond the pages of the texts on mysticism I'd been reading for years. In the company of a student with
whom I had been connected by my ultra-Orthodox friend, I went
one evening near sunset into the depths of Meah She'arim. In the
dim light, the slender, pale men in black and white we glimpsed
fluttering down the streets looked like stray piano keys.

My guide was full of trembling enthusiasm for every corner of
the neighborhood, bursting with knowledge about the renowned
inhabitants behind its crumbling walls. Up one rickety staircase lived a mystical Breslov Hasid. "That is a man who has been
through incredible suffering," he said. "His wife is literally crazy.
He had multiple children die at an early age. Yet his countenance
never creases with a single line. He is constantly, intensely happy.
People go to see him just to witness his joy. His face belongs to
man of fifty, but he is ninety-five." Down another lane, was "the
stumpless rabbi," he said. "He's a very aged man who routinely
challenges young yeshiva students to stump him on Talmud questions. They never can stump him. Never! The spectrum of men of
piety I could introduce you to…" He sighed. "It just depends what
you want. "There's a rabbi from Neturei Karta—fiercely opposed
to the idea of Jews ever having a state, even a religious one. Great
fun to talk to. You want *poskim*, who render halakhic decisions?
There are men so knowledgeable you would not believe what
their mind holds. Run-of-the-mill old Jerusalemites?" His chatter
reminded me of the patter of pushers in Washington Square Park
from days gone by. *Smoke. Acid. Ludes. Uppers.*

"Wonderful," I said.

Finally, we made our way beneath an archway into a large rubbly
courtyard. Rows of little children clung to the railings of balconies
on buildings framing that open space, peering down juristically.

We picked our way across the lot, which was scattered with the rusty debris of old strollers. A narrow set of external stairs led to a door that was opened by a tiny aged man with black-button eyes and a long, wispy beard.

This was the only rabbi my guide knew in all Jerusalem who bestowed an age-old kabbalistic blessing. Not only had the rabbi grown up in Jerusalem but his father had been among the greatest religious figures of Jerusalem in his generation. Everyone had come to the family home in the Old City when he was a child. There was no one, my guide said, who could teach me so much about Jerusalem. The problem was that he did not like talking about his father, or about Jerusalem. He did not like talking about the past at all.

This rabbi drew us gently into a room lined floor to ceiling with chocolate-colored bookcases packed with rows of carefully arranged books. In the center of the room was a heavy antique table. On its surface, beneath a sheet of glass, lay a silver-and-white satin cloth embroidered with Hebrew phrases, a Torah scroll, and birds. Perhaps here was something close to the mystical world Gershom Scholem had conjured.

The rabbi took a seat at the table and gestured for me to sit across from him. He opened his hands, asking what he could do for me. My guide explained that I had come to learn about Jerusalem, that I wanted to find whether the city had special properties, that I was trying to understand what Jerusalem was.

"*Ir Ha-Kodesh*"—the Holy City—the man said, in a quavery voice. "*Ma od?*" What more?

I said I was curious about details. How this manifests…

"Because of what happened here." The rabbi shrugged. "Because of the miracles and learning."

My guide nodded. "I know the rebbe has been responsible for some miraculous acts of healing."

"It is the blessing responsible, not me."

"The blessing is very unusual now. I thought it might be meaningful for him—"

The rabbi interrupted to ask whether I needed the blessing, whether I was ill, or whether there were loved ones of mine who needed healing.

I swallowed and said I would be grateful if the rebbe could bestow a blessing of healing through me for my children. My guide and the rabbi had a rapid exchange, which concluded with the decision that it was indeed possible to bestow a kabbalistic blessing of this nature from a distance, since the children were actually of my flesh. But before he began, my guide pressed him once more to speak of his past.

"Has the rebbe seen a change in the city over that time?" he asked. "Have things changed for the better or worse?"

The rabbi's brow crumpled. "Worse. Worse. Of course worse."

"What does the rebbe mean?"

"There was never the sinning in public when I was young."

"Ahh, never in public."

"Never. Never. People breaking the Sabbath in full view of everyone. Wearing immodest clothes. Committing lewd acts. If such things happened, they happened behind closed doors, in private. In darkness. What you see today on the street would have been unthinkable."

"Really?"

"Unthinkable. The sin in public—there was no such thing in Jerusalem."

"And what does the rebbe remember about the spirit of Jerusalem when he was young, apart from there not being public desecration? With the rebbe's father—"

But the rabbi cut him off, asking again whether I wished to receive the blessing. I nodded.

He pushed back from the table and rose. I began to stand as well, but the rabbi furrowed his brow and patted the air. Then he whisked around the table, drew out another chair, and scraped it close to mine. He skipped his left foot up onto the seat with a surprisingly youthful gesture, resting his left forearm on his thigh and placing his right hand on top of my head. Two of his fingers sank into my hair. Three rested on the yarmulke I was wearing. His face hovered just above mine.

All at once the rabbi began a moist, sibilant monologue that never quite rose to a murmur. It was a soothing, intent sound, and the feel of his hand resting on my head added to the comforting, drowsy atmosphere. I couldn't make out any individual words. I was afraid to move or even glance up to see whether his bright eyes were open or closed, out of concern that anything might break the spell.

The soft rustling chant went on and on. And the final syllables, when they came, fell from his lips like clipped feathers.

I thanked him, and when nothing more happened, I slowly rose to my feet. My guide nodded. I turned from the table to leave. The rabbi moved between me and the door, framed by enormous book-cases. Suddenly he looked straight into my eyes, his face contorted in horrible anguish, and he closed his fists before his chest, crying out: *"Become Haredi! Become Haredi!"* His voice rose and fell in a terrible tremor.

I stared at him in confusion.

"Become Haredi," he repeated, rocking back and forth, shaking his little hands. The heavy volumes around him with their jagged gold characters loomed huge. "I don't say it for myself," he said, his voice breaking. "What do I care? Who are you to me? I say it for you. *For you.* For your place in the world to come. There you will see that all this world was as nothing. A game. A joke. *Nothing. The only world is the next world. Become Haredi."* His voice rose in one last wailing, shuddering petition. This time, I thought, he was actually weeping. Then he fell silent.

We slipped past him, out the door.

I met other Kabbalists. Holding court in jammed spaces before tables cluttered with open tins of food. Rings of fluorescence humming from the ceiling. Walls hung with creepy blazes of psychedelic art. In one, the door of an old wooden wardrobe filled with a dozen black suits and white shirts hung ajar, creaking in a breeze generated by the fan of a glowing heating unit. I half expected the clothes to suddenly inflate with flesh and faces, bounding down from their hangers, dancing wildly between us. But once again, I was assailed only with stories of how corrupt Jerusalem had become. How much wretched evil there was everywhere.

Whatever mystical energy there might have been in the rebbe as he intoned the blessing, or in the sanctuaries of other Jerusalem Kabbalists I visited, it came in a compound of such pinched, stale prejudice that it was useless to me. I had wanted a glimpse of the cosmos; I was told only that I should become closed to the world.

How then might I draw nearer to the mystical dimension of experience in Jerusalem?

One day, reading an old letter, I came upon an image that brought back a memory I hadn't thought about in ages: I was married in Jerusalem. Not long after Anne and I arrived, the rabbi who'd overseen our conversion came to the city. Though we were already married in the eyes of the law, we decided that we wanted her to conduct a Jewish wedding ceremony, to complete the process we'd begun of consecrating our lives in Judaism.

Rabbi Miller proposed that we marry at the amphitheater on Mount Scopus, the steep stone crescent where Scholem had seen the university inaugurated in 1925. We were studying Hebrew there at the time, and we wanted only the simplest wedding. It was just the formality of the ritual we aspired to, with our first child soon to arrive. A relaxed administrator consented. If we didn't mind waiting until the end of a concert scheduled for the evening on which the rabbi was free to hold the ceremony, we could hold our wedding there discreetly.

For all the minimalism of our plan, I remember the dreamlike feeling as we made our way at sunset across the university campus to the site. We'd bought fruit, challah, and sweet wine at a little grocery. En route, we gathered flowers from along the road—white and pink laurel, and sprigs of rosemary.

The concert went on for hours. When it began to grow late, while the choir still exalted, the rabbi had us read and sign the *ketubah*, the official marriage contract. Finally, a few minutes before midnight, the last singers moved off the platform. Workers began clearing away the lamps and amplifiers. With our little group of friends, we rushed onto the stage, cast up a prayer shawl to serve as a chuppah, and began.

The amphitheater was still crowded with spectators and workers. As the wedding started, all the lingerers stopped to watch. We said the first prayers. Anne began circling me. We drank the wine and chanted the blessings and smashed the glass. And then—something came over us, or out of us. We found ourselves dancing round and round in the center of the stage in a ring of other dancers. Anne later said it was as if our Jewish souls, stripped of ourselves, came free. Faster and faster we whirled. While the desert spread to the east and the Old City glowed in the west, we embraced in revolutions. There was singing. Ecstasy abrupt as lightning. Blossoms flung through the air.

When it all ended, as suddenly as it began, strangers broke into tears, moving onto the stage weeping, overcome, wanting to embrace us. It was as though for that brief instant, we'd somehow become one with the extraordinary setting of Jerusalem. In our youth, and in Anne's pregnancy, and in the notion of the wedding, on that ridge between the ancient kingdom and the wilderness, our humanity became a common property of the place—transcendent in that immanence.

It was an evanescent deliverance, but it happened. And why shouldn't it be true that just as redemption can come at any moment, it can disappear at any instant also, without thereby surrendering profundity? Why should that experience of complete belonging alone be granted permanence?

Remembering our wedding, I found myself thinking again of the spectacle of birds by the Dome of the Rock. My perspective then had reversed: For a moment, all that normally appeared to be foreground in Jerusalem — places of worship and worshippers, prayers and lamentation — became the background, while the background, the birds and trees and old stones that eclipsed any one historical, ideological provenance, became foreground. All this time when I'd been wondering what kept me returning to Jerusalem, trying to dig deeper to discover some buried wonder, I might have been failing to perceive that this enchantment on the surface was itself the secret. And the next time I was at the Western Wall, I looked at life in the stones themselves.

The Wall is home to the oldest and largest colony of common swifts in Jerusalem. Some ninety nests speckle the crannies. The network of crevices in these ancient stones is so elaborate that each block stores as much as a fifth of its volume in water after the winter rains. In consequence, the stones nurture a wealth of plant life, and many of its botanical species are important avian food sources. At the center of the Wall grow jungle headdresses of ephedra, which produce a red fruit birds thrive on. Higher up are sprays of Sicilian snapdragon. Ruffled mantles of dark green packed with pointillistic yellow blossoms mark golden henbane, believed by ancient Greeks to confer the gift of prophecy. The caper's white petals unfurl everywhere. The Talmud observes that the caper bears fruit every day, as all trees will do in the era of the Messiah. Mohammed declared that hell laughed and there came forth truffles; the earth laughed and there came forth capers.

There's a kind of kabbalistic justification for this switch of focus, a type of figure-ground reversal shifting into consciousness what manifests on the face of life here.

In "Redemption Through Sin," Scholem observes that classic second-century Gnostics believed it was essential to differentiate between the benevolent but hidden God, who was exclusively worthy of being worshipped, and the Demiurge responsible for creating the physical universe. Redemption came to mankind through supernatural messengers dispatched by the hidden God to pluck the souls of the elect from the unjust laws of the material world made by the Demiurge.

Abraham Cardozo, Sabbatai Sevi's Marrano follower, took the Gnostic schema and flipped it. Every nation's philosophers had been able through intellect alone to reason out the necessity for a supreme First Cause, a being who'd set the cosmos going and who, in some fashion, correlated with the hidden God of knowledge. But Cardozo proposed that since the "gnosis" of this abstract First Principle was universally available through rational deduction, it precluded the need for revelation. "The First Cause, which was worshiped by Pharaoh and Nimrod and the wise men of India alike, is not the concern of religion at all, for it has nothing to do with the affairs of this world or its creation and exerts no influence on it for good or for bad," Scholem wrote. In Cardozo's inversion of the Gnostic scheme, "The good God is no longer the *deus absconditus*, who has now become the deity of the philosophers for whom there is no room in religion proper, but rather the God who created the world and presented it with his Torah." The true God was precisely the God rendered in the physical world of Creation, the God that the old Gnostics had considered an evil Demiurge. The true God's nature was revealed in the nature of the earth.

Perhaps this is what it means "to metamorphosize life into Scriptures."

Over the years in my travels to Jerusalem, all the different investigations I'd undertaken fell away, except for walks with my friend Adam, which I still take to this day, though his time has grown more limited since he added to his labors a new vocation as a clown in hospital pediatric wards. For years before, Adam had developed clown pieces for theater — fascinated, he told me, by the way that the clown's playing with reality permits the spectator to deal with suppressed emotions and ideas in an absurd but humane way.

One of our walks began with a drive south in his beat-up van when the sky was already deep violet. Adam's clothes and skin were caked with earth from a garden he was making for a villa being built by an American on precious land by the Natural History Museum. Adam spoke of having surreptitiously changed the landscaping order he'd received, filling the plot with plants native to Jerusalem against its owner's dictate. He does this all the time without announcing the fact—just as late at night he sometimes sneaks plants into shrines that develop around graves of wonder-working rabbis, in the hopes of persuading worshippers that these growths too are sacred and should be nurtured by the community.

As we drove, he told me that recently he'd rooted an *Ela* sapling, a local species of pistachio tree whose name means "Goddess," by a shrine that has sprung up at a mystical rabbi's grave beside the Jerusalem Bird Observatory, near the Knesset.

"*Ela* is the tree with the widest shade of all the local trees—very slow growing, very, very long living," he said. "It was probably the religious gathering place in olden times, where the goddess or oracle was. It doesn't have thorns and would have been convenient for assembling the public underneath.

"There was a time when these trees were all cut down in the fight of the Jews against other local religions. There was even a time—maybe now, too—when it was not allowed for such a tree to be planted beside a synagogue. So I thought maybe it's a good idea to root in graveyards a big, very long-living tree like this, since these places are more likely to remain untouched and not built on for a long time, especially if some important rabbi is buried there"—he turned to me, with a smile—"at least so long as the state will stand, which possibly is much shorter than the life of an *Ela*.

"The growth of the tree is faster if it gets water, so I thought to put a plaque beside it saying it is a blessing to water this plant." He laughed. "I think it will work."

We talked about how few spaces in Jerusalem have remained open land. The last uncultivated patches in the city are vanishing month by month. Adam returned to a notion he'd discussed with me in the past—that Jerusalem should harbor a continuous garden in the sky. Every roof in the city flat enough to hold soil should become a natural habitat, he suggested. Adam didn't believe this elevated ground should be cultivated. What would live on the roofs in his plan are the wildlife and plants that arrive there naturally. Different grasses and weeds would germinate first, seeded by the city's birds. While the floating garden would not be much good to the city's dwindling population of larger mammals, for the birds it would be tantamount to the creation of an enormous citywide sanctuary hovering above the earth. And not only birds—also insects, butterflies, small rodents, and reptiles would benefit. As he spoke, I saw the vision of the city's dense buildings seen from above, waving with stalks and wild blossoms, fluttering with colored wings. It would be another New Jerusalem.

In the way he reads the Scripture of the environment, I believe Adam is a kind of Kabbalist for our time.

By the time we slammed out of the car beneath the old yellow monastery where the earth dipped down into a spreading grove of trees, it was almost dark.

"Almost no one knows about this place," he said. "Even people who live in Jerusalem don't know it's here." He pointed up behind the monastery to a rising slope of rutted earth. "From up there is an amazing view. You can see all Jerusalem. The hill has always been an important point for the military because it looks down over everything. For thousands of years, actually. There were many, many fortresses here...All those ditches are trenches. The Jordanians were here most recently."

We began climbing.

It was a small landmass, a mound more than a hill, but riddled with so many winding, looping involutions it felt as though we were scaling the brain of a petrified giant. What thoughts might be held in these gnarled folds? As we rose, we spoke about the endless, repetitive struggles for Jerusalem in which Mar Elias had played the part of redoubt and overlook through the millennia.

Looking north from the hilltop, Jerusalem made a great nugget of yellow and white sparkle. Twisting south, it was possible to make out Bethlehem and tiny stabs of light marking nearby Arab villages.

Adam pointed down to where a wide road, roaring with traffic, swirled out from the base of the hill toward a new ring of glowing high-rises that could not have looked less part of the landscape if they'd been shat into place from the rear end of a spaceship.

Before they built the road to the settlement of Har Homa, Adam said, Palestinians from Sur Bahir and other villages grew wheat on the flank of this hill. "In the fall, they would come, and you would see them harvesting the grain with hand scythes. Moving slowly though the stalks. It was beautiful, magical, in a way, to have a hillside of wheat growing inside the borders of Jerusalem." But after the construction of the road, he went on, villagers stopped cultivating the grain. Maybe there were new issues with checkpoints. Maybe it was just too hard to cross that multilane highway.

It's not the moment for some romantic fantasy of side-by-side toiling in the fields. But as I talked with Adam, I reflected that there are other kinds of switches in focus that might be effected — steps not so hard to see, not so complex, that could be taken to cultivate the prospects of the Palestinians. If talks between the two sides are frozen, that doesn't mean there's nothing that can be *done*. What if the deep mystical notion of *tikkun olam*, repairing the world, were taken out of the metaphorical realm, and became an injunction to literally mend the earth — not only for the sake of making it yield a livelihood, but to vouchsafe the survival of the physical place that both people dwell on? Rather than being reduced to spoils for allocation, the land could be approached as a common trust. If not actually restored to a state of nature, the land might yet be reenvisioned from the perspective of the natural world, as a summons to conservation and renewal. On the most basic level, practices like the uprooting of olive trees for vengeance and punishment must cease. The Israeli business community could assist in finding markets for goods grown by the Palestinians. For all the resistance to accepting gestures by the State that reinforce the status quo, Palestinians might welcome tangible measures that open their position out to the world. We have to start building trust somewhere, and almost anywhere would be better than where we are now. Perhaps this other focus over time might nurture exchanges that ease the political conversation as well.

"The abyss that events have flung open between the two can be neither measured nor fathomed," Scholem wrote in one of his most poignant political essays. "Unlike many in Israel, I do not believe that the only possible means of overcoming the distance is to admit the abyss into our consciousness in all its dimensions and ramifications. There is little comfort in such a prognosis: it is

mere rhetoric. For in truth there is no possibility of comprehending what has happened — incomprehensibility is of its essence — no
possibility of understanding it perfectly and thus of incorporat-
ing it into our consciousness. This demand by its very nature cannot be fulfilled...Abysses are flung open by events; bridges are
built by goodwill. Bridges are needed to pass over abysses; they
are constructed; they are the product of conscious thinking and
willing...Where love is no longer possible, a new understanding requires other ingredients; distance, respect, openness, and
open-mindedness, and, above all, goodwill."

Scholem was writing about relations between Jews and Germans after the Holocaust. But how many lessons might be drawn
from such writing for bridging today's abyss between the Jews and
Palestinians? What might we discover going back into such texts
and kabbalistic works to mine them for insights into the contemporary predicament, when the Jews are not in exile but are instead
maintaining the exile of another people?

What, exactly, is there to be afraid of? To be revived as a morally legitimate enterprise, Zionism must be reconceived. But
wasn't Scholem always telling us that this absolute freedom to
reinvent its nature was the definition of the Jewish historical project? "There is no way of telling a priori what beliefs are possible or
impossible within the framework of Judaism," he asserted. "The
'Jewishness' in the religiosity of any particular era is not measured
by any dogmatic criteria that are unrelated to actual historical
circumstances, but solely by what sincere Jews do, in fact, believe,
or — at least — consider to be legitimate possibilities."

What disturbed Scholem most was surrendering the creative
passions to fantasies of security and stability. Writing of the world
established through Jewish Law, he declared, "It is a profound
truth that a well-ordered house is a dangerous thing." When a
little messianic apocalypticism penetrated this house, it became
"a kind of anarchic breeze. A window is open through which the

winds blow in, and it is not quite certain just what they bring in with them." This airing was vital, he insisted.

I think we must take Scholem at his word. If, as happened once before, a Jewish messiah could convert to the Muslim religion without renouncing his mission in the eyes of many of his followers, who can say what history yet holds in store? Is it inconceivable that the faith of Jews in the Land today could impel them to advocate for the Muslims in their midst?

"There's something preliminary, something provisional about Jewish history; hence its inability to give of itself entirely," Scholem wrote, in considering messianism. "There is something grand about living in hope, but at the same time there is something profoundly unreal about it." Yet there is something provisional about natural history as well, with its seasonal, migratory cycles, intrinsic to its grandeur and profoundly real. The birds with their nomadism and disrespect for borders evoke a model for rotating possession of the land. Binationalism is said now to be impossible. But the people of Jerusalem already live with bi-*naturalism*—tri-naturalism, quadri-, quinti-naturalism, ad infinitum. And one day perhaps that polysemous estate will be embraced.

Adam and I wound round and round the stony cerebellum of Mar Elias, past the shells of concrete bunkers and sweet-smelling prickly shrubs, at last threading our way down past the back wall of the monastery, dropping below the hilltop into the grove of olive trees. Only now, inside the fold, did I register the gravity of these forms. Branches splayed in wild arabesques. Huge trunks rife with dark eyes. Bark like wax drippings of a thousand candles. Ghostly, silvered fringes of trembling leaves. Each tree at once majestic and delicate.

The olive trees of Mar Elias are incredibly ancient—seven, eight hundred years, perhaps more. They may have seen the rise and fall of the Crusaders; ruins of a Crusader stronghold lay nearby. Certainly they'd been alive through the ascendancy and dissolution of kingdoms that seemed to announce a momentous shift in the order of the world. Rulers. Beliefs. The birth of the printed word. As the trees aged, they became more and more hollow, which was why they began to split and splay into more and more intricate patterns. Their vascular system pressed closer and closer to their bark sheathing. The depth of the ancient trees lay in the fact that the whole of their being had risen to the outermost layer of their skin. Their depth reflected the fact that eight hundred years of organic existence was inscribed and enacted on the level that met your eyes. Their depth was a factor of their existing entirely on the surface of being.

It felt as though we were enveloped in their bodies and arms — by limbs that might have embraced all the history of Jerusalem, impressed, however faintly, with every change in the soil and atmosphere of the city over time since they'd been planted by some forgotten hand.

We began walking again, through the glowing night, our open palms reaching out to the right and left to press the trunks of the trees as we moved, like partners in some old dance.

In his later years, Scholem liked to quote from an essay he'd written in the wake of the Wailing Wall riots: "I categorically deny that Zionism is a messianic moment and that it is entitled to use religious terminology to advance its political aims," Scholem had declared. "The redemption of the Jewish people, which as a Zionist I desire, is in no way identical with the religious redemption I hope for for the future." As a Zionist, he said, he was not prepared to satisfy political yearnings that exist only in a nonpolitical sphere, "in the sphere of End-of-Days apocalyptics." The Zionist ideal and the messianic ideal "do not touch," he wrote, "except in pompous phraseology of mass rallies, which often infuse into our youth a spirit of new Sabbatianism that must inevitably fail." Sometimes he would add that it was a particular point of pride with him that

Zionism was *not* a messianic movement. For the mix of messianic sentiments and politics was always dangerous, he said.

The words have a noble ring, and one can see why Scholem would recall them as he watched the settler movement take on ever greater apocalyptic fervor. But Scholem's position on this point is so rife with inconsistencies that I find it almost willfully unpersuasive. The very question of what Jewish messianism and redemption consist in teems with uncertainty and paradox, in part because, whatever else, deliverance is happening on this tangled earth, not in heaven. "Judaism, in all of its forms and manifestations, has always maintained a concept of redemption as an event which takes place publicly, on the stage of history and within the community," he wrote. "It is an occurrence which takes place in the visible world, and which cannot be conceived apart from such a visible appearance."

Of course there are overlaps between the idea of the Jewish people's worldly redemption through the Zionist settlement of Palestine — what Scholem called the Jews' reentry into history — and their transcendent salvation. Scholem's own writing abounds with moments when he allows the line between the two to blur. "Certain Messianic strains" had always accompanied Zionism in the background "as a sort of overtone…a sublime melody," he acknowledged. For that matter, even while professing that Zionism was a secular movement, he repeatedly asserted that it would not remain secular indefinitely. Secularity itself, he hinted, might now embrace what were formally understood as the great truths of mysticism. Scholem's cautions against the messianic ingredient in Zionism read like warnings against smoking printed on cigarette packages by their manufacturer.

It's said that when Scholem's magnum opus on Sabbatai Sevi was published in Hebrew in 1957, Prime Minister David Ben-Gurion shut his office and stayed in bed for five days and nights to read the book. Did he view the book as an admonition against coloring leadership with messianic overtones, which he'd unabashedly relied upon in achieving his own political objectives? Or did he find some endorsement in the book's last page, where Scholem abruptly questions the condemnation of the Sabbatian movement: "Was it not a great opportunity missed, rather than a big lie? A victory of the hostile powers rather than the collapse of a vain thing?" Even the failures of the Sabbatian movement were only transitional, since the aftermath of its dark fall gave birth to so many productive manifestations of Judaism, including the Jewish Enlightenment.

Herzl was seen by many as a messianic figure, and he consciously manipulated that association. Prior to Herzl, the thinkers who inspired him along with their religious forebearers dreamed of messianic salvation for the Jewish people in the land where they originated. The Labor movement was rife with messianic-utopian strains even before Ben-Gurion, who consciously nationalized messianism, calling the State merely "an instrument for the realization and implementation of the vision of redemption." Ben-Gurion's adversary Jabotinsky, meanwhile, conjured the negative messianism of an impending European apocalypse as the catalyst to the creation of the new, warrior-messiah Jew in Palestine, the Zionist Superman. Historians have traced the color spectrum of Zionist redemption fantasies: the "brown messianism" of the Revisionists, the "red messianism" of the Socialists, and the "black messianism" of the Orthodox. To these we might add the purple messianism of professors at Hebrew University.

From its inception, the project on Mount Scopus was infused with utopian-messianic expectations. "This place on which we stand—Mt. Scopus from which we can see the [remnants of the] Temple—is a sanctuary for us. This edifice and the others that will rise in the not too distant future will become for us a holy place," declared an early supporter of the Jewish Studies institute. The number of important scholars who dedicated themselves to exploring messianism there is remarkable: the Revisionist Joseph Klausner, who declared that the messianic idea was "the *original* Hebrew idea which has influenced all humanity so much"; Ben-Zion Dinur, who became minister of education and argued that messianic ferment was critical to the advance of Jewish history; Aharon Z. Aescoly, author of a pioneering survey of Jewish messianism that situates its different historical manifestations in their larger sociopolitical contexts; Jacob Talmon, who explored how political messianism grew out of the French Revolution—the list goes on. As Scholem himself stated after delivering a lecture on messianism in 1958, "Except for the miracles and wonders of the scholars of Judaism in the last fifty years, we would not know the wing-touches of history related to these movements, which were premeditatedly hidden, in all their force." Jewish messianism was excavated, analyzed, and exhibited to the people by historians, philosophers, literary scholars, and sociologists on Mount Scopus.

The messianic dimension is ubiquitous in Zionist thought—but not homogenous. Scholem overcorrected what he saw as the craven denial of Judaism's apocalyptic messianism by writing frequently as if only the apocalyptic side of that project was real. ("Jewish Messianism is in its origins and by its nature—this cannot be sufficiently emphasized—a theory of catastrophe," he claimed.) But rather than endlessly, vainly fighting and denying the messianic infusion in Zionism, one might accept that the impulse is ineradicable, then set out to cultivate those aspects of it that stir the passion for renewal beyond the nationalist camp—such as Scholem himself imagined when he was a young man cooped up in Germany, fantasizing about a Zion built from the suffering of all humanity, consisting of "the collective loneliness of people and hence the source for the messianic community." This is the messianism of the Kabbalists, who dreamed, he said, not just of receiving personal salvation but also of a "renewed condition of nature and even of the cosmos as a whole."

At the close of *Major Trends of Jewish Mysticism*, just before observing that a secret life "can break out tomorrow in you or in me," Scholem recounts a legend:

> When the Baal Shem had a difficult task before him, he would go to a certain place in the woods, light a fire and meditate in prayer—and what he'd set out to perform was done. When a generation later the "Maggid" of Meseritz was faced with the same task he would go to the same place in the wood and say: We can no longer light the fire, but we can still speak the prayers—and what he wanted done became reality. A generation later Rabbi Moshe Leib of Sassov had to perform this task. And he too went into the woods and said: We can no longer light a fire, nor do we know the secret meditations belonging to the prayer, but we do know the place in the woods to which it all belongs—and that must be sufficient, and sufficient it was. But when another generation had passed and Rabbi Israel of Rischin was called upon to perform the task, he sat down on his golden chair in his castle and said: We cannot light the fire, we cannot speak the prayers, we do not know the place, but we can tell the story of how it was done. And the story which he told had the same effect as the actions of the other three.

"You can say if you will that this profound little anecdote symbolizes the decay of a great movement," Scholem comments. "You can also say that it reflects the transformation of all its values, a transformation so profound that in the end all that remained of the mystery was the tale."

But what happens if the tale itself is forgotten? And the castle and the golden chair are lost? Then we have only the woods.

I went back to Gershom Scholem's house on Abarbanel Road one day not long ago, and where I'd once seen desolation and ruin in its state of overgrown abandonment, the sight transformed before my eyes into a wonder of natural efflorescence—a green utopian apocalypse of nature restored above the walls laid down by man. A house that was alive and wildly flourishing with variegated growth.

Come branches labyrinthine, green stalks and leaves, curling winding slashing, slanting, hanging limbs and thrusting. Thick enclosing shrub spread wide. Bright clover. Fig. Wild rose. Cactus. Palm. Carob. Myrtle. *Hadas. Rihan.* All you fluttering, pendant, interrupting fronds, thorns, stems, vines, and trunks, wrap the home of Gershom Scholem in layer upon layer of explicit nature until it vanishes, metamorphoses, radiates, proliferates, and engulfs Jerusalem, west, east, north, and south, in some new kabbalistic wilderness, where the future is unknown, again. And the spell of hopelessness is broken now, and then.

ACKNOWLEDGMENTS

Judith Gurewich, my indefatigable publisher and editor, provided crucial suggestions at many stages in the development of this book. I'm deeply thankful for her comments and the ongoing conversations we've had about the book's cast of characters and larger themes. The entire Other Press team has been, as ever, an invaluable boon to the process of bringing this book to fruition. I want to thank, in particular, Mona Bismuth for her vital help with the book's photographs, Julie Fry for her exceptional work on image placement and the overall design, Janice Goldklang and Terrie Akers for their help establishing the book's digital presence, and Yvonne Cárdenas, who had the enormous task of producing the final text. Her scrupulous attention has been essential to the completion of this work.

I couldn't be more pleased with the image Andreas Gurewich and Srijon Chowdhury created that became the cover of this book. Srijon shared the story of the inspiration he found for the painting's floral arch patterns in a mosque built by his great-great-great-grandfather on the coast of Bangladesh — and this seems a wonderfully apposite visual link to this book's syncretic ideas.

I'm also very thankful for the lucid editorial suggestions given me by Sigrid Rausing of Granta Books, who has offered thoughtful, generous support for this book throughout the process of its composition.

Various individuals at the National Library of Israel in Jerusalem have helped me over the years. Matan Barzilai, Jamie Nathan, and Rachel Misrati all assisted me with the recently digitized collection of Gershom Scholem photographs. In New York, Michael Simonson and Tracey Beck at the Leo Baeck Institute generously helped me find and arrange for the use of images that were important to the final shape of the book. Lyudmila Sholokhova at the YIVO Archives and Library kindly provided me with access to the extraordinary early copies of the Zohar in the institute's collection. I'm also thankful to many librarians at the Dorot Jewish Division of the New York Public Library. Amanda Seigel assisted me on numerous occasions.

A number of gifted writers, editors, scholars, and critics who knew Gershom Scholem gave me invaluable perspective on his personality and achievement. I'm especially thankful in this regard to Cynthia Ozick, Harold Bloom, Robert Silvers, and David Biale. I benefited as well from conversations with many scholars deeply versed in Scholem's work and the larger field of Jewish mysticism. Moshe Idel, Jonatan Meir, and Daniel Abrams offered vital help in guiding the course of my research and evolving perspective on Scholem. Itta Shedletzky and Mirjam Zadoff also generously responded to numerous queries. A conversation in Jerusalem with Adina Hoffman and Peter Cole helped point me toward useful sources and perspectives. I'm also thankful to Abe Socher for putting me in touch with David Biale, whose important book *Gershom Scholem: Kabbalah and Counter-History* was the first scholarly work to help me contextualize Scholem's achievement.

Among people I am fortunate to count as friends, this book owes its greatest debt to Adam Yakin. More than any other person, Adam has introduced me over the years to the nature of Jerusalem with a depth of knowledge and poetic insight that became critical to the development of my argument in this book—and to the persistence of my hope that the story of the Land may yet contravene the prophecies of our latter-day apocalyptists.

James Lasdun read an early draft of this book and offered enormously helpful suggestions and encouragement. Sina Najafi provided invaluable assistance in thinking about the images for this book, as well as in pointing me toward various texts and individuals who helped with the development of the book's themes. Conversations with many friends found their way into this narrative. I want to thank in particular Adam Cvijanovic, Michael Greenberg, Frederick Kaufman, William Kolbrener, Karmen Ross, Carne Ross, Jonathan Nossiter, Shari Spiegel, Alan Berliner, Adam Shatz, Marina Warner, Eyal Weizman, Hal Foster, Daniel Mendelsohn, Jonathan Rosen, and Chris Bayes.

This book owes a profound, unique debt to Anne LaFond, who not only shared the world I write about here, but also gave me incalculable help in the process of trying to reconstruct the story of those years. I hope she will find in the book some reflection of the life we led together, and the lingering resonance of the ideals we pursued.

My father, Martin Prochnik, and my siblings Ethan, James, and Elisabeth, are always supportive of my work and I'm profoundly thankful for their generosity. To my children, Yona, Tzvi, Zach, and Rafael, I would say only that your individual spirits have each played a role in the creation of these pages that goes beyond what's written here and awaits your own interpretation and fulfillment.

Rebecca Mead's immense help with this project is inscribed at every level of the book. I'm forever grateful to her for making legible my dreams.

AUTHOR'S NOTE

I want to acknowledge the great debt this book owes to *Lamentations of Youth: The Diaries of Gershom Scholem, 1913–1918*, which has been published by Harvard University Press in a vibrant translation by Anthony David Skinner. The extraordinary precocity, emotional intensity, and sheer intellectual hunger that Scholem displays in this journal is enormously revealing of his character and worldly experience in these crucial years. By humanizing the monumental scholar, Scholem's diary enables us to watch the drama of a passionate, politically radical, and sometimes psychologically desperate young man struggling to find his path out of Europe to Jerusalem. My own book could not have been written without *Lamentations of Youth,* and I hope others will have the opportunity to discover this work's magnetic power.

NOTES

INTRODUCTION

2   *"dared only a little way past"*: Ozick, "The Fourth Sparrow: The Magisterial Reach of Gershom Scholem," in Bloom, *Modern Critical Views*, 125–26.

2   *"the Kabbalah of Gershom"*: Bloom, "Scholem: Unhistorical or Jewish Gnosticism," ibid., 220.

4   *"calculated risk"*: Scholem, *On Jews and Judaism in Crisis*, 34.

5   *"The building of the land"*: Cited in Biale, *Gershom Scholem: Kabbalah and Counter-History*, 109.

5   *"which itself serves"*: Scholem, *A Life in Letters*, 135.

6   *"Oh how lucky you are"*: Ibid., 126–27.

7   the only person Scholem had ever truly loved: Cited in Scholem, *Lamentations*, 327.

8   *"No one should foster"*: Scholem, *A Life in Letters*, 145.

8   *"There would be no use"*: Buber, *Letters*, 377.

8   *"Voltairean mien"*: Steiner, *Errata*, 146–49.

9   *"unquestioningly...as forming part"*: Scholem, *On Jews and Judaism in Crisis*, 190.

9   *"I doubt it very much"*: Ibid., 191.

10   *"cursed him"*: Scholem, *Lamentations*, 326; observation by Jona Toni Sonya Simon.

10   *"He's just like me"*: Ibid., 132.

15   danced the fence: I'm referring above all to the many statements Scholem made that hint at some functional correlation between the Kabbalah and Zionism.

16   *"Even if we wish"*: Scholem, *On Jews and Judaism in Crisis*, 34.

16   *"the utopian return"*: Scholem, *The Messianic Idea in Judaism*, 35–36.

20   *"Every word of the Torah"*: See, for example, Scholem, *On the Kabbalah and Its Symbolism*, 13.

20   *"The binding character"*: Scholem, *On Jews and Judaism in Crisis*, 274.

CHAPTER ONE

25   *"Earth is a snowflake's destiny"*: Scholem, *Lamentations*, 50.

25   wealthy manufacturers of bathtubs: Scholem, *From Berlin to Jerusalem*, 8.

26 *"petty-bourgeois war"*: Scholem, *Lamentations*, 71.

26 *Arthur worked on Yom Kippur*: Scholem, *From Berlin to Jerusalem*, 10–11.

26 *Gerhard's irrepressible mother*: For Scholem's perception of his parents and his relationship to them, see ibid., 1–35.

28 *"Reason is a stupid man's longing"*: Scholem, *Lamentations*, 50.

29 *"like arrows shot from a bow"*: Roth, *What I Saw*, p. 87.

29 *exotic-sounding destinations*: Scholem, *From Berlin to Jerusalem*, 13.

30 *"We need only look"*: Buber, *On Judaism*, 66.

30 *a religious system in the Oriental spirit*: For more context on Buber and Orientalism, see Mendes-Flohr, *Divided Passions*, esp. 81–88.

31 *"diagnosed and combated"*: Scholem, *On Jews and Judaism in Crisis*, 127, 133.

31 *"comes into contact with the maternal"*: Buber, *On Judaism*, 67.

32 *"You are Orientals"*: Scholem, *Lamentations*, 40.

32 *"Revolution everywhere!"*: Ibid., 47–48.

32 *"the deep streams"*: Ibid., 49.

35 *"for my Jewish consciousness"*: Scholem, *From Berlin to Jerusalem*, 36.

35 *his religious-studies teacher introduced*: Ibid., 36–39.

36 "Kedoshim thuju": Scholem, *Lamentations*, 246.

36 *"Jews are only good"*: Scholem, *On Jews and Judaism in Crisis*, 4–6.

36 *jug handles*: Scholem, *From Berlin to Jerusalem*, 63.

36 *tracts by notorious racists*: Scholem, *Lamentations*, 23–24.

37 *"Forget my family"*: Ibid., 33.

37 *"He spoke for those"*: Scholem, "To Theodor Herzl," in *The Fullness of Time*.

38 *"I have the impression"*: Scholem, *Lamentations*, 38.

38 *"blessed lunacy"*: Ibid., 34.

38 *"I'm of the opinion"*: Ibid., 37.

39 *Uncle Theobald, kept a Jewish National Fund*: Scholem, *From Berlin to Jerusalem*, 23–25.

39 Ex Oriente Lux: Mendes-Flohr, *Divided Passions*, 109–10.

40 *"the last world-historical embodiment"*: Cited in Presner, *Muscular Judaism*, 3.

41 *The Zionist youth movement had its roots*: See, for example, Brenner, *The Renaissance of Jewish Culture in Weimar Berlin*, 46–49; and Sharfman, "Between Identities, 198–228.

41 *At the Sign of the Golden Goose*: Scholem, *From Berlin to Jerusalem*, 43–45.

42 *the new youth wing of Agudat Israel*: See, for example, Scholem, *On Jews and Judaism in Crisis*, 8–12. For the pleasure in provoking boycotts on himself, Scholem, *Lamentations*, 26.

42 *"curls resplendent"*: Scholem, *From Berlin to Jerusalem*, 57.

43   *how beautiful Jewish rituals*: Scholem, *Lamentations*, 35.

43   "Gerhardchen ist nebbich": Scholem, *From Berlin to Jerusalem*, 10.

43   *"There is no one in my immediate"*: Scholem, *Lamentations*, 33.

44   *"They just shouldn't rob youth"*: Ibid., 39.

44   *"a movement that instead"*: Ibid., 48.

44   *"In the beginning"*: Zohar, 3.

45   *he met Yetka in Treptow Park*: Scholem, *From Berlin to Jerusalem*, 57. For more of the manic tone of his emotions in this period, see Scholem, *Lamentations*, 33.

46   *"We sensed our melody"*: Cited in Biale, *Gershom Scholem*, 16.

46   *herring tamer*: Scholem, *From Berlin to Jerusalem*, 62.

46   *"Mr. Big Shot"*: Scholem, *Lamentations*, 51.

46   *In May he finally allowed himself*: Ibid., 54–58.

CHAPTER TWO

48   *"there is no such thing"*: See, for example, Belmore, "Some Recollections of Walter Benjamin," probably the most expansive, personal derogation of Benjamin's character ever written. Scholem also reports a version of this remark in *Walter Benjamin*, 55.

48   *A big woodcut of Walt Whitman*: Brooker, Bru, and Thacker, *Oxford Critical and Cultural History of Modernist Magazines*, 767.

49   *special table at the Café Grössenwahn*: Pachter, *Weimar Etudes*, 104.

49   *"cloud-cuckoo-land"*: Scholem, *Lamentations*, 33.

49   *In this instance, Hiller's cocksure*: For an account of this evening and Scholem's reaction to Hiller, see Scholem's *Walter Benjamin*, 16, and *Lamentations*, 58–61.

50   *"assumed a virtually magical appearance"*: Scholem, *Walter Benjamin*, 8–9.

50   *Judaism should not be considered*: In addition to the many references to Benjamin's positions on Judaism and Zionism that Scholem cites in *Walter Benjamin*, Benjamin delves into these subjects most notably in his correspondence with Ludwig Strauss. Some of the key points from the exchange are summarized in Steiner, *Walter Benjamin: An Introduction*, 24–25; and Rabinbach, *In the Shadow of Catastrophe*, 46–53.

51   *We go our separate ways*: Scholem, *Lamentations*, 61, and *Walter Benjamin*, 6.

51   *beside the Grunewald forest*: Boyd and Frisby, *Metropolis Berlin*, esp. 207–12.

51   *"Roaring Moses"*: Elon, *The Pity of It All*, 259.

52   *"Perhaps such intrusions"*: Nabokov, *Speak, Memory*, 303.

52   *"in a posture compounded"*: Benjamin, *Reflections*, 10.

53   *Isenheim Altarpiece*: Scholem, *Walter Benjamin*, 37.

53 *"Color is first of all"*: Walter Benjamin, "Dialogue on the Rainbow," cited in Caygill, *Walter Benjamin: The Color of Experience*, 9–10.

53 *"very respectable room"*: Scholem, *Walter Benjamin*, 6.

54 *"The arrangement of the furniture"*: Benjamin, *Reflections*, 64.

54 *"deep, inner relationship to things"*: Scholem, *Walter Benjamin*, 37.

54 *"mourning cloaks and admirals"*: Benjamin, *Berlin Childhood Around 1900*, 52–53.

55 *"I sought to limit its effect"*: Ibid., 37.

55 *"on the small and very smallest"*: Scholem, *On Jews and Judaism in Crisis*, 176–77.

56 *"Where we perceive a chain of events"*: Benjamin, *Illuminations*, 257.

57 *"If you ask me"*: Scholem, *On Jews and Judaism in Crisis*, 48.

58 *"technological assimilation"*: Ibid., 41.

58 *"steeped in elements of naturalistic"*: Scholem, *On the Possibility of Jewish Mysticism in Our Time*, 18.

58 *"not merely as a chapter of history"*: Scholem, *On Jews and Judaism in Crisis*, 46.

61 *"who is firmly convinced"*: Benjamin, *Illuminations*, 242.

63 *"I am occupying myself"*: Scholem, *Walter Benjamin*, 6–7, and *Lamentations*, 61–62.

CHAPTER THREE

66 "Mein Sohn": Scholem, *From Berlin to Jerusalem*, 19; more background on the family can be found on 1–59.

67 *"It is lonely in heaven"*: Scholem, *Lamentations*, 59–61.

67 *"toned with the colors of war"*: "Berlin Life Withers Under the Blight of War," *New York Times*, July 16, 1915, in a piece partly culled from the German paper *Vorwärts*.

67 *Ten thousand live reindeer*: "Germans to Eat Reindeer," *New York Times*, July 9, 1915.

67 *"The state is violence"*: Scholem, *Lamentations*, 63.

68 *"In these times"*: Landauer, *Call to Socialism*, "Foreword to the Second Edition."

69 *"We no longer believe"*: Ibid., "For Socialism."

69 *"the destruction and defeat"*: Cited in Rabinbach, *In the Shadow of Catastrophe*, 52.

69 *"The apocalyptists have always cherished"*: Scholem, *The Messianic Idea in Judaism*, 10.

69 *a romantic anticapitalist rebellion*: See Rabinbach, *In the Shadow of Catastrophe*, 3–65.

70 *"every atom of that power"*: Ha'am, *Selected Essays*, 294.

71 *"heaven down to earth"*: Scholem, *Lamentations*, 44.

71 *"behind everything yawns"*: Ibid., 131.

71 *"expressionless, impenetrable, and ever the same"*: Benjamin, "Experience," in *Selected Writings, Volume 1*, 3–5.

72 *There would be no basis*: For notes on these early discussions, see, for example, Scholem, *Walter Benjamin*, 11–13; also Scholem's *Lamentations*, 62–64, and *On Jews and Judaism in Crisis*, 173.

72 *"to be earned anew every day"*: Benjamin, *Correspondence*, 51–52.

73 *"Each of us has faith"*: Ibid., 56–57.

73 *"Assemblies of bourgeois intellectuals"*: Benjamin, *Reflections*, 19.

74 *"You will find us"*: Ibid., 18. I draw on Benjamin's essay "A Berlin Chronicle," in *Reflections*, in which this quote appears throughout the discussion of Benjamin's history with Heinle and the youth movement; see also Eiland and Jennings, *Walter Benjamin: A Critical Life*, esp. 60–76.

75 *"The past itself is future"*: Landauer, *Revolution and Other Writings*, 115, 121.

76 *"handle ideas like quarry stones"*: Cited in Rabinbach, *In the Shadow of Catastrophe*, 43.

76 *"Jewish aroma in our production"*: Ibid., 39.

76 *"only to the degree"*: Scholem, *A Life in Letters*, 55.

77 *"penetrating, captivating power"*: Benjamin, "Dialogue on the Religiosity of the Present," in *Selected Writings*.

77 *"if I live as a conscious human being"*: Cited in Rabinbach, *In the Shadow of Catastrophe*, 40.

78 *"would not be very comfortable"*: Scholem, *Walter Benjamin*, 11.

78 *"Next week I'll have to see"*: Scholem, *Lamentations*, 63.

81 *"Nature is the scene"*: Scholem, *Major Trends in Jewish Mysticism*, 7.

81 *"the stage on which the drama"*: Ibid., 8.

82 *"mysticism as such"*: Ibid., 6.

84 *"metaphysically positive attitude"*: Ibid., 15.

84 *"a living organism"*: Ibid., 14.

CHAPTER FOUR

89 *A plague of locusts*: The locust infestation was covered widely in the international press. See, for example, "Remarkable Details from American Consul on Palestine Locust Plague," *New York Times*, November 21, 1915.

90 *subsist on a diet of locusts*: Scholem, *Lamentations*, 87–88.

90 *knew what Zionist ideology consisted in*: Ibid., 82–84.

90 *gauge the spiritual value*: See, in particular, Walter Benjamin, "The Life of Students," in Benjamin, *Selected Writings, Volume 1*, 37–47.

90 *"the sneering face of the angel"*: Scholem, *Lamentations*, 87.

91 *They played chess*: Scholem, *Walter Benjamin*, 32.

91 *As a child, he'd often been sick*: Benjamin, *Berlin Childhood Around 1900*, 72–73.

91 *Even Benjamin's helplessness*: Benjamin, *Reflections*, 4–5.

91 *renowned Dürer prints*: For example, Benjamin, *Correspondence*, 42.

91 *vision in the Café des Deux Magots*: Benjamin, *Reflections*, 30–31.

92 *"for the suffering of individuals"*: Ibid., 71.

92 *Having discovered "Humanity"*: Scholem, *On Jews and Judaism in Crisis*, 3.

92 *"You're deluding yourself"*: Scholem discusses these debates in various places, including ibid., 3–4, and *From Berlin to Jerusalem*, 41.

94 *"'Organization' is a synonym for death"*: Scholem, *A Life in Letters*, 22–23.

94 "*The only organization Zionism has*": Scholem, *Lamentations*, 219.

94 "*Salto-mortale*": Cited in Rabinbach, *In the Shadow of Catastrophe*, 39.

94 Buber "*sought this influence*": Scholem, *On Jews and Judaism in Crisis*, 127.

95 "*You'd have to ask every Jew*": Scholem, *Walter Benjamin*, 29.

95 "*horrifying, utterly bloodless white tint*": Scholem, *Lamentations*, 84–86.

96 *"Myths, which take leave of the earth"*: Cited in Benjamin, *Selected Writings, Volume 1*, 36.

96 *In the Talmud it is said*: Scholem, *Walter Benjamin*, 21.

97 "*One does want to be understood*": Rabinbach, *In the Shadow of Catastrophe*, 46.

97 "*Ein-sof is that which* cannot": Scholem, *Lamentations*, 131.

97 *God's chariot-throne, the Merkabah*: Scholem, *Major Trends in Jewish Mysticism*, 40–97. This is my source throughout the discussion of this iteration of Jewish mysticism.

101 "*the stammering sounds*": Scholem, *Lamentations*, 93.

102 "Ausserordentlich!": Scholem, *Walter Benjamin*, 9–10.

102 *suicidal thoughts were no game*: Scholem, *Lamentations*, 68.

103 "*I am an atheist!*": Ibid., 69.

104 "*purified of all selfishness*": Zweig, *The World of Yesterday*, 223.

104 "*During the past few days*": Elon, *The Pity of It All*, 321.

104 "*Do you love Germany?*": The poet is Julius Bab, discussed and cited ibid., 322–23.

105 "*One small nation*": Gershom Scholem interview with Ehud Ben Ezer, in Ben Ezer, *Unease in Zion*, esp. 264–65.

106 "He Was His Name": Scholem, *Lamentations*, 116.

106 *their patronym emerged*: Scholem, *From Berlin to Jerusalem*, 1–2.

107 "*of the distinct and the disparate*": Cited in Pensky, *Melancholy Dialectics*, 66–67.

108 "*My God, how can you commit*": Scholem, *Lamentations*, 78–80.

109 *"We are Jews"*: Ibid., 77.

110 *"for I am a man"*: Ibid., 83.

110 *"I would shoot myself"*: Ibid., 91.

111 "Jerusalem for a Thinking Humanity": Ibid., 121.

112 *"Jewish philosophy paid a heavy price"*: Scholem, *On the Kabbalah and Its Symbolism*, 99-100.

115 *"We confront the old questions"*: Ibid., 117.

CHAPTER FIVE

Except where otherwise noted, citations from Scholem's work in this chapter are all taken from his essay "Kabbalah and Myth," in *On the Kabbalah and Its Symbolism*, 87-117.

121 *Scholem triangulated psychology with history*: Idel, *Kabbalah*, 265-66.

125 *"The mystical symbol is an expressible"*: Scholem, *Major Trends in Jewish Mysticism*, 27-28.

126 *"All names and attributes"*: Ibid., 208.

128 *"In none of their systems"*: Scholem, *On the Kabbalah and Its Symbolism*, 122.

134 *"Lately I've been preoccupied"*: Scholem, *Lamentations*, 90.

CHAPTER SIX

137 *"like a sleepwalker"*: Scholem, *Lamentations*, 139.

137 *The filthy talk of the soldiers*: Scholem, *A Life in Letters*, 46-47.

137 *reassigned to postal duty*: Ibid., 48.

138 *"and be active in Palestine"*: Scholem, *Lamentations*, 158.

138 *"Hebrew, Hebrew, and more Hebrew"*: Scholem, *A Life in Letters*, 39.

138 *"No one has the right to have 'reasons'"*: Scholem, *Lamentations*, 170.

139 *"Goethe has never spoken"*: Ibid., 212.

139 *"Obscenity blocks every passage"*: Scholem, *A Life in Letters*, 48.

139 *"heavy footsteps of anti-Semitism"*: Ibid., 47.

140 *"Holiness is the rustling"*: Scholem, *Lamentations*, 74.

140 *"between the two poles of mathematical"*: Scholem, *Walter Benjamin*, 49.

140 *"Come as soon as possible"*: Ibid., 47-48.

141 *"Your marriage is the most beautiful"*: Ibid., 51.

141 *"My son the gentleman"*: Scholem, *From Berlin to Jerusalem*, 66.

142 *"I intend to win him"*: Scholem, *A Life in Letters*, 32.

142 *"Zionism and Social Democracy"*: Scholem discusses the scene in several places, most extensively in *From Berlin to Jerusalem*, 83-85.

143 *"on a bridle"*: Scholem, *A Life in Letters*, 42-43.

143 *"a multicolored dog"*: Scholem, *From Berlin to Jerusalem*, 85; discussion of Pension Stuck, 83-89. See also Scholem, *Lamentations*, 171-72.

145 *"aesthetic ecstasy"*: See Scholem, *Lamentations*, 140-41, and *From Berlin to Jerusalem*, 75-80.

145 *"I am always inclined to favor"*: Kafka, *Letters to Felice*, 505.

145 *But now, in Jena*: For example, Scholem, *From Berlin to Jerusalem*, 98-101.

146 *"All the girls I know"*: Scholem, *Lamentations*, 182.

147 *"God has sent me"*: Ibid., 205.

147 *"walls and locks"*: Scholem, *A Life in Letters*, 70-71.

148 *Lamentation "reveals nothing"*: Cited in Barouch, "Lamenting Language Itself." I'm indebted to this essay for grounding my understanding of Scholem's theory of Lamentations, and to Itta Shedletzky for bringing this work to my attention along with Scholem's important letter to Escha and Hugo Bergmann of December, 15, 1947.

149 *"the communion of man"*: Benjamin, *Reflections*, 324; "On Language as Such and on the Language of Man," in *Selected Writings: Volume 1*, 314-22.

150 *"I can understand writing"*: Benjamin, *Correspondence*, 79-81.

150 *"The* Jewish *image of a man"*: Scholem, *Lamentations*, 179-80.

151 *Benjamin's personal glosses on Jewish commentary*: I am indebted to the excellent discussion of crisscrossing influences in Handelman, *Fragments of Redemption*, esp. 71-78.

152 *"no science can better convince us"*: Cited in Gershom Scholem's important discussion of the Christian Kabbalah, in *Kabbalah*, 196-201.

152 *"My children will speak Hebrew"*: Scholem, *A Life in Letters*, 58.

152 *"This is a profound accusation"*: Scholem, *Lamentations*, 217.

153 *"Since receiving your letter"*: Scholem, *Walter Benjamin*, 49.

153 *his doubts about God's existence*: Scholem, *Lamentations*, 203.

153 *"'A real response is like a sweet kiss'"*: Benjamin, *Correspondence*, 117.

155 *"saturated with old Hebrew books"*: Scholem, *From Berlin to Jerusalem*, 169.

155 *"One could say that outside the walls"*: Ibid., 167-69.

159 *"Good day, madam, my dear lady!"*: Scholem, *Lamentations*, 225.

CHAPTER SEVEN

160 *"I'm pleased with you"*: For the first period of Scholem's time with the Benjamins in Switzerland, see Scholem, *Walter Benjamin*, 52-67, and *Lamentations*, 234-43.

162 *suits from Arnold Müller's*: On the economy of Benjamin's childhood home, see Benjamin, *Reflections*, 36–40.

163 *"outrageous wholesomeness"*: Scholem, *Walter Benjamin*, 54.

164 *"To restore language to youth"*: Scholem, *On Jews and Judaism in Crisis*, 57; full letter, 54–60.

164 *"In such matters, the key"*: Scholem, *Walter Benjamin*, 73.

165 *"I deny that metaphysically legitimate"*: Ibid., 87.

167 *The infant Stefan began "writing" him*: Ibid., 73–75.

168 *Dora was laid up*: Scholem, *Lamentations*, 272–73.

170 *"One of the greatest cultural duties"*: Magnes, *Addresses by the Chancellor of Hebrew University*.

178 *"absolute relationship"*: Scholem, *Lamentations*, 252.

179 *"In the days of the Messiah"*: Scholem, *The Messianic Idea in Judaism*, 34–35.

179 *"That ever-flowing fountain"*: Ibid., 300.

179 *the essay he'd begun on the Book of Jonah*: For the final version of this essay, see Scholem, "On Jonah and the Concept of Justice."

CHAPTER EIGHT

184 *"Our goal is communism"*: Cited in Lutz, "The Spartacan Uprising in Germany," 79.

184 *COMMUNAL INSTITUTION!*: Scholem, *A Life in Letters*, 81.

185 *"The colossal, world-shaking"*: Kessler, *Berlin in Lights*, 10–11.

186 *"dictatorship of poverty"*: Scholem, *Walter Benjamin*, 78.

186 *"I take it into my field of vision"*: Scholem, *A Life in Letters*, 81–82.

186 *"The messianic kingdom can only unfold"*: Cited in Jacobson, *Metaphysics of the Profane*, 195; full speech, "The Bolshevik Revolution," 195–96.

187 *"a theocratic state of mind"*: Scholem, *Lamentations*, 288.

188 *"God is at best"*: Ibid., 60.

188 *"Torah is not a law"*: Ibid., 153.

189 *"Religion is the consciousness"*: Ibid., 181.

190 *"the type of mother God intended"*: Ibid., 304.

190 *"Walter and Dora's notion"*: Ibid., 284.

190 *"No one commands, no one obeys"*: Scholem, *A Life in Letters*, 82–83.

191 *"a man of declamations and parades"*: For contemporary impressions of the Spartacan uprising, see, for example, "The Sons of Spartacus," *New York Times*, December 10, 1918, and Frederick A. Smith, "German Conditions Investigated by American Writer," *New York Times*, December 26, 1918; also Lutz, "The Spartacan Uprising in Germany," 78–87.

191 *"Because you fed people an impure language"*: Scholem, *Lamentations*, 319–20.

192 *"constant putsches and riots"*: Scholem, *A Life in Letters*, 97–98.

192 *"Sorry to say, it's all over"*: Ibid., 107.

192 *"The renunciation of ambition"*: Scholem, *Walter Benjamin*, 114.

192 *"the bacillus had taken hold"*: Scholem, *From Berlin to Jerusalem*, 114.

193 *"which should be discussed only"*: Scholem, *A Life in Letters*, 78–79.

193 *"meaningless-meaningful stories"*: Scholem, *Walter Benjamin*, 83–84.

193 *"critical magic"*: Benjamin, *Correspondence*, 84.

193 *Of two Jewish works of fiction*: Scholem, *From Berlin to Jerusalem*, 40–41.

194 *"From Cervantes and Shakespeare"*: Scholem, *Lamentations*, 95.

194 *"wild men from the uncivilized East"*: Weizmann, *Trial and Error*, 40.

196 *"Everything must be done immediately!"*: Cited in Rose, *The Question of Zion*, 91.

196 *"simpliste and doomed to failure"*: Weizmann, *Trial and Error*, 44.

197 *"One has to be careful not to turn the screw"*: Weizmann, *Letters and Papers*, 264.

197 *"The problem was a personal, not a national"*: Scholem, *On Jews and Judaism in Crisis*, 23.

197 *"who had the rope around their neck"*: Weizmann, *Letters and Papers*, 253.

198 *"The British Government promised"*: Rose, *The Question of Zion*, 88.

198 *nothing but small talk*: Scholem, *Lamentations*, 317–18.

200 *a brigade of Cossacks entered*: For background on these events, see, for example, Heifetz, *The Slaughter of the Jews in the Ukraine*, and Levene, *The Crisis of Genocide*.

200 *thirty-one prominent U.S. Jews*: "Protest to Wilson Against Zionist State," *New York Times*, March 5, 1919.

202 *"The Jewish people have been waiting"*: See Weizmann, *Letters and Papers*, 221–32.

202 *"on a self-supporting basis"*: Walter Duranty, "Action of Conference Satisfies Zionists," *New York Times*, March 3, 1919.

202 *Scholem closely followed these developments*: For historical context on all these events, see Vital, *Zionism*, esp. 324–76.

203 *"Jews think linguistically"*: Scholem, *Lamentations*, 320.

CHAPTER NINE

210 *"Haunted houses can be UNhaunted"*: Goldberg's interlude as ghost hunter in Manhattan is recounted in the *New Yorker*, July 17, 1943, esp. 17.

211 *"a small, fat man who looked like a stuffed dummy"*: Scholem, *Walter Benjamin*, 96; Goldberg's background, along with Goldberg's relationship to Benjamin and himself, 95–98. Also Scholem, *From Berlin to Jerusalem*, 146–49. For further

details and context, see Robertson, *The "Jewish Question" in German Literature*, 432–35.

212 *"fascinating ugliness"*: Thomas Mann, *Doctor Faustus*, trans. John E. Woods (New York: Knopf, 1997), 294–300.

213 *Walter Moses, the leader of the Blau-Weiss*: On Scholem's relationship to the Blau-Weiss, see Scholem, *From Berlin to Jerusalem*, 152–53, and *On Jews and Judaism in Crisis*, 12–13. More context and citations from Scholem's important address on the Blau-Weiss, "Erkälung," can be found in Allman, *The German Stranger*; Sheppard, *Leo Strauss and the Politics of Exile*; Sharfman, "Between Identities."

214 *"good for the printing business"*: Scholem, *A Life in Letters*, 98.

216 *"incantations and imprecations"*: Broué, *The German Revolution*, esp. 459–60.

216 *"Don't fool yourself"*: Scholem, *From Berlin to Jerusalem*, 144–45.

217 *Gerhard's arrival in Munich*: Ibid., 116–26.

217 *"waltzing my way"*: Scholem, *A Life in Letters*, 114.

217 *using black arts*: Ibid., 113.

217 *"vast foundational philological-philosophical"*: Ibid., 112.

218 *"resembled an overgrown field of ruins"*: Scholem, *On the Kabbalah and Its Symbolism*, 2.

218 *"It is the 'form of the hand'"*: From the *Book Bahir*, in Scholem, *Origins of the Kabbalah*, 149.

219 *"I have never thought of you more often"*: Benjamin, *Correspondence*, 165.

219 *"Only the Messiah himself"*: Benjamin, "Theological-Political Fragment," in *Selected Writings, Volume 1*, 305–6.

220 *Benjamin's own inability to commit himself*: I am indebted to Anson Rabinbach for insights on Benjamin's wavering between different philosophical and ideological positions. Interview, May 28, 2015.

220 *"Age can ultimately turn the choice"*: Benjamin, *Correspondence*, 169–70.

220 *"Do not turn away from us"*: Ibid., 91.

221 *"Where is my production plant located?"*: Ibid., 232.

222 *"a flâneur of charm"*: Wolff, *Hindsight*, provides vivid reminiscences of the Benjamins and their relationship to both Ernst Schoen and Jula Cohn.

224 *"I am an unsymbolic thing"*: Scholem, "Greetings from Angelus," in *The Fullness of Time*, 65–66.

225 *"the spirit of its age"*: Benjamin, "Announcement of the Journal *Angelus Novus*," in *Selected Writings: Volume 1*, 292–96.

225 *"As far as I can tell, it is a prerequisite"*: Benjamin, *Correspondence*, 185–87.

225 *"My mind was on quite different things"*: Scholem, *Walter Benjamin*, 100–3.

227 *"a specialist outside the quota"*: Scholem, *From Berlin to Jerusalem*, 158–59.

227 *"a million-fold witches' sabbath"*: Scholem, *A Life in Letters*, 125–26.

228 *Thieves formed "storming columns"*: "Even the Funeral Flowers Stolen in Berlin Cemeteries," *New York Times*, September 2, 1923.

228 *"The air is so full of phantoms"*: Benjamin, *Reflections*, 74; full essay, 70–76.

229 *"the direction it had been taking for years"*: Scholem, *Walter Benjamin*, 116.

230 *"represents the pure, unbroken power"*: Scholem, *The Messianic Idea in Judaism*, 22–24.

233 *Goldstein was treated as a hero*: See the discussion of these events in Karpin and Friedman, *Murder in the Name of God*, esp. 15–17.

CHAPTER TEN

238 *"All festivals will one day"*: Scholem, *The Messianic Idea in Judaism*, 54–55.

240 *"Reflections on Modern Jewish Studies"*: All quotes from this essay are from Scholem, *On the Possibility of Jewish Mysticism in Our Time*, 51–71.

241 *"battered forty times in its history"*: "Gen. Storrs Tells of Jerusalem Plans: British Governor Hopes 'City of a Great Soul Will Be Preserved,'" *New York Times*, February 10, 1923.

242 *"The dirty Jewish Quarter"*: Karl Baedeker: *Palestine and Syria: Handbook for Travellers* (Leipzig: Karl Baedeker, 1906), 35. Though I'm citing the 1906 edition, the language about the Jewish Quarter was repeated verbatim for many years.

244 *"He who 'experiences' a landscape"*: Scholem, *Lamentations*, 147.

244 *The Executive had no money to pay him*: These events are recounted in Scholem, *From Berlin to Jerusalem*, 160–68.

246 *"the hope of Palestine"*: Scholem, *A Life in Letters*, 129.

246 *The so-called garden suburb neighborhoods*: For background on the development of Jerusalem under the Mandate government, see Kark and Oren-Noordheim, *Jerusalem and Its Environs*, 137–90.

247 *The postwar era inaugurated*: In addition to Kark and Oren-Noordheim, see Storrs, *Orientations*, 336–66.

247 *"like tapestry, a criterion"*: Storrs, *Orientations*, 496.

248 *"The Psalms of David"*: Ibid., 366.

248 *"plastic hours" of history*: "Irving Howe Interviews Gershom Scholem. The Only Thing in My Life I Have Never Doubted Is the Existence of God," *Present Tense* 8, no. 1 (1980): 53–57.

249 *"With our return to our own history"*: Scholem, *From Berlin to Jerusalem*, 166–67.

250 *"to the sect with apocalyptic views"*: Scholem, *A Life in Letters*, 137–38.

250 *"Seldom can any community"*: Bentwich, *Mandate Memories*, 48–49.

252 *he himself had been the "young friend"*: Scholem, *On Jews and Judaism in Crisis*, 37–38.

252 *Jerusalem's early-twentieth-century kabbalistic landscape*: I am indebted both to Jonatan Meir's enlightening essay, "The Imagined Decline of Kabbalah," 197–220, and to an interview with Meir on November 23, 2014, in which he elaborated some ideas from his ongoing work on this subject. I also drew on Magid's review essay, "'The King Is Dead.'"

254 *scribbled marginalia in Scholem's own handwriting*: I am grateful to Jonatan Meir for bringing these notes to my attention.

256 *"You say very little about Safed"*: Benjamin, *Correspondence*, 243.

256 *"holy apple orchard"*: Scholem, *On the Kabbalah and Its Symbolism*, 140.

257 *it would have been professional suicide*: Moshe Idel raised this point in an interview on March 5, 2015.

258 *"the beautiful virgin who has no eyes"*: Scholem, *On the Kabbalah and Its Symbolism*, 141.

CHAPTER ELEVEN

263 *The news beamed round the world*: See, for example, "Balfour Dedicates Hebrew University," *New York Times*, April 2, 1925. For more context on the opening of the university, see Myers, *Re-Inventing the Jewish Past*, esp. 38–76.

263 *"the cultural climax of the Jewish homeland"*: Cited in "Fete in Palestine to Have Echo Here," *New York Times*, March 29, 1925.

263 *"a nursery fostering"*: Weizmann, *Letters and Papers*, 29.

264 *"American radical"*: Scholem, *From Berlin to Jerusalem*, 171–73.

264 *"Not here Judaism, there humanity"*: Bentwich, *For Zion's Sake*, 156–57.

267 *Balfour was escorted by Governor Storrs*: Storrs, *Orientations*, 506–7.

268 *"spinsterish and architectural"*: Begbie, *The Mirrors of Downing Street*, 61–70.

268 *The Arabs called a strike when Balfour*: For one contemporary account, see "Strike as Balfour Reaches Palestine," *New York Times*, March 26, 1925.

268 *"political instrument"*: Magnes, *Dissenter in Zion*, 231–33.

269 *"It was to have been expected"*: Ibid., 234–35.

270 *"If the world could be saved by universities"*: "Rabbi Criticizes Hebrew University," *New York Times*, April 13, 1925.

271 *"the effects of intense capitalist colonization"*: Benjamin, *Correspondence*, 268.

271 *"Dr. Weizmann merely wanted research institutes"*: Quoted in Schechtman, *The Life and Times of Vladimir Jabotinsky*, 187.

272 *"Balm of Gilead"*: Schechtman, *The Jabotinsky Story*, 58–61.

272 *"Palestine is not Rhodesia"*: Cited in Lavsky, *Before Catastrophe*, 168.

272 *"No more gallant officer"*: Storrs, *Orientations*, 488.

273 *The first political essay Scholem wrote*: Ratzabi, *The Radical Circle in Brith Shalom*, 141. Many of Scholem's Brit Shalom essays were collected in *'Od Davar*, ed. Avraham Shapira (Tel Aviv: 'Am 'Oved, 1989) (Hebrew).

273 *"Palestine will be a state of two nations"*: Cited in Buber, *A Land of Two Peoples*, 72–73.

273 *bloody anti-Semitic riots*: "Violent Rioting Starts in Vienna as Zionists Meet," *New York Times*, August 18, 1925.

274 *"You know that I came to Palestine"*: Scholem, *A Life in Letters*, 145–46.

275 *"Such a man can be relied on"*: Scholem, *From Berlin to Jerusalem*, 174.

275 *delivering one of the institute's inaugural lectures*: This debut is discussed in Myers, *Re-Inventing the Jewish Past*, 160–61. I'm grateful to Daniel Abrams for providing me with the Hebrew original of this talk. I also benefited from Henry Wasserman's fascinating review essay, "A Gershom Scholem Goldmine," *Haaretz*, November 15, 2002, which contains an incisive analysis of Scholem's relationship to the questions of pseudepigraphy that surround the Zohar, and also delves into Scholem's first Brit Shalom essay against the Jewish Legion.

278 *"revelation will come to unfold"*: Scholem, *The Messianic Idea in Judaism*, 296.

278 *"love of words"*: My understanding of Scholem's relationship to philology was deepened by Andreas B. Kilcher, "Philology as Kabbalah," a compelling essay in Huss, *Kabbalah and Modernity*, 13–28.

278 *"I do believe that deep philology"*: Quoted ibid., 24.

279 *"does not share the firm faith"*: Scholem, "On the Possibility of Jewish Mysticism," in *On the Possibility of Jewish Mysticism in Our Time*, 15–16.

285 *Freud postulated that Judaism*: Sigmund Freud, "Moses the Man and Mono-theistic Religion," in *Mass Psychology and Other Writings*, 293–98.

287 *"the tree of freedom, symbolic of an age"*: Scholem, *On the Kabbalah and Its Symbolism*, 68–69.

288 *"the exile of the Shekinah"*: Ibid., 70.

CHAPTER TWELVE

289 *Sabbatai Sevi, born in Smyrna in 1626*: My principal source for the Sabbatai Sevi story is Scholem's extraordinary biographical study, *Sabbatai Sevi: The Mystical Messiah*. For important further context, see Goldish, *The Sabbatean Prophets*, and Rapoport-Albert, *Women and the Messianic Heresy of Sabbatai Zevi*.

292 *"The apostasy of the Messiah"*: Scholem, *The Messianic Idea in Judaism*, 64.

293 *"has the power of restoring"*: Ibid., 66.

293 *"It is ordained that the King"*: Ibid., 95.

294 *"The Days of the Messiah represent"*: George Foot Moore, cited ibid., 53.

294 *"at the boundary between the validity of the old law"*: Ibid., 65.

295 *"the unique psychology of these reconverts"*: Ibid., 95.

296 *"The land is a volcano"*: This extraordinary letter has been reprinted and retranslated many times. This version is from *On the Possibility of Jewish Mysticism in Our Time*, 27–29.

298 *"rather ostentatious self-assurance"*: For more on this Paris trip, see Scholem, *Walter Benjamin*, 130–42.

298 *"along with others who refused to bow"*: Scholem, *A Life in Letters*, 156–57. For further background on Werner's story, see Zadoff, "From Mission to Memory. I'm also grateful to Mirjam Zadoff for answering a number of queries about Werner Scholem I placed to her in an email exchange.

299 *So much for Arthur's legacy*: Scholem, *A Life in Letters*, 141–43.

301 *"Capitalists without capital"*: For background on this period, see, for example, Laqueur, *A History of Zionism*, esp. 270–338. For perspective on the vicissitudes of the Labor party relative to Jabotinsky and the rise of the Revisionists, see Cohen, *Zion and State*, esp. 105–60.

302 *"entirely materialistic, nationalist, acquisitive"*: Storrs, *Orientations*, 444.

303 *"including State lands and waste lands"*: Ibid., 419.

304 *"ignorant Fellah"*: See, for example, Porat, "Forging Zionist Identity Prior to 1948," 55.

304 *formally launched thereafter as the Brit Shalom*: For background on Arthur Ruppin and Brit Shalom, see Ratzabi, *The Radical Circle in Brith Shalom*; Aschheim, *Beyond the Border*; Ruppin, *Memoirs, Diaries, Letters*; Lavsky, *Before Catastrophe*.

304 *"the last flicker of the humanist nationalist flame"*: Cited in Aschheim, *Beyond the Border*, 6.

305 *chats with their gardeners*: Ibid., 35.

306 *"If I were in Palestine"*: Benjamin, *Correspondence*, 377–78.

307 *"was for 'external' purposes"*: Scholem, *On Jews and Judaism in Crisis*, 43.

307 *"You have now occupied the actual fortresses"*: Benjamin, *Correspondence*, 366.

307 *"I have long since become wedded"*: Cited in Myers, *Re-Inventing the Jewish Past*, 158.

308 *"Rest assured that this man"*: Scholem, *A Life in Letters*, 161.

CHAPTER THIRTEEN

314 *Early Friday afternoon on August 23, 1929*: Scholem, *A Life in Letters*, 172.

315 *At nightfall, the bloodshed was raging*: The events surrounding the riots/uprising

at the Wall were extensively covered in the international press. For example, "47 Dead in Jerusalem Riot; Attacks by Arabs Spread; British Troops Rush to City," *New York Times*, August 25, 1929. On the background of the riots as reported in the *Times*, see "Wailing Wall of Jerusalem Gives Rise to Controversy; Mourners at Historic Place of Lamentations Make Sharp Protest Against the Removal of a Partition," October 7, 1929. See also Storrs, *Orientations*, 466–67; and Sela, "The Wailing Wall Riots."

316 *the epicenter of Jewish lamentation*: See Giller, *Reading the Zohar*, 12–13; and Vilnay, *Legends of Jerusalem*, 159–78.

317 *The grand mufti's cohort*: "Protest to King George," *New York Times*, October 25, 1928.

318 *"recognizing unreservedly the inviolability"*: "Tries to Calm Arabs," *New York Times*, November 11, 1928.

318 *Ten thousand Jews came*: "10,000 Jews Guarded at the Wailing Wall," *New York Times*, August 16, 1929.

318 *"To sacrifice all"*: For example, "2,000 Demonstrate in Jerusalem; Demand Free Access of Jews to Wall," Jewish Telegraph Agency, August 18, 1929.

319 *a young Jewish man playing ball*: "Jews Allege Arabs Desecrate Wall," *New York Times*, August 25, 1929; "Jerusalem Clashes Result in One Death," *New York Times*, August 21, 1929.

319 *"The argument that the Arabs should not"*: Schechtman, *The Jabotinsky Story*, 118–21.

320 *"Warm regards to the servant"*: Scholem, *A Life in Letters*, 179.

320 *Arab grievances had risen*: Joseph M. Levy, "Arab Counsel Asks Mandate Revision," *New York Times*, December 27, 1929.

320 *"There seems to be a considerable body"*: Joseph M. Levy, "Zionists Assailed on Palestine Stand," *New York Times*, December 28, 1929.

321 *"expanded immigration, particularly of young people"*: Cited in Sela, "The Wailing Wall Riots," 83.

322 *Arabs were accused of poisoning grapes*: Joseph M. Levy, "Clashes Continue Palestine Unrest," *New York Times*, September 10, 1929.

322 *a statement by Chief Rabbi Yitzhak Kook*: Joseph M. Levy, "Arab Counsel Asks Mandate Revision," *New York Times*, December 27, 1929.

323 *"Precisely understood, there is nothing concrete"*: Scholem, *The Messianic Idea in Judaism*, 35.

324 *"atomized, individualized, confined"*: Cited in Aschheim, *Beyond the Border*, 15.

324 *But, as Gershom reminded his mother*: Scholem, *A Life in Letters*, 179.

324 *"the soul of this activity is Scholem"*: Cited in Aschheim, "The Metaphysical Psychologist," 921n80.

324 *He joined Brit Shalom's call*: "22 Arabs Reprieved in Palestine Riots," *New York Times*, June 1, 1930.

325 *When Menachem Ussishkin*: Cited in Aschheim, *At the Edges of Liberalism*, 45.

325 *"There should only be Jews and Hebrew"*: Ibid., 47.

325 *"Zionism never ceased to rely"*: Cited in Shapira, *Land and Power*, 169.

325 *In May 1930*: Buber, *Letters*, 176–78.

326 *Scholem refused to put his scholarly knowledge*: Ratzabi, *The Radical Circle in Brith Shalom*, 154.

326 *"Encounter with Zion and the World"*: Scholem, *The Fullness of Time*, 87–89.

327 *Betty Scholem assured her son*: Scholem, *A Life in Letters*, 187–88.

327 *She told Gershom she'd heard twelve million*: Ibid., 192.

327 *"We on our part contemplate"*: Weizmann, *Letters and Papers*; his full summing-up, 613–41. For more background on these events, see Lavsky, *Before Catastrophe*, 181–226; and Cohen, *Zion and State*, esp. 141–60.

328 *Jabotinsky's address*: See Schechtman, *The Jabotinsky Story*, 147–50.

328 *"I have no sympathy"*: Weizmann, *Letters and Papers*, 642.

328 *The congress devolved*: See Louis Stark, "Zionist Congress Halted by Uproar," *New York Times*, July 3, 1931; Stark, "Revisionists Riot in Zionist Parley," *New York Times*, July 13, 193; Schechtman, *The Jabotinsky Story*, 151–54.

330 *"a religious-mystical quest"*: Scholem, *Walter Benjamin*, 171–74.

332 *"You must bear in mind"*: Scholem, *A Life in Letters*, 194.

CHAPTER FOURTEEN

340 *Scholem and Escha planted carnations*: One of the best (and only) sources for details of Scholem's day-to-day life in these years is his voluminous correspondence with his mother, Betty, much of which is collected in Scholem, *A Life in Letters*. For the complete Hebrew edition of the exchange, see Gershom Scholem, *Gershom Scholem and His Mother, Letters 1917–1946* (Tel Aviv: Schocken Books, 1998), from *Mutter und Sohn im Briefwechsel, 1917–1946* (Munich: C. H. Beck 1989).

341 *Werner had been rearrested*: In addition to the discussion of these events ibid., there are numerous mentions of Scholem's anxieties and despair over Werner's fate in Benjamin and Scholem, *Correspondence*, esp. 43–44, 56, 75. Scholem touches on them in *From Berlin to Jerusalem*, esp. 144–46.

343 *"Kafka's world is a world of revelation"*: Benjamin and Scholem, *Correspondence*, 126.

344 *"with a prosperous cultivation"*: Byron, *The Road to Oxiana*, 38.

344 *"One recent ship alone"*: Benjamin and Scholem, *Correspondence*, 33.

344 *"the sentimental and religious values"*: "Tourist Lures in Jerusalem: Program of

Beautification to Add New Attractions to the Ancient City," *New York Times*, September 22, 1935.

344 *"More blood is spilled than the newspapers"*: Joseph Roth, "The Third Reich a Dependency of Hell on Earth," in Roth, *The Hotel Years*, 234–36.

344 *"a harrowing picture of medieval events"*: Benjamin and Scholem, *Correspondence*, 39.

344 *"The last age became"*: Scholem, *Major Trends in Jewish Mysticism*, 246.

345 *"the just revenge of the* genius loci*"*: Benjamin and Scholem, *Correspondence*, 56.

346 *"yeast seeking dough"*: Ratzabi, *The Radical Circle in Brith Shalom*, x–xi.

346 *"Our existence, our sad immortality"*: Scholem, *Walter Benjamin*, 173.

346 *"The indefiniteness of the Jewish inflow"*: Bentwich, *Mandate Memories*, 154–55.

347 *"I am uncannily attracted"*: In Scholem, *The Fullness of Time*, 95–97.

347 *"One cannot catechize him"*: Cited in Biale, *Gershom Scholem: Kabbalah and Counter-History*, 34.

348 *"enchanted kingdom of illusions"*: Gershom Scholem, "With a Copy of Kafka's *The Trial*," in *On the Possibility of Jewish Mysticism in Our Time*, 194–96.

348 *"model of a renewed humanity"*: Scholem, *The Messianic Idea in Judaism*, 13–14.

348 *"a theologian marooned"*: Scholem, *On Jews and Judaism in Crisis*, 186–87.

349 *"that his imagination had made itself independent"*: Walter Benjamin, "In the Sun," in Benjamin, *Selected Writings, Volume 2: Part 2*, 662–65.

349 *"I learned from this what honors"*: Benjamin and Scholem, *Correspondence*, 123n.

350 *"Not system but* commentary*"*: Scholem, "Tradition and Commentary as Religious Categories in Judaism."

351 *"concise exposition"*: Benjamin and Scholem, *Correspondence*, 151.

351 *"Of course, the voyage itself"*: Ibid., 152.

351 *"This has as much to do with family matters"*: Ibid., 161–62.

351 *"drastically affected"*: Ibid., 172.

352 *"Separating from Escha"*: Ibid., 176.

352 *Escha and Hugo had begun an affair*: Itta Shedletzky contributed to my under-standing of these events in a phone interview on January 9, 2015, in the course of which she described a conversation with Scholem's good friend Meta Jahr in which Jahr spoke of the affair as common knowledge.

352 *"the most succinct expression"*: Benjamin and Scholem, *Correspondence*, 188.

354 *including Scholem's colleague*: Ibid., 183–84; and "Teacher Is Killed in Palestine Home," *New York Times*, August 22, 1936.

354 *"Here we find ourselves standing"*: Scholem, *The Messianic Idea in Judaism*, 78.

354 *"the Bible is not our land registry"*: Cited in Karpan and Friedman, *Murder in the*

Name of God, 93. This book is essential for an understanding of Netanyahu's complicity in Rabin's death.

356 *OUR FATE TO BE DECIDED*: Ibid., 89–100.

357 Pulsa da-Nura: Ibid., 90–91; and Bloom, *Jewish Mysticism and Magic*, 192.

358 *"fire, fire, there is evil in Rabin"*: Karpan and Friedman, *Murder in the Name of God*, 170–71.

358 din rodef: Ibid., 105–9.

360 *"I cannot digest what is happening"*: Scholem, *A Life in Letters*, 228.

CHAPTER FIFTEEN

361 *"Once it could be claimed"*: Scholem, *The Messianic Idea in Judaism*, 99; the complete essay, "Redemption Through Sin," 78–141.

364 *"The people who came to Palestine"*: Scholem and Biale, "The Threat of Messianism."

366 *"inwardly governed by Zion"*: Scholem, *Lamentations*, 128.

367 *"Hitler came to power"*: Scholem and Biale, "The Threat of Messianism."

367 *"Those Jews we hoped for are dead"*: Ibid.

368 *"the life of Jewish youth"*: Scholem, *Lamentations*, 300.

370 *"enormous lust for destruction"*: Ibid., 34.

370 *destruction represented a positive*: Scholem, *On Jews and Judaism in Crisis*, 194–95.

370 *"I have never stopped believing"*: Ibid., 33.

371 *self-discipline might crumble at any time*: See, for example, Scholem's letter to Benjamin of June 6, 1935, in Benjamin and Scholem, *Correspondence*, 180–81.

371 *descriptions of the "soldiers"*: Anthony Skinner points out the parallels between Jabotinsky and Frank in his commentary in Scholem, *A Life in Letters*, 212.

372 *"We subordinate all human efforts"*: Cited in Cohen, *Zion and State*, 169. This book elucidates events contributing to and consequent on Jabotinsky's ascendancy.

373 *"remain free of apologetic inhibitions"*: Benjamin and Scholem, *Correspondence*, 174.

375 *the counterterror began*: Arab-Jewish violence in the mid-1930s was covered extensively in the world press. For example, Joseph M. Levy, "6 Killed, 14 Injured in Palestine Riots," *New York Times*, November 15, 1937, which mentions the Arab and Jewish construction workers attacking one another on a building site.

376 *"a wilderness inhabited"*: Agnon, *Shira*, 103.

376 *"Dirt and rock take shape"*: Ibid., 106.

377 *"like that of the leaves of trees"*: Benjamin and Scholem, *Correspondence*, 190–91.

377 *He was caught up in excitement*: Ibid., 199–201.

378 *"to make visible that abyss"*: Scholem, *Major Trends in Jewish Mysticism*, 38–39.

382 *"Who better than a nation of construction workers"*: Hass, *Drinking the Sea at Gaza*, 24–25. This remarkable book helped to broaden my perspective on the political turmoil during the years I was living in Jerusalem.

382 *"There are two aspects to the curfew"*: Agnon, *Shira*, 301.

CHAPTER SIXTEEN

387 *Dr. Joachim Prinz*: "Jews Held Doomed Under Nazi Regime," *New York Times*, October 31, 1937.

388 *"a candid word"*: Scholem, "A Candid Letter About My True Intentions in Studying Kabbalah," in *On the Possibility of Jewish Mysticism in Our Time*, 3–5.

391 *"the liquidation of apocalypticism"*: Scholem, *The Messianic Idea in Judaism*, 26–27.

391 *"a truthful representation of the historical"*: Ibid., 9.

391 *"The historical experience of the Jewish people"*: Scholem, *On the Kabbalah*, 146.

392 *"to the extent that the rationalism"*: Scholem, *The Messianic Idea in Judaism*, 26.

392 *"Since the end of the individual life"*: Ibid., 30.

394 *as Scholem contends that Maimonides did*: For more on Scholem's analysis of Maimonides, see his important essay, "Messianism — A Never-Ending Quest," in *On the Possibility of Jewish Mysticism in Our Time*, 102–13.

395 *"The psychological stimulus emanates"*: Scholem, *Major Trends in Jewish Mysticism*, 120–21.

395 *"The Quest for Truth knows of adventures"*: Ibid., 204.

396 *"downright dramatic moments"*: For the key scenes in this trip, see Scholem, *Walter Benjamin*, 205–14.

398 *"Self-deception can lead too easily to suicide"*: Ibid., 234.

398 *"sacrificed truth for the sake"*: Benjamin and Scholem, *Correspondence*, 220–26.

399 *"Benjamin was something like a bogeyman"*: Scholem, *Walter Benjamin*, 217.

399 *"For this the charms exerted on me"*: Benjamin and Scholem, *Correspondence*, 248–49.

399 *in a hotel in Nice*: In addition to Scholem's account of this period, see Eiland and Jennings, *Walter Benjamin: A Critical Life*, 376–80.

400 *Benjamin was interned as an enemy alien*: The most detailed account of Benjamin's time at the internment camp can be found in Hans Sahl, "Walter Benjamin in the Internment Camp," in Smith, *On Walter Benjamin*, 346–52.

401 *"Perhaps it is even proper"*: Scholem, *Walter Benjamin*, 221.

401 *"deprived of this soil"*: Ibid., 223.

403 *"greater creativity in the public realm"*: Scholem, *On the Possibility of Jewish Mysticism in Our Time*, 10.

403 *"the great cataclysm"*: Scholem, *Major Trends in Jewish Mysticism*, 350.

403 *"I suppose that I considered"*: Scholem, *On Jews and Judaism in Crisis*, 47.

403 *"Every line we succeed in publishing"*: Benjamin and Scholem, *Correspondence*, 262.

403 *"actually changes the whole picture"*: Hannah Arendt, "Jewish History, Revised," Arendt's review of *Major Trends in Jewish Mysticism*, in Arendt, *The Jewish Writings*, 303–11.

404 *"a most attractive country"*: Benjamin and Scholem, *Correspondence*, 234.

CHAPTER SEVENTEEN

410 *When Harold Bloom described*: Harold Bloom, interview with author, March 28, 2015.

411 *He told one visitor*: Weiner, *9½ Mystics*, 60. Weiner's full reflections on Scholem, drawn on throughout this chapter, 57–89.

411 *When Cynthia Ozick met Scholem*: Cynthia Ozick, phone interview with author, May 19, 2015.

412 *"great talent for faux pas"*: Hans Jonas, *Memoirs*, 167.

412 *"How could this be that this grand master"*: Cynthia Ozick interview.

412 *"the capacity to make one's life a surprise"*: Ozick, "The Fourth Sparrow," 133.

412 *"like a warrior ready for battle"*: Wiesel, *All Rivers Run to the Sea*, 397.

413 *"I was a listener"*: Cynthia Ozick interview.

413 *"revels in obscenity"*: Scholem's *Haaretz* review of *Portnoy's Complaint*, quoted in Judith Thurman, "Philip Roth Is Good for the Jews," *New Yorker*, May 28, 2014.

413 *"The very question was chilled"*: Steiner, *Errata*, 149.

413 *"I have no argument"*: Scholem interview with Ehud Ben Ezer, in Ben Ezer, *Unease in Zion*, 265–66.

414 *"Scholem had one weakness"*: Anson Rabinbach, interview with author, May 28, 2015.

414 *"Why am I being bribed?"*: Ozick, "The Fourth Sparrow," 132.

415 *"They use biblical verses"*: Scholem and Biale, "The Threat of Messianism."

415 *"not one, not two, but many"*: Moshe Idel, interview with author, March 5, 2015.

415 *Israeli literary critic Baruch Kurzweil*: For the Scholem-Kurzweil debate, see Myers, *Re-Inventing the Jewish Past*, 172–75; Piterberg, *The Returns of Zionism*, 178–87.

417 *"I'll never recover from this terrible blow"*: Scholem to Shalom Spiegel, in Scholem, *A Life in Letters*, 311–12.

417 *"The mystery of human life is deeper"*: Scholem, *Lamentations*, 131.

417 *"was a vacuum in which we would choke"*: Scholem, *From Berlin to Jerusalem*, 151.

417 "none of us thought of that": From a letter by Gershom Scholem to Karl Löwith, cited in Aschheim, *Scholem, Arendt, Klemperer*, 36–37.

418 *wandering alone through the graves*: See, for example, Scholem's correspondence in *A Life in Letters*, 336–39. I'm indebted to Moshe Idel for remarks he made in the course of our interview on March 5, 2015, about the impact of the postwar trip to Germany on Scholem's emotional state.

419 *"mountain of marzipan"*: Ibid., 340–41.

419 *"Only he who can change"*: Cited in Nathan Rotenstreich, "Gershom Scholem's Conception of Jewish Nationalism," in Mendes-Flohr, *Gershom Scholem: The Man and His Work*, 119.

419 *"With his thick tomes"*: Cited in Scholem, *Lamentations*, 4.

420 *"The first thing you see is this painting"*: Cynthia Ozick interview.

420 *Was there a "shadow-Scholem"?*: Ozick, "The Fourth Sparrow," 131.

420 *"A Friendship and Its Flaws"*: George Steiner, "A Friendship and Its Flaws," *Times Literary Supplement*, June 27, 1980.

421 *"That sweep of the hand"*: Cynthia Ozick interview.

422 *"created a situation"*: Scholem, *A Life in Letters*, 332.

423 *"We are asked, it appears, to confess"*: Scholem's main statement in the exchange is reproduced in *On Jews and Judaism in Crisis*, 300–06.

423 *"I have never in my life 'loved'"*: Scholem, *A Life in Letters*, 398–400.

423 *"The gentlemen enjoyed their evil"*: Ibid., 402.

423 *evil existed now only on the surface*: Ibid.

424 *"Today, following the great disaster"*: Scholem, *On the Possibility of Jewish Mysticism in Our Time*, 155; the entire important essay, "Memory and Utopia in Jewish History," 155–66.

426 *"In his final years he was very hopeless"*: Cited in Magid, "Stuck Between Berlin and Jerusalem."

427 *"exceptionally worthwhile and promising"*: Benjamin and Scholem, *Correspondence*, 224–25.

427 *"Without the key that belongs to it"*: Ibid., 135.

427 *"I think the key to Kafka's work"*: Ibid., 243.

428 *Quixote represented Sancho Panza's own demon*: Franz Kafka, "The Truth About Sancho Panza," in Kafka, *The Great Wall of China*, 179.

429 *"The absolute word is as such meaningless"*: Scholem, *On the Kabbalah*, 12; full essay, "Religious Authority and Mysticism," 1–31.

430 *No Talmudic-era scholar says any such thing*: Moshe Idel explores the Origen

citation in his fascinating essay, "Hieroglyphs, Mysteries, Keys: Scholem Between Molitor and Kafka," in Idel, *Old Worlds, New Mirrors*, 109–32.

431 *"The literal meaning is preserved"*: Scholem, *On the Kabbalah and Its Symbolism*, 15.

431 *"Everything that he did in his life"*: Cited in Ratzabi, *The Radical Circle in Brith Shalom*, 205.

431 *"Amerika is one large clown act"*: Benjamin and Scholem, *Correspondence*, 243.

431 *"the vigor and suppleness of a clown"*: Anonymous review of *Leaves of Grass, Critic* 1 (November 5, 1881): 302–3.

432 *"After having been murdered as Jews"*: Scholem, *On Jews and Judaism in Crisis*, 72.

432 *"Scholem filled the gap very nicely"*: Moshe Idel, interview with author, March 5, 2015.

433 *"A likeable fellow"*: Scholem, *On Jews and Judaism in Crisis*, 40.

433 *"Gershom Scholem wrapping his hand"*: Allen Ginsberg, *Journals*, 268.

433 *Later, Ginsberg met with Scholem*: John Freeman interview with Gershom Scholem on BBC *Face to Face*, 1994; transcript posted by the blog, "The Allen Ginsberg Project," http://ginsbergblog.blogspot.com/2011/11/bbc-face-to-face-interview-1994-asv21.html

434 *"The uninhibited optimism"*: Gershom Scholem, "Reflections on Jewish Theology," in *On Jews and Judaism in Crisis*, 291.

434 *"It was clear to them"*: Ibid., 48.

436 *"There must be something basically wrong"*: Scholem, *A Life in Letters*, 492.

436 *"For me, he was the essence"*: Ibid., 494–95.

437 *"What we learn from creation and revelation"*: Scholem, "The Name of God and the Linguistic Theory of the Kabbalah (Part 2)," 194.

CHAPTER EIGHTEEN

441 *"I share the traditional view"*: Scholem, *On Jews and Judaism in Crisis*, 34.

442 *"Three things come unawares"*: Cited in Scholem, *The Messianic Idea in Judaism*, 11.

442 *"The great enterprise of the land of Israel"*: Scholem, "A Lecture About Israel," in *On the Possibility of Jewish Mysticism in Our Time*, 39.

444 *"We are sinful not merely"*: Kafka, *Great Wall of China*, 29.

452 *"The First Cause"*: See in particular Scholem, *The Messianic Idea in Judaism*, 104–07,

457 *"The abyss that events have flung open"*: Scholem, *On Jews and Judaism in Crisis*, 90–91.

458 *"There is no way of telling a priori"*: Scholem, *Sabbatai Sevi*, 283–84.

458 *"It is a profound truth"*: Scholem, *The Messianic Idea in Judaism*, 21.

459 *"There's something preliminary"*: Ibid., 35.

460 *"I categorically deny"*: Scholem, *On Jews and Judaism in Crisis*, 44.

461 *"Judaism, in all of its forms"*: Scholem, *The Messianic Idea in Judaism*, 1.

461 *"Certain Messianic strains"*: Scholem interview with Ehud Ben Ezer, in Ben Ezer, *Unease in Zion*, 269.

462 *"Was it not a great opportunity missed"*: Scholem, *Sabbatai Sevi*, 929.

462 *"an instrument for the realization"*: Cited in Ohana, *Political Theologies in the Holy Land*, 14.

462 *color spectrum of Zionist redemption*: Ibid., 12. In addition to Ohana's important book, I benefited in formulating these thoughts from both my interview with Moshe Idel and his essay "Messianic Scholars." I was greatly helped as well by Myers, *Re-Inventing the Jewish Past*.

462 *"This place on which we stand"*: Statement by Max Margolis, cited in Myers, *Re-Inventing the Jewish Past*, 92.

463 *"Jewish Messianism is in its origins"*: Scholem, *The Messianic Idea in Judaism*, 7–8.

463 *"renewed condition of nature"*: Ibid., 13.

464 *"When the Baal Shem"*: Scholem, *Major Trends in Jewish Mysticism*, 349–50.

SELECT BIBLIOGRAPHY

Allman, William H. F. *The German Stranger: Leo Strauss and National Socialism.*
Lanham, MD: Lexington Books, 2011.

Arendt, Hannah. *The Jewish Writings.* Edited by Jerome Kohn and Ron H. Feldman.
New York: Schocken Books, 2007.

Aschheim, Steven E. *At the Edges of Liberalism: Junctions of European, German, and
Jewish History.* New York: Palgrave Macmillan, 2012.

———. *Beyond the Border: The German-Jewish Legacy Abroad.* Princeton: Princeton
University Press, 2007.

———. "The Metaphysical Psychologist: On the Life and Letters of Gershom
Scholem." *Journal of Modern History* 76 (December 2004).

———. *Scholem, Arendt, Klemperer: Intimate Chronicles in Turbulent Times.* Bloomington: Indiana University Press, 2001.

Barouch, Lina. "Lamenting Language Itself: Gershom Scholem on the Silent
Language of Lamentation." *New German Critique* 111 (Fall 2010): 1–26.

Begbie, Harold. *The Mirrors of Downing Street: Some Political Reflections by a
Gentleman with a Duster.* New York: Putnam, 1921.

Belmore, H. W. "Some Recollections of Walter Benjamin." *German Life and Letters*
28, no. 2 (January 1975).

Ben Ezer, Ehud. *Unease in Zion.* New York: Quadrangle/New York Times, 1974.

Benjamin, Walter. *Berlin Childhood Around 1900.* Cambridge, MA: Harvard University
Press, 2006.

———. *The Correspondence of Walter Benjamin, 1910–1940.* Edited by Gershom Scholem
and Theodor W. Adorno. Translated by Manfred R. Jacobson and Evelyn M.
Jacobson. Chicago: University of Chicago Press, 1994.

———. *Early Writings 1910–1917.* Translated by Howard Eiland et al. Cambridge, MA:
Harvard University Press, 2011.

———. *Illuminations.* Edited by Hannah Arendt. Translated by Harry Zohn. New York:
Schocken Books, 1968.

——. *Reflections: Essays, Aphorisms, Autobiographical Writings.* Edited by Peter Demetz. Translated by Edmund Jephcott. New York: Schocken Books, 1986.

——. *Selected Writings, Volume 1: 1913–1926.* Edited by Marcus Bullock and Michael W. Jennings. Cambridge, MA: Harvard University Press, 1996.

——. *Selected Writings, Volume 2: Part 2: 1931–1934.* Edited by Michael W. Jennings, Howard Eiland, and Gary Smith. Cambridge, MA: Harvard University Press, 1999.

Benjamin, Walter, and Gershom Scholem. *The Correspondence of Walter Benjamin and Gershom Scholem, 1932–1940.* Translated by Gary Smith and Andre LeFevere. Cambridge, MA: Harvard University Press, 1992.

Bentwich, Norman. *For Zion's Sake: A Biography of Judah L. Magnes.* Philadelphia: Jewish Publication Society, 1954.

Bentwich, Norman and Helen. *Mandate Memories, 1918–1948.* London: Hogarth, 1965.

Biale, David. *Gershom Scholem: Kabbalah and Counter-History.* Cambridge, MA: Harvard University Press, 1982.

Bloom, Harold, ed. *Modern Critical Views: Gershom Scholem.* New York: Chelsea House, 1987.

Bloom, Maureen. *Jewish Mysticism and Magic: An Anthropological Perspective.* New York: Routledge, 2007.

Brenner, Michael. *The Renaissance of Jewish Culture in Weimar Berlin.* New Haven: Yale University Press, 1996.

Brooker, Peter, Sascha Bru, and Andrew Thacker, eds. *The Oxford Critical and Cultural History of Modernist Magazines, Vol. III, Europe 1880–1940.* Oxford: Oxford University Press, 2013.

Broué, Pierre. *The German Revolution, 1917–1923.* Edited by Ian Birchall and Brian Pearce. Translated by John Archer. Chicago: Haymarket Books, 2006.

Buber, Martin. *A Land of Two Peoples: Martin Buber on Jews and Arabs.* Edited by Paul Mendes-Flohr. Chicago: University of Chicago Press, 1983.

——. *The Letters of Martin Buber: A Life of Dialogue.* Edited by Nahum N. Glatzer and Paul Mendes-Flohr. Translated by Richard and Clara Winston and Harry Zohn. New York: Schocken Books, 1991.

——. *On Judaism.* Edited by Nahum N. Glatzer. New York: Schocken Books, 1967.

Byron, Robert. *The Road to Oxiana.* New York: Oxford University Press, 1982.

Caygill, Howard. *Walter Benjamin: The Colour of Experience.* New York: Routledge, 1998.

Cohen, Mitchell. *Zion and State: Nation, Class and the Shaping of Modern Israel.* Oxford: Blackwell, 1987.

Eiland, Howard, and Michael W. Jennings. *Walter Benjamin: A Critical Life*. Cambridge, MA: Harvard University Press, 2014.

Elon, Amos. *The Pity of It All: A Portrait of the German-Jewish Epoch, 1743–1933*. New York: Picador, 2002.

Freud, Sigmund. *Mass Psychology and Other Writings*. Translated by J. A. Underwood. London: Penguin Books, 2004.

Giller, Pinchas. *Reading the Zohar: The Sacred Text of the Kabbalah*. New York: Oxford University Press, 2001.

Ginsberg, Allen. *Journals: Early Fifties, Early Sixties*. Edited by Gordon Ball. New York: Grove Press, 1977.

Goldish, Matt. *The Sabbatean Prophets*. Cambridge, MA: Harvard University Press, 2004.

Ha'am, Ahad. *Selected Essays*. Translated by Leon Simon. Philadelphia: Jewish Publication Society, 1912.

Handelman, Susan A. *Fragments of Redemption: Jewish Thought and Literary Theory in Benjamin, Scholem, and Levinas*. Bloomington: University of Indiana Press, 1991.

Hass, Amira. *Drinking the Sea at Gaza: Days and Nights in a Land Under Siege*. Translated by Elana Wesley and Maxine Kaufman-Lacusta. New York: Henry Holt, 1996.

Heifetz, Elias. *The Slaughter of the Jews in the Ukraine in 1918*. New York: Thomas Seltzer, 1921.

Idel, Moshe. *Kabbalah: New Perspectives*. New Haven: Yale University Press, 1988.

———. *Old Worlds, New Mirrors: On Jewish Mysticism and Twentieth-Century Thought*. Philadelphia: University of Pennsylvania Press, 2010.

———. "Messianic Scholars: On Early Israeli Scholarship, Politics and Messianism." *Modern Judaism* 32, no. 1 (February 22, 2012).

Jacobson, Eric. *Metaphysics of the Profane: The Political Theology of Walter Benjamin and Gershom Scholem*. New York: Columbia University Press, 2003.

Jonas, Hans. *Memoirs*. Edited by Christian Wiese. Translated by Krishna Winston. Waltham, MA: Brandeis University Press, 2008.

Kafka, Franz. *The Great Wall of China*. Translated by Willa and Edwin Muir. New York: Schocken Books, 1946.

———. *Letters to Felice*. Edited by Erich Heller and Jürgen Born. Translated by James Stern and Elisabeth Duckworth. New York: Schocken Books, 1973.

Kark, Ruth, and Michal Oren-Noordheim. *Jerusalem and Its Environs: Quarters, Neighborhoods, Villages, 1800–1948*. Detroit: Wayne State University Press, 2001.

Karpin, Michael, and Ina Friedman. *Murder in the Name of God: The Plot to Kill Yitzhak Rabin*. New York: Metropolitan Books, 1998.

Kessler, Count Harry. *Berlin in Lights: The Diaries of Count Harry Kessler, 1918–1937*. Translated and edited by Charles Kessler. New York: Grove Press, 1971.

Landauer, Gustav. *Call to Socialism*, "Foreword to the Second Edition" and "For Socialism," 1911, https://theanarchistlibrary.org/library/gustav-landauer-call-to-socialism.

———. *Revolution and Other Writings: A Political Reader*. Edited and translated by Gabriel Kuhn. Oakland, CA: PM Press, 2010.

Laqueur, Walter. *A History of Zionism: from the French Revolution to the Establishment of the State of Israel*. New York: Schocken Books, 1972.

Lavsky, Hagit. *Before Catastrophe: The Distinctive Path of German Zionism*. Detroit: Wayne State University Press, 1996.

Levene, Mark. *The Crisis of Genocide: Devastation, Volume 1: The European Rimlands, 1912–1938*. New York: Oxford University Press, 2013.

Lutz, Ralph H. "The Spartacan Uprising in Germany." *Current History: A Monthly Magazine of the New York Times* 14 (April–September, 1921).

Magid, Shaul. "'The King Is Dead [and has been for three decades], Long Live the King': Contemporary Kabbalah and Scholem's Shadow." *Jewish Quarterly Review* 102, no. 1 (Winter 2012): 131–53.

———. "Stuck Between Berlin and Jerusalem: What Kind of Zionist Was Gershom Scholem?" *Tablet*, March 10, 2015.

Magnes, Judah L. *Addresses by the Chancellor of Hebrew University*. Jerusalem: Hebrew University Press, 1936.

———. *Dissenter in Zion: From the Writings of Judah L. Magnes*. Edited by Arthur A. Goren. Cambridge, MA: Harvard University Press, 1982.

Meir, Jonatan. "The Imagined Decline of Kabbalah: The Kabbalistic Yeshiva Sha'Ar Ha-Shamayim and Kabbalah in Jerusalem in the Beginning of the Twentieth Century." In *Kabbalah and Modernity: Interpretations, Transformations, Adaptations*, edited by Boaz Huss, Marco Pasi, and Kocku von Stuckrad (Boston: Brill, 2010).

Mendes-Flohr, Paul R. *Divided Passions: Jewish Intellectuals and the Experience of Modernity*. Detroit: Wayne State University Press, 1991.

———, ed. *Gershom Scholem: The Man and His Work*. Albany: State University of New York Press, 1994.

Myers, David N. *Re-Inventing the Jewish Past: European Jewish Intellectuals and the Zionist Return to History*. New York: Oxford University Press, 1995.

Nabokov, Vladimir. *Speak, Memory: An Autobiography Revisited*. New York: Vintage Books, 1989.

Ohana, David. *Political Theologies in the Holy Land: Israeli Messianism and Its Critics*. New York: Routledge, 2010.

Pachter, Henry. *Weimar Etudes*. New York: Columbia University Press, 1982.

Pensky, Max. *Melancholy Dialectics: Walter Benjamin and the Play of Mourning*. Amherst: University of Massachusetts Press, 1993.

Piterberg, Gabriel. *The Returns of Zionism: Myths, Politics and Scholarship in Israel*. New York: Verso, 2008.

Porat, Dina. "Forging Zionist Identity Prior to 1948 — Against Which Counter-Identity?" In *Israeli and Palestinian Narratives of Conflict: History's Double Helix*, edited by Robert I. Rotberg (Bloomington: Indiana University Press, 2006).

Presner, Todd Samuel. *Muscular Judaism: The Jewish Body and the Politics of Regeneration*. New York: Routledge, 2007.

Rabinbach, Anson. *In the Shadow of Catastrophe: German Intellectuals Between Apocalypse and Enlightenment*. Berkeley: University of California Press, 1997.

Rapoport-Albert, Ada. *Women and the Messianic Heresy of Sabbatai Zevi, 1666–1816*. Translated by Deborah Greniman. Portland, OR: Littman Library of Jewish Civilization, 2011.

Ratzabi, Shalom. *The Radical Circle in Brith Shalom, 1925–1933*. Leiden, Germany: Brill, 2002.

Robertson, Ritchie. *The "Jewish Question" in German Literature, 1749–1939: Emancipation and Its Discontents*. New York: Oxford University Press, 1999.

Rose, Jacqueline. *The Question of Zion*. Princeton: Princeton University Press, 2005.

Roth, Joseph. *The Hotel Years*. Translated by Michael Hofmann. New York: New Directions, 2015.

——. *What I Saw: Reports from Berlin, 1920–1933*. Translated by Michael Hofmann. New York: W. W. Norton, 2003.

Ruppin, Arthur. *Memoirs, Diaries, Letters*. Edited by Alex Bein. Translated by Karen Gershon. New York: Herzl Press, 1971.

Schechtman, Joseph B. *The Life and Times of Vladimir Jabotinsky: Rebel and Statesman, the Early Years*. New York: Thomas Yoseloff, 1956.

Scholem, Gershom. *From Berlin to Jerusalem: Memories of my Youth*. Translated by Harry Zohn. New York: Schocken Books, 1980.

——. *Briefe I: 1914–1947*. Edited by Itta Shedletzky. Munich: Verlag C.H. Beck, 1994.

——. *Briefe II: 1948–1970*. Edited by Thomas Sparr. Munich: Verlag C.H. Beck, 1995

——. *Briefe III: 1971–1982*. Edited by Itta Shedletzky. Munich: Verlag C.H. Beck, 1999.

———. *The Fullness of Time.* Edited by Steven M. Wasserstorm. Translated by Richard Sieburth. Jerusalem: Ibis Editions, 2003.

———. *Kabbalah.* New York: Quadrangle Books/New York Times, 1974.

———. *Lamentations of Youth: The Diaries of Gershom Scholem.* Translated and edited by Anthony David Skinner. Cambridge, MA: Harvard University Press, 2007.

———. *A Life in Letters, 1914–1982.* Translated and edited by Anthony David Skinner. Cambridge, MA: Harvard University Press, 2002.

———. *Major Trends in Jewish Mysticism.* New York: Schocken Books, 1946.

———. *The Messianic Idea in Judaism: And Other Essays in Jewish Spirituality.* New York: Schocken Books, 1971.

———. "The Name of God and the Linguistic Theory of the Kabbalah (Part 2)." *Diogenes* 80 (1972).

———. *On Jews and Judaism in Crisis: Selected Essays.* New York: Schocken Books, 1976.

———. "On Jonah and the Concept of Justice." Translated by Eric J. Schwab. *Critical Inquiry* 25, no. 2 (Winter 1999): 353–61.

———. *On the Kabbalah and Its Symbolism.* Rev. ed. New York: Schocken Books 1996.

———. *On the Possibility of Jewish Mysticism in Our Time.* Edited by Avraham Shapira. Translated by Jonathan Chipman. Philadelphia: Jewish Publication Society, 1997.

———. *Origins of the Kabbalah.* Edited by R. J. Zwi Werblowsky. Translated by Allan Arkush. Princeton: Princeton University Press, 1987.

———. *Sabbatai Sevi: The Mystical Messiah.* Translated by R. J. Zwi Werblowsky. Princeton: Princeton University Press, 1973.

———. "Tradition and Commentary as Religious Categories in Judaism." *Studies in Comparative Religion* 3, no. 3 (Summer 1969).

———. *Walter Benjamin: The Story of a Friendship.* New York: Schocken Books, 1981.

Scholem, Gershom, and David Biale. "The Threat of Messianism: An Interview with Gershom Scholem." *New York Review of Books*, August 14, 1980.

Sela, Avraham. "The Wailing Wall Riots (1929): A Watershed in the Palestine Conflict." *Muslim World* 84, no. 1–2 (January–April 1994): 60–94.

Shapira, Anita. *Land and Power: The Zionist Resort to Force, 1881–1948.* Stanford: Stanford University Press, 1999.

Sharfman, Glenn R. "Between Identities: The German-Jewish Youth Movement Blau-Weiss, 1912–1926." In *Forging Modern Jewish Identities: Public Faces and Private Struggles*, edited by Michael Berkowitz, Susan L. Tananbaum, and Sam W. Bloom. Portland, OR: Valentine Mitchell, 2003.

Sheppard, Eugene. *Leo Strauss and the Politics of Exile: The Making of a Political Philosopher.* Waltham, MA: Brandeis University Press, 2006.

Smith, Gary, ed. *On Walter Benjamin: Critical Essays and Recollections*. Cambridge, MA: MIT Press, 1988.

Steiner, George. *Errata*. New Haven: Yale University Press, 1997.

Steiner, Uwe. *Walter Benjamin: An Introduction to His Work and Thought*. Translated by Michael Winkler. Chicago: University of Chicago Press, 2010.

Storrs, Sir Ronald. *Orientations*. London: Ivor Nicholson & Watson, 1937.

Vilnay, Zev. *Legends of Jerusalem*. Philadelphia: Jewish Publication Society, 1973.

Vital, David. *Zionism: The Crucial Phase*. New York: Oxford University Press, 1987.

Weiner, Herbert. *9½ Mystics: The Kabbala Today*. New York: Collier Books, 1992.

Weizmann, Chaim. *The Letters and Papers of Chaim Weizmann: Series B, Volume 1, August 1898–July 1931*. Edited by Barnet Litvinoff. New Brunswick, NJ: Rutgers University Press, 1983.

——. *Trial and Error: The Autobiography of Chaim Weizmann*. New York: Harper, 1949.

White, Ian Boyd, and David Frisby, eds. *Metropolis Berlin: 1800–1940*. Berkeley: University of California Press, 2012.

Wiesel, Elie. *All Rivers Run to the Sea: Memoirs*. New York: Schocken Books, 1996.

Wolff, Charlotte. *Hindsight: An Autobiography*. London: Quartet, 1980.

Zadoff, Mirjam, and Noam Zadoff. "From Mission to Memory: Walter Benjamin and Werner Scholem in the Life and Work of Gershom Scholem." *Journal of Modern Jewish Studies* 13, no. 1 (2014): 58–74.

Zohar: The Book of Splendor: Basic Readings from the Kabbalah. Edited by Gershom Scholem. New York: Schocken Books, 1949.

Zweig, Stefan. *The World of Yesterday*. Translated by Benjamin W. Huebsch with Helmut Ripperger. New York: Viking, 1943.

ILLUSTRATIONS

p. viii: Gershom's Scholem's house, entrance path. Photo by the author.

p. 6: Gershom Scholem in Jerusalem, 1924. Courtesy of Gershom Scholem Archive, the National Library of Israel.

p. 13: Jason's Tomb. Photo by the author.

p. 24: Newsboys waiting for "Extras," circa 1914–1915, published by Bain News Service, from the Library of Congress.

p. 27: Gershom Scholem in Berlin, 1902. Courtesy of Gershom Scholem Archive, the National Library of Israel.

p. 28: Children roller-skating in Berlin, 1910. Photo by Philipp Kester. Courtesy bkp, Berlin / Münchner Stadtmuseum / Art Resource, New York.

p. 31: A Hasidic rabbi and his followers in Karlsbad, circa 1930–1939. United States Holocaust Memorial Museum, courtesy of Raphael Aronson.

p. 40: Gershom Scholem and his brothers in costume at their uncle's wedding, 1904. Courtesy of Gershom Scholem Archive, the National Library of Israel.

p. 45: Gershom Scholem in 1913. Courtesy of Gershom Scholem Archive, the National Library of Israel.

p. 52: Grunewald. Photo by the author.

p. 62: Rifts in the Jordan River banks caused by the July 1927 earthquake in Palestine. Matson (G. Eric and Edith) Photograph Collection, American Colony (Jerusalem) Photo Department, Library of Congress.

p. 68: Female stationmaster working the rails during the war, circa 1914–1918. Bundesarchiv / Photo by o.Ang. / Scherl Agency.

p. 84: Damaged Zohar, Sefer Ha-Zohar, Zultz Bach, 1684. Volume from YIVO Institute for Jewish Research. Photo by the author.

p. 89: Cloud of locusts coming over the horizon in Palestine, 1915. Matson (G. Eric and Edith) Photograph Collection, American Colony (Jerusalem) Photo Department, Library of Congress.

p. 93: Gershom Scholem with his brothers, 1904. Courtesy of Gershom Scholem Archive, the National Library of Israel.

p. 96: A party at Martin Buber's house in Jerusalem, 1951. Courtesy of Gershom Scholem Archive, the National Library of Israel.

p. 119: Kabbalistic diagram including six levels of the created world and ten sefiroth (emanations), divine and sub-eternal. From Sefer Shef ha-tal, a work of mystical commentary by Shabtai Shefel Horowitz, 1612. Courtesy Leo Baeck Institute.

p. 130: Two Jewish men and two Jewish women standing in front of Western Wall, 1908. From the Library of Congress.

P. 136: American, British, French, and German gas masks, circa 1915–1920. The Bain Collection, the Library of Congress.

p. 149: Damaged, worm-eaten page from Zultz Bach Zohar, 1684. Volume from YIVO Institute for Jewish Research. Photo by the author.

p. 151: Syncretic diagram from the Kabbalah Denudata, a masterwork of Christian Kabbalah, 1678. Courtesy Leo Baeck Institute.

p. 161: The Mercurial Demon of the Alchemic Philosophers, from Giovanni Battista Nazari's *Della transmutatione metallica*, Brescia, 1589. Copied from *Devils, Demons and Witchcraft* by Ernst and Johanna Lehner (New York: Dover Publications, 1971).

p. 171: Aerial view of Hebrew University campus on Mount Scopus, date uncertain, perhaps 1925. Matson (G. Eric and Edith) Photograph Collection, Library of Congress.

p. 175: Large stone blocks of ancient city wall of Jerusalem, Musara Quarter, 1934–1930. Matson (G. Eric and Edith) Photograph Collection, American Colony (Jerusalem) Photo Department, Library of Congress.

p. 185: The Reichstag transformed into headquarters of the Workers and Soldiers Council during the revolution, 1918. Bundesarchiv / Photo by o.Ang. / Scherl Agency.

p. 189: Escha Scholem in Jerusalem, 1924. Courtesy of Gershom Scholem Archive, the National Library of Israel.

p. 195: Portrait of Chaim Weizmann, undated. Bain Collection, Library of Congress.

p. 205: Entrance to the courtyard of buildings where the author lived in Rehavia, Jerusalem. Photo by the author.

p. 215: Soldiers during the revolution in position with machine guns before the Berlin City Palace, 1918. Bundesarchiv / Photo by Marmulla, L.

p. 218: Kabbalistic diagram depicting hands divided into twenty-eight parts, each containing one letter. In the mystical geomatria the number twenty-eight equals *Koach*, the Hebrew word for strength. Letters at the base of the hands combine to spell the Tetragrammaton. The arrangement of the fingers is meant to evoke the Hebrew letter "Shin" — the initial for "Shadai," another of God's sacred

names. From Sefer Shef ha-tal by Shabtai Shefel Horowitz, 1612. Courtesy Leo
Baeck Institute.

p. 227: German woman overturning a basket of banknotes next to examples of
exorbitant pricing during the hyperinflation, 1923. Photo by Albert Harlingue /
Roger Viollet / Getty Images.

p. 228: Berlin's notorious White Mouse Cabaret, where guests were given a choice
of white or black masks to conceal their identities, circa 1925. Ullstein Bild /
Granger, New York City.

p. 236: Purim Festival, Safra Square, 2015. Photo by the author.

p. 239: Puppet from Adam Yakin's troupe, Purim 2015. Photo by the author.

p. 243: Jerusalem from Mount Scopus, 1942. Matson (G. Eric and Edith) Photograph
Collection, Library of Congress.

p. 245: Gershom Scholem with Escha in Sukkah, 1926. Courtesy of Gershom
Scholem Archive, the National Library of Israel.

p. 255: Gershom Scholem in Jerusalem, 1924. Courtesy of Gershom Scholem Archive,
the National Library of Israel.

p. 265: Judah Magnes as Chancellor of Hebrew University, circa 1925–1934. Matson
(G. Eric and Edith) Photograph Collection, American Colony (Jerusalem) Photo
Department, Library of Congress.

p. 266: Lord Balfour declaring Hebrew University open, April 1, 1925. Matson (G. Eric
and Edith) Photograph Collection, American Colony (Jerusalem) Photo
Department, Library of Congress.

p. 269: Front page of Arab newspaper protesting Lord Balfour's arrival, 1925. See the
notice printed in English on the left. Matson (G. Eric and Edith) Photograph
Collection, American Colony (Jerusalem) Photo Department, Library of
Congress.

p. 297: Children exercising in Tel Aviv, circa 1920–1930. Matson (G. Eric and Edith)
Photograph Collection, American Colony (Jerusalem) Photo Department,
Library of Congress.

p. 303: Jerusalem porter carrying fifty empty petrol tins on his back, circa 1914–1918.
Matson (G. Eric and Edith) Photograph Collection, American Colony (Jerusalem) Photo Department, Library of Congress.

p. 314: Jewish families fleeing violence in the Old City, 1929. Matson (G. Eric and
Edith) Photograph Collection, American Colony (Jerusalem) Photo Department,
Library of Congress.

p. 315: Muslim library looted and burned by Jews, 1929. Matson (G. Eric and Edith)
Photograph Collection, American Colony (Jerusalem) Photo Department,
Library of Congress.

INDEX

Benjamin, Walter (*cont'd*)
  Grunewald neighborhood of, 51–53
  Hiller and, 48–49
  influence on Scholem, 103, 107
  influences on, 69, 73, 221
  intellect of, 64, 96, 103
  interests of, 53, 55, 94, 298, 395, 428–429
  interned in France, 400–401
  Jewish studies of, 151, 219–220, 224, 299
  on Jews, 76, 94
  on language, 148–160
  language of, 50–51, 56, 102
  leaving Germany, 340
  letter to Schocken, 426–427
  magazine project of, 224–226, 240
  marriage of, 140–141, 166, 168–169, 222–223
  at meetings of bourgeois intellectuals,
    73–74
  opposition to war, 64, 140
  personality of, 91–92, 102
  philosophy program of, 160–161
  political activism of, 300–301
  poor health of, 395, 401–402
  relations with family, 162–165, 219–221, 227
  relationships of, 222–223, 256, 298
  reputation of, 48
  reversal in balance of power with
    Scholem, 219, 223–224
  Scholem meeting, 47, 49–50
  Scholem not taking to Jung Juda meeting,
    77–78
  Scholem trying to bring to Jerusalem, 171
  Scholem visiting, 193, 298, 395–397
  Scholem's correspondence with, 420–421
  Scholem's descriptions of, 49–50, 348, 419
  Scholem's discussions with, 63–64, 90–92,
    102, 148, 160–162, 186
  Scholem's feelings for, 147, 426–427
  Scholem's reading and, 75, 101–102, 421
  Scholem's relationship with, 72, 178, 189,
    221–222, 224, 377, 426
  settling in France, 398
  suicide of, 399–400, 417
  travel by, 91, 102
  underestimating Scholem's investment
    in Jewish traditions, 188–189

  wanting to work on Kafka, 398–399,
    426–427
  writings by, 150, 169, 224
  on Zionism, 50, 77
Benjamins
  Scholem increasingly focused on, 152–153
  Scholem reading essay on Book of Jonah
    to, 179–183
  Scholem with in Switzerland, 158–162, 165
  Scholem's disillusionment with, 162–163,
    166–169, 190
Bentwich, Norman, 346
Bergmann, Else, 340
Bergmann, Hugo, 227, 249, 273, 351, 418
  Brit Shalom and, 304, 324
  Escha and, 340, 352–353
  Scholem's friendship with, 226, 245, 340
Berlin, 29, 75, 91
  chaos in, 184–186
  Grunewald neighborhood of, 51–53, 52, 220
  revolution in, 190–191
  Scholem scheduled to work in, 431
  Scholem visiting synagogues in, 35–36, 49
  Scholem's childhood in, 26–29, 28
Betar, youth group of Revisionist party, 318
Bialik, Chaim, 249, 274
Bible, myths from, 70–71, 97–98, 121
biblical criticism, Scholem's, 179–183
Billig, Levi, 354
Blau-Weiss group, 213–214
Bleichrode, Dr., 42, 102
Bloch, Ernst, 69
Bloom, Harold, 410, 412, 414, 435, *436*
Blue-White Spectacles (journal), 25, 64–65, 95
Blum, Edgar, 43, 138
Bolshevik Revolution, 184, 186
Book Bahir, 124–128, 226
Book of Jonah
  justice and judgment in, 187, 194
  Scholem's essay on, 179–183
Book of Lamentations, 148, 152
Book of Zachariah, 230, 233–234
bourgeois
  Jewish settlement in Palestine as, 301–302
  meetings of intellectuals, 73–74
  Scholem's rejection of, 66, 75, 143–145, 199

Scholem on, 192–193, 278–279, 343–345, 389
philosophy, Benjamin's program for, 160–161
PLO, *vs.* Hamas, 381
poetry, 41, 58
  Benjamin's, 96
  Heinle's, 73
  Scholem and, 3, 437
police, Mandate, 317, 319, 347, 375, *375*, 387
Portnoy's Complaint (Roth), 413
poverty, and revolutionary power, 186–187
present, Scholem trying to escape, 101
Prinz, Joachim, 387–388
Prochnik, Anne, 33, 79, 85, 231, 310
  children of, 116, 205–206, 231–232,
    439–440
  effects of husband's religious laxity,
    282, 284
  financial worries of, 262, 312–313
  with International Committee of the
    Fourth International, 438
  Jewish wedding of, 449–451
  leaving Israel, 170, 313, 378, 383–386,
    404–409
  moving to Israel, 87, 310, 385
  pregnancies of, 112, 173, 230
  separation from husband, 439–440
  teaching job of, 280–283, 334
Prochnik, Rafael, 439–440
Prochnik, Tzvi, 205–206
Prochnik, Yona, 116, 206
Prochnik, Zachariah, 230–231
prophecy, history confused with, 181
pseudepigraphy, 275–276, 279–280, 395
psychic research, Goldberg's, 210–211
psychology, 121, 128, 166
purity
  God's, 121–122
  lack of, 139, 190–191
  loss of, 367, 384
  Scholem's idealization of, 38–39, 110,
    122, 182, 190, 278

Rabin, Yitzhak, 383
  assassination of, 338, 355–356, 336–359
  demonization of, 259–261, 355–357
Rabinbach, Anson, 414, 415

Rafiq, author's friendship with, 175–177
reading
  Benjamin and Scholem's, 75, 101–102, 421
  Benjamin's, 137, 151
  Scholem's, 137, 217, 410–411
The Reality of the Hebrews (Goldberg), 212
reason, revolt against, 69
Redeemer, restoration of the world through,
    292–293
redemption, 452, 461
  constant possibility of, 425, 442
  of Judaism, 32, 90, 203–204, 250–251, 330,
    364, 460
  Maimonides' vision of, 391–393
"Redemption Through Sin," 354, 361–367, 373,
    377–378, 452
"Reflections on Modern Jewish Studies," 240
Reform movement, 133
relationships, Scholem's, 145–146. *See also*
  under marriage
  with Escha Burchardt, 186, 188–190, 217
  with Grete Bauer, 189
  Scholem's awkwardness in, 146–148, 152
  with Yetka, 42–43, 45
religion, 81, 133
  Benjamin's, 97
  Scholem's, 58
"Religious Authority and Mysticism," 429–431
repentance, 70
restoration of the world, 292–293
resurrection, *vs.* death, 32
Revisionist party, 318, 347
  Brit Shalom supporters *vs.*, 328–330
  plan to take Palestine by force, 306, 318,
    371
  redefining Zionism, 271–273, 333
  splitting Zionists, 302, 306, 327
revolution, 397
  Benjamin intrigued by, 65, 75
  in Germany, 179, 184–185, *185*, 190–191,
    214–216, *215*
  Judaism and, 187–188
  Werner's hopes for, 65, 92–93
Romanticism, Scholem's, 102
Rosenzweig, Franz, 347
Roth, Joseph, 28–29, 345

GEORGE PROCHNIK's most recent book, *The Impossible Exile: Stefan Zweig at the End of the World*, received the National Jewish Book Award for Biography/Memoir in 2014 and was short-listed for the Wingate Prize in the United Kingdom. Prochnik is also the author of *In Pursuit of Silence: Listening for Meaning in a World of Noise* (2010), and *Putnam Camp: Sigmund Freud, James Jackson Putnam, and the Purpose of American Psychology* (2006). He has written for *The New Yorker, New York Times, Bookforum,* and *Los Angeles Review of Books,* and is editor-at-large for *Cabinet* magazine.

Also by George Prochnik

THE IMPOSSIBLE EXILE
Stefan Zweig at the End of the World

The biography of Austrian writer Stefan Zweig, the inspiration behind *The Grand Budapest Hotel*, Wes Anderson's award-winning film

"A major work of historical and cultural criticism of Europe's darkest times... Zweig's haunted talent has never been better explored than in this exemplary study." —*The Times*

"Subtle-minded and unsentimental, Prochnik makes some sense out of the enigmatic Zweig... The biography is nestled in excellent mini-essays on Zweig's world: journalism, the coffeehouse culture, Viennese snobbery, Jewish snobbery. In turn, that story is embraced by Prochnik's own: growing up in America in a family that had escaped Austria after the Anschluss. The book is in the bloodline of W. G. Sebald." —Joan Acocella, *The New Yorker*

"*The Impossible Exile* is a gripping, unusually subtle, poignant, and honest study. Prochnik attempts, on the basis of an uncompromising investigation, to clarify the motives that might have driven to suicide an author who still enjoyed a rare popularity." —Anka Muhlstein, *New York Review of Books*

"[A] superbly lyrical study... *The Impossible Exile* is not really — or not just — a biography of Zweig's final years. It is a case study of dislocation, of people who had not only lost a home but who were no longer able to define the meaning of home... Mr. Prochnik gives a very rich sense of what so many exiles experienced during the war... [his] words could not be more resonant." —André Aciman, *Wall Street Journal*

"[A]n intriguing... meditation on Zweig's last years... an intellectual feast served as a series of canapes." —*New York Times Book Review*

▌ OTHER PRESS   *www.otherpress.com*

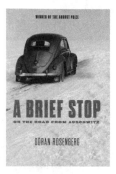

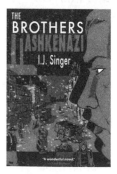